Social Movements

Critiques, Concepts, Case-Studies

Edited by

Stanford M. Lyman

Robert J. Morrow Eminent Scholar
and Professor of Social Science
Florida Atlantic University

NEW YORK UNIVERSITY PRESS
Washington Square, New York

First published in the U.S.A. in 1995 by
NEW YORK UNIVERSITY PRESS
Washington Square
New York, N.Y. 10003

Reprinted 1995

Library of Congress Cataloging-in-Publication Data
Social movements : critiques, concepts, case-studies / edited by
Stanford M. Lyman.
p.   cm. — (Main trends of the modern world)
Includes bibliographical references and index.
ISBN 0–8147–5085–0. — ISBN 0–8147–5086–9 (pbk.)
1. Social movements. 2. Social history—1945–   I. Lyman,
Stanford M.   II. Series.
HN17.5.S598 1995
303. 48'4—dc20   94–12366
                                                         CIP

Printed in Hong Kong

SOCIAL MOVEMENTS

MAIN TRENDS OF THE MODERN WORLD

General Editors: Robert Jackall and Arthur J. Vidich

Propaganda
Edited by Robert Jackall

Metropolis: Center and Symbol of Our Times
Edited by Philip Kasinitz

Social Movements: Critiques, Concepts, Case-Studies
Edited by Stanford M. Lyman

The New Middle Classes: Life-Styles, Status Claims and
Political Orientations
Edited by Arthur J. Vidich

Contents

Part IV   Contemporary Studies

Part V   The Future of Social Movements

Part VI   Coda: Social Movements in Sociological Thought

Series Preface

Main Trends of the Modern World is a series of books analyzing the main trends and the social psychology of our times. Each volume in the series brings together readings from social analysts who first identified a decisive institutional trend and from writers who explore its social and psychological effects in contemporary society.

The series works in the classical tradition of social theory. In this view, theory is the historically informed framing of intellectual problems about concrete social issues and the resolution of those problems through the analysis of empirical data. Theory is not, therefore, the study of the history of ideas about society, nor the abstract, ahistorical modeling of social realities, nor, as in some quarters, pure speculation often of an ideological sort unchecked by empirical reality. Theory is meaningful only when it illuminates the specific features, origins, and animating impetus of particular institutions, showing how these institutions shape experience and are linked to the social order as a whole.

Social analysts such as Karl Marx, Max Weber, Émile Durkheim, Sigmund Freud, Georg Simmel, Thorstein Veblen, and George Herbert Mead, whose works we now consider classics, never consciously set out to construct paradigms, models, or abstract theories of society. Instead they investigated concrete social phenomena such as the decline of feudal society and the emergence of industrial capitalism, the growth of bureaucracy, the consequences of the accelerating specialization of labor, the significance of religion in a scientific and secular age, the formation of self and the moral foundations of modern society, and the on-going rationalization of modern life. The continuing resonance of their ideas suggests the firmness of their grasp of deep-rooted structural trends in Western industrial society.

Later European and American social thinkers, deeply indebted though they were to the intellectual frameworks produced by the remarkable men who preceded them, faced a social order marked by increasing disarray, one that required fresh intellectual approaches. The social, cultural, and intellectual watershed was, of course, the Great War and its aftermath. The world's first total war ravaged a whole generation of youth. In Europe, it sowed the seeds of revolution, militarism, totalitarianism, fascism, and state socialism; in both Europe and America it signaled the age of mass propaganda. On both continents the aftermath of the war brought economic and political turmoil, cultural frenzies, widespread disenchantment and disillusionment, and social movements of every hue and description that led eventually to the convulsions of the Second World War. These later social thinkers grappled with issues such as:

- The deepening bureaucratization of all social spheres and the ascendance of the new middle classes.
- The collapse of old religious theodicies that once gave meaning to life and the emergence of complex social psychologies of individuals and masses in a rationalized world.
- The riddles posed by modern art and culture.
- The emergence of mass communications and propaganda as well as the manufacture of cultural dreamworlds of various sorts.
- War, militarism, and the advent of totalitarianism, fascism, and state socialism.
- The deepening irrational consequences and moral implications of the thoroughgoing rationalization of all life spheres.

Emil Lederer, Hans Speier, Joseph Schumpeter, Kenneth Burke, Robert MacIver, Harold Lasswell, Walter Lippmann, Robert Park, W. I. Thomas, Florian Znaniecki, George Orwell, Hannah Arendt, Herbert Blumer, and Hans H. Gerth are only a few of the men and women who carried forward the theoretical attitude of the great classical thinkers in the course of working on the pressing issues of their own day. In this tradition, social theory means confronting head-on the social realities of one's own times, trying to explain both the main structural drift of institutions as well as the social psychologies of individuals, groups, and classes.

What then are the major structural trends and individual experiences of our own epoch? Four major trends come immediately to mind, each with profound ramifications for individuals. We pose these as groups of research problems.

BUREAUCRACY AS THE ORGANIZATIONAL FORM OF MODERNITY

• What are the social and psychological consequences of living and working in a society dominated by mass bureaucratic structures? How do these structures affect the private lives of the men and women exposed to their influences?
• What is the structure and meaning of work in a bureaucratic society? In particular, how does bureaucracy shape moral consciousness? What are the organizational roots of the collapse of traditional notions of accountability in our society?
• What is the relationship between leaders and followers in a society dominated by a bureaucratic ethos? What are the changing roles of intellectuals, whether in the academy or in public life, in defining, legitimating, challenging, or serving the social order?

THE TECHNOLOGIES OF MASS COMMUNICATION AND THE MANAGEMENT OF MASS SOCIETY

• What role do public relations, advertising, and bureaucratized social research play in shaping the public opinions and private attitudes of the masses?
• What is the relationship between individuals' direct life experiences (with, for example, family, friends, occupations, sex, and marriage) and the definitions that the mass media suggest for these individual experiences? What illusions and myths now sustain the social order? What are the ascendant forms of this-worldly salvation in our time?
• What are the different origins, dynamics, and consequences of modern political, social, and cultural mass movements with their alternative visions of justice and morality?
• What social, economic, and cultural trends have made many great metropolises, once the epitomes of civilization and still the centers and symbols of modern life, into new wildernesses?

THE ON-GOING SOCIAL TRANSFORMATION OF CAPITALISM

- What are the prospects for a transformed capitalism in a post-Marxist, post-Keynesian era?
- How has the emergence of large bureaucratic organizations in every sector of the social order transformed the middle classes? What is the social and political psychology of these new middle classes?
- What transformations of the class and status structure have been precipitated by America's changing industrial order?
- What are the social, cultural, and historical roots of the pervasive criminal violence in contemporary American society? What social factors have fostered the breakdown of traditional mechanisms of social control and the emergence of violence as a primary means for effecting individual or group goals?

THE CLASH BETWEEN WORLDVIEWS AND VALUES, OLD AND NEW

- How has science, particularly in its bureaucratized form, transformed the liberal doctrines of natural rights, individual rights, and concomitant conceptions of the human person, including notions of life and death?
- How have the old middle classes come to terms with mass bureaucratic institutions and the subsequent emergence of new classes and status groups? What social forces continue to prompt the framing of complicated social issues in terms of primal antagonisms of kith, kin, blood, color, soil, gender, and sexual orientation?
- What are the roots of the pervasive irrationalities evident at virtually every level of our society, despite our Enlightenment legacy of reason and rationality and our embrace of at least functional rationality in our organizational apparatus? To what extent is individual and mass irrationality generated precisely by formally rational bureaucratic structures?

In short, the modern epoch is undergoing social transformations every bit as dramatic as the transition from feudalism to industrial capitalism. The very complexity of the contemporary world impedes fixed social scientific understanding. Moreover we may lack the language and concepts necessary to provide coherent analyses of some emerging features of our social order. Nonetheless this series tries to identify and analyze the major trends of modern times. With a historical awareness of the great intellectual work of the past and with a dispassionate attitude toward contemporary social realities, the series fashions grounded, specific images of our world in the hope that future thinkers will find these more useful than speculation or prophecy.

Each volume in this series addresses one major trend. The book in hand analyzes social movements originating in crowd actions or political and economic agitations that posed challenges to the social order. This volume also examines contemporary forms of collective protest.

ROBERT JACKALL
ARTHUR J. VIDICH

Introduction
Stanford M. Lyman

> Social Movements can be viewed as collective enterprises
> to establish a new order of life.
>
> Herbert Blumer[1]

A central aim of *Social Movements: Critiques, Concepts, Case-Studies* is to bring together classical, recent and contemporary analyses of the social-movement phenomenon. In this volume analysis is represented in several variants of its discursive form: the expository essay, the critique, the general theory, the specific case study, the futuristic meditation. The book is divided into six parts – entitled, respectively, Classical Perspectives; Disciplinary Approaches; Conceptual Issues: Debates and Critiques; Contemporary Studies; The Future of Social Movements; and a coda: Social Movements in Sociological Thought – each containing one to four essays. Although each essay was written independently and to serve its author's particular purpose, its presentation in this volume permits each to contribute to a comprehensive and thematic formulation of the subject. The editor's concluding essay provides an original and critical summation of the place of social movements in past and present sociological thought.

Part I opens with Robert E. Park's critique and reformulation of the idea of the "general will," a conceptualization which, having passed through the seminal philosophies of Hobbes, Locke, Rousseau, Fichte, Kant and Hegel, is redefined as "what is morally valid for the collectivity." However, as Park observes, the collectivity itself is subject to reformation as either a crowd or a public. The former seems atavistic; the latter modern. Yet both are creatures of post-Enlightenment societies and each contributes to the substance and direction of any social movement: "The crowd submits to the influence of a collective drive, which it obeys without criticism," while the public "is guided by prudence and rational reflection." Implicit in Park's essay is a query: whether the adherents of a social movement will revert to the kind

1

of behavior associated with an irrational crowd or raise themselves to the reasonable quality of action that the modern
social question seems to require.

Part I continues with Albert Salomon elaborating on the
theme of modern secular theodicies and their relation to social
movements. In "The Religion of Progress" (Chapter 2) he
rejects the thesis that holds that social movements are wholly
determined by material, that is, economic, forces and points
to the "spiritual horizon" that lays the foundations for both
praxis and passion in human affairs. Salomon calls attention to the faith in progress that for two centuries has provided post-Enlightenment societies with more than one secular
religion and locates the political source of these religions
of progress in French Jacobinism: "They have all been the
heirs of the religions of reason, the supreme being and
theophilanthropy . . ., [and despite] their opposition to the
French Revolution, they share its historical messianism." Such
a gospel infused the sociological eschatologies of Proudhon,
Marx, St Simon and Comte and, as Salomon observes, makes
these thinkers' works profoundly different from those of
Thucydides, Sallust or Tacitus. The social movements that
draw strength and ideology from the writings of the former
group are each heir to a tradition that brings together into
a single inner-worldly spatio-temporal trajectory "God, history, society and humanity."

In Part II the focus turns to specific intradisciplinary
approaches to twentieth-century social movements. In Chapter
3 Rudolf Heberle treats the subject from the point of view
of political sociology. As an aspect of such, a social movement must perforce participate in the "game of politics,"
influence or be influenced by political parties, and, in effect,
compete with or become one of the latter. However "a social
movement that aims at a change in the social order may,
under certain conditions, constitute a danger for the very
existence of social order . . ." Whether it will be such depends
on the extent to which the society is governed by norms of
civility and a toleration of differences. For, as Heberle concludes, "a variety of social movements can exist within a
society without endangering social solidarity, provided the
members of these movements respect their opponents as
fellow members of the larger community with whom they

are willing to debate and to search for solutions
acceptable to all . . . [T]he danger lies in the ele'
political goals to the rank and dignity of absolute, ultimate
ends."

In Chapter 4 Herbert Blumer deepens our understanding by conceiving social movements through a componential
and processual analysis. First distinguishing among general
(that is, cultural drift), specific (that is, reform and revolutionary) and expressive (for example, religious and fashion)
movements, Blumer points to the characteristic features and
specific kinds of conduct associated with each. Attention is
given to unpacking each of the intersubjective processes and
modes of social relationship conducive to the development
of a social movement. A collectivity's response to specific
dissatisfactions with the prevailing ways of society moves
through four stages – recognized social unrest, popular excitement, formalization and institutionalization. However these
stages are neither progressive nor irreversible; rather, their
very coming into being is dependent on the effectiveness of
agitation, the intensity of esprit de corps, a pervasive sense
of morale, the development of an ideology and an appropriate use of tactics. Moreover not all movements aim at
societal reform or social, cultural or political revolution. Those
that Blumer calls "expressive" aim less at reforming or revo-
lutionizing the external social order than at morally regen-
erating the world. Blumer is careful to point out that the
analytical distinctions he has made are not found in a similar
state of distinctiveness in the praxiological world. In fact
the social world that sociology seeks to investigate is likely
to meld the types such that "a revolutionary movement may
have many of the features of a religious movement, with its
success dependent to some extent upon the movement's
becoming fashionable."

Despite the prodigious efforts of such scholars as Park,
Salomon, Heberle and Blumer to formulate a clear picture
of the character and dynamics of social movements, some
sociologists remain unsatisfied with the epistemology and
methodology employed. Robert D. Benford and Scott A. Hunt
are among those who believe that the "sociology of social
movements currently lacks a conceptual framework to understand collective attempts to construct and reconstruct

definitions of power." To remedy this situation, in Chapter
5 they offer a dramaturgical approach that treats the processes entailed in the social construction of power shifts and
authority replacements. Focusing on four well-known dramatic techniques – scripting, staging, performing and interpreting – and drawing on their own and other investigators'
studies of the antiapartheid, socialist, sanctuary, labor, nuclear-
disarmament and environmental movements, Benford and
Hunt urge sociologists to adapt the theatrical perspective
to their attempts to evaluate the success and effectiveness
of these and other collective efforts that are aimed at reforming or reconstructing a social order. Their contribution calls for a paradigm shift in social-scientific research
on these phenomena.

In Part III the contributors inquire into the character of
recent social movements and critique certain new approaches
to their study. In Chapter 6 David Plotke asks, "What's so
new about new social movements?" In his answer he appraises
feminism, gay liberation, environmentalism, ethnonationalism
and opposition to nuclear-weapons development in terms
of the claim that these collective efforts differ from those of
earlier eras in that they not only eschew identification with
the labor movement but also depart from both interest-group
liberalism and classical socialism. In Chapter 7 Frances Fox
Piven and Richard Cloward weigh in with a sharp critique
of resource-mobilization theory and its emphasis on the
similarities between conventional conduct and protest
behavior. Part III closes with Chapter 8, "Social Movement
Research in the United States: A European Perspective,"
Margit Mayer's cautionary essay advising sociologists not to
synthesize "theoretical approaches that are rooted in incompatible social–theoretical frameworks" and requesting that
they apply the concept of American exceptionalism to any
international comparison of social-movement phenomena.

Turning to concrete studies of contemporary social movements, Part IV begins with Chapter 9, Edwin Amenta's and
Yvonne Zylan's exploration of three distinctive perspectives,
each of which throws a different light on the movement
begun by Francis E. Townsend during the Great Depression to obtain pensions for the elderly, but none of which,
alone, provides a comprehensive understanding of it. Mansoor

Moaddel's study, "Ideology as Episodic Discourse: The Case of the Iranian Revolution" (Chapter 10), not only adds to the perspectival collage extant in the contemporary sociology of social movements by focusing on three models of ideology in its relation to revolution, but also contributes a fourth model – episodic discourse. The latter model facilitates the historical–contextual understanding of the Iranian Revolution and shows considerable promise as an approach to other studies of religio-national revolts. Daniel Harris's critique of the role of "politically correct" rhetoric in the movement attempting to reorganize both social thinking and medical practice with respect to the AIDS crisis (Chapter 11) combines dispassionate study of a collective effort with critical engagements of the academic and postmodern orientations that might undermine its aims. A similar spirit haunts Chapter 12, Robert Brulle's analysis of environmentalism and human emancipation, but by introducing Jürgen Habermas's thesis about rhetoric and the norms and proprieties of public discourse, Brulle is able to reconceive the research question for a praxiological sociology of the environmental movement: " ... not which environmentalist discourse is right, but rather, what type of political practice these discourses engender."

In the penultimate section of this volume we turn to the future of social movements and of the discourses in which they are expressed and investigated. Considering the issue of whether such current movements as that represented by the greens are descendants of or breaks with the new left and the several revolts of the 1960s, in Chapter 13 Carl Boggs argues the thesis of legacy and continuity, but notes how much that historical lineage has been obscured by belief in what he calls the "total-break scenario." "The point is," he concludes, "that the 1960s were merely a beginning," but he concedes that "new-left politics was never more than a series of disparate, chaotic revolts against authority ..." Zygmunt Bauman (Chapter 14) moves the argument further, holding that, although the left has been the counterculture of capitalism, the extent to which it can retain that identity is now challenged by the fact that the number of industrial workers is shrinking, that poverty is no longer associated with organized labor, and that the poor are no longer the likely bearers of future progressive developments. In effect, he suggests that the current sense of disenchantment and loss of direction that characterizes the left is a consequence of its inability to find "any historical agent to complete the [anti]capitalist project." In "Beyond Social Movements?" (Chapter 15) Alain Touraine restates the issue in even larger terms than its expression in the essays by Boggs and Bauman. He writes, "The question that arises with respect to countries that have been considerably influenced by socialist, communist or anti-imperialist forms of thought, is: can the idea of a central social conflict – which I here identify with the recognition of social movements – survive what now appears as the irremediable decline of historicist thought, that is, of a form of thought that defined the social actor by his position in a social progress opposed by the forces of conservatism and reaction?" His answer is in the negative, and he urges a new historical imperative: "One must . . . rediscover the existence and efficacy of social actors, East, West and South; one must . . . strive to understand how history, far from having reached its conclusion, resumes its march."

This book concludes with a coda contributed by the editor. In "Social Theory and Social Movements: Sociology as Sociodicy" (Chapter 16) Stanford M. Lyman treats sociology's position midway between analysis of stasis and advocacy of social change as partaking of its role as the successor to religion. Just as the latter provided theodicies that vindicated the ways of God to humankind, so sociology has assumed the task of supplying sociodicies, justifying the ways of society to those who perforce must live in them. Whether a sociodicial sociology is conservative and opposed to social movements or synergistic with respect to their aims, it cannot escape its self-defined task of judging or its fate as an object of peoples' judgments.

Note

1. Herbert Blumer, "Collective Behaviour," in Robert E. Park (ed.), *An Outline of the Principles of Sociology* (New York: Barnes & Noble, 1939), p. 255.

Part I

Classical Perspectives

1 The General Will*
Robert E. Park

The concept of the general will enters modern philosophy for the first time in Rousseau's discussion about the "Volonté de tous."[1] It is true that Hobbes and Locke had already presented similar ideas. Hobbes, for example, argued that the state was a "real entity" and should be viewed as a person; but "real" in this sense can only mean that the state is the bearer of the unified power of those individuals united within it, for the state is based upon an agreement, it is an "artificial person."[2] "Person" should likewise be understood as a legal construct, the bearer of the rights given up by the individuals.[3] For Hobbes there is no "moral person" recognizing in its own consciousness the power of a higher law; the general will is so unlike the "real" will of individuals, that the state comes into existence only after individual wills subordinate themselves to the will of the ruler and accept his commands unconditionally.[4]

For man, the state of nature is a condition of mutual hostility, a *bellum omnium contra omnes*. Only when this natural state is abolished does the State come into being. With the formation of the State, individual wills are surrendered to the will of the collectivity which is represented through the person and will of the ruler. This general will always exists as something external to the individuals. According to Hobbes there is no self-government, since rule is always and necessarily coercive.[5]

This doctrine of the State's permanent opposition to individuals, of the State as an external power limiting individual freedom, appears elsewhere, even in the writings of those men who in other points do not agree with Hobbes, such as Goodwin, John Stuart Mill, and Spencer.[6] The doctrine received its classic expression in Bentham's statement: "Government is a necessary evil."[7] Common to all these writers is

* Reprinted from Robert E. Park, *The Crowd and the Public and Other Essays* (Chicago: The University of Chicago Press, 1972), pp. 63–81.

the assumption that there is a complete separation existing
between the individual and the State. However, this is not
to be understood as in Hegel's theory where the individual
finds his true self and his freedom only in the State. It means
instead that the individual must always renounce a part of
his freedom to the State, as much as is necessary for secur-
ing the same freedom for all other individuals.[8]

Rousseau's writings represent the historical transition from
the doctrine of Hobbes and Locke to that of the general
will as it appears in the political philosophy of Hegel.[9] Locke
wrote his "Essay on Civil Government" primarily to justify
the English Revolution.[10] He diverged from Hobbes's doctrine
insofar as he believed that the general will was ultimately
based in the community and was only taken over temporarily by ruler and government for the representative exercise of power.[11] The will that actually exerts its influence in
the community is thus not the will of the collectivity, but
that of the sovereign who exercises his own will under the
conditions of the constitution. This transfer of sovereignty
to the king and parliament is always conditional and can be
recalled as soon as the conditions are not fulfilled.[12] For
Locke the general will was not an "actual" will, but only the
position of individuals who agreed with or rejected the actions
of the government; he viewed these individuals not as an entity
but as separate persons. "Thus for Hobbes," Bosanquet states,
"it can be said that the political unity lies in a will which is
real but not common (not a general will); it is namely the
will of the sovereign. For Locke, on the other hand, this
unity lies in a will which although general, is not real."[13]

Rousseau often used the language of Locke and Hobbes;
in general his writings appear to vacillate between the earlier
concept of social unity which places unity above and outside
the circle of individual volitions, and the later concept which
locates this unity in a general will existing in real and substantial opinions instead of in a common agreement.[14] The
relapse into earlier doctrines is clearest where Rousseau
attempted to formulate the social mechanism through which
the state was to form this general will. For this, he prescribed
a relentless regime of public meetings that were to embody
the sovereignty of the state.[15]

In presenting his doctrine, Rousseau also used the historical fiction of the social contract. He treats this "contract" as a universal and constitutive relationship; only when it is accepted is the State called into being.[16] Where this concept of the social contract is most generally formulated, it means nothing more than the mutual recognition of individuals as persons who possess rights and duties. Here the social contract is the formal expression of the normative consciousness that constitutes the prerequisite for concrete relationships between individuals within the political body.[17]

On the other hand, Rousseau views man's original existence prior to his entering into social bonds with others as a condition of natural freedom. In earlier writings he speaks of society as if its formation meant the annulment of individual freedom.[18] But in *The Social Contract* he contrasts the natural freedom of the individual, innocent of social bonds, with the new freedom that man first gains within the State.[19] Here Rousseau's teachings oppose Hegel's, since Hegel considered the so-called natural freedom existing before the creation of the moral individual to be exactly the opposite of freedom.[20] Freedom in Hegel's sense is only attained by the moral individual who aspires to a rational ideal; freedom can therefore only be realized within the State.[21]

The essential element in Rousseau's teaching is his separation of "general will" (*volonté général*) and the "will of everyone" (*volonté de tous*), which indicates his progress beyond Locke. The will of everyone must not be interpreted as an expression of the general will.[22] Coincidental agreement among the empirical wills of individuals does not constitute the essence of the general will. Instead, it can be said to exist only when a universal goal is desired and when this desire takes the form of a law which is equally valid for everyone at all times. Only when the individual subjects himself to a general law and refrains from obeying momentary drives, is the decision resulting from a popular vote identical with the general will.[23]

It would be easy to conclude that the individual will is the same as the general will, or at least could be seen as its subjective expression. Hegel's development of this thought will be discussed below. But for Rousseau, this interpretation was impossible, since he retained the old separation of nation (the people) and the government. As a result, his doctrine (as well as Locke's) does not mention a specific organ for forming the general will. The government is not this organ; according to Locke it retains sovereignty only temporarily, while Rousseau considered it to be simply an administrative committee.[24] In order to define the general will, it is necessary to resort to the general consensus of citizens.[25]

The concept of the general will, which is only briefly sketched out in Rousseau's doctrine, was then taken up and further developed in classic German philosophy. Its most complete expression occurs in Hegel's teaching of the objective spirit.[26] Under this term, Hegel reunited the two aspects of the general will, one moral, the other legal, which Kant's somewhat one-sided insistence upon the autonomy of the individual had set into opposition. The autonomous will is the one that rises above the system of empirical drives and shapes itself solely by the law of reason. The highest moral law is: the individual should behave as if he wished that the maxims of his behavior would become general laws of nature.[27] But although this law is generally necessary and valid for all men, it is purely formal; for as Hegel emphasized, it demands nothing more than the formal accord of the individual with himself.[28] The individual yields to the law he must follow. The subjectivism of this concept is revealed in the doctrine that only the good will is good.[29] Kant's philosophy of law ascribed no inherent moral value to public institutions; this is the greatest difference between his philosophy of law and that of Hegel.

It is necessary to mention the special importance of Fichte's doctrine of State and law, for it provides the transition from the eighteenth-century to the nineteenth-century theory of the State; in other words, from the subjective concept of Kant's ethical norm to Hegel's objective interpretation.[30] For Fichte, it is the individual's duty to enact in particular the supraindividual will. "The voice of conscience, which shows everyone his particular duty, is the beam on which we emerge from the infinite and are established as individual and particular beings; this voice sets the limits of our personality; it is also our true primitive element, the basis and the ingredient of all our existences."[31]

The idea of the supraindividual life first appeared in the Kantian notion of "consciousness in general."[32] Although the

concept revealed a complete break with Enlightenment philosophy, Fichte remained on the same ground as Hobbes insofar as his closed economic state presented the State simply
as the sum of external conditions under which the individual could fulfill his destiny.[33] However, his concept of
the State developed continually in the various forms of his
teachings. Before publication of his essay on the "closed
economic state," Fichte had already prided himself in being
the first to conceive of the State as an organism.[34] Although
the idea was already contained in his theory of morals, it
was first clearly expressed in *Talks to the German People:* the
State is also an individual, it has a destiny that its actual
existence serves to realize.[35]

It has already been noted that Hegel's doctrine of the
objective spirit is the fullest development of Rousseau's
original concept of the general will. In his *Philosophy of Law*,
Hegel defined the State in the same sense as Fichte did in
Talks to the German People – a sentient individual whose essence is a particular application of the general spirit; this
spirit finds its actualization in world history.[36] Thus the State
is not a work of art nor a simple ideal floating before the
individuals in the society; instead it is something real, a sentient substance which has actualized itself in governmental
institutions.[37]

Exactly as with the individual's real will, which is his essence,
so also the State's real will is never identical with the empirical will but is only partially expressed in it. Therefore "the spirit of the nation does not speak out in the
exchange of momentary opinions, nor in the arbitrariness
of parliamentary leaders, but expresses itself instead in the
stable structure which the State achieves through its continual development."[38]

Hegel believed that the ethical substance, which he called
morality and which is here identified with Rousseau's general
will (*volonté général*), assumed three different forms. In the
family, the general will assumes its immediate form, that of
feeling and natural drive.[39] As long as the family is part of
the State, the family is the natural form of society.[40] The
unity seen here is direct; individual elements possess no independence in the face of the whole. "The right which the
individual possesses on the basis of family unity, and which

constitutes his life itself within this unity, emerges in the form of a right (only insofar as it is the abstract moment of the specific individuality) when the family is in the process of dissolving, and those who were members become independent people, both in their self-conception and in reality. In their separation, only the outer aspects of that which made them definite forces within the family is now preserved: possessions, nourishment, cost of education, etc."[41]

If the family is dissolved into its individual elements, so that in their separation members interact only in terms of external bonds, there results the form of society that Hegel called civil society.[42] In civil society individuals are conscious of their private interests wherever these are in conflict with the interests of other individuals.[43] Individuals thus become self-conscious; as their private interests press to the forefront and become the determining force of consciousness, a split develops between the individual and the totality, and the totality appears as something external and foreign to the individual. If a general consensus does exist among the members of civil society, it assures the form of the "will of everyone," for "in civic society everyone is his own end, everything else is nothing to him."[44]

It is characteristic of Hegel that he valued these forms of society in which individual differences appear, and that he saw them as an essential force in the development of the general will as it appears in the State.[45] The general will assumes the self-conscious form of reason only within the State.[46] It is precisely in the State that the general will consolidates the differences between individual elements that first appear in civil society. Because this occurs in the State, this form consists of the unity of differences.[47] It is not "the interests of individuals per se which stand as the final end of their unification," as is the case in civil society; instead, "unification itself is the true content and goal, and the destiny of the individuals is to lead a common existence. This substantive and universal life is the beginning and end of their further particular satisfaction, activity, and behavior."[48]

The concept of general will, as it appears perfected in Hegel's philosophy of the State, must be understood as a sentient substance; it appears subjectively within the individual consciousness in the form of conscience, and objectively in the form of mores.[49] The foundations of morality as well as the laws the political community applies to itself are based upon this spiritual substance.

The general will is finally to be understood as the essence of all that is valid for the social group, whether it is the family or the State, in contrast to that which operates continually in the collectivity as drives.[50] The concept of the general will in the writings of Hegel and others before and after him is not basically sociological, but ethical–legal.[51] An attempt to transfer this notion of the general will into social psychology resulted in one of the many controversial problems of the last century, for the question of the general will and its relationship to individuals in the group ran parallel to the problem of the relationship of the soul to the body.[52]

From the viewpoint of this study, the problem is purely epistemological; it concerns the question of whether psychology is to be viewed as a purely natural and phenomenological science or not. Basically, the general will would not be considered an object of social psychology, because it could never be equated with any of its manifestations. On the other hand, since the general will exists as a historic structure in society, it would have to be viewed as a product and formative element in the empirical process of society.[53] This question does not need to be answered here, for in any case the reality of the general will remains unquestioned, and that is sufficient for the present aim, the definition of the concepts "crowd" and "public."

The end of this discussion has been reached, and it is necessary to summarize what is most relevant for the concepts of crowd and public. It has been seen that the concept of reciprocity (sympathy and imitation) does not suffice for a definition of society, since reciprocity also occurs in "the war of all against all" (panic). The notion of society implies that the people it includes form a more or less permanent unity and are capable of acting as such. When society is viewed as such an entity, it assumes the category of a reality. The question is: of what does social reality consist?

The reality of society cannot be found in its external appearances because the perception of society is not limited to its external phenomena, and in addition, society does not present an homogeneous whole. The so-called organic theory was an attempt to understand society as a perceivable entity, but this idea was never seriously developed and always led to confusion. However, this should not discourage anyone from conceiving of society as a reality.

An individual's own personality consists of just such a stable combination of qualities, and this combination assumes a reality even though it is never visually perceived. What is called the personality is perceived outwardly in actions, inwardly as impulses and drives. Viewed as a cohesive whole, these impulses and drives can be called the will. The will is never identical with individual impulses and drives as they emerge in the consciousness; instead, these impulses and drives are the manifestation of the will.

It is possible to speak of a general will in the same way. General will does not merely refer to the interaction and reciprocal formation of individual wills, but more to the existence of a permanent relationship between them. Because of this relationship, people who join together at different times can be regarded not only as the same people, but also as the same society.

The general will, which is first formulated in the mores, must not be considered a third element, something apart from the individual wills, but as what is essential in them. The general will is distinguished from the drives and instincts of single individuals only when it is violated, that is, when the individual's drives or actions take a course opposed to it. In this way the moral element, which was previously expressed only as a drive, emerges as a norm in the collective consciousness.

The feelings and behavior that are awakened within the collectivity by the immoral action of one individual must be viewed as the expression of the general will – a kind of evaluation of the offensive action. A similar evaluation of immoral behavior will occur in the consciousness of the offender himself. Such an evaluation of personal behavior is expressed in feelings of embarrassment, shame, regret, etc. – or in a self-judgment. In its clearest form, this process of self-judgment is called conscience.

A double misunderstanding must be avoided here. In the first place, the general will must not be equated with the feeling and ideas actually controlling the collectivity at every moment. Nor is it simply what is active in the collective consciousness as drive and natural force. Instead, the general will is *what is morally valid for the collectivity.* Thus the differentiation between the "will of everyone" and the "general will," between empirical and normative collective will.

Secondly, it is incorrect to think that the collective consciousness that judges immoral action is determined only by personal and individual interests. If this were so, the judgment of the collectivity would have to be expressed so: "This action is opposed to our interests, therefore it is wrong." In contrast, each naive judgment of an action – if ever expressed – states: "this action does not agree with the mores, therefore it is bad." It is only when an attempt is made to justify this judgment from a philosophical outlook based on individual sense perceptions, that it is necessary to understand individually these actions of the collectivity.

In order to avoid the difficulties of explaining moral judgments on an individualist–sensualist basis, the concept of sympathy has been adopted. It has been seen that sympathetic imitation in itself is a purely formal process, the means through which men are able to experience the feelings of other people. Only in this way does the inner life of others become a motive for personal behavior.

However, the images in the consciousness of the individuals involved are only partially determined by the process of reciprocity and are not always well intended. Pleasure in another person's misfortunes (*Schadenfreude*) is as much a product of the process of sympathetic imitation as is pity. The fact that the sense of norms is not determined by sympathetic feelings is shown by the acts of pity which are frequently committed with the knowledge that it is wrong to do so. The ability to empathize at all with others assumes that something in common exists. Thus in spite of empathy, people know what right actions are. This shows that there is an element in human consciousness which is determined neither by individual sense perceptions nor through the reflected sense perceptions of other people.

Equally without basis is the claim that even if the general will cannot be equated with the sympathetic interaction of individual feelings, it must nevertheless be viewed genetically as the product of such interaction. This again is true only insofar as the sympathetic interpenetration and reconciliation of individual feelings is the precondition of a collective action. For it is always the necessity of a common action to protect common possessions that has produced a collective spirit in men.

The necessity of collective action has had other effects. Whenever a division developed within the group, it has forced individuals to examine and evaluate their individual tendencies and interests with an eye to the aims of the collectivity. It is this collective purpose, again, that has become so established in the general will that it does not simply hover in front of people as an ideal, but acts as an ideal force to inspire and drive them on.

The general psychological characteristics of social groups are: (1) reciprocity, that is, the mutual affecting and reconciling of human drives, and (2) a general will that is first expressed as a collective force overpowering and assimilating all individual drives. Existing at times as a norm, it opposes the transient individual feelings and drives of the collectivity.

The next question is: How are the many kinds of groups to be differentiated which appear and dissolve in endless variety against the background of human existence?

In spite of their great variety, this study separates groups into two classes. First, there is the category of sects, castes, classes, and groups that serve any special purpose whatsoever. These are all highly varied among themselves and must be further classified. The only characteristic they have in common is that they are not isolated, or in existence only for themselves. The existence of each group is based on that of other groups different from it. A political party, for example, assumes the existence of other political parties. Without the others, a single party would be inconceivable, and these parties are opposed in such a manner that no person can simultaneously be a member of two of them.

But the political parties, just like all other groups that have developed within society in order to serve some special interest or other, or to carry out a social function, presume the existence of a collectivity in which they are viewed as the parts. Their aims and the forces that influence them are only the particular manifestations of a general will that,

for its part, attains fuller expression in the political organization of a State or in national cults.

Crowd and public are different from all of these. They
represent the second type of association, which grows out
of and beyond the others, and they serve to bring individuals out of old ties and into new ones. Compared with those
social structures just discussed, crowd and public differ stri-
kingly from them. The historical element which plays such
an important role for the other groups is partially or completely absent for the crowd as well as the public. Instead,
the crowd and the public reveal the processes through which
new groups are formed, although they are not yet conscious
of themselves as groups. The individuals in a crowd or a
public lack a common tradition, so they have no basis for
viewing themselves as a permanent collectivity. For example,
people gather in a public square; they converse, exchange
opinions, and then go their separate ways; the intimate sense
of personal and spiritual contact and the awakened feelings
and interests that united them for a short time now dissolve.
This is the simplest form that a crowd or a public can take.

In contrast, there is the situation where a number of people
gather frequently and regularly. Here the mood that was
dominant at the first encounter is invoked again at the second,
third, fourth, etc., union, and in this way customs and traditions are built. A group so formed finally becomes conscious
of its temporal duration, and with this consciousness the
group differentiates more or less between itself and other
people. The tradition formed this way supplies the material
for a norm that is to regulate the group. When the group
finally differentiates itself from others in order to defend
its tradition, the goal of the process is reached whose beginning was seen at work in crowd formation. The group is
now changed; the collective consciousness assumes the normative form; in other words, the will of the group, which
formerly operated as a collective force dominating the drives
of individuals, develops into norm and regulation.

The relationship between crowd and public and the other
social groups can now be seen. From a standpoint of form,
or conceptually, crowd and public precede the other groups;
actually, they occur later – they are frequently the forms
that the other groups take to transform themselves into a

new, undefined whole. In addition, they are the forms individuals belonging to different established groups use to make
new groupings. Thus as crowd and public appear in modern
life, they assume the prior existence of other groups that
functionally express the varied, divided interests of men.
Wherever a new interest asserts itself amid those already
existing, a crowd or a public simultaneously develops; and
through this union of groups, or certain individuals from
among them, a new social form for the new interests is
created. In Europe a public reaching beyond the boundaries of states and nationalities has formed; and the general statement can be made that a public always develops
where the interests of people, whether political or economic,
come into conflict and seek to reconcile themselves. Further, it is precisely this contact and reciprocal adjustment
of opinion that has given rise to a tradition reaching beyond the boundaries of states and nationalities, a tradition
containing the kernel of a norm and of legislation that is
international.

It is not the content of the collective consciousness, but
rather its form, that separates crowd and public from the
other kinds of groups. Crowd and public are dominated by
a collective force, but this kind of collective will has not yet
assumed the form of a norm; therefore it cannot be viewed
as general will in the historical sense of the word, but instead
as an empirical preliminary stage to it. Neither the crowd
nor the public recognizes itself as a whole, nor do they attempt
to determine their own actions. No regulations, conscious
control, or self-consciousness exists. Crowd and public are
defined only by the conditions of reciprocal interaction, and
therefore they cannot define themselves as do all other groups.
For example, admission to a normal eating club is always
bound up with certain formalities in which the new member virtually obligates himself to adapt to the mood of the
group and respect the existing tradition.

In these respects crowd and public are alike; their difference is based on the conditions under which they develop.
Entrance to the crowd depends on the simplest conditions
imaginable, namely, possessing the ability to feel and empathize.
Admittedly, choice and selection occur even under these
conditions, but this is purely psychological, and the indi-

vidual himself is unaware of it. There is also a control here, but it is purely psychological and not normative. The individual experiences the collective will as his own internal drive.

The conditions under which one enters the public are somewhat more exacting. Not only the ability to feel and empathize is required, but also the ability to think and reason with others. That does not mean that a person is forced to bow to some procedural regulation or other; only the norms of logic must be accepted unconditionally.

There is another difference between crowd and public: the public expresses criticism. Within the public, opinions are divided. When the public ceases to be critical, it dissolves or is transformed into a crowd. This provides the essential characteristic differentiating the crowd from the public: The crowd submits to the influence of a collective drive which it obeys without criticism. The public, in contrast – precisely because it is composed of individuals with different opinions – is guided by prudence and rational reflection. However, it cannot be ignored that like the crowd, the public is to some degree influenced by the collective drive. But within the public, this collective drive has found individual expression in the various parties or individuals. The insight gained through criticism and the resulting explanation of the drive controlling the public is called "public opinion."

If an attempt is made to define crowd and public according to the form in which control is exercised, it is clear that they are, properly speaking, the only forms of society that can be called individualistic. Again, a difference between crowd and public must be recognized. Only in the crowd does anarchy in its purest form exist. As members of a public, people are at least controlled by the norms of logic. The ultimate tyranny, as Max Stirner has already noted, is that of the concept.

While crowd and public are differentiated so that in the former the instincts dominate, and in the latter reason prevails (suggesting that the public is a higher form of society than the crowd), one point must not be overlooked: this differentiation refers only to the form of the collective consciousness, and not to its content. This distinction is purely logical and cannot be viewed as a value difference.

Finally, the decisive difference between crowd and public

must be emphasized: in the crowd, both the theoretical and the practical norm are implicit in the collective impulse, while in the public – precisely because the individuals have different opinions – the two norms diverge. Here individuals are dominated by the theoretical norm even when the practical norm is held up before them as an ideal attainable only through action and discussion.

Notes

1. Bernard Bosanquet, *The Philosophical Theory of the State* (London: MacMillan, 1899), p. 13.
2. Thomas Hobbes, *Leviathan* (1651), pt. 2, chap. 17 and Foreword. Compare also Bogdan A. Kistiakowski, *Gesellschaft und Einzelwesen* (Berlin: 1899), p. 10.
3. Bosanquet, *Theory of the State*, p. 93.
4. Ibid., p. 104; Wilhelm Windelband, *Geschichte der neueren Philosophie*, vol. 1, (February, 1892), p. 154.
5. Paul Janet, *Histoire de la science politique*, vol. 2 (Paris: 1887), p. 182.
6. James Bonar, *Philosophy and Political Economy* (London: 1893), pp. 199ff; Bosanquet, *Theory of the State*, pp. 60ff., 69ff.
7. Jeremy Bentham, *Principles of Legislation*, (London: 1798), p. 48.
8. John Stuart Mill, *On Liberty* (London: 1861), chap. 4.
9. Bosanquet, *Theory of the State*, p. 13. "For it is Rousseau who stands midway between Hobbes and Locke on the one hand and Kant and Hegel on the other ... and he bequeathed to his successors the task of substituting for mere words and fictions of contract, nature, and original freedom, the idea of the common life of an essentially social being, expressing and sustaining the human will at its best."
10. Paul Janet, *Histoire de la science politique*, vol. 2, p. 199.
11. John Locke, *Essay on Civil Government* (London: 1690), chap. 7.
12. Ibid., chaps 13 and 18.
13. Bosanquet, *Theory of the State*, p. 104.
14. D.G. Ritchie, *Natural Rights* (London: 1895) p. 49.
15. Jean-Jacques Rousseau, *Du Contrat social* (Geneva: 1762), bk. 3, chap. 15. "Sovereignty cannot be represented for the same reason that it can not be alienated; its essence lies in the general will, and will cannot be represented. ... Any law not ratified by the people themselves is not a law. English people consider themselves free; they are strongly mistaken. It is only so during the election of members of parliament. As soon as they are elected, the English are slaves, that is, nothing." Compare D.G. Ritchie, *Natural Rights*, p. 50; Windelband, *Geschichte der neueren Philosophie*, p. 436.
16. Rousseau, *Du Contrat social*, bk. 1, chap. 8. "This transition from the state of nature to the civil state produces a very remarkable trans-

formation in man. Justice is substituted for instinct in his conduct, and his actions take on morality, which was lacking before then. It is only when the voice of duty replaces physical impulse, and law replaces appetite, that man, who up to then only looked after himself, finds himself forced to act upon other principles and to consult his reason before listening to his desires."

17. Windelband, *Präludien*, "Was ist Philosophie?" (Tubingen: J. C. B. Mohr, 1924). "The validity of the normative consciousness as the absolute measure for logical, ethical, and esthetic judgments, lies as an inevitable assumption at the basis of all man's higher functions, and especially at the basis of those functions which are the product of social culture and have as their content the production and preservation of that which stands above the desires of the individual."

18. Rousseau, *Discours sur l'origine de l'inégalité parmi les hommes*, pt. 1. "It is thus the same with man; while becoming socialized and enslaved, he becomes weak, fearful, and cringing."

19. Rousseau, *Du Contrat social*, bk. 1, chap. 8. "What man loses in the social contract is his natural liberty and an unlimited right to everything that tempts him and that he can obtain; what he gains is civil liberty along with ownership of all that he possesses. . . . moral liberty can be added accordingly to his gains within the civil state; only this can make man truly master of himself, for domination by the appetites alone is slavery; and obedience to the law that one has prescribed for himself is freedom." Compare Georg Wilhelm Friedrich Hegel, *Philosophie des Rechts* (Berlin: 1821), sec. 258.

20. Hegel, *Philosophie des Rechts*, sec. 194.

21. W. Wallace, *Lectures and Essays*, "Person and Personality," in *Lectures and Essay on Natural Theology and Ethics* (Oxford: Clarenden Press, 1898), p. 266. "Personality, in short, is a quality of the human being that expresses his moral nature. And the moral nature of man lies in his being subordinate to a general law, or being a member of a community, in which he forms an integral part and performs a function. Or, personality, like morality, only belongs to man in so far as, though a physical individual, he is implicitly universal."

22. Rousseau, *Du Contrat social*, bk. 2, chap. 3. "It follows from the above that the general will is always right, and that it always tends toward the public good. But it does not follow that the deliberations of the people always result in good; this is not always understood. The people can never be corrupted, but they can often be deceived and thus they only appear to desire what is evil.There is often a great difference between the 'will of everyone' and the 'general will.' The latter only concerns what is of common interest. The former expresses private interests; it is only the sum of individual desires.'

23. Ibid., bk. 2, chap. 6.

24. Locke, *Civil Government*, chap. 2, sec. 22; Bosanquet, *Theory of the State*, p. 105. "Locke feels that actual government is a trust and that the ultimate supreme power remains in the community as a whole. . . . But the trust is conditional and theoretically revocable; the ultimate supreme power is in the community at large, which may withdraw

the trust if its conditions are violated. Of course, no determinate means of doing this in a lawful manner is or can be suggested and therefore the will of the people is not expressed by Locke as a real or actual will." Rousseau, *Du Contrat social*, bk. 3, chap. 1.

25. Bosanquet, *Theory of the State*, p. 116. "Now all this makes it clear that in endeavouring to point out the sign of the general will, Rousseau is really enthroning the will of all.... By reducing the machinery for the expression of the common good to the isolated and un-assisted judgment of the members of the whole body of citizens, Rousseau is ensuring the exact reverse of what he professes to aim at. He is appealing from the organized life, institutions and selected capacity of a nation to that nation regarded as an aggregate of iso-lated individuals. And, therefore, he is enthroning as sovereign, not the national mind, but that aggregate of private interests and ideas, which he has himself described as the will of all."

26. Windelband, *Geschichte der neueren Philosphie*, 2:326ff. "Hegel's doc-trine of the objective spirit includes in the widest sense the entire area to which the tasteless name of sociology is applied today.... The essence of the objective spirit is completed only when its outer and inner forms coincide. This synthesis of legality and morality was called public morality [*Sittlichkeit*] by Hegel; it is expressly dif-ferentiated from morality [*Moralität*]."

27. Ibid., 2:116.

28. Hegel, *Philosophie des Rechts*, sec. 135. "As important as it is to em-phasize the pure unconditional self-determination as the root of duty – through Kant's philosophy, knowledge of the will gained its se-cure basis and point of departure by reflection upon the infinite autonomy of the will – adherence to a purely moral standpoint which is not transformed into a conception of ethics reduces this gain to an empty formalism; it reduces the science of morals to mere talk of duty for its own sake. And from this last standpoint, no imma-nent doctrine of duty is possible. (Of course, something can be brought in from outside, and specific duties can be derived from this.) But from that definition of duty seen as the lack of contradiction, as the formal agreement with itself – this is nothing but confirma-tion of an abstract indefiniteness – specific duties cannot proceed. When a specific content for behavior is examined, the foregoing principle does not provide a criterion of whether it is or is not a duty. On the contrary, all wrong and immoral behavior can be jus-tified in this manner."

29. Windelband, *Geschichte der neueren Philosophie*, 2:326. "It is a credit to Hegel's wisdom, that he treated ethics from an objective rather than a subjective standpoint. Precisely the subjectivism of Kant's and Fichte's moral philosophy has shown that the principle of ethics must be sought for at a level above the individual. Moral consciousness and moral legislation can never be derived from the individual 'I.' It is rooted instead in the relationship wherein the individual realizes he is subordinate to a general reason."

30. Windelband, *Fichtes Idee des deutschen Staates*, p. 9. "Where the previ-

ous century rationalized, this one wants to nationalize. Between these two stands Fichte – Janus-faced, he sounds the rousing cry to the future but still is filled with thoughts of the past."

31. Johann Gottlieb Fichte, *Die Bestimmung des Menschen*, p. 299.
32. Windelband, *Geschichte der Philosophie*, pp. 445, 448.
33. Windelband, *Geschichte der neueren Philosophie*, 2:222. "As he [Fichte] published his *Grundlage des Naturrechts* in 1796, he still was formally under the influence of the 18th century. Out of the principle of the theory of science, he deduced the plurality of physically organized personalities, and he discovered that in outward community life, the freedom of every individual must be limited by that of all others. But when he viewed the State as the means for obtaining this, he applied its functions only to outer relationships and not to moral ends."
34. Fichte, *Grundlage des Naturrechts*, p. 209. Compare Wallace, *Lectures and Essays*, "The Relations of Fichte and Hegel to Socialism," p. 427.
35. Fichte, *Reden an die deutsche Nation*, p. 381. "In the higher meaning of the word, taken from the standpoint of a general spiritual world, this is a nation: the totality of people surviving with each other in society and perpetuating themselves continually, both physically and spiritually; it stands as a whole under a certain special divine law of development. It is the common quality of this special law which both in the eternal world, and thus also in the temporal one, binds this group of people into a totality that is natural and homogeneous." Compare Windelband, *Geschichte der neueren Philosophie*, p. 224; Bosanquet, *Theory of the State*, p. 244.
36. Hegel, *Philosophie des Rechts*, sec. 258, Supplement. "Whether man knows it or not, this being (the State) actualizes itself as an independent power in which single individuals are only moments; the existence of the State is the march of God; its basis is the power of the intelligence actualizing itself as will." Compare ibid., pt. 3, div. 3, p. 423.
37. Ibid., sec. 258. "The State is as the reality of the substantial will which is contained in the special self-consciousness raised to its universality; it is intelligence in and for itself."
38. Windelband, *Geschichte der neueren Philosophie*, p. 329.
39. Hegel, *Philosophie des Rechts*, sec. 158.
40. Ibid., sec. 151.
41. Ibid., sec. 159.
42. Ibid., secs. 157, 184 and 238.
43. Ibid., sec. 184, Supplement.
44. Ibid., sec. 182.
45. Ibid., sec. 187.
46. Ibid., sec. 258.
47. Ibid.
48. Ibid.
49. Bosanquet, *Theory of the State*, p. 93. "We find that the essence of human society consists in a common self, a life and a will, which belong to and are exercised by the society as such, or by the individuals in society as such; it makes no difference which expression

we choose. This reality of this common self, in the action of the
political whole, receives the name of the 'general will. Ibid., p. 298.
"In institutions, then, we have that meeting point of the individual
minds which is the social mind. Rather let us say we have the ideal
substance, which, as a universal structure, is the social, but in its
differentiated cases is the individual mind." Compare Windelband,
Präludien, "Vom Prinzip der Moral," p. 308.

50. Bosanquet, *Theory of the State*, p. 39. "A strong sentiment, as such, is
a mere fact, a mere force, and as such the sociologist regards it; a
law involves the pretention to will what is just, and is therefore a
sentiment and something more, vis., the point of view of social good.
Kistiakowski, *Gesellschaft und Einzelwesen*, p. 154. "In all research into
social processes, it is very important to differentiate betwen the general
spirit which forms a totality or a collectivity to which the individual
spirits are related as parts, and the general spirit which, as norm or
laws, controls all individual spirits, and represents, in a special sense,
a generic term for all its effects on individual consciousnesses. The
difference is already clear from the fact that moral–legal order or
norms always remain the same for all individuals who originate in
the same society, regardless of their number; on the other hand,
patriotic or other social feelings or desires are highly dependent in
their social meaning and effect upon the number of individuals."

51. Windelband, *Präudien*, 1st ed., "Normen und Naturgesetze," p. 176.

52. Windelband, *Geschichte der Philosophie*, pp. 516ff., 529.

53. Hugo Münsterberg, *Grundzüge*, pp. 93 and 203. Windelband, *Präludien*,
1st ed., "Normen und Naturgesetze," p. 246.

2 The Religion of Progress*
Albert Salomon[1]

Modern social movements in the industrial age have been carefully analyzed with regard to their social causes and collective motives. For a century, historians and sociologists have taught that the movements are determined by material, and in particular by economic, forces. Such theories, however, cannot stand the test of comprehensive empirical scrutiny. Economic institutions are not living and autonomous things. They are composed of human beings whose actions are conditioned by a variety of motives. All empirical research makes it evident that the social process is not a simple evolution that can be inspired or explained by any single motive.

It is a commonplace truth that man's action in society is determined by material interests. In politics and in economic development, in social advancement and in intellectual competition, men are deeply conditioned by brutal and material interests. But if we attempt to measure the dynamics of social action, we have to investigate the elements that constitute the intensity, the density, and the power of social movements. Such inquiry will reveal that societies refer their material needs, desires, and deficiencies to a frame of meaning that provides the criteria for social action and social change. Such a frame of reference is a context of values regarding the whole of individual and social life. It is the spiritual horizon that establishes the foundations of human action and passion as meaningful in a larger whole. In measuring material interests with such systems of meaning, men are able to fill material and economic requirements with the explosive power of radical action. Men live not by bread alone; they need a meaning for their acting and being acted upon to which they can refer their sufferings and hopes.

* Reprinted from *Social Research*, vol. 13, no. 4 (December 1946), pp. 441–62.

There have been misery, exploitation, and injustice as long as societies have existed. And the humiliated and oppressed classes have tolerated such domination most of the time because of human inertia. They rise in revolutionary action only under two sets of conditions. The unprivileged classes succeed in building up a revolutionary group when they can appeal to their rights which have been abolished by the ruling elite. This is the pattern of all pre-industrial revolutions from the time of Solon to the Peasants' War of the sixteenth century. These revolutions remained in the orbit of the political and legal spheres. The second type of revolution is the modern one. In modern times, social movements result in an integrated revolutionary class when certain groups have gained the absolute conviction of their historical mission in the progress of mankind. Modern revolutions do not take place in the frame of politics, but in the frame of religion. They are radical in the literal sense of the word, transforming the lives of societies at their roots, that is, totally. Modern social movements and revolutions gain their revolutionary power not from the motives of economic requirements, but from their religious and messianic frame of reference.

One of the great accomplishments of Max Weber's sociology of religion was the investigation of the interrelationships between interest-motives and meaning-motives in social action. This approach must be applied to the secular and revolutionary religions that paved the way for the totalitarian world. We speak of secularization as a characteristic feature of the modern world. The term indicates that the supernatural religions and churches are losing their constructive and guiding power over modern technical and industrial societies. It implies that the decline of these religions is identical with the end of religion in general. The sociologist, however, should not apply notions with a specific theological meaning. He must use categories that are not value-determined. For this reason the sociologist should speak of the religion of progress as a social phenomenon in the revolutionary nineteenth century. The religious beliefs and spiritual creeds of the industrial world have been the dynamic power in modern social movements and a vital reality in the constituents of the totalitarian world. We can formulate our theses in two sentences. The nineteenth and twentieth centuries are deeply religious epochs. The social and economic issues of modern movements cannot be separated from the religious meaning that men have attributed to their revolutionary action.

The religions of progress are a universal phenomenon of the post-French Revolution world. It is necessary, therefore, to describe briefly the general phenomenon before limiting the analysis to the topic at hand. The desire for a new religion is a characteristic of romanticism. Romanticism is not only a literary movement; in its fullest sense, it is a philosophical and social attitude. It is an international phenomenon with conspicuously national differentiations. It is a movement of intellectuals, of philosophers and poets who experience two antagonistic tendencies as constructive and destructive in their lives. They are enthusiastic about the tremendous progress that philosophers, scientists, and poets have made in extending the sovereignty of human thought, action, and sensibility. They are in despair because they feel the forlornness and solitude of the modern intellectual living in a world of philistines, of pedants, and of bourgeois.

From this specific experience of the power of the human mind and the solitude of the modern intellectual has emerged Romantic Messianism, which is a common feature in Schlegel and Saint-Simon, in Novalis and Comte. Their religions are religions of progress. They intend to unify intellectual progress and social orders as a communion of progressive learning and emerging spirit in a society in which everyone has his objective place, function, and meaning in the whole. They take seriously the idea of constructing a religion of progress. Schlegel's formulation is valid for all subsequent religions:[2] "The revolutionary desire to realize the Kingdom of God is the flexible element of progressive learning and the beginning of modern history." Schlegel postulates the Realm of God in the Here and Now and rejects the idea of mankind as realizing itself in the infinity of the historical process. The romantic idea of a *religion* of progress is absolutely different from previous *philosophies* of progress.

During the seventeenth century, thinkers discovered the superiority of the modern, over the classical, mind, and considered this indicative of intellectual progress. This made it possible to challenge the authority of the classics. Turgot's and Condorcet's philosophies of progress united intellectual and political progress in the comprehensive idea of total evolution without imposing religious dignity on their theories. Nor is Spencer's sociology of progress a religion, whatever might have been its influence on the Protestant churches in the Anglo-Saxon world. The theories of the Enlightenment were definitely antireligious and purely philosophical. They illuminated the thinking of the philosophically minded person.

The religions of progress were destined to have a practical effect on the whole of society and to reestablish meaningful bonds of superiority and subordination, of hierarchy and discipline in an all-embracing spirit. These new religions hoped to recreate a catholic universe of meaning to give spiritual and moral security to the individual. They responded to the general trend of materialism and atheism that prevailed throughout the eighteenth century. They had to answer the question: who will take over the functions of the transcendent God as ultimate reality that is, as final constitutor of legitimacy in history? They knew that they had to establish a new ontology after transcendence had gone. They discovered two social realities – humanity and history. Some speak of people or nation rather than humanity, but all consider Society the bearer of absolute meaning – the bearer of progress as the total and true reality. People, nations, humanity are the manifestations of truth and present the reality of the Divine. The romantics have made history and society the demiourgoi of the world of progress. For Schlegel and Saint-Simon, for Comte and Bonald, for Proudhon and DeMaistre, the true reality is in history. History is the self-realization of the emerging absolute.

This general phenomenon of the vision of a new religion in the romantic movements finds its specific expressions in the religions of progress as they refer to the industrial and social movements of the nineteenth century. It is indicative of uprooted European civilization that all social movements, even those rejecting revolutionary action, appear as religions. They are in need of doctrines that affect human wills and attitudes by establishing the absolute meaning of the social and historical process. Four types of religion appear in the social movements of the modern industrial world.

Saint-Simonian religion appears as the gospel of a pantechnocollectivism. Comte's religion of humanity expresses a scientific and sentimental catholicism, which proclaims the gospel of the harmony of totally planned and totally guided industrial societies. The founders of these religions hoped to spread their gospel and transform the world through their religious teaching.

Even the atheistic revolutionary doctrines appear as negative religions. They establish an unimpeachable theology, a body of priests who interpret the holy writ authentically and bar heretical doctrines. Whatever might have been Marx's personal opinion of his work, Marxism in the Russian version has become a gospel of progress and final meaning, a religious belief and a militant church. More radical still are the atheistic religions that Bakunin and Proudhon introduced in their revolutionary struggle against the binding institutions of the past. They felt most seriously that there were no social and political questions that were not deeply intertwined with theological problems. In the modern world, revolutions are not restricted to the constitutional frame of reference. There is a new mankind arising from the roots of history, remaking the totality of the human institutions as it fulfils the meaning of progress.

In all four types of the religion of progress, this fundamental principle of religion is visible. We need a spiritual power, apart from the temporal power, able to guide and direct the mind and soul, in order to reestablish tranquillity, serenity, and order within the unending progress of humanity in history. This principle of a dynamic order is the normative idea of a perfect world, the unification of progress and order and the synthesis of the antagonisms become the focusing elements of the new religions.

With the vision of an absolute harmony, all these religions considered the contemporary state of affairs as anarchy – a chaos they referred to the French Revolution. Intellectual, moral and economic anarchies are the recurrent terms for describing the contemporary world as sinful and ripe for salvation. It is to be noted that the category of anarchy as coined by Saint-Simon and accepted and enlarged by Comte, Enfantin, and Marx, cannot be considered a scientific conception. Rather is it a mythical notion, which replaces the idea of original sin and the political concept of a state of nature. It indicates the state of corruption in the language of the new theology of history, in which the unity of progress and order describes the earthly paradise of the universe of history. For this reason no one can fail to recognize the messianic and eschatological terror in the description of these intellectual, moral, and social states of chaos.

This leads us to the political source of the religions of progress.[3] All of them have taken up the religious heritage of French Jacobeanism. They have all been the heirs of the religions of Reason, the Supreme Being, and Theophilanthropy. In spite of their opposition to the French Revolution, they share its historical messianism. The revolutionary cults inaugurated all those subsequent religions that proclaimed through reason and progress the spiritual mission of the historical classes in industrial humanity. The Jacobins began this historical messianism as a religion of progress. The eschatological vision of the human situation made it possible to view the enemy as atheist or heretic, and to classify mankind as believers and unbelievers. Revolutions and religions divided society into good and bad, friends and enemies. Modern society does not recognize legal and political status as decisive for social classification. In modern revolutionary radicalism is implied the fanaticism and terror of monopolistic religions. The term "aristocrat" was a category of obscene sinfulness to the "citizen," almost like the notion of the devil. This mythical classification of society indicates that modern revolutions identify their struggle with the fight for the victory of truth and the absolute in the historical progress of society. This religious and revolutionary attitude is still alive in the eschatological opposites of bourgeois–proletarian and Jew–Aryan in the bolshevik and national socialist worlds, respectively.

Nobody has expressed the eschatological vision of a decaying world more clearly and more nobly than Proudhon. He sees his struggle with constitutionalism and socialism as a decisive battle of destruction. He speaks frequently of the Napoleonic battle in order to indicate the ultimate character of the revolutionary conflict. He sees the decay of the bourgeoisie and, as a sequel, the similar disappearance of Christianity. He remembers the benefits of this religion in what he terms "its last hour," for it is going to perish along with the social and political institutions of the modern world. "All traditions are abused, all beliefs abolished, while the new gospel has not yet entered the mind of the masses. That is what I call the dissolution. It is the most atrocious moment in the history of society. Everything merges in order to depress the people of good will . . . I have no illusions and I do not expect to see reappearing in our country . . . intelligence among the bourgeois and common sense among the plebeians. . . . The killings are going to come and will be followed by a terrifying prostration. We are not going to see the work of the new period. We are going to fight in the dark . . ."[4]

There are similar passages in Marx, Saint-Simon, Comte, and in Saint-Simonian writings, which describe their historical situation in such eschatological terms. But nowhere in classical writings can one find anything like that. When Thucydides describes the fall of Athens, he explains and understands this tragic event in terms of human motives and of social laws. Sallust, analyzing the corruption of Roman nobility, and Tacitus, depicting the imperial court, never leave the spheres of historical and psychological explanation and understanding. Even when they are deeply moved by visualizing the decline of what they cherish most, they remain in the orbit of human action and human attitudes. It was necessary to have passed through Christian dogmatism before it was possible to confuse the *pax terrena* and *pax coelestis* and to indulge in the romantic identification of God, history, society, and humanity.

This universally recognized state of anarchy in the modern world makes the new religions indispensable for reestablishing the context of meaning that transforms the chaos of the historical process into the universe of progress. This again is something new. The Scottish philosophers, who were certainly no longer Christian, were extremely suspicious of history as the sphere of all human irrationalities and passions. Perfectibility and progress were categories of personal achievement, not generalizations for the historical process *in toto*. Here again the French Revolution opened the avenues for identifying history with the meaning of social evolution and imposing spiritual dignity on the classes that carry on progress.

Among the new religions, the Saint-Simonian theology and church deserve special attention for two reasons: first, most of the French socialists passed through this experience and incorporated it into their own theories of social salvation; second, all technocratic religions have started from this pioneering vision of the redemption of the world through a perfect industrial and technological society.

Saint-Simonianism has a special value also because it exhibits modern society before the capitalistic antagonisms came out into the open. The meetings of this church were visited by bankers, engineers, industrialists, professional revolutionists, leaders of labor, philanthropists, and social reformers. They were all willing to cooperate in bringing about an harmonious industrial order.

It is interesting to note, furthermore, that the founders of Saint-Simonianism discarded completely the principles of a Divine Being or the substance of a Holy. According to their belief, religion is the synthesis of knowledge for the practical purpose of guiding and directing the minds and souls of men in all situations. It is the spiritual power without which no temporal power can establish discipline, hierarchy, order, and obedience. This spiritual power does not derive its religious dignity from a transcendental God: it derives its message from the identity of scientific and humanitarian thinking in man. Positive science hypothesizes a providential plan of the universe. Hence scientists are the main body of the new clergy. They are supported by poets and artists. The scientists are able to derive final truth from the laws of nature, which enable men to know the code of interests and the sequence of needs. Poets will teach men the potentialities of their imagination, sentiments, and sensibility. Both will direct men to a wise and social use of their intellectual and emotional faculties by establishing order and making progress in the control of nature and society. The spiritual power, composed of scientists and artists, will take the initiative in planning the industrial world meaningfully in support of the temporal power of the industrialists. Thus, religion appears again as the all-embracing and leading institution in the social world, as the trustee of the final and absolute meaning of the whole. This whole, however, is no longer the world of creation or the universe of nature, it is now the narrow universe of total evolution of historical mankind, the universe of social progress.

The new clergy will determine and prescribe the conduct of society and the individual in all details because it alone is able to understand and to explain the historical situation of mankind. The clergy will elaborate the fundamental religious norms, the gospel of labor, the gospel of brotherhood, and the gospel of the poor. The gospel of labor is the spiritual recognition of industrial societies. Labor is blessed as the universal agent of productivity, which makes progress possible. All activities are included even the productive investment of capital in useful enterprises. He who contributes to the constructive effort of an industrial world, whether worker, foreman, manager, banker, or engineer, is in a state of bliss since he helps to bring about a harmonious order of progress. Only the idle, the remnants of feudal society who live off their rents, are amoral and antireligious. This is the first stride toward a religion of technocracy and of socialisms which is to establish a humanitarian paradise.[5]

Up to this point the Saint-Simonians are entitled to consider scientists a valuable body in the new clergy. The gospel of brotherhood, however, and the religious transfiguration of the poorest and most numerous class cannot be derived from scientific knowledge, but only from sentiments of humanitarian love. This is a utilitarian transfer of the spiritual principles of charity and poverty to the plane of social reality. To improve the physical and moral conditions of the poorest and most numerous class is a religious norm that pertains to the gospel of labor. Saint-Simon founded his challenge to Christian religion on the necessary relationship between scientific industry and humanitarian progress. We would not be in need of a new Christianity if the Church had promoted science and technology with a view to raising the standards of the masses. But this connection between technology and social ethics is neither natural nor logical. It is the optimistic belief that the spiritual principles of the supernatural religion have become natural concerns of mature mankind in its unending progress.

The world of industrial brotherhood does not mean liberty and equality. It means a hierarchy of mutuality. The stronger and wiser take the responsibility for the weaker and ignorant, who in their turn recognize the ranks and order in society. This order is not founded on justice, but on love. Mutual responsibility and service can exist only where society is united in one common purpose of realizing progressive harmony through the humanitarian love of one's fellow man.

This gospel was transformed into a church and cult by disciples and followers. Among them were young bankers – some of them emancipated Jews – engineers, and social reformers. They exerted a powerful influence on all strata of society – industrialists, bankers, and workers alike.

The Saint-Simonians were convinced that in the dialectics of progress from one organic period to another their religion surpassed monotheism by eliminating the last remaining antagonisms of spirit and matter. This is truly a gospel of a materialistic technical society. It appears in their own terminology as pantheism, for they define their dogmatic position as follows: "God is one, he is all that is. . . . He manifests Himself under two main aspects, spirit and matter."[6] According to their sermons, however, divinity and true religion are possible only when they have their foundation in social reality and in the progress of society. For this reason the term "pantheism" is confusing. There is no divine substance that pervades the All, there are only human passions and human thoughts that express the complex unity of human nature and its identity with the divine Human nature reveals the trinity of the Saint-Simonian religion: truth, usefulness, and beauty are its highest goods. They reveal the spiritual nature of man who strives for knowledge, searches for security, and longs for love.

The Saint-Simonian gospel can be summarized in the two blessings: the glorification of labor and the transfiguration of the passions. Both present the complex unity of the antagonistic forces of matter and spirit. This led to propaganda for the rehabilitation of the flesh, for the elimination of the antagonisms of the sexes by the idea of total person, and for the search for the divine mother. It is important to know such details in order to understand fully that all these efforts toward identifications and syntheses that are called religions have one purpose – to establish the total meaning of history and of social evolution and to grant religious dignity to the intellectuals who constitute and create this universe of social progress. The Saint-Simonian gospel did not transform the world as believers had hoped. But its vision has tremendously influenced technological and social-istic progress, and it has inspired engineers and bankers as much as radical workers.

Comte's religion of humanity[7] repeats the Saint-Simonian theology in a more distinct and systematized manner. This makes it possible to see how much this new theocracy pre-pared the way for the subsequent totalitarian philosophies. From the beginning, the philosophy of positivism contains in its basic intention the religion of humanity. For Comte, science and religion are the two aspects of the teleology inherent in human nature. Both point toward unity and harmony; both discover and recognize religious reality in order to satisfy it. Both establish order: the one in the sequence of the sciences, in order to know how to control nature; the other in the sequence of the feelings, in order to make possible subordination and discipline in the organiz-ation of society. There are two areas of religion – the intellec-tual and the moral. On the one plane, Comte finds intelligence as expressed in faith and dogmatism; on the other, the heart and love as manifest in worship, devotion, and service. Faith is described as the intellectual affirmation of dogmatism. It gives intellectual security by knowing the universe, and this makes it possible to improve the conditions of mankind: it is a universe, not revealed, but demonstrated. It makes us understand life as a mixture of fatalism and spontaneity – a *fatalité modifiable.* In manifestations of love, we apply the truth of dogmatism in living for others, devoting our efforts to the service of humanity as family, group, country, humanity at large. The three types of worship and the patterns of prayer are symbols and techniques for expressing the disci-pline and the blessing of subordination as the liberation from individual independence. They are described as the techniques that enable man to manipulate his organism and to concentrate on his work.

This is Comte's religion: the cult of industrial and mana-gerial humanity as administered by humanitarian engineers, social and scientific. He wished to establish his church as the industrial version of Catholicism: a spiritual power that is superior to all political institutions, a moral power that reduces individuals to subjects of society and reforms human animality to sociability. It is catholic in the literal sense because it unites sciences and religion by demonstrating man as a finalistic animal. For this reason, morals are higher than sociology in the final hierarchy of the sciences. It is the empirical division of the religion of humanity. Living for others, working for mankind, this is the religious truth. Thus mankind merging in the process of history is the continuous unity of the dead and of the unborn in the living. In this experienced and understood dependency and service, mankind reveals its religious character.

In the narrow universe of total evolution we are master and servant, god and historical man simultaneously. This is the religion of humanity, the self-adoration of mankind. It establishes new bonds and old obligations beyond the traditional churches and the vanishing states. This religion builds a new universe of meaning after the world of creation is gone and political constitutions have lost their moral and social reality. The fiat of the first sociologists creates the modern world as fatality of progress and proclaims the religious mission of the industrial classes to be the carrying on of the logical and spiritual progress. Modern natural sciences destroyed the classical cosmos when they discovered the infinite and open nature of the universe. Modern sociology as the religion of humanity transferred the Christian process of salvation to the history of society. By doing so, they made social and political progress a spiritual concern. This implied that their idea of order was of a final and absolute character.

Comte's work shows in all its details the intention of re-establishing a universe of meaning in order to guide and shelter forlorn and helpless modern mankind. It is a distinctly grim religion of total control – totalitarian thinking in a nutshell. Comte and the Saint-Simonians, too, praised the reign of Louis Napoleon as the necessary transition to the positive state of order and meaning. Comte, in particular, celebrated all details for the future administration of the positivistic society. In dealing with the cultural budget and with the freedom of the press, he gives concrete evidence that his early conviction of the negative character of freedom has ruled his thought throughout. His establishment of a new calendar and his designation of positivistic saints for every day in the year are in imitation of the Jacobin religion. His administrative ideas for organizing the Republic of the West are likewise inspired by Jacobin and Napoleonic patterns of radical abolition of traditional boundaries.

In these new religions merge the traditions of the Jacobin cults, the enthusiasm and discipline of the Empire, the vision of the engineers and scientists, and the philosophies of Bonald and Condorcet. It is indicative for the revolutionary situation of the modern epoch that the doctrines of progress and revolution appeared as religions. It is a symbol of this situation that the founders of these religions were the most lonesome and the most asocial members of a society that they described as anarchical. Because of this precarious situation, they were able to visualize the desperate position of the intellectual in a disintegrating world. And so they postulated order, communion, and religion. As Napoleons of the engineering and scientific age, they proclaimed their *sic volo, sic jubeo* for the purpose of reestablishing amity, tranquillity, and social and spiritual security. It is necessary to see these religions of the social and revolutionary movements in the general context of romanticism. In all its manifestations, romanticisms means to rebuild and to reconquer the world as a unity of meaning and order. Whether the romantics visualized the new order as a return to the medieval order or to a scientific and industrial catholicism, their religions had the special function of establishing the frame of reference within which obedience, subordination, and service again receive value and meaning.

It is essential to mention the system of Marx among the religions of progress. His scientific socialism is romantic and eschatological as revolutionary dogmatism, whatever may be the scientific qualities of the work for economics and sociology. As a revolutionary force, Marx's work has fascinated millions of workers, not by its scientific truth, but by the religious hopes and spiritual security it grants. Throughout the Marxist socialist movement this religious element has prevailed in the writings of the great political leaders. In Bebel's books it is conspicuous that the pathos of his language stems from the religious certainty of his socialistic faith. It is worth comparing the many editions of Bebel's work to see how slowly the religious fervor vanishes in the routine of everyday politics. All the simplifications and vulgarizations of the *Zukunftstaat* derive from concepts that Marx never abolished though they indicate a romantic and eschatological affinity to Hegel. The dialectics of freedom and its final achievement is merely a metaphysical substitute for the theological principles of grace and providence. Even Marx's early categories of "true democracy" and "true humanism" transfer the Augustinian concepts of the *civitas coelestis* to the secular process of history and confound it with the *civitas terrena.*

Marx's work shows most distinctly that under modern conditions religions of progress and revolutions must merge, for modern revolutions are total in character and radical by nature. There is no religious or political frame of reference left that would guide the revolutionary masses in their destructive or constructive work. They themselves are acting and being acted upon, conditioning and being conditioned. They themselves create a new world, that is, they themselves establish meaning and values in thought, sentiment, and action. That is why all modern revolutions must be religions of progress.

Proudhon and Bakunin handled the religious problem in a different and more radical way. Both must be considered the ancestors of anarchism and syndicalism rather than of socialism. Both made the war against Christian religion one of the main issues of their revolutionary doctrines. Both were firmly resolved to abolish the fundamentals of religious transcendence.

Bakunin, in particular, practiced a most radical naturalism in the war against theology. He hated the effects of theological sociology on the institutions of control, subordination, and discipline. His fury was directed chiefly against the categories of original sin, fall, and corruption. Such principles, and according to Bakunin, only such principles make possible domination and exploitation, superiority and obedience. All patterns of control derive from Christian pessimism regarding human nature, for all moral values lead toward theological foundations. And all social and political authorities refer to, and are justified by, spiritual conceptions of human nature that distort and displace the immanent truth and beauty of life. Bakunin saw the roots of this perverted thinking in greed and the lust for power on the part of those who are the stronger and smarter. He saw such unnatural thinking resulting in the universal corruption of rulers and ruled alike. He challenged the theological doctrines by proclaiming the radical and absolute goodness of man.[8]

Proudhon was more clearly aware that his struggle against God was not merely an element in his combat against the social and political institutions of the bourgeoisie. He felt that fighting God could take place only on a spiritual plane. Imbued with a genuine spirit of despair and radical negation, his revolt comes close to a new religious insight. This is remarkable because he shares some of the general presuppositions of the religions of progress. He shares the general belief in the law of progress, the logic inherent in humanity to which philosophers must submit in order not to fall into the errors of arbitrary subjectivism. Only society as a collective being can follow its instincts wisely and abandon itself to its free will without fear of committing an absolute error. In the dynamics of humanity superior reason leads in the right direction. Hence truth, instincts, reality, and history coincide in the progress of humanity which includes the evolution of labor.

Thus far Proudhon agrees with the romantics and the socialists on the totality of progress with humanity as its bearer. But he rejects violently the social pantheism of the Saint-Simonians and the total immanentism of the socialists. He hates the deification of humanity; he ridicules the reintroduction of mysticism under the name of humanism. He resents the subjection of the moral world to the authority of custom and the subordination of economy to the rule of communism. In these diverse types of religious dogmatism in the industrial world, he recognizes an effort to escape freedom and human independence in order to reintroduce more complex patterns of authority and exploitation than the world has ever seen. His whole attack is directed toward extirpating all the institutions of domination and dependency that degrade natural freedom and corrupt good instincts. He therefore assails violently the idea of God as the unified and centralized monopoly of meaning. From this principle spring all other patterns of centralized authority, such as the centralized state and the unified monopoly of academic truth. Despite, or because of, his recognition of the hypothesis of an infinite being, he rejects the total immanentism of the romantics. For the same reason he considers the infinite being as the hostile power against which he has to struggle unto death. Proudhon explicitly affirms that in God is the principle of evil, in man the principle of good. Human and divine powers are two potent rivals in deciding the principle that should rule the world. It is the duty of man to conquer God, who as the enslaving principle is man's enemy, and to erect the principle of human goodness in order to establish freedom. Proudhon was dimly aware that his struggle against God was still concerned with genuine religion as one of the deepest roots of human societies.[9]

More profound and wiser than Marx, Proudhon understood that radical revolutions in modern times must be total. They must attack the structure of society at its roots and foundations. Proudhon was keenly aware that religion is a constituent element in the foundations of all political and social constitutions. Therefore, the more he was willing to grant the principle of an infinite being, the more important it was to destroy the principle of Christian transcendence. He felt certain that with this principle defeated he could conquer the bourgeois world, because he himself was following a spiritual principle that integrated his revolution. Thus he challenged the existing order by proclaiming the Kingdom of Satanas. Proudhon and Bakunin both identified their revolutionary combat with spreading Satanas.

No one reads Proudhon and Bakunin any more except historians of socialism and of the social sciences. Their writings and ideas are no longer alive. There remains, however, a symbol of their radical anti-Christian religion in Baudelaire's enthronement of Satanas. Baudelaire created the symbol of Proudhon's and Bakunin's spiritual class-warfare with the image of Satanas ascending the throne. Satanas appears as "the adoptive father of all those whom God the Father has chased from the terrestrial paradise in his dark anger . . .[10] Satanas' kingdom is supported by Cain, the murderer, in revolt against the bourgeois Abel, who warms his belly at the patriarchal fireside. Baudelaire expresses perfectly the essential meaning of Proudhon's religious battle:

Race de Cain, au ciel monte
Et sur la terre jette Dieu.[11]

According to these revolutionists, the God of the churches cannot be the true spiritual principle. If He were, He could not tolerate the misery, humiliation, and exploitation of the majority of mankind. For this reason they fight the revolutionary battle against misery, exploitation, and humiliation.

In contrast to Saint-Simonian pantheism and Comte's totalitarian Catholicism, Proudhon is moved by a truly eschatological despair over a last battle of Napoleonic dimensions, and by a spiritual desire for reuniting life and the divine.

It is indicative for the modern revolutionary situation that Proudhon's greatest opponent – the Catholic philosopher of total authority, Donoso Cortés – fully recognized the unique and religious character of modern revolutions. This is remarkable because he knows Proudhon to be the archenemy. He agrees with Proudhon, however, on all aspects of modern liberalism and on most of modern collectivism; he appreciates the noble and superior mind of Proudhon and understands him as the greatest enemy. "The revolutions of modern times," he writes, "have an unconquerable and destructive force which the revolutions of ancient times did not possess; and this force is necessarily satanic since it cannot be divine."[12]

The student of sociology cannot use the same terms as the Christian philosopher. But he can grant that Satanas was a fallen angel. Thus modern societies liberated themselves from the God of creation, from original sin and divine grace. Instead they adored their own power and creativity in the technological potentialities of the industrial age. They identified the historical and social process with the meaning of divine providence. They were not yet able to see what the student of the social sciences affirms in the contemporary world – that lords and gods of the industrial and technological creation become the slaves of their own works and that the creators are going to be slain by their creation. For this reason the student of sociology sees the religions of progress as demonic phenomena. They are demonic because they praise the unleashed powers of man as meaningful in themselves and identical with absolute meaning. They are demonic because they do not recognize a frame of reference beyond the nature of man. Thus they become symbolic of the revolutionary situation of the nineteenth century in which the Hobbesian state of nature reappeared. The brave new world is demonic in its tremendous power to control nature and in its weakness in controlling its power. In the final analysis, satanism and demonism coincide.

The religions of progress are manifestations of a general state of uprootedness and universal revolution. As such, they attempt to offer a radical cure for a radical situation. Religion is the radical cure that establishes the rules of conduct and the meaning of humanity. The philosopher-priests of the industrial societies do this by fiat. It is the first effort toward total planning of man and society in the modern world. In these religions of progress, the structures of modern revolution and past Catholicism merge and coincide. Both share the same absolute knowledge of a state of salvation, both have the same radical conception of a state of sinfulness and corruption, both have the characteristic fanaticism of the possessors of a monopolistic truth.

The religions of progress express most distinctly one aspect of total revolution that has been going on since 1789. The man who saw this connection clearly was Alexis de Tocqueville. He spoke frequently of the ceaseless revolution. He was well aware that the French Revolution had opened the avenues leading to a total transformation of Western mankind. He made it plain that the revolution would change all ways of thinking and feeling and would completely reverse the traditional patterns of conduct. He understood the satanic and demonic elements in the socialist and industrialist movements. He predicted that they would lead toward a despotism of unheard-of dimensions. He was dimly aware that the total revolution was heading toward total peace. He wanted, therefore, to bring it back into the frame of Christian principles and to solve its social problems in the sphere of politics and constitutionalism.

All religions of progress have certain affinities to specific types of historical religions. Saint-Simonianism and Comte's religion of humanity transfer the pattern of the Catholic church and its institutions to their irenic and scientific re-

ligions. The Marxist creed is definitely social Mohammed-
anism, while Proudhon has been classified as Manichean.[13]
In spite of all these differences, there remains in all the
systems a general trend toward catholic and totalitarian planning of the lives of the individual and of societies. The
merging of total revolution and religion was inescapable in
a world that had lost the vision of a larger whole and had
limited its perspectives to the historical evolution of mankind. This process cannot be attributed to any one single
cause. The development of science did not necessitate the
negation of traditional religion. Rationalism and Enlightenment were still considering the world of man under a
transhistorical horizon of normative reason and intellectual
and moral perfectibility. In the French Revolution, these
trends merged in a definite anti-Christian religion of progress
and historicism. What the French Empire meant to these
religions has never been thoroughly analyzed. At least, Saint-
Simon and Comte understood well the blessings of a dicta-
torial order of progress. But the main contribution to these
religions came from the technological and scientific thinking of the industrial societies. All these trends merge in the
romantic movement which reveals the constructive and destructive force of total revolution. As a constituent element
of this revolution, the religion of progress is no less real
than its material interests. It is even more real because these
militant societies would never have gained the explosive power
of their integrated force if they had not referred their needs
and postulates to the religion of progress.

Notes

1. Paper prepared for the Seventh Conference on Science, Philosophy
   and Religion, held in Chicago, 9–11 September 1946.
2. See Friedrich von Schlegel, in *Athenaeum*, vol. 1, no. 2 (Berlin 1798),
   p. 60, and vol. 3, no. 1 (Berlin 1800) pp. 4, 5, 6, 10 ff., 13.
3. See Henri Gouhier, *La jeunesse d'Auguste Comte et la formation du
   positivisme*, Bibliothèque d'histoire de la philosophie, 2 vols. (Paris,
   1936), and *La vie d'Auguste Comte* (Paris 1931).
4. Proudhon, *Oeuvres complètes*, new ed., vol. 10 (Paris 1927) pp. 205 ff.
5. See Henri de Saint-Simon, *Oeuvres, Textes choisis*, ed. by C. Bouglé
   (Paris, 1925), and *Oeuvres de Saint-Simon et d'Enfantin* (Paris 1865–78);

for Saint-Simonian religion and sermons see especially vols. 23, 27–29, 42–46. See also *Doctrine de Saint-Simon, Exposition, première annèe 1829,* new ed. by C. Bouglé and E. Halévy (Paris 1924), and S. Charléty, *Histoire du Saint-Simonisme* (Paris 1931).

6. *Doctrine de Saint-Simon,* op. cit., p. 251.
7. Auguste Comte, *System of Positive Polity,* vol. 4 (Paris 1854); it may be worth mentioning that the subtitle of this volume is "Treatise on Sociology, instituting the Religion of Humanity. . . . containing the synthetical presentation of the Future of Man."
8. Michael Bakunin, *Oeuvres,* 5 vols. (Paris 1895–1912); see especially vol. 2.
9. See especially Proudhon's *Systèmes des contradictions économiques, ou Philosophie de la misère* (Paris, 1848), *Les confessions d'un révolutionaire* (Paris, 1850), and *De la justice dans la révolution et dans l'église,* 3 vols. (Paris, 1861).
10. Baudelaire, *Les Fleur du Mal,* ed. by Paul Valéry (Paris 1926) p. 252.
11. Ibid., p. 249.
12. Donoso Cortés, *An Essay on Catholicism, Authority and Order* (New York 1925) p. 264.
13. Ibid., p. 111.

Part II

Disciplinary Approaches

3 Social Movements and Social Order*
Rudolf Heberle

ON THE PREMISES OF PARTY GOVERNMENT

Any kind of party government presupposes the existence of genuine political parties; it ceases to work if the parties become mere pressure groups or political orders. A political party is by definition a part of the larger political community; it must therefore have a political action program that takes into consideration all important questions of policy that are live issues in the state;[1] it should be ready to assume responsibility; and it must respect the other parties not merely as opponents and competitors but also as partners who share certain basic political principles. One might say, genuine parties should be in relation to each other like two football teams: each of them certainly wants to win, but both have also the common purpose of playing the game, and therefore they are bound to observe certain rules and certain standards of fairness. So-called parties that aim at a monopoly of power for their own membership and intend to exclude the opposition from participation in the formation of the political common will are not true parties.

In a modern democracy each party plays the game of politics according to rules they all acknowledge; the game is a serious one, but the differences and conflicts between parties are never taken in deadly earnest; the antagonism between parties is not supposed to transgress the limitations and restrictions of a true $agon$[2] – a competitive game. Under the rules of parliamentary procedure individuals or groups who spoil the game by violating rules of order are subjected to various penalties (removal from the Chamber of the Legislature, suspension, temporary denial of the right to speak, and so on) by the presiding officer of the Legislature.[3]

* Reprinted from Rudolf Heberle, *Social Movements: An Introduction to Political Sociology* (New York: Appleton-Century-Crofts, 1951), pp. 447–59.

This relationship is possible because each of the teams acknowledges a higher aim than winning the game: namely, to keep the government functioning. This is the real meaning of the game, and the game can be played only if the parties are not so definitely opposed to one another that victory for the party becomes the primary aim. The system presupposes that the members of all parties are fundamentally united in a profound and strong sense of community, which enables them to place national unity above all party interests.

Although this conception of the party and party antagonism belongs to a very recent phase in the development of political institutions, it may be worthwhile to trace it back into the archaic phases of society. We know the dualism of primitive society, where a tribe is split into two exogamic phratries that have different totems and where an antagonistic but "agonal" relationship exists between these two totemistic phratries.[4] We know, furthermore, that the two political parties of the Blues and the Reds (a symbolism still in use in military maneuvers) in Byzantium sprang from the clubs that contested at the races. They managed the races (*Ludi*) and were at the same time political organizations.[5]

Nobody who has watched a presidential or gubernatorial campaign in the United States, from the prenomination contests to the final election, can fail to recognize the sportive or game element; the voters at least take it large like a game of chance, or like a match between various teams and champions; the very fact that wagers are made and that the prevalent odds are used (together with polls) in predicting the chances of the contestants, is highly significant. The game, however, may turn deadly earnest when the sociological premises change. Huizinga, the great Dutch historian who was perhaps the first to point out the elements of play in British and American party politics, saw the danger. Writing in the days of the imminent world domination by authoritarian political orders, he made the following melancholic comments:

> More and more the sad conclusion forces itself upon us that the play-element in culture has been on the wane ever since the 18th century, when it was in full flower. Civilization today is no longer played, and even where it

still seems to play it is false play – I had almost said, it plays false, so that it becomes increasingly difficult to tell where play ends and non-play begins. This is particularly true of politics.

Not very long ago political life in parliamentary democratic form was full of unmistakable play-features. One of my pupils has recently worked up my observations on this subject into a thesis on parliamentary eloquence in France and England, showing how, ever since the end of the 18th century, debates in the House of Commons have been conducted very largely according to the rules of a game and in the true play-spirit. Personal rivalries are always at work, keeping up a continual match between the players whose object is to checkmate one another, but without prejudice to the interests of the country which they serve with all seriousness. The mood and manners of parliamentary democracy were, until recently, those of fair play both in England and in the countries that had adopted the English model with some felicity. The spirit of fellowship would allow the bitterest opponents a friendly chat even after the most virulent debate. It was in this style that the "Gentleman's Agreement" arose.... There can be no doubt that it is just this play-element that keeps parliamentary life healthy, at least in Great Britain, despite the abuse that has been lately heaped upon it. The elasticity of human relationships underlying the political machinery permits it to "play," thus easing tensions which would otherwise be unendurable or dangerous – for it is the decay of humor that kills. We need hardly add that this play-factor is present in the whole apparatus of elections.

In American politics it is even more evident. Long before the two-party system had reduced itself to two gigantic teams whose political differences were hardly discernible to an outsider, electioneering in America had developed into a kind of national sport. The presidential election of 1840 set the pace for all subsequent elections.... The emotionality of American politics lies deep in the origins of the American nation itself: Americans have ever remained true to the rough and tumble of pioneer life. There is a great deal that is endearing in American politics, something naïve and spontaneous for which we look in vain in the dragoonings and drillings, or worse, of the contemporary European scene.[6]

In the meantime, two of the game-spoiling political orders have succumbed to the combined forces of democratic, game-playing powers and the non-charismatic order of the Bolshevists.

Present-day Communists, like the fascistic political groups, are not good sports from the point of view of party government. Because, for them, the essence of politics is the friend–foe relationship (a formulation invented by Carl Schmitt), instead of seeking to attain a compromise, they seek to annihilate the political adversary. Transferring the sociological pattern of international relations to the scene of domestic politics, these political orders deny the existence of a community between the adherents of different political creeds. No longer is the opposition regarded as acting presumably in good faith – it becomes the absolute enemy.

But even within the orbit of Western democracy, certain symptoms of a deep-seated inner crisis of party-government are discernible. The parliamentary system in its classical form was developed in England at a time when the old and the new ruling classes had settled most of their differences and had merged to a great extent by intermarriage and business connections.[7] There persisted the old antagonism between church and chapel, and that between the country squires and their retainers on the one side and the merchant and manufacturing classes on the other side. The latter, in their nonconformist anti-ecclesiastic attitude, were supported by the high nobility of reformation origin, which had enriched itself at the cost of the church. But there were no very fundamental differences of opinion with regard to the constitution or basic political institutions. Thus the parties were really factions within the ruling class of landed proprietors and industrial and commercial entrepreneurs. In such a situation, each party can be confident that the opposition party, if it should come to power by a shift in the party preferences of the voters, will not do anything that would seriously upset the established social and political order.[8]

The gradual extension of the franchise during the nineteenth century and the rise of the Labor Party in the twentieth century seemed to endanger this system.[9] For now a new class, opposed to the political dominance of land owners and capitalists, had entered the political arena and was sending into Parliament men who did not share the economic interests and political ideas of the ruling classes. In Italy, Germany, Spain, and other countries without a long experience of participation in political life by the broad masses of the people, an analogous situation had been or was soon to become the doom of constitutional government. In Great Britain, the system, in spite of Mosley's attempt to create a British Fascist party, survived the two severe crises of the depression of 1927–33 and the Second World War. The explanation may be found partly in the training and traditions of the political elite, including the leaders of the Labor Party. The same is true of the Scandinavian countries.

The system can function even where antagonistic social classes compete for political dominance, provided that all parties are agreed upon the necessity of preserving certain basic political institutions (even at the price of postponement of ultimate political aims) and provided that the anti-democratic activists of various denominations can be kept out of the ranks of political leadership.

The integration of the many particular wills in the modern "great society" (Graham Wallas) into a united group-will depends in the last analysis on the existence of a general respect for compromise. This can spring only from a fundamental, deep-seated sense of community. It has been the good fortune of the British that they have developed and preserved this sense of community.

Readiness and willingness to compromise are not merely matters of expedience and tactics. There are, in political affairs, situations in which a good politician and an upright citizen should not compromise, but rather stick to convictions and principles. When we speak of the will to compromise that springs from a sense of community, we mean the willingness to sacrifice the pursuit of particular groups' interests for the benefit of the common good, the willingness to see the good reasons in the antagonist's point of view and to search, together, for a solution acceptable to both parties. In this sense, the will to compromise and the respect for compromises agreed upon are essential for the formation of a common political will.

Throughout the nineteenth and twentieth centuries so far, the British ruling classes seem to have been more free from fear of the lower classes than any other European ruling class, and at the same time they have been more willing to let the leaders of the rising lower classes have a share in political responsibility. As a result, the lower social classes, especially labor, in Britain seem to have put more confidence in reform and adjustment than those in other large nations of Europe.[10] In this respect, the political scene of Great Britain has much in common with that of the Scandinavian countries.

Another important factor in these countries was the broadening of the labor parties into real people's parties, whereas in Germany and Austria they remained essentially parties of the proletariat with an insecure fringe among the lower ranks of salaried workers and civil servants.[11]

Apart from the threat of class antagonism, there are certain tendencies in party structure that may turn out to be fatal for party government. We refer to those previously discussed tendencies that may impair the independence of individual members within the party. The very essence of democracy can be endangered if political parties are too elaborately organized. If the party, in becoming a big organization, has attracted a large body of permanent members who develop many ties with party-sponsored institutions, the leaders will manage to gain effective control over the members. In other words, the voter's freedom of choice between candidates or parties will be impaired. The high commands of each party, being able to count on certain blocs of voters, will become less and less willing to strike genuine compromises than if they had to compete with other parties for a large mass of independent voters.

One of the most astute critics of party government has expressed this idea as follows: an election can either result in genuine representation if it is meant to select the best men, or it can mean a mere appointment of agents for special interests; in this latter case the elected delegate is the dependent and subordinate employee of the electors. "As soon as permanent party organizations dominate as fixed, always present entities in parliament, the latter is no longer a representation of the people but a body of agents."[12]

This statement of a contemporary political scientist sounds very much like the earlier liberal arguments against parties that we discussed in the beginning of this chapter. But it was not meant that way. A few years later, its author became a councillor of state for a modern dictator. Nevertheless, if we take the statement at its face value, it deserves serious consideration. Modern democracy is confronted with a dilemma: it cannot function, at least not in times of international tensions and crises, without a certain amount of discipline in the political parties – and yet one feels that party discipline ought not be carried too far. The voter should have the freedom to bolt from his party without fear of recrimination, and the elected representative of the people should have the freedom to vote according to his conviction – even against the majority of his party.

Seen in this light, a relative looseness of party ties, as it exists in the United States Congress and in the state legislatures, may in the long run prove to be a healthy condition.

SOCIAL MOVEMENTS AND THE SOCIAL ORDER

The rise of social movements in a society is a symptom of discontent with the existing social order. Political parties can come into existence because of antagonism between groups of power-desiring people who, though not at all dissatisfied with the existing social order, want to occupy positions of control and remunerative public offices. Genuine social movements aim at changes in the social order. They arise therefore among people who are dissatisfied with the order that is in operation.

Dissatisfaction with a social order arises when individuals no longer consider the values and norms on which the order is based to be the best or only possible values and norms. The agreement on social values and norms is the essence of social solidarity or of the sense of community. The sense of community is the foundation of any social order. Even certain social entities that come into existence through mere purposive or utilitarian motivations – like most purely contractual relations and associations – can not be maintained unless there is an underlying minimum sense of community among the partners. Otherwise the mutual confidence would be lacking that makes contractual relations possible and worthwhile. In the political field, a regime based solely upon fear is not a true social order; it is more like an armistice between hostile powers. A genuine social order is possible only where a set of values and a code of conduct are shared by the entire society. This does not mean that *all* values must be shared by every member of the society, nor that *all* norms must be valid for all members of the society. We know of very firmly established social systems – like the medieval Christian society or the old Hindu society – in which various status groups or ethnic and religious groups lived together, each adhering to its specific set of values and its particular code of conduct. A social order of this kind is possible if the *basic* values and the *fundamental* norms are shared by all groups and if the particular values and codes of each group are respected by those who do not recognize them as valid for themselves. This is what we mean by a fundamental sense of community or by *concord*, as we called it before.

From these premises it follows that a social movement that aims at a change in the social order may, under certain conditions, constitute a danger for the very existence of the social order, and we shall presently indicate what those conditions are. On the other hand, we also know that a society is not a static system; we know that external as well as immanent factors – such as an increase in population density – produce changes in the basic conditions of social life, and that codes of conduct and values will be affected by such changes. In many cases adjustments of the value and norm systems as well as adjustments in social organization will be inevitable if the society is to survive at all. If the dominant minority in a society is unwilling to make the necessary adjustments, these will have to be achieved by concerted action of other groups – in other words, by a social movement. In this kind of situation, a social movement is the force that saves the society from destruction, although the dominant minority may not realize that at the time. This is probably one reason why it is so difficult to oppress permanently a movement whose aims are in harmony with *tendencies* of social change that are immanent in a given society. If repression is at all successful, it may result in a high degree of conformity of overt behavior and in the illusion of preserved or restored social solidarity.

[Actually such repression will not extinguish the fire of discontent that smolders on under the surface, and the atmosphere of mutual distrust that is created will lead to further disintegration of the community.] The experiences of the Nazi regime have shown this very clearly. While the Nazis achieved a high degree of conformity in behavior, they left, after their fall, the German nation in a state of disintegration, of mutual distrust and disunity worse than ever before.[14]

When a dominant minority resorts to repression (which it may do with the aid of a mass movement), it is usually a symptom of fear resulting from weakness. The very fact that a movement like that of the National Socialists was nursed along by certain groups in the economic, military, and political elite of the German nation because it promised restoration of national solidarity (the ethnic community of the people, or the *Volksgemeinschaft*), was symptomatic of the sense of weakness in those elite groups. By way of contrast, the British and the Scandinavian nations were able to overcome and disperse similar movements before they had gained too much force. And this was achieved with a minimum of repression. These are nations in which the basic sense of community is very strong. Perhaps it is symptomatic that in the Swedish parliament the members are seated, not by parties, but in geographic order, according to the districts they represent; if the leader of the Conservatives and the leader of the Social Democrats are both elected in different districts of Stockholm, they will occupy seats next to each other. The British institution of "His Majesty's opposition" is well known. Before the elections of 1950 the press carried a photograph showing the leaders of the three major parties – Winston Churchill, Mr Attlee, and the leader of the Liberals, Mr. Davies – in attendance at a prayer meeting in St. Paul's Cathedral, sitting side by side in the front row, facing the high altar. This, we thought, was a most moving symbolization of the deep and strong sense of community among the British people.

In a society where there is this basic sense of community, the free and public expression of various and diverse opinions on public affairs is not regarded as a danger to the social

order, as long as the various voices of public opinion respect one another and are willing to debate in sincerity with
their opponents. Similarly, a variety of social movements can
exist within a society without danger to social solidarity,
provided the members of these movements respect their
opponents as fellow members of the larger community with
whom they are willing to debate and to search for solutions
that are acceptable to all. This is possible as long as political action – in the broadest sense – is regarded as a means
and not as an end. Depending on how much a social movement comes to pursue its goals as if they represented ultimate values in themselves instead of means to higher ends,
it will constitute a real and serious danger to the society.
Thus the danger lies in the elevation of political goals to
the rank and dignity of absolute, ultimate ends. It is, as a
rule, not difficult to reach agreement on means, but ultimate ends are usually beyond rational discussion.

We may therefore say that social movements and political
parties whose members do not claim to be in the possession
of the absolute truth are no threat to the social order; they
may be on the contrary a sign of vitality of a society. The
intransigents, especially the totalitarian movements and their
political orders, on the other hand, are bound to destroy
the solidarity of a society because they are devoid of that sense
of community that includes even the political opponent. But
these movements, while they are led and supported in their
beginnings only by small groups of fanatics or enthusiasts,
do not spring from nowhere. They have their causes in the
conditions of a society, they are not only destroyers of a
given social order, they are also symptoms of a disintegration
that is quite independent of their actions. While any sensible statesman who believes in the existence of values that
are of greater importance than political goals will curb such
movements, it is not always possible to do this, or to do it
successfully. Forcible repression is usually the least appropriate
course of action. One has to cure the causes, not the symptoms.
Movements of this sort arise when large masses of individuals
begin to feel that under the existing social order, in particular under the existing economic and political institutions,
they do not have a full stake in their society; they develop
the idea that they are only *in* but not really *of* the society.

Those Western nations that enjoy a high degree of stability and solidarity in their social order have had political elites who knew how to prevent the spreading of such sentiments. Adequate and well-timed reforms in social institutions can take the wind out of the sails of a radical movement. Almost equally important is the rise of leaders of the discontented groups into the political elite. Again it must be emphasized that the latter policy cannot be applied in dealing with the leaders of totalitarian political orders, because they are not willing to play the game according to the rules of an integrated community.

Notes

1. Not merely land reform or monetary reform or limited goals of similar kind.
2. The Greek word *agon* means an athletic contest.
3. A. Lawrence Lowell, *The Government of England* (New York: Macmillan, 1926), ch. XII on procedure in the House of Commons.
4. J. Huizinga, *Homo Ludens: A Study of the Play-Element in Culture* (London: Routledge & Kegan Paul, 1949), pp. 53 ff.
5. Ibid.
6. Ibid., pp. 206–8.
7. R. B. Smellie, *A Hundred Years of English Government* (London, 1937), pp. 67 ff.
8. Lowell, op. cit., ch. XXIV.
9. Ibid., pp. 350 f.
10. Smellie, op. cit., p. 353, observes that the underlying unity upon which the two-party system rested was endangered after the First World War. However, a new unity seemed to be developing between Conservatives and Labor, both agreeing that some kind of an economic plan had to be adopted.
11. Compare ibid., p. 355.
12. Carl Schmitt, *Verfassungslehre* (München und Leipzig, 1928), p. 219.
13. The only exceptions are those movements that represent a reaction against the original movement – the conservative movements that profess to defend the status quo. Actually, these intend to hold up changes in the social structure that are already in the making, and *in this sense* they too want to change the present order by restoration of an older order.
14. See R. Heberle, *From Democracy to Nazism* (Baton Rouge: Louisiana State University Press, 1945), p. 20.

4 Social Movements*

Herbert Blumer

General, specific, expressive.

Definition of social movements

Social movements can be viewed as collective enterprises to establish a new order of life. They have their inception in a condition of unrest, and derive their motive power on one hand from dissatisfaction with the current form of life, and on the other hand, from wishes and hopes for a new scheme or system of living. The career of a social movement depicts the emergence of a new order of life. In its beginning, a social movement is amorphous, poorly organized, and without form; collective behavior is primitive and the mechanisms of interaction are elementary and spontaneous. As a social movement develops, it takes on the character of a society. It acquires organization and form, a body of customs and traditions, established leadership, an enduring division of labor, social rules and social values – in short, a culture, a social organization, and a new scheme of life. Our treatment of social movements will deal with three kinds – general social movements, specific social movements, and expressive social movements.[1]

GENERAL SOCIAL MOVEMENTS

New Cultural Trends

By general social movements we have in mind movements such as the labor movement, the youth movement, the women's movement, and the peace movement. Their background is constituted by gradual and pervasive changes in the values of people – changes that can be called cultural drifts. Such cultural drifts stand for a general shift in the ideas of people, particularly along the line of the conceptions people have of themselves, and of their rights and

* Reprinted from Alfred M. Lee (ed.), *New Outline of the Principles of Sociology*, 2nd edn, revised (New York: Barnes & Noble, Inc., 1951), pp. 199–220.

privileges. Over a period of time many people may develop a new view of what they believe they are entitled to – a view largely made up of desires and hopes. It signifies the emergence of a new set of values, which influence people in the way in which they look upon their own lives. Examples of such cultural drifts in our own recent history are the increased value of health, the belief in free education, the extension of the franchise, the emancipation of women, the increasing regard for children, and the increasing prestige of science.

Indefinite Images and Behavior

The development of the new values that such cultural drifts bring forth involve some interesting psychological changes that provide the motivation for general social movements. They mean, in a general sense, that people have come to form new conceptions of themselves that do not conform to the actual positions that they occupy in their life. They acquire new dispositions and interests and, accordingly, become sensitized in new directions; conversely, they come to experience dissatisfaction where before they had none. These new images of themselves, which people begin to develop in response to cultural drifts, are vague and indefinite; and correspondingly, the behavior in response to such images is uncertain and without definite aim. It is this feature that provides a clue for the understanding of general social movements.

Characteristics of General Social Movements

General social movements take the form of groping and uncoordinated efforts. They have only a general direction, toward which they move in a slow, halting, yet persistent fashion. As movements they are unorganized, with neither established leadership nor recognized membership, and little guidance and control. Such a movement as the women's movement, which has the general and vague aim of the emancipation of women, suggests these features of a general social movement. The women's movement, like all general social movements, operates over a wide range – in the home, in marriage, in education, in industry, in politics, in travel – in each area of which it represents a search for an arrangement that will answer to the new idea of status being formed by women. Such a movement is episodic in its career, with very scattered manifestations of activity. It may show considerable enthusiasm at one point and reluctance and inertia at another; it may experience success in one area, and abortive effort in another. In general, it may be said that its progress is very uneven with setbacks, reverses, and frequent retreading of the same ground. At one time the impetus to the movement may come from people in one place, at another time in another place. On the whole the movement is likely to be carried on by many unknown and obscure people who struggle in different areas without their striving and achievements becoming generally known.

A general social movement is usually characterized by a literature, but the literature is as varied and ill-defined as the movement itself. It is likely to be an expression of protest, with a general depiction of a kind of utopian existence. As such, it vaguely outlines a philosophy based on new values and self-conceptions. Such a literature is of great importance in spreading a message or view, however imprecise it may be, and so in implanting suggestions, awakening hopes, and arousing dissatisfactions. Similarly, the "leaders" of a general social movement play an important part – not in the sense of exercising directive control over the movement, but in the sense of being pace-makers. Such leaders are likely to be "voices in the wilderness," pioneers without any solid following, and frequently not very clear about their own goals. However, their example helps to develop sensitivities, arouse hopes, and break down resistances. From these traits one can easily realize that the general social movement develops primarily in an informal, inconspicuous, and largely subterranean fashion. Its media of interaction are primarily reading, conversations, talks, discussions, and the perception of examples. Its achievements and operations are likely to be made primarily in the realm of individual experience rather than by noticeable concerted action of groups. It seems evident that the general social movement is dominated to a large extent by the mechanisms of mass behavior. Especially in its earlier stages, general social movements are likely to be merely an aggregation of individual lines of action based on individual decisions and selections. As is characteristic of the mass and of mass behavior, general social movements are rather formless in organization and inarticulate in expression.

The Basis for Specific Social Movements

Just as cultural drifts provide the background out of which emerge general social movements, so the general social movement constitutes the setting out of which develop specific social movements. Indeed, a specific social movement can be regarded as the crystallization of much of the motivation of dissatisfaction, hope, and desire awakened by the general social movement and the focusing of this motivation on some specific objective. A convenient illustration is the antislavery movement, which was, to a considerable degree, an individual expression of the widespread humanitarian movement of the nineteenth century. With this recognition of the relation between general and specific social movements, we can turn to a consideration of the latter.

SPECIFIC SOCIAL MOVEMENTS

Characteristics

The outstanding instances of this type of movement are reform movements and revolutionary movements. A specific social movement is one with a well-defined objective or goal. In this effort to reach this goal it develops an organization and structure, making it essentially a society. It develops a recognized and accepted leadership and a definite membership characterized by a "we-consciousness." It forms a body of traditions, a guiding set of values, a philosophy, sets of rules, and a general body of expectations. Its members form allegiances and loyalties. Within it there develops a division of labor, particularly in the form of a social structure in which individuals occupy status positions. Thus, individuals develop personalities and conceptions of themselves, representing the individual counterpart of a social structure.

A social movement, of the specific sort, does not come into existence with such a structure and organization already established. Instead, its organization and its culture are developed in the course of its career. It is necessary to view social movements from this temporal and developmental perspective. In the beginning a social movement is loosely organized and characterized by impulsive behavior. It has no clear objective; its behavior and thinking are largely under the dominance of restlessness and collective excitement. As a social movement develops, however, its behavior, which was originally dispersed, tends to become organized, solidified, and persistent. It is possible to delineate stages roughly in the career of a social movement that represent this increasing organization. One scheme of four stages has been suggested by Dawson and Gettys.[2] These are the stage of social unrest, the stage of popular excitement, the stage of formalization, and the stage of institutionalization.

Stages of Development

In the first of these four stages people are restless, uneasy, and act in a random fashion. They are susceptible to appeals and suggestions that tap their discontent, and hence, in this stage, the agitator is likely to play an important role. The random and erratic behavior is significant in sensitizing people to one another and so makes possible the focusing of their restlessness on certain objects. The stage of popular excitement is marked even more by milling, but it is not quite so random and aimless. More definite notions emerge as to the cause of their condition and as to what should be done in the way of social change. So there is a sharpening of objectives. In this stage the leader is likely to be a prophet or a reformer. In the stage of formalization the movement becomes more clearly organized with rules, policies, tactics, and discipline. Here the leader is likely to be in the nature of a statesman. In the institutional stage, the movement has crystallized into a fixed organization with a definite personnel and structure to carry into execution the purposes of the movement. Here the leader is likely to be an administrator. In considering the development of the specific social movement our interest is less in considering the stages through which it passes than in discussing the mechanisms and means through which such a movement is able to grow and become organized. It is convenient to group these mechanisms under five headings: (1) agitation, (2) development of *esprit de corps*, (3) development of morale, (4) the formation of an ideology, and (5) the development of operating tactics.

The Role of Agitation

Agitation is of primary importance in a social movement. It plays its most significant role in the beginning and early stages of a movement, although it may persist in minor form in the later portions of the life-cycle of the movement. As the term suggests, agitation operates to arouse people and so make them possible recruits for the movement. It is essentially a means of exciting people and of awakening within them new impulses and ideas that make them restless and dissatisfied. Consequently, it acts to loosen the hold on them of their previous attachments, and to break down their previous ways of thinking and acting. For a movement to begin and gain impetus, it is necessary for people to be jarred loose from their customary ways of thinking and believing, and to have aroused within them new impulses and wishes. This is what agitation seeks to do. To be successful, it must first gain the attention of people; second, it must excite them, and arouse feelings and impulses; and third, it must give some direction to these impulses and feelings through ideas, suggestions, criticisms, and promises.

Agitation operates in two kinds of situations. One is a situation marked by abuse, unfair discrimination, and injustice, but a situation wherein people take this mode of life for granted and do not raise questions about it. Thus, while the situation is potentially fraught with suffering and protest, the people are marked by inertia. Their views of their situation incline them to accept it; hence the function of the agitation is to lead them to challenge and question their own modes of living. It is in such a situation that agitation may create social unrest where none existed previously. The other situation is one wherein people are already aroused, restless, and discontented, but where they are either too timid to act or else do not know what to do. In this situation the function of agitation is not so much to implant the seeds of unrest, as to intensify, release, and direct the tensions people already have.

Agitators seem to fall into two types corresponding roughly to these two situations. One type of agitator is an excitable, restless, and aggressive individual. His dynamic and energetic behavior attracts the attention of people to him; and the excitement and restlessness of his behavior tends to infect them. He is likely to act with dramatic gestures and to talk in terms of spectacular imagery. His appearance and behavior foster the contagion of unrest and excitement. This type of agitator is likely to be most successful in the situation where people are already disturbed and unsettled; in such a situation his own excited and energetic activity can easily arouse other people who are sensitized to such behavior and already disposed to excitability.

The second type of agitator is more calm, quiet, and dignified. He stirs people not by what he does, but what he says. He is likely to be a man sparing in his words, but capable of saying very caustic, incisive, and biting things – things that get "under the skin" of people and force them to view things in a new light. This type of agitator is more suited to the first of the social situations discussed – the situation where people endure hardship or discrimination without developing attitudes of resentment. In this situation, his function is to make people aware of their own position and of the inequalities, deficiencies, and injustices that seem to mark their lot. He leads them to raise questions about what they have previously taken for granted and to form new wishes, inclinations, and hopes.

The function of agitation, as stated above, is in part to dislodge and stir up people and so liberate them for movement in new directions. More specifically, it operates to change the conceptions people have of themselves, and the notions they have of their rights and dues. Such new conceptions, involving beliefs that one is justly entitled to privileges from which he is excluded, provide the dominant motive force for the social movement. Agitation, as the means of implanting these new conceptions among people, becomes, in this way, of basic importance to the success of a social movement.

A brief remark relative to the tactics of agitation may be

made here. It is sufficient to say that the tactics of agitation vary with the situation, the people, and the culture. A procedure that may be highly successful in one situation may turn out to be ludicrous in another situation. This suggests the problem of identifying different types of situations and correlating with each the appropriate form of agitation. Practically no study has been conducted on this problem. Here one can merely state the truism that the agitator, to be successful, must sense the thoughts, interests, and values of his listeners.

The Development of Esprit de Corps

Agitation is merely the means of arousing the interest of people and thus getting them to participate in a movement. While it serves to recruit members, to give initial impetus, and to give some direction, by itself it could never organize or sustain a movement. Collective activities based on mere agitation would be sporadic, disconnected, and short-lived. Other mechanisms have to enter to give solidity and persistency to a social movement. One of these is the development of *esprit de corps*.

Esprit de corps might be thought of as the organizing of feelings on behalf of the movement. In itself, it is the sense that people have of belonging together and of being identified with one another in a common undertaking. Its basis is constituted by a condition of rapport. In developing feelings of intimacy and closeness, people have the sense of sharing a common experience and of forming a select group. In one another's presence they feel at ease and as comrades. Personal reserve breaks down and feelings of strangeness, difference, and alienation disappear. Under such conditions, relations tend to be of co-operation instead of personal competition. The behavior of one tends to facilitate the release of behavior on the part of others, instead of tending to inhibit or check that behavior; in this sense each person tends to inspire others. Such conditions of mutual sympathy and responsiveness obviously make for concerted behavior.

Esprit de corps is of importance to a social movement in other ways. Very significant is the fact that it serves to reinforce the new conception of himself that the individual has formed as a result of the movement and of his participation in it. His feeling of belonging with others, and they with him, yields him a sense of collective support. In this way his views of himself and of the aims of the movement are maintained and invigorated. It follows that the development of *esprit de corps* helps to foster an attachment of people to a movement. Each individual has his sentiments focused on, and intertwined with, the objectives of the movement. The resulting feeling of expansion he experiences is in the direction of greater allegiance to the movement. It should be clear that *esprit de corps* is an important means of developing solidarity and so of giving solidity to a movement.

How is *esprit de corps* developed in a social movement? It would seem chiefly in three ways: the development of an in-group–out-group relation, the formation of informal fellowship association, and the participation in formal ceremonial behavior.

The In-Group–Out-Group Relation

The nature of the in-group–out-group relation should be familiar to the student. It exists when two groups come to identify each other as enemies. In such a situation each group regards itself as the upholder of virtue and develops among its members feelings of altruism, loyalty, and fidelity. The out-group is regarded as unscrupulous and vicious, and is felt to be attacking the values the in-group holds dear. Before the out-group the members of the in-group not only feel that they are right and correct, but believe they have a common responsibility to defend and preserve their values.

The value of these in-group–out-group attitudes in developing solidarity in a social movement is quite clear. The belief on the part of its members that the movement is being opposed unjustly and unfairly by vicious and unscrupulous groups serves to rally the members around their aims and values. To have an enemy, in this sense, is very important for imparting solidarity to the movement. In addition, the "enemy" plays the important role of a scapegoat. It is advantageous to a movement to develop an enemy; this development is usually in itself spontaneous. Once made, it functions to establish *esprit de corps*.

Informal Fellowship

Esprit de corps is formed also in a very significant way by the development of informal association on the basis of fellowship. Where people can come together informally in this way they have the opportunity of coming to know one another as human beings instead of as institutional symbols. They are then in a much better position to take one another's roles and, unwittingly, to share one another's experiences. It seems that in such a relationship, people unconsciously import and assimilate into themselves the gestures, attitudes, values, and philosophy of life of one another. The net result is to develop a common sympathy and sense of intimacy that contributes much to solidarity. Thus, we find in social movements the emergence and use of many kinds of informal and communal association. Singing, dancing, picnics, joking, having fun, and friendly informal conversation are important devices of this sort in a social movement. Through them, the individual gets a sense of status and a sense of social acceptance and support, in place of prior loneliness and personal alienation.

Ceremonial Behavior

The third important way in which social movements develop *esprit de corps* is through the use of formal ceremonial behavior and of ritual. The value of mass meetings, rallies, parades, huge demonstrations, and commemorative ceremonies has always been apparent to those entrusted with the development of a social movement; the value is one that comes from large assemblages, in the form of the sense of vast support that is experienced by the participant. The psychology involved here is the psychology of being on parade. The individual participant experiences a feeling of considerable personal expansion and therefore has a sense of being somebody distinctly important. Since this feeling of personal expansion comes to be identified with the movement as such, it makes for *esprit de corps*. Likewise, the paraphernalia of ritual possessed by every movement serves to foster feelings of common identity and sympathy. This paraphernalia consists of a set of sentimental symbols, such as slogans, songs, cheers, poems, hymns, expressive gestures, and uniforms. Every movement has some of these. Since they acquire a sentimental significance symbolizing the common feelings about the movement, their use serves as a constant reliving and re-enforcement of these mutual feelings.

Esprit de corps may be regarded, then, as an organization of group feeling and essentially as a form of group enthusiasm. It is what imparts life to a movement. Yet just as agitation is inadequate for the development of a movement, so is mere reliance on *esprit de corps* insufficient. A movement that depends entirely on *esprit de corps* is usually like a boom and is likely to collapse in the face of a serious crisis. Since the allegiance it commands is based merely on heightened enthusiasm, it is likely to vanish with the collapse of such enthusiasm. Thus, to succeed, especially in the face of adversity, a movement must command a more persistent and fixed loyalty. This is yielded by the development of morale.

The Development of Morale

As we have seen, *esprit de corps* is a collective feeling that gives life, enthusiasm, and vigor to a movement. Morale can be thought of as giving persistency and determination to a movement; its test is whether solidarity can be maintained in the face of adversity. In this sense, morale can be thought of as a group will or an enduring collective purpose.

Morale seems to be based on, and yielded by, a set of convictions. In the case of a social movement these seem to be of three kinds. First is a conviction of the rectitude of the purpose of the movement. This is accompanied by the belief that the attainment of the objectives of the movement will usher in something approaching a millennial state. What is evil, unjust, improper, and wrong will be eradicated with the success of the movement. In this sense, the goal is always overvalued. Yet these beliefs yield to the members of a movement a marked confidence in themselves. A second conviction closely identified with these beliefs is a faith in the ultimate attainment, by the movement, of its goal. There is believed to be a certain inevitability about this. Since the movement is felt to be a necessary agent for the regeneration of the world, it is regarded as being in line with the higher moral values of the universe, and in this sense as divinely favored. Hence, there arises the belief that success is inevitable, even though it may only be after a hard struggle. Finally, as part of this complex of convictions, there is the belief that the movement is charged with a sacred mission. Together, these convictions serve to given an enduring and unchangeable character to the goal of a movement and a tenacity to its effort. Obstructions, checks, and reversals are occasions for renewed effort instead of for disheartenment and despair, since they do not seriously impair faith in the rectitude of the movement nor in the inevitability of its success.

It is clear from this explanation that the development of morale in a movement is essentially a matter of developing a sectarian attitude and a religious faith. This provides a cue to the more prominent means by which morale is built up in a movement. One of these is found in the emergence of a saint cult which is to be discerned in every enduring and persisting social movement. There is usually a major saint and a series of minor saints, chosen from the popular leaders of the movement. Hitler, Lenin, Marx, Mary Baker Eddy, and Sun Yat-sen will serve as convenient examples of major saints. Such leaders become essentially deified and endowed with miraculous power. They are regarded as grossly superior, intelligent, and infallible. People develop toward them attitudes of reverence and awe, and resent efforts to depict them as ordinary human beings. The pictures or other mementos of such individuals come to have the character of religious idols. Allied with the saints of a movement are its heroes and its martyrs. They also come to be regarded as sacred figures. The development of this whole saint cult is an important means of imparting what is essentially a religious faith to the movement and of helping to build up the kind of convictions spoken of above.

Similar in function is the emergence in the movement of a creed and of a sacred literature. These, again, are to be found in all persisting social movements. Thus, as has been said frequently, *Das Kapital* and *Mein Kampf* have been the bibles respectively, of the communist movement and of the National Socialist movement. The role of a creed and literature of this sort in imparting religious conviction to a movement should be clear.

Finally, great importance must be attached to myths in

the development of morale in a social movement. Such myths may be varied. They may be myths of being a select group or a chosen people; myths of the inhumanity of one's opponents; myths about the destiny of the movement; myths depicting a glorious and millennial society to be realized by the movement. Such myths usually grow out of, and in response to, the desires and hopes of the people in the movement and acquire by virtue of their collective character a solidity, a permanency, and an unquestioned acceptance. It is primarily through them that the members of the movement achieve their dogmatic adherence to their convictions, and seek to justify their actions to the rest of the world.

The Development of Group Ideology

Without an ideology a social movement would grope along in an uncertain fashion and could scarcely maintain itself in the face of pointed opposition from outside groups. Hence, its ideology plays a significant role in the life of a movement; it is a mechanism essential to the persistency and development of a movement. The ideology of a movement consists of a body of doctrine, beliefs, and myths. More specifically, it seems to consist of the following: first, a statement of the objective, purpose, and premises of the movement; second, a body of criticism and condemnation of the existing structure that the movement is attacking and seeking to change; third, a body of defense doctrine which serves as a justification of the movement and of its objectives; fourth, a body of belief dealing with policies, tactics, and practical operation of the movement; and fifth, the myths of the movement.

This ideology is almost certain to be of a twofold character. In the first place, much of it is erudite and scholarly. This is the form in which it is developed by the intellectuals of the movement. It is likely to consist of elaborate treatises of an abstract and highly logical character. It usually grows up in response to the criticism of outside intellectuals, and seeks to gain for its tenets a respectable and defensible position in this world of higher learning and higher intellectual values. The ideology has another character, however – a popular character. In this guise, it seeks to appeal to the uneducated and to the masses. In its popular character, the ideology takes the form of emotional symbols, shibboleths, stereotypes, smooth and graphic phrases, and folk arguments. It deals, also, with the tenets of the movement, but presents them in a form that makes for their ready comprehension and consumption.

The ideology of a movement may be thought of as providing a movement with its philosophy and its psychology. It gives a set of values, a set of convictions, a set of criticisms, a set of arguments, and a set of defenses. As such, it furnishes a movement with (1) direction, (2) justification, (3) weapons of attack, (4) weapons of defense, and (5) inspiration and hope. To be effective in these respects, the ideology must carry respectability and prestige – a character that is provided primarily by the intelligentsia of the movement. More important than this, however, is the need of the ideology to answer to the distress, wishes, and hopes of the people. Unless it has this popular appeal, it will be of no value to the movement.

The Role of Tactics

We have referred to tactics as the fifth major mechanism essential to the development of a social movement. Obviously tactics are evolved along three lines: gaining adherents, holding adherents, and reaching objectives. Little more can be said than this, unless one deals with specific kinds of movements in specific kinds of situations. For, tactics are always dependent on the nature of the situation in which a movement is operating and always with reference to the cultural background of the movement. This functional dependency of tactics on the peculiarity of the situation helps to explain the ludicrous failures that frequently attend the application of certain tactics to one situation even though they may have been successful in other situations. To attempt revolutionary tactics these days in terms of the tactics of two centuries ago would be palpably foolish. Similarly, to seek to develop a movement in this country in terms of tactics employed in a similar movement in some different cultural setting would probably bring very discouraging results. In general, it may be said that tactics are almost by definition flexible and variable, taking their form from the nature of the situation, the exigencies of the circumstances, and the ingenuity of the people.

We can conclude this discussion of the five mechanisms considered merely by reiterating that the successful development of a movement is dependent on them. It is these mechanisms that establish a program, set policies, develop and maintain discipline, and evoke allegiance.

Reform and Revolution

Mention has been made of the fact that specific social movements are primarily of two sorts: reform and revolutionary movements. Both seek to effect changes in the social order and in existing institutions. Their life-cycles are somewhat similar, and the development of both is dependent on the mechanisms we have just discussed. However, noteworthy differences exist between the two; some of these differences will now be indicated.

The two movements differ in the *scope of their objectives.* A reform movement seeks to change some specific phase or limited area of the existing social order; it may seek, for example, to abolish child labor or to prohibit the consumption of alcohol. A revolutionary movement has a broader aim; it seeks to reconstruct the entire social order.

This difference in objective is linked to a *different vantage point of attack.* In endeavoring to change just a portion of the prevailing social order, the reform movement accepts the basic tenets of that social order. More precisely, the reform movement accepts the existing mores; indeed, it uses them to criticize the social defects it is attacking. The reform movement starts with the prevailing code of ethics, and derives much of its support because it is so well grounded on the ethical side. This makes its position rather unassailable. It is difficult to attack a reform movement or reformers on the basis of their moral aims; the attack is usually more in the form of caricature and ridicule, and in characterizing reformers as visionary and impractical. By contrast, a revolutionary movement always challenges the existing mores and proposes a new scheme of moral values. Hence, it lays itself open to vigorous attack from the standpoint of existing mores.

A third difference between the two movements follows from

the points already made. A reform movement has *respectability*. By virtue of accepting the existing social order and of orienting itself around the ideal code, it has a claim on existing institutions. Consequently, it makes use of these institutions such as the school, the church, the press, established clubs, and the government. Here again the revolutionary movement stands in marked contrast. In attacking the social order and in rejecting its mores, the revolutionary movement is blocked by existing institutions and its use of them is forbidden. Thus, the revolutionary movement is usually and finally driven underground; whatever use is made of existing institutions has to be carefully disguised. In general, whatever agitation, proselytizing, and maneuvers are carried out by revolutionary movements have to be done outside the fold of existing institutions. In the event that a reform movement is felt as challenging too seriously some powerful class or vested interests, it is likely to have closed to it the use of existing institutions. This tends to change a reform movement into a revolutionary movement; its objectives broaden to include the reorganization of the institutions that are now blocking its progress.

The differences in position between reform and revolutionary movements bring in an important distinction in their *general procedure and tactics*. A reform movement endeavors to proceed by developing a public opinion favorable to its aims; consequently, it seeks to establish a public issue and to make use of the discussion process considered above. The reform party can be viewed as a conflict group, opposed by interest groups and surrounded by a large inert population. The reform movement addresses its message to this indifferent or disinterested public in an effort to gain its support. In contradistinction, the revolutionary movement does not primarily seek to influence public opinion, but instead tries to make converts. In this sense it operates more like a religion.

This means some difference as to the groups among which the two movements respectively conduct their agitation and seek their adherents. The reform movement, while usually existing on behalf of some distressed or exploited group, does little to establish its strength among them. Instead, it tries to enlist the allegiance of a middle-class public on the outside and to awaken within them a vicarious sympathy for the oppressed group. Hence, generally, it is infrequent that the leadership or membership of a reform movement comes from the group whose rights are being espoused. In this sense a revolutionary movement differs. Its agitation is carried out among those who are regarded as in a state of distress or exploitation. It endeavors to establish its strength by bringing these people inside its ranks. Hence, the revolutionary movement is usually a lower-class movement operating among the underprivileged.

Finally, by virtue of these characteristic differences, the two movements diverge in their functions. The primary function of the reform movement is probably not so much to bring about social change as to reaffirm the ideal values of a given society. In the case of a revolutionary movement, the tendency to dichotomize the world between those who have and those who have not, and to develop a strong, cohesive, and uncompromising group out of the latter, makes its function that of introducing a new set of essentially religious values.

A concluding remark may be made about specific social movements. They can be viewed as societies in miniature, and as such, represent the building up of organized and formalized collective behavior out of what was originally amorphous and undefined. In their growth a social organization is developed, new values are formed, and new personalities are organized. These, indeed, constitute their residue. They leave behind an institutional structure and a body of functionaries, new objects and views, and a new set of self-conceptions.

EXPRESSIVE MOVEMENTS

The Distinctive Feature of Expressive Movements

The characteristic feature of expressive movements is that they do not seek to change the institutions of the social order or its objective character. The tension and unrest out of which they emerge are not focused upon some objective of social change that the movement seeks collectively to achieve. Instead, they are released in some type of expressive behavior that, however, in becoming crystallized, may have profound effects on the personalities of individuals and on the character of the social order. We shall consider two kinds of expressive movements: religious movements and fashion movements.

Religious Movements

Religious movements begin essentially as cults; they have their setting in a situation that, psychologically, is like that of the dancing crowd. They represent an inward direction of unrest and tension in the form of disturbed feelings that ultimately express themselves in movement designed to release the tension. The tension does not then go over into purposive action but into expression. This characteristic suggests the nature of the situation from which religious movements emerge. It is a situation wherein people are upset and disturbed, but wherein they cannot act; in other words, a situation of frustration. The inability to release their tension in the direction of some actual change in the social order leaves as the alternative mere expressive behavior.

It is well to recall here the most prominent features of the dancing crowd. One of these is a feeling of *intense intimacy* and *esprit de corps.* Another is a heightened feeling of *exaltation* and ecstasy which leads individuals to experience personal expansion and to have a sense of being possessed by some transcendental spirit. Individuals feel inspired and are likely to engage in prophetic utterances. A third mark is the *projection of the collective feelings on outside objects* – persons, behavior, songs, words, phrases, and material objects – which thereby take on a sacred character. With the recurrence and repetition of this crowd behavior, the *esprit de corps* becomes strengthened, the dancing behavior formalized and ritualized, and the sacred objects reinforced. It is at this stage that the sect or cult appears. Since the growth of a religious movement is patterned after that of the sect, let us consider some of the important features of the sect.

First it should be noted that the members of a sect may be recruited from an heterogeneous background, showing differences in wealth, rank, education, and social background.

These differences and distinctions have no significance in the sect. In the milling and in the development of rapport everyone is reduced to a common level of brotherhood. This fact is shown not only by the feelings and attitudes the members have for one another, but also by the manner in which they refer to one another and the way in which they address one another.

Around the feelings of exaltation and the sacred symbols in which these feelings become crystallized, there grow up a series of beliefs and rites that become the *creed and the ritual of the sect.* The whole life of the sect becomes centered around this creed and ritual, which comes to acquire a sacred character. Since it symbolizes the intense feelings of the group, it becomes absolute and imperative. The prophet plays an important role here. He is a sacred parsonage and he tends to symbolize in himself the creed and ritual of the group. Also, he is the primary guardian of this creed and ritual.

The creed of the group becomes elaborated into an extensive body of doctrine as the sect becomes cognizant of criticisms made by outsiders and as it seeks to justify its views. It is in this way that a *theology* arises; a large part of it is in the form of an apologia. Accompanying this is some change in the ritual, primarily in the form of addition. Those features of its practices and modes of living that subject the sect to criticism and even persecution at the hands of outsiders are likely to be cherished by the sect as the marks of its own identity and thus acquire a special significance.

Another important feature of the sect that arises from its peculiar experience and sacred character is the belief that it is divinely favored, and that it consists of a *select group of sacred souls.* The transformation experienced by members of the sect and the new moral and communal vistas that it yields, readily lead them to this conviction. People on the outside of the sect are regarded as lost souls; they have not been blessed with this rectifying experience.

The feeling the sect has of itself as a community of saved souls easily disposes it to aggressive proselyting of outsiders. Frequently, it feels it has a divine mission to save others and to "show them the light." Hence it seeks *converts.* In order to become a member, an outsider has to have a conversion experience – a moral transformation similar in character to that of the original members. The public confession is a testimonial of such an experience, and is a sign that the individual is a member of the select. These remarks point to a particularly significant characteristic of the sect – the intense conflict relation in which the sect stands with reference to the outside world. The sect may be said to be at war with the outside world, yet it is a peculiar kind of conflict relation, in that the sect is not concerned with seeking to change the institutions or the objective social order, but instead seeks the moral regeneration of the world. It aims, at least originally, not to change the outside existence, but to change the inner life. In this sense, the sect might be thought of as profoundly revolutionary, in that it endeavors to inculcate a new conception of the universe instead of merely seeking to remake institutions or the objective structure of a social order.

A religious movement tends to share these features of the sect: Its program represents a new way of living and it aims at a moral regeneration of the world. As it develops from the amorphous state that it is likely to have in the situation of the dancing crowd, it tends to acquire a structure like that of the sect, and so develops into a society. In this way it becomes analogous to specific social movements except that its aims are of a profoundly different nature.[3]

Fashion Movements

While fashion is thought of usually in relation to clothing, it is important to realize that it covers a much wider domain. It is to be found in manners, the arts, literature, and philosophy, and may even reach into certain areas of science. In fact, it may operate in any field of group life, apart from the technological and utilitarian area and the area of the sacred. Its operation requires a class society, for in its essential character it does not occur either in an homogeneous society like a primitive group, or in a caste society.

Fashion behaves as a movement, and on this basis it is different from custom which, by comparison, is static. This is due to the fact that fashion is based fundamentally on differentiation and emulation. In a class society, the upper classes or so-called social elite are not able to differentiate themselves by *fixed* symbols or badges. Hence the more external features of their life and behavior are likely to be imitated by classes immediately subjacent to them, who, in turn, are imitated by groups immediately below them in the social structure. This process gives to fashion a vertical descent. However, the elite class finds that it is no longer distinguishable, by reason of the imitation made by others, and hence is led to adopt new differentiating criteria, only to displace these as they in turn are imitated. It is primarily this feature that makes fashion into a movement and which has led one writer to remark that a fashion, once launched, marches to its doom.

As a movement, fashion shows little resemblance to any of the other movements considered above. While it occurs spontaneously and moves along in a characteristic cycle, it involves little in the way of crowd behavior and it is not dependent upon the discussion process and the resulting public opinion. It does not depend upon the mechanisms of which we have spoken. The participants are not recruited through agitation or proselyting. No *esprit de corps* or morale is built up among them. Nor does the fashion movement have, or require, an ideology. Further, since it does not have a leadership imparting *conscious* direction to the movement, it does not build up a set of tactics. People participate in the fashion movement voluntarily and in response to the interesting and powerful kind of control that fashion imposes on them.

Not only is the fashion movement unique in terms of its character, but it differs from other movements in that it does not develop into a society. It does not build up a social organization; it has no personnel or functionaries; it does not develop a division of labor among its participants with each being assigned a given status; it does not construct a set of symbols, myths, values, philosophy, or set of practices, and in this sense does not form a culture; and finally, it does not develop a set of loyalties or form a we-consciousness.

Nevertheless, the movement of fashion is an important form of collective behavior with very significant results for the social order. First, it should be noted that the fashion movement is a genuinely expressive movement. It does not have a conscious goal that people are trying to reach through collective action, as is true in the case of the specific social movements. Nor does it represent the release of excitement and tension generated in a dancing crowd situation. It is expressive, however, of certain fundamental impulses and tendencies, such as an inclination toward novel experience, a desire for distinction, and an urge to conform. Fashion is important especially in providing a means for the expression of developing tastes and dispositions; this feature establishes it as a form of expressive behavior.

The latter remark provides a clue for understanding the role of fashion and the way in which it contributes to the formation of a new social order. In a changing society, such as is necessarily presupposed for the operation of fashion, people are continually having their subjective lives upset; they experience new dispositions and tastes which, however, are vague and ill-defined. It seems quite clear that fashion, by providing an opportunity for the expression of dispositions and tastes, serves to make them definite and to channelize them and, consequently, to fix and solidify them. To understand this, one should appreciate the fact that the movement and success of fashion are dependent upon the acceptance of the given style or pattern. In turn, this acceptance is based not merely upon the prestige attached to the style but also upon whether the style meets and answers to the dispositions and developing tastes of people. (The notorious failures that attend efforts to make styles fashionable upon the basis of mere prestige provide some support for this point.) From this point of view, we can regard fashion as arising and flourishing in response to new subjective demands. In providing means for the expression of these dispositions and tastes, fashion acts, as suggested before, to shape and crystallize these tastes. In the long run fashion serves, in this manner, to construct a *Zeitgeist* or a common subjective life, and in doing so, helps to lay the foundation for a new social order.

REVIVAL MOVEMENTS AND NATIONALISTIC MOVEMENTS

The Merging of Specific Movements

In our discussion so far, we have been treating separately specific social movements, religious movements, and fashion movements. Yet it should be clear that they can be merged, even though to very different degrees. Thus a revolutionary movement may have many of the features of a religious movement, with its success dependent to some extent upon the movement's becoming fashionable.

Revival Movements

Revival movements and nationalistic movements are particularly likely to have this mixed character. We shall devote a few remarks to them. In revival movements people idealize the past, venerate the ideal picture that they have, and seek to mold contemporary life in terms of this ideal picture. Such movements are explainable, apparently, as a response to a situation of frustration. In this situation people are experiencing a loss of self-respect. Since the future holds no promise for them to form a new respectful conception of themselves, they turn to the past in an effort to do so. By recalling past glories and achievements they can regain a modicum of self-respect and satisfaction. That such movements should have a strong religious character is to be expected. Nationalistic movements are very similar in these respects.

Nationalistic Movements

Most nationalistic movements have a strong revivalistic character in which the past of the people is glorified. This aspect is intimately associated with the motivation that is so characteristic of this kind of movement – namely a feeling of inferiority. Those who initiate the movement have usually had distressing personal experiences in which they have been made to feel inferior and as not privileged enough to enjoy a respectable status. Their wounded self-feelings and their desire to re-establish self-respect lead them to efforts to improve the status of the group with which they are identified. In such a movement there is not only the creation of an objective, such as the gaining of national autonomy, but usually also an idealization of some past epoch in the lives of the people.

Notes

1. Attention is called, in passing, to spatial movements, such as nomadic movements, barbaric invasions, crusades, pilgrimages, colonization, and migrations. Such movements may be carried on as societies, as in the case of tribal migrations; as diverse peoples with a common goal, as in the case of the religious crusades of the Middle Ages; or as individuals with similar goals, as in most of the immigration into the United States. Mechanisms of their collective operation will be dealt with in the following discussion of social movements. In themselves, such movements are too complicated and diversified to be dealt with adequately here.
2. C. A. Dawson and W. E. Gettys, *Introduction to Sociology* (rev. ed.; New York: Ronald Press Co., 1935, chap. 19).
3. There are political as well as religious sects. The difference is that the political sect seeks to bring about political revolution as well as change in the fundamental philosophy of life.

5 Dramaturgy and Social Movements: The Social Construction and Communication of Power*

Robert D. Benford and
Scott A. Hunt[1]

INTRODUCTION

The sociology of social movements currently lacks a conceptual framework to understand collective attempts to construct and reconstruct definitions of power. This deficiency highlights a paradox. On the one hand, movement activists devote considerable time articulating their understanding of power relations. Movement scholars, on the other hand, have generally neglected the processes by which these meanings are developed, sustained, and transformed.

To address this shortcoming we offer a dramaturgical framework that examines how movements construct and communicate power, focusing on intersubjective and interpretive factors. This framework is grounded in research of and experiences in various social movements including antiapartheid, socialist, sanctuary, labor, nuclear disarmament and environmental.[2] Drawing on these observations, this chapter analyzes and illustrates how movement actors collectively define, redefine and articulate power via four dramatic techniques: (1) scripting, (2) staging, (3) performing and (4) interpreting. The chapter concludes by suggesting the utility of dramaturgical analyses and proposing directions for future research.

* Reprinted from *Sociological Inquiry*, vol. 62, no. 1 (February 1992), pp. 36–55.

POWER, SOCIAL MOVEMENT AND DRAMATURGY

The very existence of a social movement indicates that differences exist regarding the meaning of some aspect of reality. At the core of these contests over meaning are differences regarding conceptions of power (cf. Gamson 1968; Gerlach and Hine 1970; Piven and Cloward 1977; Moore 1978; Tilly 1978). What is it? Who has it? Who doesn't? How is it wielded? Who ought to have it? How should it be used? While movement actors attempt to raise and answer these questions, institutional elites seek to maintain their "hegemonic ideology" by sustaining their definitions of the situation (Gitlin 1980; cf. Gramsci, 1971; Hall 1972), by " . . . shaping . . . perceptions, cognitions and preferences in such a way that . . . [people] accept their role in the existing order of things . . ." and by controlling the agenda (Lukes 1974, pp. 24, 25).

Although the outcomes of such contests hinge to some extent on how movements define and communicate power, a thorough understanding of how these dynamics work is lacking. In part, this lacuna was a consequence of the highly restrictive focus on resources (McCarthy and Zald 1973; 1977), a focus that neglected interpretive factors associated with social movement mobilization. But power has not only an objective basis, it is also grounded in the subjective,[3] as implied by the recent development of a number of concepts including Rude's (1980) "inherent" and "derived" ideology, McAdam's (1982) "cognitive liberation," Gamson, Fireman, and Rytina's (1982) "injustice frames" and Snow, Rochford, Worden, and Benford's (1986) "frame alignment processes."

While these contemporary efforts alert scholars to the importance of ideology and grievance interpretation and their relation to power, a conceptual framework illuminating the processes by which movements construct and communicate power is still needed. As McAdam, McCarthy, and Zald (1988, pp. 728–9) point out, movement scholars have tended to neglect "the dynamics of collective action past the emergence of a movement" and "the ongoing accomplishment of collective action." A dramaturgical approach facilitates an understanding of such dynamics. It does so by focusing on social acts and emergent meanings, recognizing that " . . . meaning is a continually problematic accomplishment of human interaction and is fraught with change, novelty, and ambiguity" (Brissett and Edgley 1990, p. 2). Finally, the analytical scope of dramaturgy is quite broad. It goes beyond the study of rhetorical strategies (Snow, Rochford, Worden, and Benford 1986; Gamson and Modigliani 1989) to consider a plethora of additional processes associated with the social construction and communication of meaning, including formulating roles and characterizations, managing performance regions, controlling information, sustaining dramatic tensions and orchestrating emotions. Dramaturgy can not only be employed to study crowd behavior, collective action related to particular events and the everyday interaction of movement participants, it can also be used to analyze movement careers as well as the ebb and flow of social change.

With these considerations in mind, social movements can be described as dramas in which protagonists and antagonists compete to affect audiences' interpretations of power relations in a variety of domains, including those pertaining to religious, political, economic or life style arrangements. Movement and countermovement activists, targets of change, and the media present divergent interpretations of extant and ideal power relations, desiring some audience to accept and act upon their particular presentation as if it were unquestionably real (Mauss 1975; Gitlin 1980; Gusfield 1981; Hunt 1991b).

However, what is real is itself problematic. Similarly, what constitutes power is subject to differential interpretation. Some activists see power as a means, others see it as an end, and still others see it as both. Given such diversity of meanings as well as the lack of scholarly consensus on the topic,[4] this chapter does not seek to define or operationalize power. Rather, it seeks to understand power from the perspective of movement actors – how they collectively construct their images of power and how they struggle to alter extant power relations.[5]

DRAMATIC TECHNIQUES AND POWER

To communicate power movement actors employ a variety of dramatic techniques. We identify and elaborate four broad techniques: scripting, staging, performing and interpreting. These are sequentially arranged and treated as though they are discrete processes for analytical purposes only. Empirically, two or more may be employed simultaneously by social movements. Moreover, since movement dramas are emergent and ongoing phenomena, activity associated with any one technique affects the unfolding of subsequent techniques.

Scripting

Scripting refers to the development of a set of directions that define the scene identify actors and outline expected behavior. Scripts are not rigid texts that movement participants are required to follow. Rather, they are interactionally emergent guides for collective consciousness and action, guides that are circumspect enough to provide behavioral cues when unanticipated events arise yet sufficiently flexible to allow for improvisation. Thus, while the bulk of scripting activity occurs prior to a performance, it can be improvised as actors interact with each other and the audience.

Scripts are built upon "frames" that provide a collective definition of the situation (Snow, Rochford, Worden, and Benford 1986; Snow and Benford 1988, 1989). Scripting is a social process that encompasses all of the various framing activities and alignment strategies. It differs from framing in that scripts attempt to integrate and coordinate movement activity. While framing provides actable ideas, scripting moves these ideas one step closer to enactment. It casts roles, composes dialogue and directs action.

Social movement scripts are about power relations. They include ideas, attributions, norms, values, beliefs and a universe of discourse. Scripts also provide performers with (1) diagnoses that identify problematic dimensions of power relations that are in need of amelioration, (2) prognoses that articulate an alternative vision of power arrangements, (3) compelling rationales for changing power relations and participating in movement dramas and (4) strategic and tactical direction delineating the most effective means to obtain power (Wilson 1973; Ladd, Hood, and Van Liere 1983; Snow and Benford 1988). The first two processes center around developing dramatis personae, that is constructing identities and roles for a cast of characters associated with movement dramas. The latter two entail generating dialogue and direction for movement performances and actors.

Developing Dramatis Personae

Social movement scripting begins with the development of dramatis personae or what Zurcher and Snow (1981, p. 472) refer to as "the cast of characters." Movement organizers help construct identities and roles for antagonists, victims, protagonists, supporting cast members and audiences (Hare 1985; Snow, Rochford, Worden, and Benford 1986; Snow and Benford 1988), including scripting their own identities and roles (Alinsky 1971).

In identifying an antagonist, movement actors usually point to a specific event or situation as problematic and attribute blame to some person, group, social institution or idea (Snow and Benford 1988). They frequently vilify the identified antagonist by invoking caustic labels such as "capitalist pigs," "male chauvinists," "baby killers," "warmongers," "fascists" and "scabs." Typifications of opponents as immoral, evil or villains serve to "galvanize and focus sentiment" (Snow, Rochford, Worden, and Benford 1986, p. 470; cf. Coser 1956; 1969; Lang and Lang 1961; Klapp 1962). An American labor song, "Talking Union," epitomizes such attributional processes:

> He's puffing a big seegar, feeling mighty slick
> 'Cause he thinks he's got your union licked.
> Well, he looks out the window, and what does he see
> but a thousand pickets, and they all agree
> He's a bastard . . . unfair . . . slave-driver . . .
> Bet he beats his wife (Almanac Singers 1947).

The "evil" actions of an antagonist are usually presented as directed against some group activists identify as undeserving victims or potential victims. Without victims there would be no social movement dramas (cf. Burke 1954; Holstein and Miller 1990). A number of scholars have observed as well that movement participation requires the development of a sense of injustice among a critical mass of structurally connected actors (Turner 1969; Piven and Cloward 1977; Moore 1978; Gamson et al. 1982; McAdam 1982; Snow, Rochford, Worden, and Benford 1986). These writers tend to neglect, however, the basis for movement claims about injustices and victimage. Movement dramas demonstrate how antagonists have violated cultural norms regarding the proper use and distribution of power. The imputed victims of such abuses of power can be protagonists, part or all of the identified audience, the supporting cast, or some "innocent" bystander such as fetuses, the homeless, children, aged, handicapped, minorities, or one's self.

Those identified as having the capability of overcoming injustice or solving the problematic situation are the protagonists. They are scripted as the embodiment of good, the negation of all that the antagonists represent. Protagonists articulate a more just world, one devoid of innocent victims, and claim to have the capacity to alter existing power relations. They can be idolized or charismatic figures, such as Martin Luther King, Jr., Cesar Chavez, Angela Davis or Jerry Falwell, an entire movement, a specific movement organization or some combination of the three.

A successful performance usually requires enlisting and empowering a supporting cast. Though the size of the supporting cast varies considerably across movements, typically a large number of auxiliaries are needed to perform numerous front- and backstage roles such as peacekeepers, writers, emcees, leafletters, fundraisers and the like. This involves recruiting cast members via persuasion (Snow, Rochford, Worden, and Benford 1986) or by offering "selective incentives" (Olson 1976; Fireman and Gamson 1979; Oliver 1980).

The final type of dramatis personae is the audience. Movement performances can be directed toward a variety of audiences, ranging from those who hold and wield power to the victims of extant power relations. More typically, performances are for the benefit of those who have the potential to alter existing power arrangements, even though they may not be cognizant of their capacity. Indeed, supporting cast members are frequently recruited from audiences. At a 1986 campus anti-apartheid sit-in the senior author observed, for instance, several of those arrested began as spectators but were eventually persuaded by the demonstrators to join the action.

Dialogue and Direction

While movement participation literature tends to focus exclusively on recruitment processes, sustaining the cast's involvement is equally crucial to an ongoing production. This is contingent in part on empowering the cast. Empowerment refers to an interactive process of convincing individuals or groups that they have the capacity to affect power relations. Social movements facilitate empowerment in a variety of ways (Carmichael and Hamilton 1967; Alinsky 1971; Dellinger 1975), many of which are predicated upon the construction of a universe of discourse (Mead 1934; Snow and Machalek 1984) and a vocabulary of motives (Mills 1940; Scott and Lyman 1968).

Vocabularies of motive supply adherents with compelling reasons or rationales for taking action and provide participants with justifications for actions undertaken on behalf of the movement's goals, particularly when their behavior is called into question by friends, family or coworkers. Social movements construct and nurture vocabularies of motive concerning the severity and urgency of the problem as well as the efficacy and propriety of taking action. A vocabulary of motive helps participants answer such question as: Why take any action? Why take action now? What is to be done? Will my actions make any difference?

Evidence of the promotion of rationales for taking action can be found across a variety of social movements. In *The Feminine Mystique*, for example, Friedan (163, p. 10) seeks to instill in women a vocabulary of efficacy convincing them that they have the capacity to alter power relations:

> women can affect society, as well as be affected by it; that, in the end, a woman, as a man, has the power to choose, and to make her own heaven or hell.

Scripting also provides direction for appropriate performances. This includes the scripting of emotion, as Zurcher's (1982b; 1985) work suggests (cf. Shott 1979; Hochschild 1979; 1983; Lofland 1985). Movement performers offer facial and verbal cues as well as utilize props intended to define and evoke the appropriate emotion or mood. The following excerpts from field notes of a carefully orchestrated disarmament event staged during the 1985 Pantex Peace Encampment illustrate the organizational scripting and staging of emotions:

> About 175 people gathered around the stage. By the smiles
> and chatter ... I judged the mood to be festive. The emcee
> [a peace activist], four Japanese, and an Anglo man filed
> onto the stage. The emcee smiled, and as she spoke, her
> expression turned solemn. The expressions of those watch-
> ing were now solemn. The emcee introduced two of the
> Japanese as 'hibakusha' [A-bomb survivors] and the other
> two as translators.
>
> The hibakusha related their experiences on the day of
> the bombing, their struggle to survive, and their subsequent
> treatment as social outcasts. ... I felt pity for them. I could
> see pained expressions on most faces. A few rocked their
> upper bodies. Their eyes began to fill with tears ...
>
> The emcee then introduced the Anglo as 'the first Ameri-
> can to witness the destruction of Hiroshima'. ... He ex-
> plained how he was assigned to fly over Hiroshima
> immediately after the bombing to determine its effective-
> ness and to film the devastation. At first, he appeared in
> control of his emotions. But soon his voice began to quiver.
> He broke down completely and began sobbing. He reached
> out, grabbed both the hibakusha, embraced them, and
> wailed, 'Oh God! What did we do to these lovely people?'
>
> Everyone I could see through my own tear-filled eyes
> was weeping. Several sobbed aloud. The emcee stepped
> forward and proclaimed, 'This is a wonderful occasion!
> What we have witnessed here today is an extraordinary
> reconciliation! ... Each of us must take that spirit ... back
> to our communities and put its power to work so that
> there will never be another Hiroshima or Nagasaki
> again!' ... The audience stood and applauded. ... The
> joyous mood had been restored.

The foregoing also illustrates how emotions can be scripted
to dramatize ideas regarding the exercise of power. The
performers' accounts of the abuses of power and the Air
Force officer's conversion from antagonist to protagonist
served as forceful affective prods for those who witnessed
the event. The emotions served to empower observers by
instilling in them both a sense of propriety and efficacy –
propriety by exemplifying the sacrifices others are making

for peace, efficacy by demonstrating that even antagonists can be converted to the disarmament cause.

Furthermore, the performance calls attention to the on-going dialectical tension between passion and organization (Zurcher and Snow 1981, p. 479). Managing this tension is a key to the survival of a movement organization. Too little passion with too much organization fails to inspire partici-pants; but too much passion with too little organization reduces a potentially powerful group to an undirected crowd.

A similar tension exists regarding the scripting of unique and routine events. Tactical innovations provide variety for movement participants, attract media coverage (Tuchman 1978; Molotch 1979; Gitlin 1980) and impede attempts by antagonists and authorities to damage or control movement performances (McAdam 1983); but too many unique actions suggest that the movement organization lacks focus and purpose. Routine events and movement rituals provide op-portunities to reinforce group values, goals and images of power relations. Too much routine, on the other hand, suggests that the movement organization is static, unimagin-ative and hence lacks the capacity to affect change. Whether performers and audiences view movement dramas as sus-penseful, captivating and persuasive or predictable, boring and uninspiring often depends upon the management of unique/routine and passion/organization tensions.

One peace movement organization studied, for example, had a longstanding reputation for mobilizing hundreds of participants on short notice by scripting and staging novel events usually characterized by enthusiasm and excitement. They staged die-ins and sit-ins, performed street theater, erected human billboards, and presented Lockheed with a "Bad Neighbor Award." Each dramatically portrayed prob-lems associated with existing power relations. In 1983, mem-bers turned to restructuring the organization. By focusing exclusively on organizational matters, the only participation opportunities the group offered were meetings that most of the supporting cast found boring. Gradually, the number of active members declined. Six months later, after finally completing their reorganization plans, the group disbanded, never to meet again. It had organized itself to death.

Staging

Nevertheless, some organization is needed to stage movement performances. Staging refers to appropriating, managing and directing materials, audiences and performing regions. This involves the maintenance and expansion of an organization's capacity to communicate its ideas about power. It requires that movement organizations concern themselves with garnering and managing money and other material resources (McCarthy and Zald 1977). Goffman (1974, p. 1) makes a similar point: "Whether you organize a theater or an aircraft factory, you need to find places for cars to park and coats to be checked. . . ."

Although staging frequently entails such logistical matters, a dramaturgical approach suggests that activists must also attend to developing and manipulating symbols. One central dramatistic task, for instance, involves the staging of performances that are consistent with the script, including engaging appropriate audiences and using "politically correct" symbols. To illustrate, one peace movement coalition studied attempted to prevent the local Revolutionary Communist Party from displaying symbols of guns, burning American flags, and clenched fists at an event. Organizers considered those props to be antithetical to the nonviolent scripts of the peace movement and thus inappropriate displays of the exercise of power.

Another major staging task involves promotion and publicity activities. Social movement dramas require audiences. Unless a performance is staged where people are already assembled for other purposes such as sporting events, conventions or near pedestrian or vehicular arteries, movement organizers must publicize upcoming performances and solicit attendance. A plethora of specialized and labor-intensive tasks are required to produce newsletters, brochures, pamphlets, leaflets, posters, letters to the editor, press releases, print and electronic media ads, mass mailings, door-to-door campaigns and phone banks.

The final staging problems presented here concern the interrelated issues of audience segregation and backstage control. The content of performances are often tailored to specific audiences. Movement actors, for example, typically stage a different performance for elites than for the masses. This reflects a common sense notion shared by most movement activists that institutional elites interpret displays of power differently than the powerless. However, it may not be possible to control audience homogeneity.

Moreover, as Goffman (1959) suggests, performances can be architecturally and temporally organized so as to prevent audiences from witnessing backstage activity or earlier performances that could undermine the image or message being fostered frontstage. Activists frequently encounter difficulty segregating regions, because their performances are staged in spaces designed for other purposes and controlled by authorities. Movement organizers sometimes devise creative means for concealing backstage activity in public places. Antiapartheid activists, for instance, had to hide their role in organizing an "illegal" rally or otherwise be banished from campus. They also wanted the demonstration to appear to be an impromptu reaction to arrests of protesters by campus police. As the rally began, the senior author joined a dozen gagged protesters standing on a wall facing a main walkway and was discretely handed an instruction sheet by a rally organizer that read, "STRESS SPONTANEITY, NO GROUPS ARE PARTICIPATING AS ORGANIZATIONS." The instruction leaflet thus served as a backstage communication medium in the absence of physical barriers segregating regions.

The foregoing example also illustrates how staging is an interactive process in which organizers and antagonists adjust to each others' actions (McAdam 1983). Frequently, antagonists control or limit the places where movement performances are staged (cf. Snow, Zurcher, and Peters 1981). University of Texas officials attempted to prevent mass demonstrations by erecting architectural barriers, restricting "free speech" to specific times and places, requiring assembly permits and sanctioning and even arresting violators of these rules. One reason antagonists seek to control such spaces is that they are typically involved in managing their own dramas, including preventing counterperformances that might upstage or disrupt their performances.

In 1984, for example, Dallas city officials attempted to prevent protesters from demonstrating near the Republican

National Convention in hopes of avoiding an encore of the spectacle of the 1968 Democratic Convention. Cognizant of the lack of drama associated with nominating an incumbent president, officials feared that the throngs of reporters would find the protesters' performances more interesting and newsworthy. A lengthy court battle ensued over the distance from the convention center the city would be permitted to erect a hurricane fence preventing "undesirables" from getting too close to the main performance.

Not only must those who stage movement dramas deal with problems associated with the segregation of regions during specific performances; they must also be concerned with overall backstage control. As Marx (1974, 1979) reports, agents provocateurs infiltrated various U.S. movements for purposes of damaging their performances, exacerbating or instigating internal conflict and encouraging defections. These counteragents were able to do dramatistic damage because of the privileged information regarding scripting and staging they acquired by virtue of having been accepted backstage as loyal performers.

Performing

Performing involves the demonstration and enactment of power. It concretizes ideas regarding the struggle between protagonists and antagonists and reveals to audiences ways they can achieve or preserve desirable power relations. Furthermore, performing is itself empowering. By taking action to alter or sustain power arrangements, movement participants experience a transformation of self, moving from a person who is acted upon by external forces to an agent actively shaping the scene.

Presenting a movement performance that effectively communicates power to audiences and empowers actors requires the coordination of a variety of dramatic techniques. Here dramaturgical loyalty, discipline and circumspection will be considered. Although these techniques often emerge from movement scripts and are frequently rehearsed, they are also skills that actors employ while performing.

Dramaturgical Loyalty

Dramaturgical loyalty refers to allegiance to a movement's constructed definitions or emergent norms (Turner and Killian 1987). Successful movement dramas require its performers to " . . . act as if they have accepted certain moral obligations," that is, they must display dramaturgical loyalty (Goffman 1959, p. 212). It requires commitment on the part of participants to keep the secrets of the group, to check criticisms of the team so as to present an image of solidarity to outsiders, to avoid exploiting their presence in the front region, to accept minor roles within the group, and to be taken in by their performance enough to appear sincere but not so much as to become overinvolved.

Actors who become overinvolved, for example, such as prolifers who bomb abortion clinics, antinukers who remove railroad tracks serving nuclear weapons facilities, or Christians who believe they are the next Messiah, perhaps share the movement's general views regarding macro-level power arrangements. From the perspective of other participants, however, the disloyal fail to understand their appropriate roles, misframe the tenor of the unfolding drama and use power illegitimately. Their actions thus not only upstage or parody collective performances, they tend to discredit movement attempts to sustain a unified image.

Dramaturgical Discipline

Loyalty to the underlying values expressed in the movement's script and to the collectively constructed images of power being fostered does not by itself insure a successful performance. Participants must also exercise dramaturgical discipline. This involves sustaining self-control so as to behave in ways that maintain the movement's affective line: avoiding involuntary disclosure of secrets, having the presence of mind to " . . . cover up on the spur of the moment for inappropriate behavior . . ." (Goffman 1959, p. 216), taking seriously that which is defined as serious and taking as humorous that which is defined as such.

An encounter we observed at a campus rally illustrates such dramatistic concerns. A woman in the process of being arrested for illegal assembly responded to reporter's questions regarding her motives by stating, "It's what's happening!" Upon continuing to indicate that she was participating because it was exciting and "the thing to do," one of the protest organizers pushed his way between her and the television camera and interrupted with:

> That's not the main reason why we're out here. We're here to protest U.T.'s eight-hundred and fifty million dollar investment in companies that do business in South Africa!

This not only illustrates the need for espousing an appropriate vocabulary of motive, one that conveys the gravity of the situation, but also the importance of having the stage presence to save the show when actors are perceived as muffing their roles.

Dramaturgical Circumspection
The success of a social movement drama also frequently hinges upon dramaturgical circumspection, the ability to prepare for performances in advance and to adapt an ongoing performance to unforseen circumstances (Goffman 1959). Regarding the first concern, this includes recruiting actors who are loyal and disciplined, targeting an appropriate audience for each performance, attending to the logistical details of staging and anticipating various contingencies that might arise.

Equally essential to the smooth flow of movement dramas is the capacity to adjust or improvise performances as unexpected developments or incidents occur. Thus rather than strictly adhering to every detail of movement scripts, actors must be adept at fashioning new performances out of the emergent scene.

One contingency a core company of movement players frequently must confront is stigmatization. In the context of social movements, stigmatization typically involves the labeling of an organization as unfit to hold or wield power. Activists seek to manage stigma by neutralizing discreditable actions, disassociating the organization from embarrassing actions and actors, purging the organization of disreputable characters and conducting face work once the organization has been given a discreditable label (Goffman 1955; 1959; Snow 1979). The Ku Klux Klan, for example, engages in impression management in order to overcome its unfavorable image. A Klan public relations director expressed awareness of their discreditable label: "People think we are hoodlums, but we ain't" (Williams 1961, p. 46). One face work strategy is to emphasize that the movement is part of "respectable" society. A Klan member articulated this ploy:

> You have heard about irreligiousness of the Klan and its being composed of hoodlums. . . . Maybe there have been some that entered the Klan that were unworthy; there have been . . . But of the thirteen men who compose the governing body of our Klan, . . . eleven are bona fide members of the Gospel of Jesus Christ, many of them with more than thirty years in the ministry. That's the kind of Klan we are trying to build (Williams 1961, pp. 47–8).

Finally, movements face a unique staging concern in that they must be prepared to manage counterperformances and piggy-backers. Any social movement that attempts to challenge or reinforce existing power relations is likely to encounter opposition often in the form of another group staging a countervailing performance. Furthermore, extramovement individuals and organizations present dramatistic problems when they exploit a movement's audience by promoting their own interests, selling products, proselytizing, and vying for media attention. Dramaturgical circumspection requires that the sponsoring movement groups handle such piggy-backers in ways that do not undermine the theme of the main performance.

Returning to an earlier illustration, several agents of a peace coalition advocated limiting Revolutionary Communist Party (RCP) members' participation in the Pantex Peace Pilgrimage. This created a dramaturgical dilemma. On the one hand, the peace movement could risk being stigmatized as illegitimate power contenders by allowing "pinkos" to exploit the peace movement's performance. This might jeopardize their image with local media and citizens, an image that had been carefully constructed over a two-year period. On the other hand, the peace coalition could contradict fundamental movement precepts regarding appropriate uses of power, including rights of free speech and assembly, by attempting to exclude the RCP actors from the stage. After considerable internal debate, the coalition allowed the RCP to participate but distanced themselves from the "communists." Ultimately, such dramatistic decisions rest on the negotiation of interpretations of the scene.

Interpreting

Thus far the dramatic techniques social movements employ have been discussed as though they were discrete, time-bound stages. However, these techniques are inextricably linked and temporally fused. There are, for example, scripting processes operating throughout the application of staging and performing techniques. The same could be said for interpreting. However, interpreting is fundamentally different from the other dramatic techniques in that it is the basis of all social activity. No other domain of social life is more pervasive and problematic than interpreting, the process of individually or collectively making sense out of symbols, talk, action and the environment, or, more succinctly, determining what is going on (Mead 1934; Blumer 1969; Goffman 1974). It is particularly problematic given the possibility of diverse interpretations and hence "multiple realities" (Schutz 1962; cf. Gusfield 1981).

According to Burke (1945), audiences and performers must interpret the act, scene, agency and purpose as well as the relations among them in order to develop a line of action, which in turn is interpreted by self and others, and so forth. Hence, interpreting is a never-ending social activity that makes movement scripting, staging and performing possible. For each dramatic technique, activists seek to develop a line of action they perceive to be consistent with their collectively negotiated reality interpretations, idealistic visions and readings of the audiences' interpretations. Movement scripts, for instance, represent the collective construction of meaning, particularly concerning real and ideal power arrangements, taking various audiences' interpretations into account. Staging techniques, too, are predicated upon interpreting elements of the scene and imagining how a specific performance might appear to others. Finally, no movement performance could occur unless the actors were constantly monitoring their social and physical environments, especially the reactions of other performers and the audience, and adjusting their performances accordingly.

Interpretations are not only central to producing movement dramas, they are the very object of those productions. Performances seek to affect audiences' interpretations of reality, interpretive work that fundamentally concerns power relations. It identifies who had and who lacks power, portrays how it is wielded, presents an alternative vision of power arrangements and articulates how such transformations might be realized. Movement interpretive work thus stimulates audiences to redefine their situations as unjust and mutable so that existing power structures can be altered.

Yet movement scripts and performances do not have intrinsic meaning. Meaning is derived in part from audiences' interpretations, and these in turn are affected by personal biographies as well as by understandings of the wider social context (Mills 1959). According to Snow and Benford (1988) there are three such contextual factors that affect audiences' interpretations. First, events may occur that undermine the empirical credibility of movement claims. Second, audiences filter such evidence through an interpretive screen based on their personal experience. A movement presentation may be too far removed from experiences of the audience for them to identify with or develop empathy toward the protagonists. Finally, an audience's cultural heritage, that is, their folk wisdom, narrations and myths, affects its interpretations. In sum, movement performances incongruent with audience interpretations of their empirical, experiential and cultural realities may fail to resonate or move them to participate actively in the collective drama.

To illustrate, one attempt by Austin Peace and Justice Coalition actors to recruit minorities entailed sponsoring a barbecue at a lower-class neighborhood community center. One of the peace activists recounted:

> I was serving food to people, when this middle-aged black guy walked up and asked if he could have some chicken to take home to his family. I said, 'sure', and he asked me what we were doing there. I told him about the march and rally and explained why we were trying to stop the deployment of missiles in Europe. I wish you could have

heard what he said to me. He goes 'Lady, a nuclear war is about the best thing that could happen to us, because we'd finally be on an equal footing with white folk.'

In short, the peace coalition's communications about national and international power relations failed to resonate with the audience's interpretations of everyday life experiences involving power relations between whites and blacks.

Factors beyond the control of social movements can also distort or otherwise modify the desired interpretations of the intended audiences. Producers of modern movements frequently find that their audiences' interpretations are filtered by media agents and agencies who take an active role in the reality construction business. Thus many are exposed only to those movements or performances deemed newsworthy, and when media outlets choose to cover movements they often trivialize them or demean their participants (Tuchman 1978; Gitlin 1980). For example, a magazine article, based on in-depth interviews with several Austin peace activists who worked for nine months to stage a statewide disarmament march and rally, focused on the "hippies" in the movement referring to their "beards and sandals," while neglecting the performance's central theme. The activists felt that the media had in effect reduced a drama about global power relations and the survival of our species to a "cute" human interest story.

Members of the audience who articulate their interpretations essentially provide reviews or critiques of social movement dramas. Activists interpret audience reactions and decide either (1) to make subsequent scripting, staging and performing adjustments to fit the targeted audience, (2) to target a different audience or (3) to discount the reviews as unrepresentative, ill-informed or flat out wrong (cf. Snow, Rochford, Worden, and Benford 1986). Activists who completely ignore audience interpretations risk being discounted as a fringe group, while those who continually compromise their scripts to accommodate audience reviews risk being seen as a movement without principled direction and hence an unsuitable contender for power.

CONCLUSION

Activists and revolutionaries have long appreciated both the objective and subjective bases of power. Alinsky (1971, p. 127), for example, proclaims that "power is not only what you have but what the enemy thinks you have." By recognizing the subjective bases of power, this essay illuminates how social movement actors socially construct and communicate their conceptions of power. It does so by identifying and elaborating four interrelated dramatistic techniques social movements employ – scripting, staging, performing and interpreting.

This effort makes several theoretical and empirical contributions. First, it adds to an understanding of how movements actually acquire and mobilize resources. Though resource mobilization theory has advanced understanding of social movement processes in a number of ways, it has begged the question of how movements and movement organizations acquire resources from members, conscience constituents and third party supporters (Jenkins and Perrow 1977; McCarthy and Zald 1977). Dramaturgy provides a framework for analyzing the dynamics of resource acquisition and deployment.

While extant theories and research have contributed to an understanding of the factors affecting movement emergence and decline as well as the correlates of recruitment, commitment and participation, they have failed to illuminate adequately the processes associated with these phenomena. Consequently, most literature tends to depict movements as relatively static. By extending the temporal span of analyses and attending to the ongoing flow of interaction among actors, events and performances, dramaturgy captures more fully than heretofore the dynamic qualities of movements.

One set of dynamics frequently overlooked concerns the intense emotions, dramatic tensions and heightened sense of expectancy associated with movement activities. This recent neglect of emotions is attributable in part to resource mobilization theory's domain assumptions regarding rationality. In reaction to the psychopathological models, which characterized collective behavior as irrational, resource mobilization theorists recast movement participants as

ultrarationalistic actors devoid of feeling. But movement
actors are neither psychotics nor computers. Participants
must be more than mobilized to act; they have to be inspired.
Indeed our observations suggest that passion is crucial to
constituent mobilization. Dramaturgy attends to this shortcoming by providing a foundation for analyzing how affect
can be orchestrated as well as for the role emotions play in
movement mobilization (Zurcher, 1982a).

The dramaturgy of social movements has additional utility
in that it inspires a somewhat different genre of research
questions than suggested by other perspectives. One set of
issues concerns the relationship between dramatic techniques
and outcomes. This essay represents an initial attempt to
delineate several factors associated with producing an effective
movement performance. Future research could move forward along these lines by examining the conditions under
which various movement dramas succeed in mobilizing supporters, neutralizing antagonists and affecting power relations. We suspect, for example, that a variety of movement
outcomes, from resource mobilization to longevity, depend
upon scripting and sustaining agon. Mobilization is more
difficult if the antagonist is not particularly susceptible to
vilification or the protagonist is not very likable.

Furthermore, the more thematically consistent a movement's dramatic techniques appear to audiences the more
likely they will consider the movement a legitimate contender for power. Some potential pro-life sympathizers, for
instance, might call into question the movement's life
affirming theme upon hearing about abortion clinic bomb-
ings, and thus doubt its sincerity and legitimacy.

The above illustration suggests another set of issues to be
explored. Frequently, fundamental differences erupt among
a movement's organizations regarding the most appropriate and effective ways to communicate power (Benford and
Zurcher 1990). What happens when intramovement disputes
take an acrimonious turn? While research suggests that some
infighting is beneficial (Gerlach and Hine 1970; Anderson
and Dynes 1973; Meier and Rudwick 1973), it can be detri-
mental when it incessantly diverts audience attention from
the movement's principal theme. When movements fail to
present a unified front they are perhaps more vulnerable

to countervailing tactics of antagonists. Future research ought to attend more fully to how movement factions negotiate basic dramatic elements so as to present an image of a unified effort. On the other hand, what happens when such unity is not desired by all factions? Attending to the dramatistic techniques employed could illuminate how some actors use movement diversity and internal conflict to their advantage.

Notes

1. An earlier version of this chapter was presented at the annual meetings of the Society for the Study of Symbolic Interaction, San Francisco, August 1989. We are indebted to Nicholas Babchuk, Jay Corzine, Bill Gamson, Tom Hood, Michael G. Lacy, Michelle Miller, Helen Moore, Dave Snow, Hugh Whitt, Mayer Zald and several anonymous reviewers for their insightful comments and assistance with earlier drafts.

2. The six movements were investigated using multi-method, grounded theory approaches including overt participant observation, interviews, and document analyses. For more extensive descriptions of the methods employed, see Snow, Benford, and Anderson (1986), Benford (1987) and Hunt (1991a). For elaborations of grounded theory, see Glaser and Strauss (1967), Lofland and Lofland (1984) and Strauss and Corgin (1990).

3. Weber (1978, pp. 53 and 212ff.) seemed to suggest as much in his discussions of power (*macht*) in terms of "probability" as well as his distinction regarding "legitimate domination." Numerous writers since Weber have called attention to other subjective dimensions of power, particularly processes of maintaining or challenging legitimate authority via the manipulation of symbols, language and myths (Edelman 1964; 1971; Gramsci 1971; Lukes 1974; Young and Massey 1978; Gaventa 1980).

4. For reviews of controversies on power, see Lukes (1974; 1986) and Wrong (1979).

5. Social construction refers to the notion that the meaning and sometimes the very existence of "things" in the human environment are collectively derived via sustained social interaction (Berger and Luckmann 1966; Blumer 1969). Once meaning has been attributed to some thing, it obtains the status of objective reality, that is people tend to act toward it as though it were real. However, to use the term social construction, does not imply that meaning is fashioned ex nihilo. At any given point in time, extant meanings are subject to reconstruction. Thus, the term social construction refers not only to the initial collective attribution of meaning, but to the ongoing and frequently contentious processes of negotiation, renegotiation, and reconstitution of meanings.

References

Alinsky, Saul D. (1971) *Rules for Radicals; A Pragmatic Primer for Realistic Radicals* (New York: Random House).

Almanac Singers (1947) *Talking Union* (Stormking Music Inc.)

Anderson W. A. and R. R. Dynes (1973) "Organizational and Political Transformation of a Social Movement: A Study of the 30th of May Movement in Curacao." *Social Forces*, vol. 51, pp. 330–41.

Benford, Robert D. (1987) *Framing Activity, Meaning and Social Movement Participation: The Nuclear Disarmament Movement*, unpublished PhD dissertation, University of Texas-Austin.

Benford, Robert D. and Louis A. Zurcher (1990) "Instrumental and Symbolic Competition Among Social Movement Organizations." in *Peace Movement Dynamics: Sociological Views*, Sam Marullo and John Lofland (eds), (New Brunswick, NJ: Rutgers University Press).

Berger, Peter L. and Thomas Luckmann (1966) *The Social Construction of Reality: A Treatise in the Sociology of Knowledge* (New York: Doubleday).

Blumer, Herbert (1969) *Symbolic Interactionism* (Englewood Cliffs, NJ: Transaction).

Brissett, Dennis and Charles Edgley (1990), (eds), *Life as Theatre: A Dramaturgical Source Book*, 2nd (New York: Aldine de Gruyter).

Burke, Kenneth (1945) *A Grammar of Motives* (Berkeley: University of California Press).

Burke, Kenneth (1954) *Permanence and Change: An Anatomy of Purpose* (Indianapolis: Bobbs-Merrill).

Carmichael, Stokely and Charles V. Hamilton (1967) *Black Power: The Politics of Liberation in America* (New York: Vintage Books).

Coser, Lewis (1956) *The Function of Social Conflict* (New York: Free Press).

Coser, Lewis (1969) "The Visibility of Evil," *Journal of Social Issues*, vol. 25, pp. 101–9.

Dellinger, Dave (1975) *More Power Than We Know: The People's Movement Toward Democracy* (Garden City, NY: Doubleday).

Edelman, Murray (1964) *The Symbolic Uses of Politics* (Chicago: University of Illinois Press).

Edelman, Murray (1971) *Politics as Symbolic Action: Mass Arousal and Acquiescence* (Chicago: Markham Publishing).

Fireman, Bruce and William H. Gamson (1979) "Utilitarian Logic in the Resource Mobilization Perspective," in Mayer N. Zald and John D. McCarthy (eds), *The Dynamics of Social Movements* (Cambridge, MA: Winthrop).

Friedan, Betty (1963) *The Feminine Mystique* (New York: Dell).

Gamson, William A. (1968) *Power and Discontent* (Homewood, IL: Dorsey Press).

Gamson, William A., Bruce Fireman and Steven Rytina (1982) *Encounter With Unjust Authority* (Homewood, IL: Dorsey Press).

Gamson, William A., and Andre Modigliani (1989) "Media Discourse and Public Opinion on Nuclear Power: A Constructionist Approach." *American Journal of Sociology*, vol. 95, pp. 1–37.

Gaventa, John (1980) *Power and Powerlessness: Quiescence and Rebellion in an Appalachian Valley.* (New York: Oxford University Press).

Gerlach, Luther P. and Virginia H. Hine (1970) *People, Power, Change: Movement of Social Transformation* (Indianapolis: Bobbs-Merrill).

Gitlin, Todd (1980) *The Whole World is Watching* (Berkeley: University of California Press).

Glaser, Barney G. and Anselm Strauss (1967) *The Discovery of Grounded Theory* (Chicago: Aldine).

Goffman, Erving (1955) "On Face-work: An Analysis of Ritual Elements in Social Interaction." *Psychiatry*, vol. 18, pp. 213–31.

Goffman, Erving (1959) *The Presentation of Self in Everyday Life* (Garden City, NY: Doubleday).

Goffman, Erving (1974) *Frame Analysis. An Essay on the Organization of Experience* (Boston: Northeastern University Press).

Gramsci, Antonio (1971) *Selections from the Prison Notebooks of Antonio Gramsci*, edited by A. Hoare and G. N. Smith (New York: International Publishers).

Gusfield, Joseph (1981) *Drinking-Driving and the Symbolic Order* (Chicago: University of Chicago Press).

Hall, Peter M. (1972) "A Symbolic Interactionist Analysis of Politics." *Sociological Inquiry*, vol. 42, pp. 35–75.

Hare, A. Paul (1985) *Social Interaction as Drama: Applications From Conflict Resolution* (Beverly Hills: Sage).

Hochschild, Arlie Russell (1979) "Emotion Work, Feeling Rules, and Social Structure." *American Journal of Sociology*, vol. 85, pp. 551–75.

Hochschild, Arlie Russell (1983) *The Managed Heart: Commercialization of Human Feelings* (Berkeley: University of California Press).

Holstein, James A. and Gale Miller (1990) "Rethinking Victimization: An Interaction Approach to Victimology." *Symbolic Interaction*, vol. 13, pp. 103–22.

Hunt, Scott A. (1991a) *Constructing Collective Identity in a Peace Movement Organization*, unpublished PhD dissertation, University of Nebraska-Lincoln.

Hunt, Scott A. (1991b) "Critical Dramaturgy and Collective Rhetoric: Cognitive and Moral Order in the *Communist Manifesto.*" *Perspectives on Social Problems*, vol. 3, pp. 1–18.

Jenkins, J. Craig and Charles Perrow (1977) "Insurgency of the Powerless: Farm Worker Movements (1946–1972)." *American Sociological Review*, vol. 42, pp. 249–68.

Klapp, Orrin E. (1962) *Heroes, Villains, and Fools: The Changing American Character* (Englewood Cliffs, NJ: Prentice-Hall).

Ladd, Anthony, Thomas C. Hood and Kent D. Van Liere (1983) "Ideological Themes in the Antinuclear Movement: Consensus and Diversity." *Sociological Inquiry*, vol. 53, pp. 252–72.

Lang, Kurt and Gladys Engel Lang (1961) *Collective Dynamics* (New York: Thomas Y. Crowell).

Lofland, John and Lyn H. Lofland (1984) *Analyzing Social Settings: A Guide to Qualitative Observation and Analysis*, 2nd ed (Belmont, CA: Wadsworth).

Lofland, Lyn H. (1985) "The Social Shaping of Emotion: The Case of Grief." *Symbolic Interaction,* vol. 8, pp. 171–90.

Lukes, Steven (1974) *Power: A Radical View* (London: MacMillan).

Lukes, Steven (1986) *Power* (New York: New York University Press).

Marx, Gary T. (1974) "Thoughts on a Neglected Category of Social Movement Participation: The Agent Provocateur and the Informant." *American Journal of Sociology,* vol. 80, pp. 402–42.

Marx, Gary T. (1979) "External Efforts to Damage or Facilitate Social Movements: Some Patterns, Explanations, and Complications." in Mayer N. Zald and John D. McCarthy (eds), *The Dynamics of Social Movements* (Cambridge, MA: Winthrop).

Mauss, Armand L. (1975) *Social Problems as Social Movements* (Philadelphia: J. B. Lippincott).

McAdam, Doug (1982) *Political Process and the Development of Black Insurgency, 1930–1970* (Chicago: University of Chicago Press).

McAdam, Doug (1983) "Tactical Innovation and the Pace of Insurgency." *American Sociological Review* vol. 48, pp. 735–54.

McAdam, Doug, John D. McCarthy and Mayer N. Zald (1988) "Social Movements," pp. 695–737 in Neil J. Smelser (ed.), *Handbook of Sociology* (Newbury Park, CA: Sage).

McCarthy, John D. and Mayer N. Zald (1973) *The Trend of Social Movements in America: Professionalization and Resource Mobilization* (Morristown, NJ: General Learning Press).

McCarthy, John D. and Mayer N. Zald (1977) "Resource Mobilization and Social Movement: A Partial Theory." *American Journal of Sociology,* vol. 82, pp. 1212–41.

Mead, George Herbert (1934) *Mind, Self, and Society* (Chicago: University of Chicago Press).

Meier, August and Elliot Rudwick (1973) *CORE: A Study in the Civil Rights Movement, 1942–1968* (New York: Oxford University Press).

Mills, C. Wright (1940) "Situated Actions and Vocabularies of Motive." *American Sociological Review,* vol. 5, pp. 404–13.

Mills, C. Wright (1959) *The Sociological Imagination* (London: Oxford University Press).

Molotch, Harvey (1979) "Media and Movements." in Mayer N. Zald and John D. McCarthy (eds), *The Dynamics of Social Movements* (Cambridge, MA: Winthrop).

Moore, Barrington (1978) *Injustice: The Social Bases of Obedience and Revolt* (White Plains, NY: Sharpe).

Oliver, Pamela (1980) "Rewards and Punishments as Selective Incentives for Collective Action: Theoretical Investigations." *American Journal of Sociology,* vol. 84, pp. 1356–75.

Olson, Mancur, Jr (1965) *The Logic of Collective Action* Cambridge, MA: Harvard University Press).

Piven, Frances and Richard Cloward (1977) *Poor People's Movements: Why They Succeed and How They Fail* (New York: Pantheon).

Rude, George (1980) *Ideology and Popular Protest* (New York: Pantheon Books).

Schutz, Alfred (1962) *The Problem of Socially Reality* (The Hague: Nijhoff).

Scott, Marvin and Stanford Lyman (1968) "Accounts." *American Sociological Review*, vol. 33, pp. 46–62.

Shott, Susan (1979) "Emotion and Social Life: A Symbolic Interactionist Analysis." *American Journal of Sociology*, vol. 84, pp. 1317–34.

Snow, David A. (1979) "A Dramaturgical Analysis of Movement Accommodation: Building Idiosyncrasy Credit as a Movement Mobilization Strategy." *Symbolic Interaction*, vol. 2, pp. 23–44.

Snow, David A., and Robert D. Benford (1988) "Ideology, Frame Resonance and Participant Mobilization." *International Social Movement Research*, vol. 1, pp. 197–217.

Snow, David H. and Robert D. Benford (1989) "Schemi Interpretativi Dominanti E Cicli Di Protesta." [Master Frames and Cycles of Protest.] *Polis: Ricerche E Studi Su Societa E Politica*, vol. 3, pp. 5–40.

Snow, David A., Robert D. Benford and Leon Anderson (1986) "Fieldwork Roles and Informational Yield: A Comparison of Alternative Settings and Roles." *Urban Life*, vol. 14, pp. 377–408.

Snow, David A. and Richard Machalek (1984) "The Sociology of Conversion." *Annual Review of Sociology*, vol. 10, pp. 367–80.

Snow, David A., E. Burke Rochford, Jr., Steven K. Worden and Robert D. Benford (1986) "Frame Alignment Process, Micromobilization, and Movement Participation. *American Sociological Review*, vol. 51, pp. 464–81.

Snow, David A., Louis A. Zurcher and Robert Peters (1981) "Victory Celebrations as Theater: A Dramaturgical Approach to Crowd Behavior." *Symbolic Interaction*, vol. 4, pp. 21–41.

Strauss, Anselm and Juliet Corbin (1990) *Basics of Qualitative Research: Grounded Theory Procedures and Techniques* (Newbury Park, CA: Sage).

Tilly, Charles (1978) *From Mobilization to Revolution* (Reading, MA: Addison-Wesley Publishing).

Tuchman, Gaye (1978) *Making News: A Study in the Construction of Reality* (New York: Free Press).

Turner, Ralph H. (1969) "The Theme of Contemporary Social Movements". *British Journal of Sociology*, vol. 20, pp. 390–405.

Turner, Ralph H. and Lewis M. Killian (1987) *Collective Behavior*, 3rd ed (Englewood Cliffs, NJ: Prentice Hall).

Weber, Max (1978) *Economy and Society: An Outline of Interpretive Sociology*, translated by Guenther Roth and Claus Wittich (Berkeley: University of California Press).

Williams, Donald E. (1961) "Protest Under the Cross: The Ku Klux Klan Presents Its Case to the Public." *Southern Speech Journal*, vol. 27, pp. 43–55.

Wilson, John (1973) *Introduction to Social Movements* (New York: Basic Books).

Wrong, Dennis H. (1979) *Power: Its Forms, Bases and Uses* (New York: Harper and Row).

Young, T. R. and Garth Massey (1978) "The Dramaturgical Society: A Macro-Analytic Approach to Dramaturgical Analysis." *Qualitative Sociology*, vol. 1, pp. 78–98.

Zurcher, Louis A. (1982a) "Collective Behavior: From Static Psychology to Static Sociology?", *Free Inquiry in Creative Sociology*, vol. 10, pp. 1–9, 12.

Zurcher, Louis A. (1982b) "The Staging of Emotion: A Dramaturgical Analysis." *Symbolic Interaction*, vol. 5, pp. 1–22.

Zurcher, Louis A. (1985) "The War Game: Organizational Scripting and the Expression of Emotion." *Symbolic Interaction*, vol. 8, pp. 191–206.

Zurcher, Louis A. and David A. Snow (1981) "Collective Behavior: Social Movements." in Morris Rosenberg and Ralph H. Turner (eds), *Social Psychology: Sociological Perspectives* (New York: Basic Books).

Part III

Conceptual Issues: Debates and Critiques

6 What's So New About New Social Movements?*

David Plotke

In the last three decades important new social movements have emerged in the United States and elsewhere. Though levels of mobilization are now modest, there is good reason to think that movements and interest groups now on the scene may gain force at future points. And there is also good reason to expect further movements as yet unnamed to appear. Yet these forces only partly resemble what is analyzed and advocated in recent theories of new social movements.

This essay argues that accounts of a widespread "new social movement discourse" are wrong in crucial ways. Dubious claims about the movements, about what they are and should be, are politically significant because they are taken seriously both by analysts and by some participants in the movements. Inasmuch as theories of new social movements influence the political choices of analysts and (less directly) of groups within the movements, they influence the political development of what they aim to understand. Thus, theories matter for politics. In this case, "new social movement discourse" overstates the novelty of the movements it analyzes, selectively depicts their aims as cultural, and exaggerates their separation from conventional political life in this country. Due to these deficiencies, new social movement discourse generates normative and strategic perspectives that disparage political engagement in favor of a marginality conceived as stringent sociocultural criticism.

One source of these problems has been an uncritical adaptation of theoretical approaches developed in a Western European political context that differs crucially from the US setting. A deeper problem derives from the logic of conflict

* Reprinted from *Socialist Review*, vol. 20, no. 1 (January–March, 1990), pp. 81–102.

between those who have proposed various forms of new social movement discourse in the last two decades and those who have advocated a more-or-less orthodox Marxism. The location of this conflict mainly on relatively orthodox Marxist terrain has had unfortunate consequences for proponents of new social movement perspectives. It has led them to formulate their positions as reversals and denials of Marxist orthodoxy, and to do so in often dramatic and hyperbolic terms. When Marxist orthodoxy has lost most of its grip on political and social realities, denying its claims is not very fruitful (though analytically better than assenting to them). Framing their positions in this manner has helped leave proponents of new social movements unprepared to engage in theoretical and political debate in the United States, where neoconservative interpretations became dominant in the late 1970s and 1980s.

The starting point for assessing accounts of new social movements is the 1960s. The movements of the 1960s were, on balance, radical reform movements that achieved considerable success. The social and political movements that took shape first in the civil rights movement and later in the antiwar, feminist, and other movements took major steps toward attaining their political and social objectives. They won major legal changes (centrally in civil rights), expanded social and political entitlements, and managed to open wide new areas for ongoing political and cultural debate. The movements won less than their most radical sections wanted, less even than the minimal aims that held them together. But that should not be surprising, as movements rarely achieve all their aims.

Yet at the time, the movements were too often measured with respect to their potential for generating an imagined revolutionary project. Despite considerable rhetoric, in general they were neither interested in nor capable of such a role. The arguments of the 1960s about the "revolutionary nature" of one or another movement had little relation to any likely political agenda. Yet critiquing the new movements for lacking sufficient revolutionary potential – conceived mainly in orthodox terms – was a basic element of the response made by more-or-less orthodox Marxist intellectuals. That judgment prepared the way for a reactive valorization of new social movements, by participants and sympathetic analysts, in which their transformative potential was affirmed. The result, for theory of new social movements, was a defensive response to orthodox Marxism that has left them increasingly unable to engage with the main relevant political and theoretical questions. Even when no manifest debate with Marxism seems to be happening, this framing has been sufficiently powerful to shape the presuppositions of much new social movement discourse.

WHAT ARE NEW SOCIAL MOVEMENTS?

From at least the mid-1970s to the present, an influential current of critical thought has understood itself to be making a distinctive political statement through claims about "new social movements." There have been many empirical referents for these claims: "new social movement" has been used to designate feminist movements, the gay movement, the environmental movement, (sometimes) movements among racial minorities, and anti-nuclear-weapons efforts.

Like most political categories that matter, the concept is not only descriptive; it has also been a means of arguing about how those political forces ought to proceed to realize their aims. Thus "new" has a different meaning from the interest-group liberalism of the mid-decades of the century and from classical socialist conceptions. (In both cases, "new" also means different from the labor movement). "Social movement" means concerned with changes in ways of life, in norms – posing objectives that not only go beyond routine political reforms but also may be impossible to achieve through conventional political channels.

Rather than presenting a detailed history of the emergence of accounts of new social movements in both Europe and the United States, I will present two summary statements of the core claims of new social movement discourse. Both try to draw basic lines between the themes of contemporary movements and those of the recent past; both formulations identify elements that have been important for the self-understanding of parts of these new movements.

In his influential work, Michel Foucault stressed the novelty of emergent social forces. Though he primarily focused on the operation of power rather than on forms of resistance, he provided an important framework for thinking about contemporary movements. In his view, the conflicts in which such movements have been engaged

identity

> are struggles which question the status of the individual: on the one hand, they assert the right to be different and they underline everything which makes individuals truly individual. On the other hand, they attack everything which separates the individual, breaks his links with others, splits up community life, forces the individual back on himself and ties him to his own identity in a constraining way... they are struggles against the 'government of individualization'.
>
> They are an opposition to the effects of power which are linked with knowledge, competence, and qualification: struggles against the privileges of knowledge. But they are also an opposition against secrecy, deformation, and mystifying representations imposed on people.... What is questioned is the way in which knowledge circulates and functions, its relations to power. In short, the *regime du savoir*.
>
> Finally, all these present struggles revolve around the question: Who are we? They are a refusal of these abstractions of economic and ideological state violence which ignore who we are individually, and also a refusal of a scientific or administrative inquisition which determines who one is.
>
> To sum up, the main objective of these struggles is to attack not so much "such and such" an institution or power, or group, or elite, or class, but rather a technique, a form of power.[1]

This account claims that new forces are individualizing without being egoistic; that they oppose concentrated forms of power; and that they are preoccupied with defining and valorizing individual and collective identities. Foucault's assertions derive partly from an argument with orthodox Marxism; the opposition to Marxist accounts of working-class political movements is sharp and central. For the latter, the workers' movement was communal (if not wholly collectivist) in form and aims; its aim was to gain political power and redirect its application; and on the basis of a more or less clear class-political aim, it sought to transform the distribution of power and resources.

Another theorist who has made important efforts to identify what is distinctive in new social movements is Claus Offe. Offe counterposes new and old paradigms of political action. The old paradigm is associated with issues of "economic growth and distribution; military and social security; social control," while the new paradigm is linked to "preservation of the environment, human rights, peace, and unalienated forms of work." The old paradigm privileges the values of "freedom and security of private consumption and material progress"; the new favors "personal autonomy and identity, as opposed to centralized control."

Internally, the old paradigm is based on "formal organization, large-scale representative associations," while the new paradigm entails "informality, spontaneity, low degree of horizontal and vertical differentiation." Externally, the old paradigm focuses on "pluralist or corporatist interest intermediation, political party competition, majority rule"; the new emphasizes "protest politics based on demands formulated in predominantly negative terms." Finally, the actors differ. In the old paradigm, the actors were "socioeconomic groups acting as groups (in the group's interest) and involved in distributive conflict." In the new paradigm, actors are "socioeconomic groups acting not as such, but on behalf of ascriptive collectivities."[2] The main referent in Offe's analysis is the socialist and communist tradition, and in particular the large socialist party–trade union complexes of postwar politics.

Offe and Foucault converge in depicting new movements as concerned mainly with quality-of-life issues, and with the definition and valorization of personal and collective identities. Such movements often have a mainly negative character, not because they are destructive, but because they oppose the manipulation and distortion imposed by large-scale institutions and the compromises and routinization required in conventional forms of interest representation and mediation. Together these claims by Foucault and Offe provide a condensed statement of the main themes of new social movement discourse. (Politically, however, the two should be distinguished: when Foucault is willing to recommend any politics at all, it is one of strengthening new social movement impulses against power. Offe proposes a strategic alliance between the new forces and "old" party–union actors.)

New social movement discourse was not invented by either theorist, but arose from many theoretical and practical sources over the last two decades. Yet their arguments are clear and exemplary. In the United States, typical formulations of new social movement discourse have incorporated sociological themes similar to those found in Offe's work within a framework similar to Foucault's.[3]

This conception of new movements – as embodying resistance to power, motivated by cultural aims, fundamentally differing from the labor and socialist traditions, uninterested in conventional forms of political participation – has been widely influential in the United States in the last two decades. It has appeared in many strands of "cultural" or "radical" feminism from the late 1960s to the present; in nationalist impulses within the black movement and to some extent in movements of other racially-dominated groups; in the radical sections of the environmentalist movement from the 1970s on; in parts of the peace movement of the late 1970s through the mid-1980s; and in radical sections of the gay rights movement, especially before the full onset of the AIDS crisis. It would be valuable to trace out the specific forms of new social movement discourse within the various movements; but here I will limit myself to pointing to the set of common formulations about what it meant to be a social movement that emerged with many different inflections within parts of these new forces. While this discourse has never wholly dominated any particular movement, it has been one influential current among others within and around them. By abstracting from the range of specific formulations of new social movement discourse, I hope to focus attention on characteristics that appear across movements.

Needless to say, if one surveys the US political landscape for major forces that in a pure form exemplify the themes developed by Foucault or Offe, the results are disappointing. Yet the themes of new social movement discourse are part of contemporary collective action, present in a wide range of political and social interest groups and movements. New social movement discourse, unfortunately, is not a good guide to the important changes in collective action it partially identifies. As I indicated earlier, a major source of misconceptions has been a protracted conflict with Marxism. This conflict, in journals, books, conferences, and sometimes in small political organizations, continues to influence the formulations even of analysts of new social movements who are not explicitly concerned with Marxist claims.

At the most general level, Marxist theories claim that "capitalism" is an analytically useful way of conceptualizing the emergence of modern industrial societies in the West; attempt to define the normative and structural limits to capitalism as a system; and propose that those limits might be surpassed by other forms of modern social organization. Within this general framework, the contemporary Marxist theories take class and mode of production as central concepts, view politics primarily as an expression of socioeconomic processes, and assess political projects in terms of their contribution to movements led by the working class and aimed at establishing social ownership of the primary means of production. This definition combines orthodox Marxism and various neo-Marxisms both to underline their common elements and to stress the inability of the new Marxist efforts of the last two decades to generate a coherent alternative to orthodox positions. Most recent Marxisms deny that basic social changes have occurred (on the grounds that capitalism still exists) and then reject new social movement discourses for not taking the conventional production/class/politics nexus as the central referent for critical theory and political practice.

New social movement discourse more accurately identifies the contemporary terrain of collective action than Marxist claims that nothing "basic" has changed. The former is more attuned to ongoing changes in political and social life, less constrained by pieties, and less inclined to become immersed in terminological quagmires. Despite these advantages, the formation of new social movement discourse in critical opposition to more-or-less orthodox Marxism has entailed major costs. Overturning wrong positions does not produce an adequate response to what is probably the key question: does what we know of the actual movements and their context justify the political claims of new social movement discourse?

NEW SOCIAL MOVEMENTS AND MARXISM

To ask what really can be said about new forces, and how much of what new social movement discourse says is right, requires trying to articulate central problems around which the discourse emerged: Is the secular decline of the socialist and communist movement's conception of class and political/social transformation a definite, enduring outcome? If so, does that mean the "end of ideology" is finally upon us?

There is a wide range of compelling evidence, from sociological studies of the class structure to studies of voting and ideology, indicating that the post-1960s decline of social-democratic and communist politics has deep structural roots. Whether that decline might somehow be reversed is hard to know, but at least in the visible future, no renewal based on industrial class politics seems likely. Yet, for many on the left, acknowledging the permanent decline of radical political movements based on the industrial working class seems to capitulate to a claim that the movements of the 1960s once seemed to disprove: that the material progress and sociocultural integration of the years after World War II had forever consigned Marxism and other radical critiques of advanced industrial societies to the margins of political and cultural life.

New social movement discourse recognizes the impossibility of sustaining "classical" notions of industrial class politics in the United States today. Here the reference to Marxism is both beneficial and costly. It illuminates what is at stake in the decline of class politics, and permits a thoughtful rejection of the traditional class–party–socialism schemas. Yet the Marxist referents seem to create an enduring temptation to recreate the same logic, now transposed onto new agents; if the old working-class stories are untenable, they can be re-told with new social movements taking the leading role.

The crucial move that social movement discourse makes is to deny any end of ideology. Thus it can reject both Marxist orthodoxy and "bourgeois" accounts of the decline of working-class politics by relocating radical agency in political forces whose novelty itself then becomes a sign of escape from a conformist political and social logic. But there is a fine line between mirroring the logic of classical Marxist analyses, now with a new/imaginary proletariat, and making fruitful arguments about contemporary politics. When new social movement discourse inverts and restates a rejected Marxist orthodoxy, it distorts important claims that the presence of new social and political forces really can be held to support.

These claims assert the persistence of deep social conflict; the durability of conflict over norms as well as distribution; the production of new identities and collectivities; and the continued importance of sites of conflict other than those of routinized workplace negotiation and legislative/electoral politics. Such claims are unconventional, probably true, and encourage theoretical and political innovation. New social and political forces do exist, and are important. Yet noting their presence does not solve many theoretical or political problems. The next sections of this essay consider how new social movement discourse treats three major issues: the role of cultural themes in contemporary collective action; the status of legal–egalitarian objectives; and the prospects of a radical social and political autonomy. In each case, I have a dual purpose: to show how conflicts with orthodox Marxism have encouraged the articulation of untenable positions, and to argue that important elements of new social movement discourse are valuable, if reframed in more modest and secular terms.

THE NOVELTY OF CULTURE

What about the claim that new social movements are new because of their extensive cultural concerns? Empirically this claim is not very persuasive. US history has repeatedly seen sharp cultural conflicts: over religion in the eighteenth and early nineteenth centuries; over the proper definition of American culture with respect to immigrant groups in the nineteenth and early twentieth centuries; over race in the late nineteenth century and intermittently into the present; about gender and sexual norms from the earliest part of the century into the present. Given this history, the equation of cultural themes with novelty reveals the extent to which new social movement discourse has been formed by insular struggles with Marxism. For the latter, major movements are always basically class movements, even if they claim to be something else.

Proponents of new social movement discourse are right to insist that contemporary collective action really is about culture, not merely about the cultural expression of class elements. But this is not very new. In the US class conflict has always existed alongside cultural, ethnic, and racial struggle, never as a pure form for other movements to express.

It is understandable that the explosion of cultural themes in political conflict in the late 1960s appeared dramatically new. The New Deal had replaced cultural and sectional cleavages with socioeconomic conflicts to an unprecedented degree. After World War II, the politics of the next two decades mainly focused on claims for more by established interest groups or new ones similar in form. Thus the powerful return of cultural themes in politics seemed to mark a radical departure both from pluralist accounts of interest-group liberalism and Marxist treatments of the same political dynamics.

There are significant novel elements in both the context and the substance of the cultural emphases of new forces. First, explicitly cultural elements have more weight in new movements than was the case in most prior periods of US history, even if cultural efforts have always been present. Second, these cultural concerns are increasingly framed in terms not only of general social values and norms, but also of the definition and maintenance of identities for individuals. The notion of a conflict over culture necessarily entails a conflict over identity, as norms have to be lived. Nonetheless, the question of identity has often been submerged under the assumption that it would be given by whatever set of cultural orientations triumphed. In contemporary conflicts, no general resolution is in principle adequate to fix individual identities, which remain contested and unstable.

Third, cultural conflicts have intensified because of new links between cultural and socioeconomic processes. The location of individuals and groups within socioeconomic hierarchies is increasingly dependent on access to education and skills, for example; this access is shaped by conceptions of the merit and potential of different groups. Thus conflicts over the cultural practices through which groups are distinguished and stratified help to shape socioeconomic relations. (As an obvious example, efforts by blacks to contest racial stereotyping are intertwined with efforts to gain improved education and better treatment in diverse work settings.)

Taken together, these changes signal a substantial increase in the importance of culture in the concerns of contemporary political forces. They do not suffice to take the recent period out of history, however, nor do they do the work of political argument in determining which cultural practices to defend.

To underline novelty, new social movement discourse sharply contrasts efforts to attain legal equality and distributive equity with efforts at cultural change, derogating the former in favor of the latter. This argument misses basic realities of US politics, when discourses that have developed mainly in Europe are reproduced in the United States without much attention to differences in context.

In Western Europe, as Offe's formulation makes clear, new social movement arguments center on a contrast between sociocultural concerns with "post-material" values and the distributive and legal aims of social-democratic and socialist labor movements. This opposition of distributive and egalitarian to cultural aims corresponds to a distinction between the traditional labor movement and contemporary forces that presume its accomplishments. In such a context, the question arises: is democratic change more likely to occur through the advance of labor toward distributive justice, or through a cultural critique by new social movements?

Where the labor movement is powerful and dominates a broadly defined left, this question is a reasonable one to debate. In the United States, the question is much less pertinent, and when it is combined with a counterposition of equity against cultural change, the result is to generate confusion. Why?

In the United States, the labor movement was unable to win on its own some of the crucial victories presumed by Offe's dichotomies, such as general legal equality or a minimal welfare state. Given that history, the important fact that the power of the labor movement is limited and not on the verge of being renewed does not mean that cultural elements (pointing beyond equality) will predominate in the themes of new forces.

The relevant differences between the United States and Western Europe are clear regarding racial divisions and the course of the civil rights movement. New social movement discourses on race typically stress the cultural politics of opposition to racism, derogating or even ignoring prior and current efforts at legal and economic equity. Yet this opposition distorts the course of the US civil rights movement.

The weakness (and sometimes collusion in racial division) of the labor movement was key: it could not win a full extension of voting rights to the adult population when it was preeminent among popular forces in the first half of the twentieth century. Thus the black movement of the 1950s and 1960s could not presume civic equality, much less economic equity. Its primary aims involved an end to physical terror against blacks in the South, the attainment of civil rights, and the practical extension of voting rights. New social movement discourse is right to insist on the importance of cultural themes within that movement, and wildly wrong to treat it (then or now) as mainly a cultural movement uninterested in legal and distributive issues. The coexistence of legal, distributive, and cultural elements in the themes of the black movement is evident. Perhaps this complexity is one reason that the black movement sometimes drops out of accounts of new movements, because it cannot reasonably be assimilated to a model that starkly counterposes cultural concerns to "old" issues.

Relations between feminism – always a central example of a new social movement – and social policy underline this point. In Sweden, a labor movement initiated welfare-state measures (often as family policy) to protect large parts of the middle and working classes against the worst dangers of labor markets. Given such measures, to pose a cultural feminism against or at least beyond a laborist social policy is credible, whether or not it is judicious. In the United States, the labor movement could not enact more than a partial and rudimentary welfare state, leaving women very vulnerable in the labor market as family ties weakened and female labor-force participation exploded.

Thus to insist that feminism in this country is (should be) a cultural movement, beyond (even against) issues of legal equity and socioeconomic distribution, simply misses much of what has occurred in the last two decades. Efforts at "conventional" forms of equity have preoccupied the attention of large parts of the feminist movement, which have sought to win reforms that the labor movement did not.

For new social and political forces, the weakness of the US labor movement poses a difficult problem. They are caught between the need to attain "conventional" reforms and the need to articulate a cultural and social critique that assumes the reality of those same reforms. But if it makes sense to criticize analyses that conceive contemporary movements as aimed purely at a narrowly defined equality, we should not deny the importance of egalitarian aims in collective action, as though equality were already achieved.

BEYOND STATE POLITICS?

What of claims that new social movements want autonomy? That they express a radical alternative to the rational-technical logic of big political and economic institutions? That they aim to refuse power rather than take it? That their aims are local and focused on defining and sustaining identities?

Once again, a partially obscured argument with Marxism frames these claims, and limits their merit for the United States. For more-or-less orthodox Marxism, the political expressions of the workers' movement had to be organized on a large scale as a means of overcoming the many obstacles to working-class action imposed by the strength of the opposition and the conditions of working-class life. The aim was not to refuse power, much less destroy it, but to take and reshape it. The problem of identity was in theory already settled, with reference to class position. What remained was the problem of enhancing and guarding identities in practice.

New social movement discourse proceeds too often as though the choice were between embracing orthodox Marxism and simply reversing its terms. On balance, an inverted Marxism, in the form of new social movement discourse, does a better job of making contact with contemporary political and social choices. Against rationalistic notions of collective action, of which orthodox Marxism is an example, we can insist that identities with normative elements matter, that people fight not only for more but for the possibility of defining a way of life expressive of deeply held values. Identities that logically or practically transcend class seem likely to emerge with every new social movement, and are linked to real social relations irreducible to class. When such identities become a stake of political conflict, demands for autonomy are also demands for self-determination.

These points might be a sufficient assessment if new social movement discourse in the United States articulated the efforts of movements to survive against a powerful Communist Party on the one hand and a highly centralized state and homogeneous culture on the other. In that case, strong claims about the autonomy and irreducibility of particular identities, even obscurantist arguments about a radical otherness beyond any notion of democratic citizenship, deserve sympathy. But in this country, no Communist Party dominates its small left, and political institutions are relatively decentralized, even fragmented. Power is relatively dispersed. And despite the weight of national mass cultural institutions, there exist considerable regional diversity and room for local initiatives.

Political and theoretical efforts that negate Marxist orthodoxy by reversing its terms become hostage to a partly imaginary adversary in the name of a partly imaginary conception of the movements being defended. Serious problems arise, for example, when analysts propose radical autonomy as a central concept for new movements – autonomy from what, and for what? If new social movement discourse preserves the totalizing imagery of Marxist orthodoxy, while rejecting most of Marxist politics, then autonomy refers to parties, unions, and the state. This stance might make sense if there were only one social movement challenging the logic of such institutions; politics would then mean affirming its identity, autonomy,. and worth, and its capacity to help renew a vibrant civil society.

Yet there will be no unification of new (and/or old) social and political movements into a single entity with a coherent, totalizing identity. Such a unification is wholly incompatible with the complexity and diversity of the United States and similar societies. Given the permanence of this plurality, claims of autonomy lose much of their force, and easily take on an anti-political cast. What are new forces supposed to be autonomous from? If autonomy simply means independence, this aim seems valid, but insufficient to generate political or cultural choices. Such independence is in any case available, if not always easily, in a political culture that encourages interest group competition. If autonomy means radical separation from other political and social actors, it seems both undesirable and at a mass level probably impossible to attain.

Thus autonomy cannot function as the central political concept it is often claimed to be. Given a Stalinist opposition and leviathan state, stressing autonomy might be enough; given cultural and political fragmentation and competition it is important to know what autonomy is supposed to signify.

Few proponents of new social movement discourse really want to argue that autonomy and identity are private goods to be enjoyed by their owners in a separate social space. If not, then it becomes necessary to develop autonomy and identity into concepts that can indicate what relations are envisaged between their bearers and the rest of the society. No autonomy is absolute and permanent; its terms require renegotiation with other agents and institutions. Once this point is recognized, political questions quickly arise (how to negotiate, with whom, for what aims, etc.).

Similarly, identities cannot be frozen or lived outside of interaction with other identities. Individuals occupy multiple social positions, and no interpretation of those positions could long endure that dissolved all of them into a single, totalizing identity. People may for a while make political and social choices overwhelmingly with reference to one dimension of their social position (as black, for example). But nothing fixes identities in such a way as to rule out future reinterpretations (for example, an interpretation framed by gender relations or occupational structures). The impermanence of political–social identities is further guaranteed by social change that puts in question identities established at the individual level.

Social change and social complexity are intertwined in blocking the reduction of all identities to a durable binary opposition. Such oppositions may emerge for brief episodes; that they open some political possibilities does not mean that radical polarization (over race, or region, or even class) is the secret truth of sociopolitical development. The real secret is more secular: a permanence of multiple oppositions, sometimes briefly fused.

Thus in the United States today and in the foreseeable future, it is wrong from the perspective of democratic and egalitarian norms simply to stress the radical autonomy (or irreducibility) of identities. It evades the political reality of plural political and social forces, a reality that helps shape any practical form of autonomy or identity. Reference to the concepts of identity and autonomy cannot justify disdain for "normal" politics, in which it is necessary to make endless compromises, distinguish good and bad deals, and identify friends and enemies. In all these matters, political dialogue and debate are crucial, meaning communication across and beyond movements with very differently situated social and political forces. (Even if somehow all emergent movements had already secured everything they needed in legal and distributive matters, they could not avoid conventional forms of political engagement, as part of their self-definition and efforts to achieve minimal objectives.) If politics is important for individual movements because of the plurality and diversity of movements, it is also important because there is a polity. Making full provision for the dispersal of politics throughout social life, there is still a political space containing state institutions and a variety of actors. If movements want to attain their objectives – and maintaining autonomy and upholding the legitimacy of their identities count as objectives – they are compelled to seek allies and discern adversaries. The place where most of this must be done – and sometimes is – is a polity already full of activity.

However, just as arguments for the centrality of cultural politics and the limits of egalitarian and distributive struggles have some merit, emphasizing autonomy and identity has its value. Such objectives do appear in collective action in a society organized by large institutions with powerful homogenizing tendencies, and they will have normative meaning for the imaginable future. Rather than standing outside conventional political channels and processes, however, autonomy and identity depend on the prior attainment of a partially functioning pluralist framework. Their recognition and maintenance entail expanding the flexibility and inclusiveness of the political system.

Maybe there is a country where new social movements are radically new simply by virtue of expressing cultural themes; where they begin and struggle beyond the framework of liberal-democratic equality; and where the effort to valorize and sustain identities can occur wholly outside "regular" politics. Perhaps in such a country, new social movement discourse makes good political sense in debating an orthodox Marxism (or social democracy) implanted in a large party or parties and leading sections of a trade union movement. But the United States is not that country. Here cultural conflict has been repeatedly crucial, equality remains problematic, and collective identities involve political negotiation. On balance, new social movement discourse does not provide a very good guide to understanding new social movements, nor is it promising as a normative framework for political projects. If new social movement discourse mistakes actual movements and interest groups for something more exotic, the responsibility lies not just with those who advance such interpretations. It also lies with a history of Marxist disparagement of those movements in favor of an imaginary renewal of orthodox politics.

NEW SOCIAL MOVEMENTS AND MODERNIZATION

While new social movement discourse was being developed and debated, US society experienced a turbulent transition in the last decade and a half. While various lefts debated the class nature of new middle strata and the character of new movements, neoconservative intellectuals and politicians were often more directly attentive to the problems of defining a postindustrial politics and culture. They waged a surprisingly successful campaign for a conservative modernization, involving some of the very groups about which various lefts were debating.

As volumes argue, major problems of economic and social integration appeared from the early 1970s. While Marxists debated whether real growth was possible, neoconservatives presumed it could occur but required the active participation of new middle strata. This followed neoconservative alarm over "the 1960s," viewed as involving an eruption of new class sympathies for irrational and hedonistic opposition to modernization.

The neoconservative project drew on Daniel Bell's distinction between cultural and economic spheres and his argument that rationalizing economic tendencies collide with unrestrained impulses toward gratification unleashed in capitalist culture.[4] Neoconservatives aimed to stigmatize the radicalisms of the 1960s not out of an inflated view of their immediate political prospects but as part of a fight for the political future of emergent middle strata. They aimed for a conservative modernization, with renewed assertions of order and authority amidst a rapidly changing socioeconomic order. This project entailed fierce attacks on political and cultural impulses that question the need to channel individual and group desires for spontaneity, self-expression and accomplishment into bureaucratic and hierarchical forms.

Neoconservative writers devoted little attention to a direct critique of Marxism, but rather focused on left-liberalism in general, or specific adversaries such as populism, black militancy, or feminism. There are several ways to read this choice. One, perhaps flattering to some Marxists, is that neoconservatives tried to find the most vulnerable expressions of "radical" positions; thus Marxism's more rigorous formulations escaped. More likely, neoconservatives attacked what they meant to.

The new movements within the middle strata from the late 1950s to the present have been anti-bureaucratic, egalitarian, and communal rather than purely individualistic and meritocratic; they have been reluctant to draw a sharp line between personal development and the exigencies of work and public life. These themes mean trouble for a conservative modernizing project, though they by no means constitute the simplistic opposition to modernization that neoconservatives charged. They question the loyalty of middle strata to the more conservative and hierarchical forms of organization that might characterize a postindustrial capitalism. And they promise different political–cultural subjects than those viewed as desirable by neoconservative analysts.

There is nothing intrinsically "revolutionary" about the

gap between neoconservative modernization projects and the radical themes of new middle strata, though some neoconservative analysts and proponents of new social movement discourse have for different reasons claimed as much. Nonetheless, the conflicts between neoconservative aims and arguments for individual autonomy, organizational flexibility, and democratic modes of authority are great enough to have inspired angry assaults on the new movements.

The war neoconservatism has waged is cultural and political, aimed at rebuilding a network of durable alliances out of the raw material thrown up by dramatic processes of class and social recomposition. Diverse left currents have had a chance to enter these political and theoretical conflicts, whose outcomes will help determine the forms of transition and the shape of a postindustrial capitalism.

Yet neither Marxists nor proponents of new social movement discourse have been able to have much influence on these conflicts. The Marxist tradition provides grounds for refusing to accept that the only choices are a conservative modernization (development that reshapes while preserving prior class and other inequalities, framed by commitments to authority and order) and a radically utopian (and/or nostalgic) rejection of growth and development. Despite this potential, Marxism was marginal in the key political and intellectual fights. This absence was encouraged by core concerns of the neo-Marxism that arose in the 1960s: the fear of cooptation, a longing for the return of classical scenarios, and drift toward conservative cultural critique. For the most part, Marxism missed its opportunities in the 1960s and 1970s to make a positive contribution to building a democratic postindustrial left.

While neoconservativism was winning many political and intellectual victories against the popular radical currents of the 1960s and 1970s, Marxists were largely preoccupied with figuring out how those movements could be further radicalized and linked to an imaginary renewal of class struggle. In the 1970s and 1980s, neoconservatism succeeded in stigmatizing the movements of the 1960s and their successors. This effect was achieved partly by drawing a line between narrowly-conceived legal equality (recognized as legitimate) and broader cultural or political change (deemed

irrational and in effect antidemocratic). Neoconservatism,
along with a broader right, reworked themes present in
postwar mainstream liberalism – growth, freedom, order,
international power – to structure the political terrain around
a new series of oppositions:

- Growth/no growth
- Liberty/statism
- Authority/ultrademocracy
- Order/hyperindividualism
- Community/fragmentation
- International power/weakness

Each opposition defined – and stigmatized – the second term
as that of a new left. "No growth" identified the environmental movement and even parts of the unions (regarding
productivity); "statism" designated the commitment of racial
minorities and unions to welfare state policies; "ultra-democ-
racy" meant anti-bureaucratic and antiauthoritarian impulses;
"hyperindividualism" disparaged feminism; and national "weakness" named opponents of US efforts in Vietnam and similar policies.

These oppositions were built through years of conflict, in
journals, books, conferences, media events, and election
campaigns. They condensed a wide array of experiences into
polarities that operated to recommend a conservative
modernization to any reasonable person. Proponents of new
social movement discourse were generally unable to offer a
very effective resistance to this strategy. Sometimes they were
distracted from even trying to do so, preoccupied with internal conflicts or battles with orthodox Marxism. At other
points, the antipolitical elements of new social movement
discourse made it hard even to engage the issues that
neoconservatives raised. Some attention was paid to criticiz-
ing neoconservative arguments, but for the most part it
focused on making the true but rather obvious point that
the latter were "ideological," suggesting a fear of straight-
forward political debate.

At another level, arguments of new social movement discourse seem committed to restating, almost innocently, the
oppositions neoconservatives have sought to construct. They
thus unintentionally offer neoconservatism the left it needs

as an inviting and vulnerable target, one suitable for polemical efforts to make conservative modernization an acceptable if unexciting alternative. To make his own dubious positions seem more sensible, Allan Bloom needs Foucault, or at least his US proponents; Irving Kristol needs analysts who call for redistribution via disruption, or simply for disruption; and William Bennett (as Secretary of Education) needed adamant critics of "Western rationalism."

BEYOND NEW SOCIAL MOVEMENT DISCOURSE?

If Reaganism had been wholly successful politically, or if neoconservatism had emerged entirely victorious from the intellectual conflicts it entered, one might end here and conclude that new social movement discourse is finished, referring only to a history of possibilities briefly opened and now beyond reach. This conclusion would be wrong. As noted earlier, new social movement discourse identifies emergent cultural and political realities that are important and have been undervalued in prevalent accounts of contemporary politics.

Is it possible, then, to dismantle the oppositions that neoconservatism managed to construct and employ so effectively? This would entail rearticulating the conceptions from which they were constructed, reinterpreting the salient experiences, and starting to create a new field of political conflict. This restructuring could identify the first term of new oppositions with a neoconservative choice and the second with a democratic alternative. "Growth/no growth," for example, could be transformed into rigidity/development, emphasizing social efficiency and the expansion of social and individual capacities. "Liberty/statism" might be redrawn as authoritarianism/democracy, addressing themes of public access and government responsibility.

Such shifts cannot be conceived in purely tactical terms, as though all that were entailed were renaming current arguments to the advantage of presently weak positions. Redefining a political and theoretical field means reinterpreting past experiences, gauging responsibility for failures and successes, proposing new policies and programs. Given these tasks, could

new democratic political and social forces develop widely
and offer alternatives to the conservative modernization that
is well underway? Could the democratic themes of the movements of the last two decades be elaborated and concretized
without being stigmatized as selfishly modernist and economically anti-modernizing?

To help supply positive answers to these questions, it would
be necessary for proponents of new social movement discourse to address perhaps its most serious problem, its denial of politics. This denial is rarely formulated directly as
such, but emerges repeatedly at the many points noted above:
in the Foucaultian account of resistance to power, in the
elaboration of apolitical conceptions of autonomy and identity;
in efforts to place new movements beyond equality and welfare; and in the sharp opposition posed between cultural
and political–economic issues.

Yet actual movements are thoroughly political, concerned
not only with winning reforms but also with gaining and
employing power. And they ought to be. In seeking equity,
autonomy, and cultural change, contemporary collective action
is immersed in politics, both in the forms of its action and
its aims. Movements and interest groups are political – concerned with shaping social relations – at the level of the
state and elsewhere. They politicize previously uncontested
relations, or repoliticize previously settled relations. In doing
so, they become involved with the national and local state,
with legislatures and courts, with all the routine forms of
political decision-making. That they are political means they
aim to gain and exercise power in the service of objectives,
but does not imply that they must express aspirations to
global power. The pure movements of (cultural) resistance,
for which politics means only the affirmation of identity against
intrusion, could not really exist for long. During their brief
existence they would fail to meet the articulated needs of
their members, who would rapidly dwindle to a sectarian
fragment of the initial movement.

Once we accept the permanent reality of multiple political forces aiming to gain objectives and affirm identities,
what relations are feasible and strategically effective among
them? How can communication take place across interest
groups and movements? How can durable alliances be con-

structed in which the endless compromises and tactical choices required for action are possible, without marginalizing weaker forces? The last question is of course the contemporary form of the Gramscian problem of hegemony – but there is no longer any particular agent naturally entitled to be hegemonic, nor any reason that groups should be sublimated within hegemonic formulations to nearly the extent that has been presumed even within the most liberal Gramscian positions. The term itself is now yet another question rather than an answer: how can durable, authentic relations of cooperation be established among diverse political and social forces of widely varying capacities, relations that persist without becoming pure domination by a single force or episodic interest-group bargaining among many?

All these questions lead toward politics, rather than opening an imaginary space for the consolidation and expression of identities. And if no single totalizing identity is or should be on the horizon, nor any means of subsuming diverse objectives and self-conceptions in an enduring unity, then the indicated politics is a radical, democratic pluralism. Here pluralism reflects the permanent diversity of oppositional movements, alongside their interests in exercising power. It signals the acceptance of a critique of statism that would preclude any single movement or bloc of movements from aspiring to merge state and society in accord with the essential principles of their own identity (e.g., a workers' state or a feminist polity). There are at least two and probably more starting points for theorizing its forms and logic: the least statist variants of social-democratic and Eurocommunist arguments, and the most egalitarian variants of liberal–democratic theory. At its best such theorizing will be able to recognize and to some extent incorporate the most powerful themes of new social movement discourse. That prospect does not imply a disappearance of the latter, however, but an enduring dynamic between a flexible and open political system and a social order in which innovation and change are positively valued. In such a dynamic, new variants of social movement discourse will push at the limits of politics and articulate emergent identities, disrupting even the most seemingly democratic political orders in the name of individual and social development and democracy.

Notes

1. Michel Foucault, "The Subject and Power," in Hubert L. Dreyfus and Paul Rabinow, eds., *Michel Foucault: Beyond Structuralism and Hermeneutics* (Chicago: University of Chicago Press, 1983), pp. 211–212.
2. Claus Offe, "Challenging the Boundaries of Institutional Politics: Social Movements since the 1960s," in Charles Maier, ed., *Changing Boundaries of the Political* (New York: Cambridge University Press, 1987), p. 73.
3. It would be easy to fill several pages with recent books and especially articles that make a contribution to or are significantly influenced by new social movement discourse. And the list could be extended vastly by beginning from the mid-to-late 1960s, when the initial formulations of this perspective appear. Some recent relevant books include: Henry Louis Gates, Jr., *Black Literature and Literary Theory* (New York: Methuen, 1984); Joan Cocks, *The Oppositional Imagination* (New York: Routledge, 1989); Joan Wallach Scott, *Gender and the Politics of History* (New York: Columbia University Press, 1988); Cary Nelson and Lawrence Grossberg, eds., *Marxism and the Interpretation of Culture* (Chicago: University of Illinois Press, 1988); John D'Emilio, *Sexual Politics, Sexual Communities: The Making of a Homosexual Minority in the United States, 1940–1970* (Chicago: University of Chicago Press, 1983); Michael Omi and Howard Winant, *Racial Formation in the United States: From the 1960s to the 1980s* (New York: Routledge, 1986); and Seyla Benhabib and Drucilla Cornell, eds., *Feminism as Critique* (Minneapolis: University of Minnesota Press, 1987).
4. Daniel Bell, *The Cultural Contradictions of Capitalism* (New York: Basic Books, 1976).

7 Collective Protest: A Critique of Resource-Mobilization Theory*

Frances Fox Piven and Richard A. Cloward

INTRODUCTION

Over the last two decades, "resource mobilization" (RM) analysts have emphasized the importance of institutional continuities between conventional social life and collective protest.[1] There is much about this interpretation with which we agree. It is a corrective to some of the malintegration (MI) literature in which movements are portrayed as mindless eruptions lacking either coherence or continuity with organized social life. Nevertheless, we shall argue that RM analysts commit a reverse error. Their emphasis on the similarities between conventional and protest behavior has led them to understate the differences. They thus tend to "normalize" collective protest.

Blurring the distinction between normative and nonnormative forms of collective action is the most fundamental expression of this tendency, as if rule-conforming and rule-violating collective action are of a piece. To be sure, RM analysts are obviously aware that some forms of protest violate established norms, and are therefore illegitimate or illegal. Indeed, a good deal of their work deals with electrifying examples of defiance of normative structures. Nevertheless, in the course of examining the institutional continuities between permissible and prohibited modes of collective action, they often allow this distinction to disappear. But an exposition of the similarities between the structure of everyday

* Reprinted from *International Journal of Politics, Culture, and Society*, vol. 4, no. 4 (Summer 1991), pp. 435–58.

life and the structure of protest is not an explanation of
why people sometimes live their everyday lives and other
times join in collective defiance. And it is, of course, precisely
this theoretical problem that is central to the MI analyses
that RM disparage; it is nonnormative collective action –
disorder and rebellion – that MI analysts want to explain.
Other problems in the RM literature are consistent with
this normalizing tendency. Protest is often treated by RM
analysts as more organized than it is, as if conventional modes
of formal organization also typify the organizational forms
taken by protest. And some RM analysts normalize the political impact of collective protest, as if the processes of influence set in motion by collective protest are no different
than those set in motion by conventional political activities.

These criticisms, which are discussed in this chapter, do
not detract from the generalization that institutional arrangements pattern both conventional and unconventional collective action. Still, the differences must be explained. And
once the problem of explaining differences is brought back
into view, the wholesale rejection of the MI tradition by RM
analysts may be seen as premature.

NORMATIVE AND NONNORMATIVE COLLECTIVE ACTION

In his recent appraisal of theories of civil violence, Rule
says RM analysts define violent action as "simply a phase in
other forms of collective action, caused by the same forces
that move people to other, 'normal' assertions of collective
interest" (Rule, 1988, pp. 170–1). Thus the Tillys object to
"sociological interpretations of protest, conflict, and violence
that treat them as occurring outside of normal politics, or
even *against* normal politics" (Tilly *et al.*, 1975, p. 240; emphasis in original). It is true, as the Tillys say, that protest is
a form of politics. But does it really make sense to treat
protest and violence as if they were simply "normal" politics? To do so is to ignore the powerful role of norms in
the regulation of all social life, including relations of domination and subordination.

Ongoing struggles for power continually stimulate efforts

by contenders to promulgate and enforce rules that either proscribe the use of specific political resources by their antagonists, or define conditions limiting their use (e.g., the conditions under which labor can be withheld in industrial conflict, or sexual access withheld in mating conflict). Thus conceived, rule-making is a strategy of power. Moreover, it is a strategy that creates new and lasting constraints on subsequent political action. Once objectified in a system of law, the rules forged by past power struggles continue to shape ongoing conflicts by constraining or enhancing the ability of actors to use whatever leverage their social circumstances yield them. That is why new power struggles often take the form of efforts to alter the parameters of the permissible by challenging or defying the legitimacy of prevailing norms themselves (Piven, 1981). Nevertheless, protest is indeed "outside of normal politics" and "against normal politics" in the sense that people break the rules defining permissible modes of political action. Of course, the distinction between normative and nonnormative is not always easy to draw because norms themselves are often ambiguous, and no more so than when they become the focus of conflict and renegotiation. Still, a riot is clearly not an electoral rally, and both the participants and the authorities know the difference.

There are several important ways in which some RM analysts direct attention away from rule-violations. One is to treat collective protest as if it were merely interest group politics, a proclivity that marks the work of McCarthy and Zald (1977; cf. also McCarthy, Wolfson, Baker, and Mosakowski, in press, on citizens organizing against drunk driving). Another is to conflate the normative and nonnormative. In his study of crowd behavior, McPhail (1991) not only conflates political gatherings (e.g., urban riots) with such other collective actions as sports and religious events, but does not consider it important to explain why the crowd which is the audience for a sports event is sometimes transformed into a riotous mob. Even Tilly, whose work shows appreciation of the distinctive features of protest, frequently lumps normative and nonnormative collective action together. His definition of "contention" covers all "common action that bears directly on the interests of some other acting groups," such as collective violence ("that sort of contention in which someone seizes or damages persons or objects"), and conventional political action, such as electoral rallies and campaigns (Tilly, 1986, pp. 381–2). His classification of contemporary forms of collective political action includes:

– Strikes
– Demonstrations
– Electoral rallies
– Public meetings
– Petition marches
– Planned insurrections
– Invasions of official assemblies
– Social movements
– Electoral campaigns (ibid., p. 393).

A similar conflation occurs in the survey essay on "social movements" prepared by McAdam, McCarthy, and Zald for Smelser's *Handbook of Sociology* where they define virtually all forms of collective action as "social movements" – from mass civil disobedience to "burial societies" and "PTAs" (McAdam *et al.*, 1988, p. 704).[2]

A still further expression of this normalizing tendency occurs when analysts focus on those aspects of protest that are normative and even ritualized (thereby illuminating the continuities between everyday institutional processes and collective protest), but then make much less of the non-normative aspects (thereby obscuring the discontinuities between everyday institutional process and collective protest). Here, for example, is Tilly's characterization of preindustrial food riots:

> If we ignore the intimate relation of the food riot to the politics of the old regime, we shall neglect the coherent political action the riot represents. Far from being impulsive, hopeless reactions to hunger, bread riots and other struggles over the food supply took a small number of relatively well-defined forms .... The work of the crowd embodied a critique of the authorities, was often directed consciously at the authorities, and commonly consisted of the crowd's taking precisely those measures its members thought the authorities had failed their own responsi-

bility to take – inventorying grain in private hands, setting a price, and so on (Tilly, 1975, p. 386).

But as this description makes clear, humble villagers did
not just act in the traditional role of the authorities; they
usurped their powers. Surely this feature of their action
demands explanation.[3] Yet even when Tilly and his collaborators provide such dramatic examples of defiance, it is the
socially patterned character of such protest events that commands their theoretical attention.

Finally, consistent with their predisposition to think of
collective violence as "normal politics," some RM analysts
characteristically deemphasize violence by protestors and instead single-out violence by the authorities. On the basis of
their historical studies, the Tillys claim that most

> collective violence will ordinarily grow out of some prior
> collective action which is not intrinsically violent: a meeting,
> a ceremony, a strike.... To an important degree, the
> damage to objects and, especially, to persons consisted of
> elite reactions to the claims made by ordinary people:
> troops, police, and thugs acting under instructions from
> owners and officials attacked demonstrators, strikers,
> and squatters (Tilly *et al.*, 1975, pp. 49, 288).

Similarly, Snyder and Tilly (1972, p. 526) conclude that
"Where governments have substantial force at their disposal,
in fact, these specialists ordinarily do the major part of the
damaging and seizing which constitutes the collective
violence". This leads to the generalization that "collective
violence should rise and fall with the nonviolent political
activity" (ibid., p. 527). Granted that government is the main
perpetrator of violence, this does not warrant the implication that people themselves do not engage in various forms
of nonnormative collective action, including violence against
persons and property. And if that is so, then governmental
repression should also rise and fall partly in reflection of
the amount of defiant behavior in which protestors themselves engage.

THE PACE AND TIMING OF COLLECTIVE PROTEST

A critical reason for calling attention to these normalizing tendencies is that they invalidate much of the work by RM analysts that deals with the prerequisites of protest – with the conditions under which people are led to defend or advance their interests by taking defiant actions that violate rules and risk great reprisals. We first criticize the grounds on which RM analysts have rejected traditional MI explanations of protest origins; then we show that the RM explanation, which emphasizes socially structured opportunities for protest, is inadequate.

Grievances and Protest

One insignia of RM work is the argument that there is little or no relationship between variations in relative deprivation and the pace and timing of collective protest. Oberschall asserts that "Grievances and disaffection are a fairly permanent and recurring feature of the historical landscape" (Oberschall, 1978, p. 298), suggesting a "constancy of discontent" (McAdam *et al.*, 1988), which in turn justifies shifting "from a *strong* assumption about the centrality of deprivation and grievance to a *weak* one" in explanations of collective protest (McCarthy and Zald, 1977, p. 1215; emphasis in original). It is largely on this ground that RM analysts claim to have won the debate with MI analysts: "Useless Durkheim," Tilly says (1981: Chapter 4).[4]

The empirical basis for this claim rests in no small degree on the widely-accepted evidence presented by Tilly and his collaborators, especially their time-series studies of the relationship between "breakdown" variables, such as intensified hardship or rapid urbanization, and the pace and timing of collective protest. However, MI analysts do not claim that breakdown is a necessary precondition of normative forms of group action. What they emphasize instead is that breakdown is a precondition of collective protest and violence, of riot and rebellion. Any effort to test breakdown theories must therefore employ a dependent variable in which normative and nonnormative forms of collective action are disaggregated, which Tilly and his collaborators do not do.

In effect, the MI tradition is being dismissed for an argument it never made.

Shorter and Tilly's study of strike frequencies in France illustrates this problem. They claim that strike rates correlate with good times, and not with economic downturns, thus presumably invalidating the hardship variant of the relative deprivation version of the MI tradition. However, strikes were legal in France beginning in 1865 (Tilly *et al.*, 1975, p. 73), and thus for the entire 1865–1965 period of the Shorter and Tilly study. Or at least Shorter and Tilly do not separate out legal strikes from strikes that include illegal activity (e.g., violence and sabotage initiated by workers, or other strike actions that violate government regulations, or "wildcat strikes" in violation of union contracts). Taken as a whole, this corpus of research does not answer the question of the conditions under which ordinary people do in fact resort to violence or defiance, and the findings cannot therefore be taken to refute the MI perspective.

We quickly acknowledge that time-series studies that distinguish between normative and nonnormative action will be more difficult to conduct. Not only is the distinction itself sometimes elusive, but norms change over time, in part as the result of successive challenges that produce new balances of power, reflected in new structures of rules. Forms of collective action impermissible in one period may be permissible in another, or the reverse. Moreover, caution has to be exercised in aggregating collective actions that occur in different institutional contexts, simply because different norms may apply, as when land occupations by urban squatters acquire tacit legitimacy while factory takeovers usually do not.

This problem and the obfuscation it creates is worsened by the fact that normative collective action occurs much more frequently than nonnormative action, and perhaps more so in the modern period with the granting of political rights and the vast increase in permissible forms of conflict. The sheer quantity of conventional political action overwhelms the more irregular and episodic incidents of unconventional protest. Electoral rallies occur with great frequency, for example, but riots are infrequent. For this reason, unless normative and nonnormative forms are disaggregated, the conventional will overwhelm the unconventional, thus blotting out any possible relationship between "breakdown" and collective protest. The point is that collective violence and defiance must be operationalized in ways that are true to the MI argument, however difficult that may be, if the relevance of MI ideas to the origins of collective violence and defiance is to be fairly tested.

A second and equally fatal source of confounding results from a criticism we made earlier – the failure to distinguish between violence initiated by protestors, and violence initiated by the authorities. The MI tradition seeks to predict violence by the former, not violence by the latter. Consider Lodhi and Tilly's time-series analysis of collective violence in France between 1830 and 1960 which has generally been accepted as puncturing MI explanations by showing that the pace and timing of collective violence does not increase with "the rate at which social ties are being dissolved" through urbanization (Lodhi and Tilly, 1973, p. 316). Their dependent variable includes "771 incidents of collective violence occurring in France from 1830 to 1860, consisting of every event involving at least one group of 50 persons or more in which some person or object was seized or damaged over resistance" (ibid., p. 305). But Lodhi and Tilly do not go into "the nature of the actions" that comprise their "grand totals of collective violence," limiting themselves instead to "aggregate levels . . . of collective violence" (ibid., p. 305) measured by "the number killed, wounded or arrested" (ibid., pp. 298–9). And these data, they say, "measure, in effect, how rigorously police and troops put down protests and demonstrations" (ibid., p. 306). The same problem arises in the Snyder and Tilly time-series study on hardship and collective violence in France during the same years. Again, the dependent variable is "the extent of governmental repression" (Snyder and Tilly, 1972, p. 520), indicated by the number of killings and arrests by the authorities. The question, then, is what is being measured? Is it resort to violence by ordinary people, or is it violence inflicted by the authorities? But this question cannot be answered because the dependent variable is clearly not an uncontaminated measure of the extent to which people themselves initiated violence prior to governmental responses.

In sum, given both the failure to disaggregate normative

and nonnormative collective action, and the failure to distinguish between the perpetrators of violence, none of these studies can be taken as refuting the MI tradition. Hardship and dislocation may yet be shown to correlate with what Kerbo (1982; cf. also Kerbo and Shaffer, 1986) calls "movements of crisis." Moreover, malintegration ideas are now enjoying a certain renaissance among some RM analysts. What seems to be provoking this shift is the contradiction between the theoretical dismissal of the breakdown tradition, on the one hand, and the empirical descriptions of the actual conditions preceding protest episodes that RM analysts themselves describe, on the other. RM accounts almost always begin by identifying precisely the sorts of antecedent conditions to which MI analysts attribute stress. These conditions – far from being recurrent, permanent, and ubiquitous, as RM analysts usually insist – are often awesome, new, and fearsome. For example, preindustrial food rioters, land squatters, and machine smashers were reacting to social and economic forces of such transforming scale as to threaten the destruction of their way of life. And perhaps for just this reason, some RM analysts are now breaking ranks over this issue. Thus there is a growing tendency in the RM literature to reintroduce such terms as "intensified grievances" and "suddenly imposed grievances" (Walsh, 1981), together with renaming traditional such concepts as legitimacy and delegitimacy with terms like "cognitive liberation" (McAdam, 1982) and "ideological anger" (Exum, 1985, p. 14).

Lateral Integration and Protest

We come now to the RM quarrel with the social disorganization strand in the MI tradition. RM analysts claim that protest is normal because it grows out of everyday social organization that creates collective capacities. Tilly takes this argument to its logical extreme. Following White's use of the term "catnet" to define "organization" – that is, the degree of organization depends on the extent to which categories of people (e.g., blacks) are bound together by internal networks (e.g., religious) – Tilly argues that the more categories are laced with networks, the more they can "in principle, mobilize" (Tilly, 1978, p. 64). Hence one of the RM school's most fundamental causal propositions: "The greater the density of social organization, the more likely that social movement activity will develop" (McAdam, McCarthy, and Zald, 1988, p. 703).

But even as social integration is exalted in explanation of protest, so too is its absence. Sometimes protest is attributed to the fact that people are integrated in the social order, and sometimes to the fact that they are not. On the one hand, if social categories of people lack a "veritable lattice work" of internal networks (ibid., p. 711), their "infrastructure deficits" impede mobilization (McCarthy, 1987). On the other hand, multiple group memberships impose role obligations, thus raising the costs of participation in movements. Consequently, McCarthy and Zald (1973) direct attention to the disproportionate participation in the movements of the 1960s by persons with few social ties, or what are called the "biographically available": students and "autonomous" professionals, for example. Students in particular are singled out because their pre-existing ties to the social order are no longer binding, nor have they formed new and enduring ties. Thus students could be drawn to the Freedom Summer project during the civil rights movement because they were "remarkably free of personal constraints that might have inhibited participation" (McAdam, 1986, p. 83). Much the same point could be made for ghetto rioters who were predominantly young and at best loosely involved in the usual array of marital, occupational, and related roles.

The proposition that the probability of protest varies directly with the degree of lateral integration is badly flawed for a another reason: although collective defiance is episodic and infrequent, the lateral integration requisite to protest is ubiquitous. By not seeing this, RM analysts end by using a double standard in evaluating the MI tradition. On the one hand, they fault MI analysts for failing to concede that grievances do not necessarily lead to protest. Thus the Tillys accuse relative deprivation analysts of using a constant to explain a variation, since they give in to

> [T]he temptation . . . to ignore the places, times, and populations in which nothing happened. When conflict is at issue, why waste time writing the history of harmony? The simple

answer: an explanation of protest, rebellion, or collective violence that cannot account for its absence is no explanation at all; an explanation based only on cases where something happened is quite likely to attribute importance to conditions which are actually quite common in cases where nothing happened. That is the characteristic defect of many theories being bandied about today which treat rebellion as a consequence of frustrated rising expectations without specifying how often (or under what conditions) rising expectations are frustrated without rebellion (Tilly *et al.*, 1975, p. 12).

On the other hand, RM analysts also use a constant to explain a variation, since they too "ignore the places, times, and populations in which nothing happened." Tilly (1986) has culled four centuries of French history for episodes of collective protest, but he has not told us about those that should have erupted but did not. Here is a population of people; they had sufficient solidarity to act on their grievances, and protest might not have been met with outright repression; nevertheless, they remained inert. Surely such occasions were numerous. But the opposite impression is conveyed when these four centuries of French protests, or a century of protests in Italy, Germany, and France (Tilly *et al.*, 1975), are compressed between the covers of a single book. Gamson's (1975) study of "challenging groups" in American suffers from the same defect. He tells us about those groups who protested, but not about those who could have but did not.

This illogic pervades the RM literature. Wilson and Orum claim that "conventional psychological theories," such as relative deprivation, do not explain the ghetto riots of the 1960s, and that instead "social bonds ... i.e., friendship networks, drew many people to become active participants" (Wilson and Orum, 1976, p. 198), but they do not wonder why riots before the 1960s were so rare or why there have been so few since, despite pervasive friendship bonds in both periods. Similarly, McAdam, McCarthy and Zald suggest that the concentration of students in institutions of higher education has created the "organizational potential for chronic student movements ... even if [the student movement of the 1960s] has presently waned" (McAdam *et al.*, 1988, p. 712). The student movement certainly did wane; it has turned out to be anything but chronic. Most of the time most people try to make their ordinary lives, not to make history (Flacks, 1988).

RM analysts are led away from this problem because they overstate the structural requisites of protest. To be sure, people have to be related to one another: some sense of common identity; some sense of shared definitions of grievances and antagonists; some ability to communicate; and so on. But these requisites do not depend on the dense and enduring lateral relationships posited by the RM school. On this point, Oberschall agrees: "collective protest actions . . . are possible even in a state of disorganization . . . the minimum requirements for collective disturbances are shared sentiments of collective repression and common targets of oppression" (Oberschall, 1973, p. 133). Consequently, some forms of protest are more or less universally available. Arson, whether in the fields of the preindustrial world or in the streets of the urbanized world, requires technological rather than organizational resources, and not much of the former, either. Riots require little more by way of organization than numbers, propinquity, and some communication. Most patterns of human settlement, whether the preindustrial village or modern metropolis, supply these structural requirements. In fact, the movements of the 1960s and 1970s often mobilized people who were previously only weakly or fleetingly related to one another, whether students activists, or direct action participants in the peace and environmental struggles. And the ghetto rioters may not have been riff-raff, but neither were they drawn from the highly integrated sectors of the black community.

Moreover, the minimal structural requirements for protest are likely to be available even during the periods of rapid social change to which Durkheimians attribute breakdown and collective disorder. In this sense, RM analysts may have overstated breakdown ideas, as if what is meant is the total shredding of the social fabric, making it akin to complete atomization. Durkheim spoke of the way the suicide rate varies with degrees of cohesion (rural vs. urban; married vs. single, widowed, and divorced, and so forth). Bonds are strong, moderate, or weak; whether Durkheim also meant to suggest that bonds can disappear altogether is debatable. But whatever Durkheim intended, the point is that total atomization, if it ever exists, is at most a fleeting phenomenon: where there are human beings, there are networks. Because people are averse to being alone, they construct relationships, even under the most disorganized conditions, and they do so rapidly. In short, lateral integration, however fragile, is ubiquitous, thus making opportunities for protest ubiquitous.

These observations also suggest that the generalization that the forms of protest change as societies change is overstated, and for the same reason: the requisite degree of lateral integration is overstated. The Tillys claim that urbanization and industrialization caused the small-scale, localistic, and diffuse modes of pre-industrial collective protest to give way to largescale, associational, and specialized forms. Thus, from the eighteenth

> to the nineteenth century either in Europe or America, we discover significant further changes in the prevailing forms of contentious gatherings. We notice the food riot, machine breaking, invasions of common fields, and their companion forms of collective action peaking and then disappearing. We find the demonstration, the strike, the election rally, the public meeting, and allied forms of action taking on more and more prominence (Tilly, 1981, p. 99).

The main generalization follows: "The organizational revolution reorganized violence" (Tilly *et al.*, 1975, p. 49).

However, since at least some forms of protest only require minimal integration, these protest forms display remarkable continuity. "The riot," for example, "is the characteristic and ever-recurring form of popular protest" (Rude, 1964, p. 6). More generally, preindustrial food riots, grain seizures, land invasions, and machine smashing have rough parallels in the modern period with urban riots, mob looting, squatting, sitdowns, sit-ins, rent strikes, and industrial sabotage. This suggests that Tilly's argument that repertoires of protest change as societies change – old forms out, new forms in – needs qualification. Even as changing modes of social organization bring into being new forms of protest, certain persisting features of social organization facilitate continuities in other protest forms.

Finally, the predictive value of lateral integration is weakened because the same structural capacities provide people with more than one way of reacting to their lot in life. The factors to which RM analysts attribute various forms of contention – interests, organization, mobilization – are also associated with the rise of religious movements, for example, or of organized racketeering. Consider the social bonds of friendship: Wilson and Orum (1976) attribute ghetto riots to them; and Ianni (1974) notes that blacks, lacking the ethnic/familial solidarities that make the Italian Mafia possible, nevertheless developed a Black Mafia because of friendship solidarities forged in street gangs and prisons. And perhaps there is even an interactive effect between crime and protest: the rise and spread of organized networks of drug entrepreneurship and consumption may help explain the low level of protest in the black ghettos since the 1960s. In other words, social integration does not dictate that people will seek solutions to felt grievances in politics at all, whether by conventional or unconventional means.

In general, then, *organizational capacity does not predict anything* – except that the violation of rules *might* take collective form and, if collective, that it *might* take political form.[5] We have elsewhere referred to this as the problem of "indeterminacy" – that given objective conditions, such as structural opportunity, do not necessarily determine given behavioral outcomes (Cloward and Piven, 1979, p. 654, and 1989). Plainly, the question of the correlates of the pace and timing of collective protest remains open.

Vertical Integration and Protest

People who are organized laterally are also typically connected to other groups vertically. But hierarchical bonds usually constrain collective protest, and that is still another reason why lateral integration does not predict protest. Tocqueville (1955) noted that it was only with the weakening of ties between nobility and peasantry that the French Revolution became possible. Moore subsequently analyzed variations in the "institutional links binding peasant society to the upper classes," and argued that weaker linkages were more conducive to peasant revolution (Moore, 1966, pp. 477–8). Oberschall also follows this line of thinking by suggesting that protest potential is enhanced when societies are "segmented" so that lower-stratum collectivities have "few links and bonds" to higher stratum groups – for example, where landlords are absentee, or when forms of colonial rule generate "few links between colonizer and colonized," or in self-contained farm-belts that are "cut-off from the power centers... except for market relations." By contrast, Oberschall continues, if there are strong "vertical social and political bonds between upper and lower classes, mobilization into protest movements among the lower classes is not likely to take place" (Oberschall, 1973, pp. 119–20).[6]

Because hierarchical integration is more the rule than the exception, the important problem is to identify the conditions under which its constraining influence weakens. On this point, the ideas of MI analysts may be relevant. Vertically-integrated institutions probably only become settings for protest under exceptional conditions – when grievances intensify, or when linkages weaken.

Prior to the advent of the RM school, the black church, with its "other-worldly" oriented clergy who were dominated by white influentials, was thought to divert people from political action, as indeed it did. RM analysts have since rehabilitated the black church by arguing that it provided a crucial nexus for the civil rights mobilization, and indeed it also did that. The same point can be made for the Catholic church in Latin America whose centuries-long alliance with the landed oligarchies has only recently begun to give way. And a similar shift of the church's role also occurred in Poland. It was probably constituency discontent that forced the shift to "activist" theologies by the black church in the South, and by the Catholic churches in Latin America and Poland. Otherwise, church leaders risked the loss of legitimacy in the eyes of parishioners. Similarly, the shift by white Protestant fundamentalist clergy in the United States from a theological doctrine prescribing the separation of religion and politics to one calling for secular political protest in the name of maintaining religious values (e.g., civil disobedience at abortion clinics) may reflect, at least in part, rising discontent among many parishioners in the face of threats to their traditional way of life raised by greater cultural permissiveness (Ginsberg, 1989; Piven, 1984). Electoral institutions also illustrate the dual effects of institutional integration. The ideology of democratic political rights, by emphasizing the availability of legitimate avenues for the redress of grievances, delegitimizes protest; and the dense relationships generated by electoral politics also divert people from protest. However, rising popular discontent sometimes sets in motion a process that, at least temporarily, transforms electoral politics itself. For instance, when deteriorating economic circumstances produce voter volatility, the short term concerns of political leaders with re-election may lead them to cope with unstable majorities by symbolically identifying with the grievances of discontented groups, thus fueling anger and legitimating protest (Piven and Cloward, 1977, p. 18).

In many situations, protest only becomes possible when vertical controls weaken owing to large scale processes of social change. In the 1930s, the craft unions associated with the dominant American Federation of Labor issued charters to industrial workers who were clamoring for unions, but the AF of L oligarchs were less than enthusiastic in welcoming their new constituents. Given their level of discontent and their loose ties to the AF of L, industrial workers broke free, and strike waves followed. A similar process occurred in company unions that had been established to inhibit protest, particularly in the steel industry. And only as strikes escalated did a few enterprising union leaders, sensing the possibilities of the moment, create "organizing committees" to form industrial unions (Piven and Cloward, 1977, p. 153). On this point, Hobsbawm agrees: "Mass union organization, in the US of the 1930s as in all analogous 'explosions' of labor unionism with which I am familiar, was the *result* of worker mobilization and not its cause" (Hobsbawm, 1978; emphasis in original). Another example of breakout is provided by the postwar drives by public employees for the right to unionize and strike, which occurred only after the historically close ties between civil service associations and local political parties had weakened (Piven, 1969). And the postwar black protest movement was not imaginable until the modernization of the plantation system led to mass evictions of blacks from the land and from a system of semi-feudal controls (Oberschall, 1973; Piven and Cloward, 1977).[7] In short, *breakdown is often prerequisite to breakout.* Perhaps Durkheim is not so useless after all.

NORMALIZING PROTEST ORGANIZATION

Some among the Durkheimians tend to think of collective protest as purposeless disorder. RM analysts think it has purpose, and that its purpose is political – the effort to exercise power in contests with other groups. In this large sense, protest is "normal" because politics is normal, as we would agree. However, in recasting collective protest as politics, RM analysts have both normalized the organizational forms typically associated with protest, especially with lower-stratum protest, and they have normalized the political processes generated by protest.

Both of these tendencies appear in Tilly's work, and are linked to his understanding of historical change as progress. Thus, in the preindustrial world, the possibility of exerting influence depended on "the willingness of [challenging groups] to inflict and endure harm," but the "grant of legality [to many previously proscribed forms of political action] lowers the group's costs of mobilization and collective action" (Tilly, 1978, p. 167). Consequently, what now "tells more" than inflicting and enduring harm is "the group's capacity to organize, accumulate resources, and form alliances," especially within the electoral system (Tilly *et al.*, 1975, p. 285). The implication is that ordinary people can now form organizations to pursue their goals through normal politics.

This conclusion strikes us as altogether too sweeping. True, with the granting of legality, the risk of repression no longer inhibits many forms of mobilization. At the same time, however, legalization increases the costs of mobilization because it imposes additional resource requirements. Tilly himself implies as much in his discussion of the way legalization transformed strikes: elements of "standardization," "routinization," and "bureaucratization" were introduced, and "spontaneity" declined (Tilly, 1978, p. 161). Moreover, legalization also "muzzles" or "encapsulates" strike power (Piven and Cloward, 1977, pp. 155–75), as McCammon reminds us in her update of the way U.S. labor relations law "severely crippled, if not negated," the power of the strike (McCammon, 1990, p. 225). In other words, to use conventional methods of influence effectively, people must be able to muster the resources both to organize bureaucratically and to overcome the influence of other groups in regular political contests. Those resources, Tilly says, are "the economist's factors of production: land, labor, capital, and perhaps technical expertise as well" (Tilly, 1978, p. 69). By these criteria, however, lower-stratum challengers are obviously left with serious resource deficits (Piven, 1963).

RM analysts have tried to solve this problem in two ways, and each fails. One has been to treat formal organization as if it compensates for lack of political resources. Unfortunately for lower-stratum groups, organization is a pale substitute for resources. Gamson's check list of what it takes for a group to become "combat ready" shows why. Since the antagonists are bureaucratically organized, challengers must create parallel organizations with three characteristics: (1) a constitution; (2) an internal division between officers, committees, and rank and file; and (3) a formal membership list. In addition, it is important that there be sufficient centralized authority to quell factionalism in the group or, if the group is more decentralized, some other mechanism to control internal dissension. "Each of these variables – bureaucracy, centralization of power, and [limited] factionalism – make a contribution to success.... There are, then, definite advantages for a challenging group, inevitably engaged in conflict with an organized antagonist, to organize itself for facility in political combat" (Gamson, 1975, p. 108).

Gamson bases these conclusions on his study of 53 "challengers" in American history between 1800 and 1945, all of which were formally-organized groups existing, on average, for eight years. Two-fifths of them were occupationally-based, mainly unions; one-third were assorted "reform groups," including abolitionists, political parties, civil rights organizations, and peace groups; another fifth were socialist groups, such as the International Workingmen's Association; and the remainder were rightwing or nativist groups, such as the German–American Bund (ibid., p. 20).

Protest actions that were not sponsored by formally organized groups did not turn up in the sample.[8] "Perhaps that tells us something," Gamson says, thereby implying that collective protest episodes are always sponsored by organizations.[9] But even the most casual perusal of collective action events – whether the ghetto riots in the American cities of the 1960s, or the mass demonstrations in Eastern Europe, or the food riots in Latin America – makes clear how dubious that thesis is, and especially how dubious it is for the kinds of collective protest and disorder that are of concern to Durkheimians. (Of course, formal organizations do often come to be associated with protest events in various ways, sometimes because outside observers erroneously attribute these events to pre-existing formal organizations, and sometimes because protests stimulate the emergence of organizations by "social movement entrepreneurs", who are then given credit retroactively for the protests.)

Protest is also depicted as overorganized in a good many RM case studies. The rise of movements is signified by organizational paraphernalia, such as the formation of social movement organizations with leaders who make demands and call for demonstrations or lobbying. In the absence of these manifestations, RM analysts often do not recognize the existence of movements. Thus the two major recent RM accounts of the civil rights movement barely touch on riots: Morris (1984) does not mention them (except for a brief reference to the riot in Birmingham), and McAdam (1982) ignores the question of why they occurred. Similarly, in the recent survey of the social movement literature by McAdam, McCarthy, and Zald (1988), riots are mentioned only once, nor do many other modes of disruptive protest figure much in their survey. Their discussion of "social movement organizations" ranges across such issues as inclusivity and exclusivity, federation and chapter structures, and competition within social movement "industries", which exert pressure for "product differentiation." The "professional social movement organization" is singled out; in "pure" form, it's distinguishing characteristic is that it "communicates with

adherents or members through the mails or the mass media"
(McAdam *et al.*, 1988, pp. 716–18).

These portrayals may well have validity for groups with
the resources to construct enduring formal organizations,
and with still further resources that can be converted into
political power. But can those with few resources form influential organizations successfully? Indeed, do they even have
the resources to form stable formal organizations, influential or not? Lower-stratum groups often act as though they
think so, and do their best to adopt constitutions, elect officers,
divide responsibilities among committees, compile membership lists, hold conventions, seek alliances, and garner external financial and expert resources. But such formal
organizations cannot be wished into existence; it takes
resources to create them, and especially to sustain them.
Labor organizations solve this problem with mechanisms to
coerce membership and contributions – such as the union
shop and dues check-off – but lower-stratum groups typically lack the capacity to coerce participation. Consequently,
efforts by lower-income people to build formal organizations
generally fail, as the most cursory reading of the history of
poor people's organizations reveals. Naison's account of tenant
organizing in New York City during the 1930s ends by noting
that the city-wide structure that coordinated local tenant
organizations "proved fragile":

> Never did City-Wide's fund-raising produce over one thou-
> sand dollars per year. . . . The slum tenants . . . lacked the
> resources to subsidize it, or the political skills and inclina-
> tions to build the kind of stable organizations that could
> give City-Wide real permanence. City-Wide survived on the
> politically-motivated idealism and skills of underemployed
> professionals, both of which were vulnerable to shifts in
> political climate and improvements in the economy (Naison,
> 1986, p. 127).

The same point can be made for welfare rights organizing
in the 1960s: the National Welfare Rights Organization only
lasted about five years because local groups throughout the
country could not sustain themselves once external resources
from the anti-poverty program, such as organizers drawn
from the ranks of Vista Volunteers, began to contract. A

serious defect of Gamson's sample is that the vast number
of failed organization-building episodes by lower-stratum
people is not represented, since most such efforts never
resulted in fully formed organizations, or the resulting organizations were so puny and short-lived that they were not
available to be sampled. Had there been a way to sample
these episodes, Gamson might not have been so quick to
advance a formal organization prescription, especially for
lower-stratum groups. In short, the resources necessary to
develop permanent mass-based bureaucratic organizations
are not equally distributed in the class structure. The preoccupation with formal organization thus inadvertently contributes to the class bias in the work of RM analysts which
has been remarked upon by Kerbo (1982).

RM analysts have also tried to solve the problem of lower-
stratum resource deficits by emphasizing the importance of
coalition politics in which "third parties" make up for resource deficiencies.[10] Here the problem is not so much that
lower-stratum groups lack resources to form stable organizations, but that their organizations, even when formed, command few of the kinds of resources that can be converted
into regular political influence. Organization, in short, is not
necessarily a source of power.

The role of third parties in making up for the lack of
political influence by lower-statum groups was highlighted
by Lipsky in his analysis of the 1963–4 New York City rent
strike (Lipsky, 1968, 1970). He concluded that the essence
of the politics of protest is "showmanship" or "noise" in which
leaders curry sympathy and support from potential "reference public." His findings, which have been widely accepted,
are summarized by the Tillys:

> Lipsky makes a strong case that the strike movement owed
> what success it had (which was not enormous) to the fact
> that dramatic protests activated powerful third parties who
> then put pressure on responsible authorities to respond
> to the grievances of the protestors (Tilly *et al.*, 1975, p. 294).

None of this was true. The so-called "rent strike movement"
consisted of a mere flurry of rent-withholding activity between November 1963 and March of the next year. The only
sense in which the episode was "dramatic" is that Jesse Grey,

the citywide strike leader, knew how to attract press coverage with groundless announcements that thousands of build-
ings were about to go on strike, and by conducting tenement
tours for sympathetic reporters who wrote stories deploring
housing conditions. As a factual matter, no powerful third
parties put pressure on anyone (Piven and Cloward, 1967).[11]
How then can people without conventional political resources exert influence? In our own work on unemployed
and labor movements, rent strikes, welfare rights organizing, and the civil rights movement, we have tried to show
that lower-stratum protestors have some possibility of influence – including mobilizing third party support – if their
actions violate rules and disrupt the workings of an institution on which important groups depend.[12] When lower-stratum groups form organizations and employ conventional
political strategies, they can easily be ignored. But institutional disruptions cannot so easily be ignored. Institutional
disruptions provoke conflict; they arouse an array of "third
parties," including important economic interests, and may
even contribute to electoral dealignment and realignment.
To restore institutional stability and to avoid worsening polarization, political leaders are forced to respond, whether
with concessions or repression. To suppose that "normal"
or conventional political strategies can have these effects is
to underestimate the maldistribution of political resources
and to trivialize the consequent realities of power.

Even when the resources are available to create them,
formally organized groups are not likely to undertake disruptive protests. Gamson's formal organization prescription
ignores the problems that disruptive or rule-breaking protests create for formal organizations. It is not that disruption and violence are never employed by formally organized
groups; it is that, in general, organization constrains against
such tactics: Protests can provoke severe repression which
formal organizations will not usually risk (secret or underground organizations are better positioned in this respect).
This is a point made by E. P. Thompson when he speaks of
the English crowd's

> capacity for swift direct action. To be of a crowd or a mob
> was another way of being anonymous, whereas to be a

member of a continuing organization was bound to expose
one to detection and victimisation. The 18th century crowd
well understood its capacities for action, and its own art
of the possible. Its successes must be immediate, or not
at all. It must destroy those machines, intimidate those
employers or dealers, damage that mill . . . before troops
come on the scene (Thompson, 1974, p. 401).

Scott puts the same point this way:

> Mob action . . . may represent a popular tactical wisdom
> developed in conscious response to political constraints
> realistically faced. Spontaneity and a lack of formal or-
> ganization then become an enabling mode of protest rather
> than a reflection of the slender political talents of popu-
> lar classes (Scott, forthcoming).

And Oberschall again breaks with the main RM currents of
thought to argue that "the degree of organization varies
inversely with the magnitude of violence in confrontations"
(Oberschall, 1973, p. 340).

Protest is also inhibited by constraints that result from
the vertical integration upon which organizational maintenance by relatively resourceless groups often depends. Thus
McAdam, McCarthy, and Zald claim that "a principal goal
of [RM analysts] is understanding how emergent movement
organizations seek to mobilize and routinize – frequently
by tapping lucrative elite resources of support – the flow of
resources, which ensures movement survival" (McAdam *et al.*,
1988, p. 697), without acknowledging that this dependency
generally turns movement organizations away from protest.
This is a problem we have tried to address in our own work
(Piven and Cloward 1977, especially the Introduction to the
paperback edition), but McAdam dismisses as "pessimistic"
our conclusion that organization (in the sense of formal
organization) tends to mitigate against disruptive tactics
(McAdam, 1982, p. 54). Nevertheless, McAdam concludes
his own discussion of these issues in words that could have
been our own:

> the establishment of formal organizations . . . sets in mo-
> tion . . . the destructive forces of oligarchization, cooptation,
> and the dissolution of indigenous support . . . [all of which]

tames the movement by encouraging insurgents to pursue only those goals acceptable to external sponsors. . . . The long list of movements that have failed to negotiate these obstacles attests to the difficulties inherent in the effort (ibid., 1986, pp. 55–6).

NORMALIZING POLITICAL INFLUENCE

In democratic polities, whether protestors win or lose depends on the interaction between disruptive political tactics and electoral politics. However, the influence resulting from the interaction between institutional disruptions and the electoral system cannot be understood by the usual mode of analysis that focuses, as the Tillys do, on the forming of alliances (Tilly *et al.*, 1975, p. 285). Lower-stratum disruptive movements tend to emerge at junctures when larger societal changes generate political volatility and dealignment, and new political possibilities. On this point, we agree with the line of analysis in much RM literature that attributes protest from below in part to the opportunities generated by the fragmenting of elites and by realigning processes. Still, the impact of protest during these periods is not simply that it contributes to subsequent coalition building and realignment. What needs to be understood is that disruptive protest itself makes an important contribution to elite fragmentation and electoral dealignment. Indeed, we think the role of disruptive protest in helping to create political crises (or what we have called "dissensus politics") is the main source of political influence by lower stratum groups (Cloward and Piven, 1966, 1968; Piven and Cloward, 1967, 1977: Chapter 4; Piven and Cloward, 1988, Introduction).

The sharp contrast between our "dissensus politics" analysis and a good number of RM analyses can be illustrated by examining explanations of civil rights successes. For example, McAdam (1982, p. 221) correctly emphasizes that a "significant disruption of public order" was essential to insure federal responses to the civil rights movement. Despite this promising beginning (and despite its clear difference with Lipsky's "noise" and showmanship"), McAdam goes on to explain federal responses in the usual coalitional terms: protestors won because of the growing influence of the black vote coupled with the support of sympathetic northern white liberals. Something like this coalitional process did indeed happen. It was not more important, however, than the fact that the tactics of the civil rights movement helped cleave the Democratic party's north – south alliance. This alliance was already weakening owing to southern opposition to New Deal labor and social welfare policies, and owing to the expansion of the white middle class generated by economic modernization in the south during the postwar period. The result was to stimulate neopopulist movements and to revive the southern wing of the Republican party. Democratic leaders only tipped decisively toward supporting civil rights legislation when it became clear that black protests were also helping to swell the volume of southern white defections to the Republican party. With the white South alienated, it was finally in the interests of the national Democratic party to enfranchise blacks in an attempt to rebuild its shattered southern wing. For McAdam, however, the Democratic party's southern regional base was "a relatively small, politically expendable segment of the population" (McAdam, 1982, p. 215), which did not figure in the calculations of national Democratic party strategists. Of course, the South was not expendable and national Democratic party leaders knew it was not, which is why they resisted civil rights concessions for as long as they did. But civil rights protests – by activating northern liberals and the growing concentrations of black voters in the northern cities, *and especially by enlarging the tide of southern white defections* – changed the political calculus. Generally speaking, then, disruptive tactics force concessions, not by enlarging and consolidating coalitions, but by exacerbating electoral "dissensus" during periods when electoral divisions are already widening (Cloward and Piven, 1966, 1968; Piven and Cloward, 1967, 1977: Chapter 4; and Piven and Cloward, 1988, Introduction).

After two decades of work by analysts associated with the RM school, protest by lower-stratum people is as marginalized and deviant as it ever was. Despite a substantial volume of work on the civil rights movement, for example, we know

little more than we did before about the riot of 11 May
1963 in Birmingham – perhaps the single most important
episode in the black movement to that date – or of the
subsequent riots in which 169 were killed, 7000 wounded,
and 40,000 arrested, except that the participants were not
"riff-raff."

When RM analysts talk about these riots, they reveal the
biases of a normalized, overorganized, and conventionalized
conception of political protest. The riots are not so much
analyzed as regretted. McAdam considers that Jacobs and
Landau "accurately summed up the situation" when they
explained that "neither SNCC nor any other group has found
a form of political organization that can convert the energy
of the slums into political power" (quoted in McAdam, 1982,
p. 191). But if such efforts to organize the black lower-class
had been undertaken – at least if they had been undertaken early enough and forcefully enough in the 1960s –
there might have been no riots. As it was, the main role
played by various social movement leaders during the rioting was to try to quell it, and RM analysts unfailingly ap-
prove. When riots broke out in Birmingham in June 1963,
Morris says that civil rights leaders "hit the streets at once
in order to persuade members of the black community not
to engage in violence" so as to "save the agreement" with
the economic elites of Birmingham. With the rioters sub-
dued, "the agreement stood, and the planned exercise of
"people power" had been successful" (Morris, 1984, p. 273).
McAdam correctly notes that the early riots triggered a veritable northward stampede by movement leaders to establish organizational footholds in the ghetto as a means of
regaining control over a movement that was slipping away
from them" (McAdam, 1986, p. 191). And Oberschall expresses the same outlook when he concludes that "The single
most important failure of the middle-class black and the
civil rights organizations was their failure to mobilize and
to organize the lower-class community" (Oberschall, 1973,
p. 213).

So there we have it again. Like many malintegration analysts
before them, resource mobilization analysts have also reduced
lower-stratum protest politics to irrational and apolitical
eruptions.

Notes

1. This contemporary development in the literature on protest follows a similar but much earlier development in the literature on property crime, or crimes against persons with income as the goal. Consider that Edwin H. Sutherland thought that "the processes which result in systematic criminal behavior are fundamentally the same in form as the processes which result in systematic lawful behavior" (Sutherland, 1939, p. 4), and thus that "criminal behavior is a part of human behavior, has much in common with non-criminal behavior, and must be explained within the same general framework as any other behavior" (Sutherland, 1947, p. 4). For a comparative analysis of these kindred but sequential theoretical perspectives in the study of crime and protest, see Piven and Cloward, "Crime and Protest: Discovery and Rediscovery," forthcoming.

2. Rule is quite critical of the work on collective behavior by Park (1921), and especially by Turner and Killian (1957) for failing "to distinguish between collective and 'normal' behavior" (Rule, 1988, p. 102). He also claims that the problem of distinguishing "collective behavior from the rest of social life" is one of two central questions with which he will be preoccupied in his book (ibid., p. 115). But in his extensive and sympathetic discussion of RM work, Rule does not note that RM analysts also blur this distinction.

3. Elsewhere, Tilly acknowledges this extraordinary normative violation: "The frequent borrowing – in parody or in earnest – of the authorities' normal forms of action . . . often amounted to the crowd's almost literally taking the law into its own hands" (Tilly, 1981, p. 161). Nevertheless, it is the role of norms in shaping the modes of defiance, not the defiance of norms as such, that is emphasized.

4. This overall conclusion seems illogical even within the RM framework which postulates continuity between normal and defiant activity. It is well-established, for example, that worsening economic conditions lead to voting shifts, imperiling incumbents, and sometimes causing dramatic political realignments (cf., for example, Tufte, 1978). Since economic deterioration produces changes in conventional political behavior, the logic of the RM analysis would lead one to expect a similar correlation between worsening economic conditions and protest.

5. And even if people are in fact inclined to seek solutions to their problems through politics, variations in social integration may predict the forms of protest better than the incidence of it. For example, disciplined civil disobedience occurred more often in the South and rioting occurred almost exclusively in the North during the 1960s. A possible explanation is that northern ghettoes were less cohesive than southern black communities, making it more difficult to promote disciplined protest, especially in the face of provocations by the police.

6. On this point, see also Eric Wolf's (1969) discussion of the constraining effect of clan ties that crossed class lines in prerevolutionary China.

164   *Collective Protest*

7. For further examples of this general point and the literature bearing on it, see Kerbo (1982, p. 652).
8. "In theory," Gamson says, "a collective behavior listing might have yielded a challenging group, in the absence of any other appropriate organizational listing, but this, in fact, never occurred. Thus, all of our final sample listings are organizations" (Gamson, 1975, p. 156).
9. Personal communication.
10. Morris (1984) has taken exception to this view in his discussion of the civil rights movement by summoning evidence of the substantial resources that the black community itself supplied, but his own data make clear that these internally-generated resources, including especially leadership resources, were contributed mainly by middle-class blacks.
11. The strike failed to rally significant third-party support because the organizers followed Gamson's prescription: they first built tenant committees. Then, together with tenant leaders, they tried to induce tenants to use the procedures for legal redress laid out by the housing agencies. They canvassed apartments for housing violations; filled out official forms; scheduled visits by building inspectors to record hazardous violations; checked that the inspectors actually filed these forms; arranged for rents to be placed in escrow; contacted lawyers, shepherded tenants through the courts, not once but over and over again in the face of delaying tactics by landlords. And for all of that, only a few victories were won. As tenants and organizers were increasingly overwhelmed and worn down by these procedures, the strike faltered and then collapsed, only a few months after it began (Piven and Cloward, 1967).
12. The essential importance of institutional disruptions for the exercise of political influence by resourceless groups is set out in Piven (1963), and in Cloward and Piven (1966). For theoretical elaborations and applications to particular social movements, see Piven and Cloward (1967 and 1977), and Cloward and Piven (1968). The role of disruption is debated in Gamson and Schmeidler (1984), and Cloward and Piven (1984).

References

Cloward, Richard A. and Frances Fox Piven (1966) "A Strategy to End Poverty." *The Nation*, 2 May. Reprinted in Richard A. Cloward and Frances Fox Piven (1974) *The Politics of Turmoil* (New York: Pantheon).
Cloward, Richard A. and Frances Fox Piven (1968) "Dissensus Politics: A Strategy for Winning Economic Rights." *The New Republic*, 20 April. Reprinted in Richard A. Cloward and Frances Fox Piven (1974) *The Politics of Turmoil* (New York: Pantheon).
Cloward, Richard A. and Frances Fox Piven (1979) "Hidden Protest: The Channeling of Female Innovation and Resistance." *Signs: Journal of Women in Culture and Society*, vol. 4, p. 41.

Cloward, Richard A. and Frances Fox Piven (1984) "Disruption and Organization: A Rejoinder to Gamson and Schmeidler." *Theory and Society*, vol. 13 pp. 587–99.

Cloward, Richard A. and Frances Fox Piven (1989) "Why People Deviate in Different Ways, in *New Directions in the Study of Justice, Law and Social Control*, edited by the Arizona State University School of Justice Studies Editorial Board (New York: Plenum).

Exum, William H. (1985) *Paradoxes of Black Protest: Black Student Activism in a White University* (Philadelphia: Temple University Press).

Flacks, Richard (1988) *Making History: The Radical Tradition and the American Mind* (New York: Columbia University Press).

Gamson, William A. (1975) *The Strategy of Social Protest* (Homewood, Il: Dorsey).

Gamson, William A. and Emilie Schmeidler (1984) "Organizing the Poor: An Argument with Frances Fox Piven and Richard A. Cloward, *Poor People's Movements: Why They Succeed, How They Fail.*" *Theory and Society*, vol. 13, pp. 567–85.

Ginsberg, Faye (1989) *Contested Lives: The Abortion Debate in an American community* (Berkeley, CA: University of California Press).

Hobsbawm, Eric J. (1978) *The New York Review of Books*, vol. xxv, no. 4 (23 March).

Ianni, Francis A. J. (1974) *Black Mafia: Ethnic Succession in Organized Crime* (New York: Simon & Schuster).

Kerbo, Harold R. (1982) "Movements of 'Crisis' and Movements of 'Affluence'. A Critique of Deprivation and Resource Mobilization Theories." *Journal of Conflict Resolution*, vol. 26, no. 4 (December).

Kerbo, Harold R. and Richard A. Shaffer (1986) "Unemployment and Protest in the United States, 1890–1940; A Methodological Critique and Research Note." *Social Forces*, vol. 64, pp. 1046–56.

Lipsky, Michael (1968) "Protest as a Political Resource." *American Political Science Review*, vol. 62, pp. 1144–58.

Lipsky, Michael (1970) *Protest in City Politics: Rent Strikes Housing and the Power of the Poor* (Chicago: Rand McNally).

Lodhi, Abdul Qaiyum and Charles Tilly (1973) "Urbanization and Collective Violence in 19th-Century France." *American Journal of Sociology*, vol. 2, no. 79 (September).

McAdam, Doug (1982) *Political Process and the Development of Black Insurgency 1930–1970* (Chicago: University of Chicago Press).

McAdam, Doug (1986) "Recruitment to High Risk Activism: The Case of Freedom Summer," *American Journal of Sociology*, vol. 92. no. 1, pp. 64–90.

McAdam, Doug, John D. McCarthy and Mayer N. Zald (1988) "Social Movements," in Neil J. Smelser (ed.), *Handbook of Sociology* (Beverly Hills, CA: Sage Publications).

McCammon, Holly J. (1990) "Legal Limits on Labor Militancy: Labor Law and the Right to Strike since the New Deal." *Social Problems*, vol. 37, no. 2.

McCarthy, John D. (1987) "Pro-Life and Pro-Choice Mobilization: Infrastructure Deficits and New Technologies," in Mayer N. Zald and John

D. McCarthy (eds), *Social Movements in an Organizational Society*. (New Jersey: Transaction Books).

McCarthy, John D., Mark Wolfson, David P. Baker and Elaine M. Mosakowski (in press) "The Foundations of Social Movement Organizations: Local Citizens' Groups Opposing Drunken Driving," in Glenn R. Carroll (ed.), *Ecological Models of Organization*. (Cambridge, MA.: Ballinger).

McCarthy, John D. and Mayer Zald (1973) *The Trend of Social Movements in America: Professionalization and Resource Mobilization* (New Jersey: General Learning Press).

McCarthy, John D. and Mayer Zald (1977) "Resource Mobilization and Social Movements." *American Journal of Sociology*, vol. 82, pp. 1212–41.

McPhail, Clark (1991) *The Myth of the Madding Crowd* (New York: Aldine de Gruyter).

Moore, Barrington (1966) *The Social Origins of Dictatorship and Democracy: Lord and Peasant in the Making of the Modern World*. (Boston: Beacon Press).

Morris, Aldon (1984) *The Origins of the Civil Rights Movement* (New York: Free Press).

Naison, Mark (1986) "From Eviction Resistance to Rent Control: Tenant Activism in the Great Depression," in Ronald Lawson (ed.), with the assistance of Mark Naison, *The Tenant Movement in New York City, 1904–1984* (New Brunswick, NJ: Rutgers University Press).

Oberschall, Anthony (1973) *Social Conflict and Social Movements* (Englewood Cliffs, NJ: Prentice-Hall).

Piven, Frances Fox (1963) "Low-Income People and the Political Process," published by Mobilization for Youth. Reprinted in Richard A. Cloward and Frances Fox Piven (1974), *The Politics of Turmoil* (New York: Pantheon).

Piven, Frances Fox (1969) "Militant Civil Servants." *Transaction*, vol. 7, no. 1 (November). Reprinted in Richard A. Cloward and Frances Fox Piven (1974) *The Politics of Turmoil* (New York: Pantheon. 1984).

Piven, Frances Fox (1981) "Deviant Behavior and the Remaking of the World." *Social Problems*, vol. 28, no. 5.

Piven, Frances Fox (1984) "Women and the State: Ideology, Power and the Welfare State," in Alice Rossi (ed.), *Gender and the Life Course* (New York: Aldine).

Piven, Frances Fox, and Richard A. Cloward. (1967) "Rent Strike: Disrupting the Slum System," 2 December, *The New Republic*, reprinted in Richard A. Cloward and Frances Fox Piven, (1974), *The Politics of Turmoil*. (New York: Pantheon).

Piven, Frances Fox and Richard A. Cloward (1977) *Poor People's Movements* (New York: Pantheon).

Piven, Frances Fox and Richard A. Cloward (1988) *Why Americans Don't Vote* (New York: Pantheon).

Rude, George (1964) *The Crowd in History* (New York: John Wiley and Sons).

Rule, James B. (1988) *Theories of Civil Violence* (Berkeley, CA: University of California Press).

Scott, James (undated) unpublished, *The Hidden Transcript of Subordi-*

nate Groups(New Haven, CT: Department of Political Science, Yale University).

Shorter, Edward and Charles Tilly (1974) *Strikes in France, 1830 to 1968* (NY: Cambridge University Press).

Snyder, David and Charles Tilly (1972) "Hardship and Collective Violence in France, 1883–1960," *American Sociological Review,* vol. 37.

Sutherland, Edwin H. (1939) *Principles of Criminology,* third edition (Chicago: University of Chicago Press).

Sutherland, Edwin H. (1947) *Principles of Criminology* fourth edition (Philadelphia, PA: J. B. Lippincott Company)

Thompson, E. P. (1974) "Patrician Society, Plebian Culture," *Journal of Social History,* vol. 7, no. 4.

Tilly, Charles (1975) "Food Supply and Public Order in Modern Europe," in Charles Tilly (ed.), *The Formation of National States in Western Europe* (Princeton University Press).

Tilly, Charles (1978) *From Mobilization to Revolution* (Reading MA: Addison-Wesley).

Tilly, Charles (1981) *As Sociology Meets History* (New York: Academic Press).

Tilly, Charles (1986) *The Contentious French* (Cambridge, MA: Harvard University Press).

Tilly, Charles, Louise Tilly and Richard Tilly (1975) *The Rebellious Century* (Cambridge: Harvard University press).

Tufte, Edward R. (1978) *Political Control of the Economy* (Princeton University Press).

Wilson, Kenneth L. and Anthony M. Orum (1976) "Mobilizing People for Collective Political Action." *Journal of Political and Military Sociology,* vol. 4, pp. 187–202.

Wolf, Eric (1969) *Peasant Wars in the Twentieth Century* (New York: Harper & Row).

8 Social Movement Research in the United States: A European Perspective*

Margit Mayer

In the effort to create a general, encompassing theory of social movements, a flurry of proposals for "synthesis" have recently been submitted. At first, suggestions were made to reintroduce social–psychological perspectives to the resource mobilization approach (Klandermans, 1984; Ferree and Miller, 1985). Now, the integration of even the resource mobilization and classical perspectives is urged (McAdam, McCarthy and Zald, 1988; Rule, 1989). And in the international debate, a synthesis of European (structural) and American (resource mobilization) traditions is proposed. (Kriesi, 1988; p. 364; Klandermans and Tarrow, 1988; Tarrow, 1991). These propositions, no doubt, reflect researchers' growing awareness of the particular limitations within each perspective to fully account for the emergence, dynamic, and characteristics of these movements. Thus, it is hoped that the systematic silences within the theory of resource mobilization (RM) on the role of norms, beliefs, or emotions might be filled by a return to some of the explanations offered within the collective behavior or mass society tradition. Or, in a somewhat parallel fashion, that the recent European new social movement theories, which link social movements to large-scale structural or cultural change, might nicely complement the American resource mobilization approach, as the latter focuses more exclusively on mobilization processes at the group and individual level.

* Reprinted from *International Journal of Politics, Culture, and Society*, vol. 4, no. 4 (Summer 1991), pp. 459–80.

However, such matchmaking will work only if the underlying premises, the basic assumptions about society and social
change that each theory holds, aren't contradictory or incompatible with each other. While this issue should be examined for each suggested linkage of different theories, this
chapter questions particularly the last case, the synthesis
between European structural and American resource mobilization paradigms. It is frequently observed that resource
mobilization theory explains the "how", whereas European
social movement theory focuses on the "why" of mobilizations,
so linking the two seems to promise a more complete account
of the whole phenomenon: an analysis of mobilization processes linked to more encompassing theories of social and
political change that seek to account for the development
of crisis situations. The problem with such linkage consists
in the fact that resource mobilization, while showing little
regard for structural or cultural change, for studying the
"why" of social movements, is not void of assumptions about
social and political theory. Even though it is not a macro
theory but consists of middle range concepts about mobilization potentials and movements, the meaning of these concepts is dependent on broader societal, political and cultural
contexts that are not specified in the approach but can be
distilled from its underlying socio-theoretical framework.

Resource mobilization's implicit assumptions about social
structure and social change may not match the theories of
social change embedded in the European theoretical approaches, vitiating a possible synthesis. Moreover, the research tools congruent with those assumptions may have been
appropriate and useful only for the analysis of the American
movements of the 60s, and 70s, for which they were originally
developed. The belief systems of many of these movements
were extensions of the basic liberal concepts hegemonic in
American public philosophy. Hence, their motivating force
and ideology did not then seem to require explanation,
whereas the methods of organization and mobilization did.
However, the categories developed for the interpretation of
methods of mobilization and organization may be inadequate
for an analysis of movements before or after that period,
movements that for example, do not exhibit the characteristics of the professional "social movement organization"

(SMO) or do not seem to be governed by strategic rationality. Before any "synthesis" of theories can take place, attention must therefore be paid to the presuppositions and implications of each analytical approach. To this end, we start with the dominant American approaches, focusing particularly on resource mobilization, and seek to "deconstruct" the epistemologies and methods of U.S. research by relating them both to the particular character of social movements and to the unique political culture and national style of politics in the United States. By accounting for the historicity and national specificity of the assumptions and theoretical premises of the dominant American approaches to social movements, we explain why these American theories are so unique, different, and – as yet – incompatible with European approaches.

IMPLICIT ASSUMPTIONS IN THE CLASSICAL AND RM APPROACHES

While the various macrosociological and cultural paradigms of European social movement research, which focus on the structural causes of social movements, their ideologies, or their relation to the culture of advanced capitalist society,[1] have produced a definition of social movements limited basically to emancipatory social-change oriented actors, American authors have looked at a far larger variety of phenomena under the heading of "social movements." For them, the term includes social protest as well as collective behavior (such as voluntary associations and interest groups), crowds and militant action as well as inner-directed movements such as cults. While no definition can seriously embrace this wide range of phenomena, a filtering out of the tacit assumptions within the dominant American approaches may be undertaken. For this purpose, the classical and RM approaches[2] are analyzed along two analytical dimensions: (1) what assumptions are made about the origin or rise of social movements, i.e. why do societies generate this phenomenon? (2) In what type of political model are the movements located, i.e. what assumptions about the political constitution of society underlie the model?

Classical Approaches

First, in the classical–functionalist approaches, which were dominant in American social movement research until the early 70s, collective behavior was triggered by societal strain, hence disorganization, and mediated via social "uprootedness" and anomie (Smelser, 1962) or via frustration and fear (Gurr, 1970). According to Smelser, collective behavior is an irrational, exceptional and cognitively inadequate response to structural strains emerging from modernization, while for Kornhauser (1959), collective behavior results from participants' disconnectedness from normal or traditional social relations. Underlying the notion of system strain is the (Parsonian) notion of societal integration, which seemed threatened either by revolutionary agitation or totalitarian movements (Parsons, 1964).

Different variants of this approach[3] all share the basic assumption that individual deprivations, breakdowns of the social order, and homogenizing ideologies are important preconditions for the emergence of social movements. These theories, while often politically preoccupied with preventing a rise of authoritarian (or otherwise alarming) mass movements, used the category "social movement" to encompass fascist movements as well as communist ones, regressive ones as well as emancipatory ones. In each case, the defining feature of the "aberrant" behavior is that it occurs not only outside the national consensus (for example the Cold War), but also outside established institutions, and that it does not follow prevailing social norms. The actors for this noninstitutional politics are the backward, marginal, alienated elements of society.

According to these theories, the life cycle of a social movement moves from spontaneous crowd action to the formation of publics and social movements. Structures associated with this process and their consequences receive little attention. If growth and expansion of the movement occurs, it is understood to be the result of crude processes of communication such as contagion, rumor, circular reaction and diffusion, for which homogenizing ideologies play an important role. Viewing this expressive type of resistance against modernization as irrational, classical theorists have primarily focused on the micro level of social psychological analysis: the origins of social movements are explained by reference to the same dynamics that account for individual participation in movement activities. Hence, answers to micro questions of individual participation *and* answers to macro questions of movement emergence are sought in the characteristic profile of the participants and the presumed psychological functions attendant to participation.

While not all theorists in this tradition deem collective behavior to be an irrational response of atomized individuals to change, they all share an emphasis on the psychological dimension of the reactions to breakdown, crude modes of communication, volatile goals and the transitory nature of social movements. The underlying assumption being that, if modernizing elites are not overwhelmed by the resistance and institutions are successfully defended, the resistance is bound to fail. Modernization will eventually provide the blessings of progress to all.

Second, the political system, within which social movements are located in this model, is an approximation to the pluralist ideal of an open polity (see Smelser, 1962; Bell (1976) Parsons, 1964). Because this assumed pluralist model of politics allows for rational pursuit of interests on the basis of decentralized channels of political articulation and access, movements appear as superfluous and irrational. Political leaders are seen as receptive, the political system as permeable, and no group capable of blocking access to another. Hence, extra-institutional forms of action can only be a matter of marginal, deprivileged groups who lack the cognitive or temporal resources to use the access. As spontaneous, essentially expressive outbursts, social movements are not accorded, in the long run, the capacity to influence societal development or policy outcomes. Only parties, interest organizations and leadership strata have this capacity. Hence, the political processes and actual political change do not need to enter the scope of social movement analysis.

Resource Mobilization Approach

First, as a reaction to the explanatory weaknesses of the classical tradition, which became transparent with the outbreak of the civil rights, antiwar, women's and black movements of the 60s, the so-called resource mobilization approach was developed. Those massive social movements stimulated a shift in theoretical assumptions and analytical emphases, which then were formalized in the theory of resource mobilization.[4] The actors in those movements were largely from the middle classes and even when they were from the lower classes (as in the case of the welfare rights or farm workers movements), they hardly conformed to the image of anomic and deviant behavior held by the classical approaches: the dynamic of these movements could neither be explained by reference to deprivations nor to individual fear reactions. In order to arrive at meaningful explanations of (and supportive interventions into) the observable movements, resource mobilization theorists dismissed structural strain and grievances as explanatory variables for the emergence of social movements. Since the long-standing discontent of Blacks, women, Native Americans and other deprived minorities did not afford much analytical leverage for explaining the widespread mobilization of the 60s and early 70s, RM theory assumes that mobilizing grievances are ubiquitous and constant. Furthermore, RM authors thought that the role of ideology could be downplayed since the belief systems of most movements of the 60s and 70s were recognized as extensions of the basic liberal concepts that dominate American public discourse. Ideological orientations and motivations are taken for granted and do not play a role in the mobilization process. Instead of stressing the factors of objective tensions, deprivations, and belief systems, *variability of resources* became the key factor in explaining the emergence and development of insurgency. Aided by newly available or improved resources, deprived groups can be mobilized into collective political behavior. Empirical research by RM investigators found that social movements arise when necessary resources become available, when the political opportunity structure for collective action improves, and when facilities and leaders become available.

Given these conditions, social movements are not distinct and apart from political parties, lobbies and interest groups, as they were conceived in the classical approaches. Rather they are equally legitimate players in basically the same field. A fundamental continuity between institutionalized and movements politics was thus posited: "In place of the old duality of extremist politics and pluralist politics, there is simply politics. . . . Rebellion, in this view, is simply politics by other means." (Gamson, 1975, pp. 138–142) The political scientists coined the concept of "protest as a political resource" (Lipsky, 1968), a resource that may be exchanged for "policy goods", thereby fundamentally transforming the relationship between protesters and their adversaries: it is now understood as a bargaining process between rational actors on both sides.

Second, RM theory locates social movements in an elitist model of politics. While this is not necessarily how RM theorists would phrase it, the image that is over and over invoked is one of insiders vs excluded groups, i.e. of elites vs. non-elites. In contrast with the classical approaches, the social groups excluded from the political process are disposed towards a rational form of interest politics: they form a collective means of interest realization not in spite of open political structures, but because of blocked political arenas. In this image of politics, both the regular channels for interest realization as well as the resources for political action are unevenly distributed. Hence, the resources for the deprived or excluded groups must come from outside their own sphere – either from reform-oriented factions of the elite or from intermediary agencies in the political environment. Therefore in this model movements correspond to neither the short-term riot nor totalitarian mass movements. Instead, the model assumes that, in the course of their careers, social movements generate the attributes of formal organization and centralization. They are defined as well-organized SMOs striving to maximize their power through skillful use of resources, balanced cost-benefit calculations, and assign a crucial role to the "organizer". According to theorists such as Gamson (1975), McCarthy and Zald, (1973, 1977), Freeman, (1979) and Jenkins (1983), social movements that are "successful" (i.e. gain formal acceptance and tangible benefits) possess the attributes of hierarchical formal organization: professional full-time organizers, and the capacity for effective mobilization of external support. These attributes are seen as responsible for movements' strategic effectiveness and combat readiness. Their view is that "Victories generally begin with policy successes and culminate in distributional goals" (Jenkins, 1985, p. 21) and that social movements are about distributional interests interjected into the centers of economic and political power so that they may be implemented through state policy. Thus, this viewpoint privileges politically oriented types of movements seeking distributional gains over and against others that do not wish inclusion into the polity, for example movements that challenge or broaden the very definition of what is "political". These tacit assumptions about the relationship between movement and polity narrow the range of movements to one visible type, making all others invisible.

On the other hand, these same assumptions also produce too broad and vague a definition of social movements because the model embraces all groups that are in some way "excluded". Since the approach is indifferent to the type of insurgency, the kind of practice, the substance of ideology, and the idea of society envisioned by the movements, it lumps social movements together with routine and sporadic collective action as well as with interest group organizations. Its basic image leads it to focus on excluded groups organizing and pooling resources in response to increased opportunities. Since such collective action is studied without specification of structure and its relation to agency, the (whole) population is conceived of as an aggregate and as such a target of mobilization efforts. Since this diffuse population of potential followers does not need to have any autonomous reasons for overcoming their inertia, they have to be constantly persuaded, directed, stimulated, and manipulated by the movement leaders. In fact, different SMOs are seen as competing for their allegiance, support, and membership: all of them apply "frame bridging", "frame extension", and "belief amplification" in their competitive efforts to attract "otherwise disinterested individuals" (Snow *et al.*, 1986, p. 18).

Over time, the resource mobilization approach began to split into two competing perspectives, one intensifying the organizational focus (the professional SMO that transforms existing discontents and demands into goal-oriented social movements)[5], the other developing a political process emphasis, within which, in addition, the collective interpretation of the situation plays a more significant role.[6]

The first (RM I) conceives of the social movement sector in free competition with other sectors of society on an open market place of groups and ideas. This market is without biased structural rigidities. In it, SMOs compete with non-movement organizations for the allegiance and resources of the population, they calculate and execute actions that give themselves notoriety and expand their membership in the same way a corporation would engage in advertising campaigns to increase sales and profits (McCarthy and Zald, 1977, p. 1229). Not surprisingly, their actors appear as "rational corporate bureaucrats devoid of passion and meaning" (Snow, 1988, p. 604).

The second (RM II) is more concerned with the structure of political opportunities and with the degree of organization within the deprived social groups; it argues from the presupposition of endogenous networks of interaction. Based on empirical work particularly about the early civil rights movement, authors committed to this position argue that two sets of macrostructural factors facilitate (or hinder) the generation of social insurgency: the level of organization within an aggrieved population, and the political realities confronting members and challengers. (Cf. McAdam, 1982, 1983; Tarrow, 1983.)

THE CORRESPONDENCE BETWEEN SOCIAL MOVEMENT THEORIES AND PRACTICE

Further variations of the resource mobilization approach, which seek to balance some of the weaknesses and problems of the paradigm, have been developed in recent years. These have attempted in particular to make up for two lacunae: (1) the neglected process of grievance *interpretation*, for which the emphasis on instrumental, purposive rationality had left no space, and (2) the lack of concern for the role of the political system. Concerning the first, Snow *et al.* (1986) and Snow and Benford (1988) expanded the RM approach to include interpretive resources, meanings, and other ideational elements, and found that occurrence, intensity, and duration of protest cycles are also due to the presence or absence of a potent innovative masterframe. Concerning the second limitation which became more and more apparent as the theory developed, political scientists began to expand the RM approach to include Eisinger's concept of political opportunity structure. Tarrow (1988), for example, interprets the unfolding of a process of policy innovation in the political system, which addresses the protesters' stated demands, as evidence for successful goal achievement of a social movement, and uses it as the basis for detecting waves of policy innovation coinciding with waves of social protest (cf. Tarrow, 1989).

In spite of these "expansions" or qualifications, RM theory remained, however, committed to the basic assumptions of the approach,[7] i.e.

– The emergence and development of social movements are primarily explained in terms of variability in resources and in the political opportunity structure.
– Underlying this view is an implicit elitist model of politics.
– Movements are always measured by the criteria of strategic effectiveness.

These key assumptions reflect both the practice of American social movements generally and those of the 60s in particular, when the failure of liberal politics provided the trigger for a wave of protest movements that could hardly be read as irrational outbursts of deviant or marginal citizens. The emphasis the RM paradigm places on rationality, resources, formal organization, and combativeness (including nonconventional and militant methods), aptly captures what appeared as significant and new about these movements and highlights some of the qualities that traditional approaches did not account for, i.e., movements that engage in rational behavior, guided and structured by movement organizations that play a crucial role in translating grievances into collective action, and which include contingent "opportunity structures" that aid or prevent mobilization. This image of what a social movement is could not be more opposite to that of the classical approaches where collective action was seen as something occurring outside established institutions and not following prevailing social norms. In the face of the experience with the 60s movements, which demanded the application of the basic liberal concepts to themselves (up to then excluded groups), the propositions of the classical approaches made no sense at all. The latter may have made sense with regard to movements that supported Stalinism or Naziism, but could not explain movements that "merely" demanded a fuller realization of democracy, even if by means that seemed unconventional. Thus, the classical approaches were replaced by others, in which social movements operate more on the level of pressure group politics associated with the utilitarian liberalism of middle class American democracy. While invoking the promises of liberal democracy, these movements also challenged its then current embodiment, the Cold-War national consensus, and envisioned instead a consensus in a hoped for future that would include the demands of the social movements.

Nonetheless, important continuities remain between these two styles of American movement research. It is striking that both the classical approaches as well as RM operate with a concept of society that is either openly pluralistic or conceived as a relatively static relationship between elites and non-elites: in neither case is society seen as structured by class relations or the logics of production and reproduction. These conceptions of social movements are accounted for not only by the specific historical movements their researches happened to be studying (i.e. very frequently "non-displacement" movements, which neither challenged the monopoly of force of the state nor the hegemonic cultural code), but also by the methodological individualism with which they view society: society seen not as forms of social organization possessed of classes and ownership relations, but as a static arrangement of (relatively homogeneous) elites and (undifferentiated) non-elites, of political insiders vs. excluded groups. The objective of the excluded groups is to "strive to scramble aboard" (Jenkins, 1985, p. 227), making the object of study the conditions under which this climbing aboard will succeed. In the pluralist case, where permeability and openness of the social and political structures are presumed, the movement's objective succeeds if and when the groups are efficiently organized (Gamson, 1975); in the more radical "social-democratic" case, where the concept of the state exhibits an institutional bias against rebellious groups (i.e., where an immanent restrictiveness of the political system is assumed), it succeeds only in exceptional instances, when realignments and political turmoil force the state to become a "facilitative agency for the institutionalization of genuine social reforms" (Jenkins, 1985, p. 228). The ultimate goal of the movement is assumed to be tangible gains for movement participants, not reform or change of society, nor rejection of the hegemonic definition of growth and efficacy, nor alternative cultural codes.

While this orientation, in fact, captures a prevailing type of social movement practice in the USA, it excludes others. For example, some contemporary movements that entertain visions of changing society do not fit the model since they do not have (or only secondarily have) distributional goals. The experience and success of groups such as direct action oriented anti-nuke groups (e.g. Livermore Action or Clamshell Alliance) or the more submerged activity of countless women's, peace, or ecological groups, apparently defy the typical pattern of the "dominant" SMO: they are decentralized and loose, consist of affinity groups and clusters, occupy construction sites and risk jail, and have belief systems and ideologies that play an important role in the mobilization process: none of these fit the image projected in the RM approach.[8] In fact, according to the RM paradigm, such movements theoretically should not experience the resonance they do insofar as RM has "demonstrated" and "proven" that a clear internal division of labor, efficient decision making, centralized resource management, and low-risk activities guarantee both significance and success of the movement (cf. Gamson, 1975, pp. 89–110).

However, since such movements appear to be "invisible" in the American public sphere, this failure to recognize them does not seem to be much of a problem: local movements especially, which do not achieve media recognition, tend to be confined in space and time, and never acquire the successful social and/or lobby influence that otherwise capture the attention of the researchers. In other cases, less marginal movement behavior, not so easily overlooked, but yet not wholly conforming with the "typical" pattern, has been "fitted" (if somewhat forcefully) into the conceptual apparatus of RM. The riots of the black ghetto populations are a case in point. To avoid falling back into the framework of

the older collective behavior approaches models were postulated that interpreted even this spontaneous rebellious
behavior as "rational politics by other means". By replacing
SMOs with "ecological units" and labelling the spontaneous
riots as "situational assembling" (Snyder and Kelly, 1979;
McPhail and Miller, 1973), the researchers invented a new
casuistry that allowed them to remain within the framework
of the RM approach.

The tenets gained from the study of this dominant type
of American social movement, those about formal organization and the role of the "organizers" especially,[9] tend to
exclude from view other, newer phenomena. This exclusion
becomes more obvious when the American situation is contrasted with that of Europe, where the "novelty" of the social
movements of the 70s and 80s has been a primary object of
interest. In the ecology, peace, and women's movements that
exploded in Western Europe during the 70s and 80s, the
working class is no longer the actor. Neither are legal/political
equality or economic demands central to their concerns.
And their organizational forms are, so it appeared to many
observers, more informal and egalitarian than those in earlier
movements.[10] This European scholarship sensitizes us to
deeper, underlying shifts in the concept of "the political"
that these new social movements seem to both articulate
and reflect: They erode the classical boundaries of political
discourse[11], and create a new political arena between the
state and civil society[12]. Though clearly not replacing the
working class movement that was seen as *the* historical actor
in the Western European case, the ecology, feminist, peace,
gay and lesbian, antinuclear movements, and so on, have
also appeared in the 80s in the United States. It is doubtful
whether their characteristics, dynamics and significance can
be grasped within the perspective provided by either one of
the dominant American approaches.

A further blind spot in both American approaches is a
failure to study the relationship between movements and
the state. In both the permeable and elitist version of the
state this relationship is more or less taken for granted. Hence,
the state's functions, reactions, and the many possible relations between social movements and the state remain outside the perceptual horizon of the research. Only recently

has Tarrow demanded that state reactions be included for consideration, but even in his proposal such relations remain limited only to positive "elite responses", i.e., those state innovative responses that constitute policy success for the movements. For Tarrow, the effects of control and of repressive state force on the movements remain outside the picture, even though it is obvious that they play a crucial role for movement development.[13] Furthermore, Tarrow's onesidedness is misleading, for the history of social conflicts shows that policy success is never a matter of direct adoption of movement goals, without compromise. But little research in the framework of American social movement theory considers the institutionalization of movement demands and the effects of these processes of institutionalization both on the movements and the political system as a whole.[14]

Within the American research paradigms, questions about the effects of innovation and state restructuring due to the introduction of new bargaining structures (e.g. New Deal, Civil Rights legislation, or responses to participatory demands) are not asked. RM theory does not consider such questions as whether new channels of access are stabilizing or destabilizing for the movements, whether the role of parties is weakened by them, or whether new modes of conflict management emerge due to the incorporation of movement representations. These questions are relevant for the study of social movements because they address the roles that social movements themselves play in the dynamics of the crisis of societal forms of reproduction.

While these examples point to structural blind spots and deficits in the dominant American approaches, it is the case that these paradigms also correspond to a uniquely American style of politics that has shaped social movements throughout American history. Even its experience of its latest movements in the 80s continues to confirm the peculiarly American characteristics of social movement practice. On the one hand, direct action movements (such as anti-nuclear weapons) are transformed into institutional politics (such as the Freeze), and SMOs seek to garner the support of "middle America", whether the movement be Freeze or Moral Majority. On the other hand, the all-pervasive American entrepreneurial habit and practice pervades not only voluntary associations and interest groups, but also social movements. Commodification of everyday life takes place at a speed and scope far greater than the decommodifying effects of social movements can achieve. Even the so-called "post-acquisitive" and "nonnegotiable" values expressed in some contemporary movements turn out to be quite marketable and useful for capital innovation. For instance, movements like those that focus on nuclear energy policy, which started out as radical critiques of state policies, have come to embrace the solar or soft technology of energy markets.

These tendencies in the American social movement sector point us in the direction we must look to explain why the resource mobilization approach has enjoyed such a splendid and fashionable career in recent American social movement research. Given the pervasiveness of these trends, the dominance of the resource mobilization approach among the various interpretations makes sense because it locates the "business" of social movement "industries" in the acquisition of resources to the neglect of movement goals and the motives of its participants.

UNIQUE AMERICAN POLITICAL STYLES AND CULTURE

Why it is that RM approaches have enjoyed such a successful career in American social movement research? Why have they become so influential and pervasive in the field of sociology, history, and political science?

A movement-internal answer to these questions would start from the observation that theories arise at certain historical conjunctures and thus represent a theoretical rationalization of historically concrete contradictions and of their corresponding praxis. In other words, RM emerged in an effort to analyse the movements of the 60s, and as a consequence reflects their conditions of emergence, dynamic of development, structure of organization, etc., in contrast with the classical approaches which were intended to explain the mass movements of the 20s and 30s, which were wholly different types of movements.

This type of explanation allows us to derive some of the

internal differences between the various strands of theory from the various movements that served as basis for the respective analysis of each. The following examples illustrate three varieties of conclusions that have been drawn from factors internal to the specific movements studied:

1. Those analyzing the early civil rights movement emphasized endogenous networks and internal resources, over and against the role of external resources. Thus, Morris (1984) could demonstrate that indigenous Black leaders and resources generated the civil rights movement and independently forced the Southern power structure to accede to their demands. In the analysis of the major campaigns, he as well as McAdam (1982, 1988a, 1988b) found a complex network of "local movement centers" rather than the handful of charismatic leaders celebrated in standard histories.

2. Those looking at non-displacement movements, which do not put forth a radical challenge to the system, emphasized the SMOs and their task of mobilizing resources. For example, Gamson's 1975 study of 53 challengers in American history (all of which were formally organized groups) has been challenged by Goldstone (1980), who reanalyzed Gamson's data and found that organizational and strategic considerations were irrelevant once controls were introduced for the goals and the political context. Hence, nondisplacement movements were found to consistently succeed in the American polity. Many of the 60s and 70s movements that served as the basis for RM analysis (McCarthy and Zald, 1973; 1977; Jenkins, 1977; West, 1981), also seemed to provide evidence for the crucial role of the professional SMO, external sponsorship, and institutional resources. Within the welfare rights and farm worker movements, and the older wing of the women's movement, these trends were increasingly observable, just as they were in the environmental, consumer rights, and public interest "movements" of the 1970s.

3. But those who used the *early* welfare rights movement (Piven and Cloward, 1977) or the community work of the New Left (Breines, 1982) as the subjects of their study, arrived at an opposite conclusion about the role of formal

organizations and professional organizers, leading them to argue that formalized organizations *divert* energies from mass defiance.

Such explanations based on the internal structure of specific movements cannot, however, account for why other countries, which also witnessed high mobilization in the 60s and parallel developments in the 70s, did not elicit a theoretical paradigm like that of RM. Another explanation is needed to account for the degree to which the studied movements and their developmental patterns reflect American society and its political culture. This explanation relates the implicit premises and assumptions inherent in the dominant American approaches to the particular social and political conditions of the United States.

The assumptions guiding collective behavior and RM theories and the incompatibility between American and European research are primarily attributable to some particular features of American politics:

1. Its relatively open, fluid and decentralized political system that has typically prevented an antagonistic polarization between movements and the political establishment.
2. The reintegration, again and again, of insurgent, innovative reform movements in the course of American history into the dominant American ideology, utilitarian liberalism, emphasizing instrumental rationality and pragmatic problem solving that prevent the formation of groups who would be unalterably opposed to the system itself.

This typical style of politics has a material foundation. The conditions of the historical emergence of American society allowed for far-reaching expressions of egalitarian power and political participation, on whose basis a rich civil society, shaped by communitarian practice and a libertarian political culture, could flourish. A precondition for the development of this society of independent citizens and their rich public–communal sphere was the restriction of the civil rights of Blacks, Native Americans, newer immigrants and women, and the appropriation of their labor. In spite of these exclusions from full civic participation, the salience of this far-reaching "self-management" and local democracy exerted a powerful influence on the cultural dispositions and organization of the American political system. Not only were political institutions designed to be weak and fragmented at their very conception, but the tradition of disobedience to established authority was raised to the level of a moral duty. Civil disobedience, supported by the founding myths and liberal theories of dissent, is legitimated as part of the traditions of anti-statist and local self-government. These traditions encourage and taint radical movements with libertarian hues, and have led throughout American history to the legitimation of uprisings against authority. At the same time, the strength of liberalism and individualism encouraged types of social movements favoring populist models of independent, self-organized projects.

Wave after wave of new ethnic immigrants exercising their right to social struggles and pressure group politics were absorbed into the open and increasingly fragmented political system. The flexibility of the party system on the one hand, and the heterogeneity of living conditions on the other, encouraged the appearance and intervention of a multitude of special movements and interest groups – from voluntary associations as described by Tocqueville to culturally/morally oriented protest movements – all of which complemented the formal political party system in their unconventional forms of expression and in their self-limitation to specific innovations (cf. Lipset, 1977).

The open and fragmented structure of the American political system further facilitated responses, even if selective, to publicized grievances by granting concessions or inclusion of movement representatives, and thus provides an inviting environment for the emergence of social movements. While this system facilitates the cooptation of protest movements into the system by flexibly allowing both material and psychic concessions to newer claimants, not all protest movements have been coopted. Those movements, like the Communist Party or other militant left groups such as the Weathermen or the Black Panthers that refused to be coopted, were instead systematically harassed.

ACCOUNTING FOR THE CENTRAL ASSUMPTIONS IN THE AMERICAN THEORIES

The specific social and political features of the United States allow us to draw out how the central assumptions in the dominant American theories are shaped by both these particular conditions and by the distinctive movement patterns that they have encouraged. There are at least five important ways, in which a direct correspondence between the theoretical assumptions and the particular historical reality of social movements in the U.S. can be seen. Viewed in this way, the apparatus of categories developed for the U.S. social movement experience not only becomes transparent in its limitations but, more positively, also contributes to our understanding of the pattern of social movement practice in the United States.

First, American conditions are receptive to the permanent *coexistence*, side by side, of social movements and interest groups with the established institutions of the political system. Because of this, analysts have concluded that there is a continuous existence of mobilization potentials, which, as such, do not require further explanation (RM). Conversely, the approximation of the ideal of the open polity could be taken as evidence for placing social movements *outside of* this polity, providing a reason to marginalize them academically and argue their repression politically (collective behavior theories). In any case, the concept of "social movement" does not refer to *the* social movement (the working class movement, as in the European contexts), but comprises a multitude of social protest and reform movements, always coexisting with parties and interest groups without challenging any institution's claim to represent political interests. This all-embracive concept of social movements seems, therefore, consistent with the dynamic of U.S. history. It does not imply that class relations were marginally important for social conflict, but it overdetermines demographic, ethnic, political, religious and sociocultural variables in ways that shape a unique social movement pattern.

Second, the United States has produced a pervasive pattern of self-limiting movements that focus on single issues, achievable success, and individual self-reform. Movements aiming to become part of the American mainstream by demanding equal opportunities or integration into established institutions tend to flourish, as do those that struggle for (partial) autonomization of various subcultures. Disaggregated and issue-specific movements that refrain from totalizing their demands flourish all over this country, but movements demanding radical societal change have always remained relatively marginal. Such radical or socialist currents were once even more marginalized by their omission in social movement research. Questions pertaining to their development and dynamic hardly appear in recent American social movement research. Much the same applies to contemporary new social movements which, to the extent that they do not conform to the canon and hence do not visibly participate in the pluralist process, are easily overlooked, or cannot even be incorporate into the categories of RM.

Third, the dominant political rhetoric of American society nourishes high-flying democratic expectations and thus provides encouragement to ever more social groups to disrupt the precarious balance between the "founding myths" (i.e. the ideals of the formative period) and the institutional realities of American politics. This tension in American liberalism, according to Huntington (1981), produces "naturally" regular periods of "creedal passion". As a consequence, the social movements articulating these tensions have not needed to define themselves *outside* the hegemonic American discourse; in fact, Jeffersonian democracy, communitarian self-reliance and decentralized, participatory forms of politics are constitutive parts of "Americanism" itself. Even movements such as those of the students (cf. the Port Huron Statement of SDS) or the antinuclear direct action movement (cf. Livermore Action Group) could claim these values.

Fourth, the heterogeneous and segmented societal pattern underlying America's high degree of civic voluntarism, self-reliant public participation and self-regulative communitarianism, implies at the same time a pronounced sectoral unevenness and sharp economic disparities. Underdeveloped welfare state policies (underdeveloped in comparison with Western Europe) have not mitigated these disparities. A very incomplete representation of the working class exacerbates the unevenness. As a consequence, social movements in the U.S. up to the present tend not only to raise the particular issues their members feel aggrieved about, but they also implicitly raise, or are quickly forced to confront, an unfinished class, race and ethnic agenda. "New", "post-material" and "life-world" oriented movements emerge in alliance with "traditional" discriminated class and racial groups. This mixture of grievances and of conflict levels makes it difficult to speak of and to detect so-called new social movements. So long as problems of economic inequality remain so uniquely unresolved because relevant parts of American society remain excluded from its established class compromises, distributive demands will be primary. The prognosis for new social movements that challenge prevailing concepts of industrial growth and progress and that concern themselves with environmental or identity problems, are unlikely to become decisive in the U.S.

Fifth, the all-pervasive businesslike entrepreneurial ideology and practice guide not only interest groups, voluntary associations, and the large professional movement organizations, which continue to gain the bulk of publicity, especially those with a religious and socially-conservative style. The entrepreneurial spirit also characterizes countercultural social movements. Almost all American movements have been quick to adopt strategies of sales and advertising firms and instrumental ways of fundraising, and have become adept in using the mass media, especially TV, to broadcast their messages. This utilitarian attitude is mirrored and reproduced in the construction of theory. Rather than exploring why movements in the U.S. are more entrepreneurial, more competitive, and less "ideological" than elsewhere, American movement research reflects uncritically these attributes in the kinds of questions asked, the problems perceived, and the language and methods used. Thus, again and again it (re)confirms and (re)verifies its assumptions in countless empirical projects:

– It is the "business of social movement industries to acquire and increase resources.
– Insurgencies that restrict their goals to single issues and leave the existing structure of authority uncontested, are

more likely to secure tangible gains (Gamson, 1975, pp. 38–55).

- The mobilization potential is weak, if the values and beliefs a movement seeks to promote are of low hierarchical salience within the larger belief system; hence the task of consciousness raising becomes more central (Snow and Benford, 1988).
- Formal organization provides a more flexible tactical repertoire, and therefore sustained mobilization.
- Hence movements acquire, in the course of their career, formal organization, centralized control etc.

The peculiarity and specific applicability of such findings to the American context is not usually acknowledged. Yet the widespread use of these assumptions and generalizations has been possible because the American scholarly community deals with social movements in an extremely self-referential way; it can afford to do so, because a huge English-speaking market offers ample opportunity for exchange and debate and need not induce scholars to confront comparative international data.

This "advantage" of the English speaking world's insularity is likely to be lost in the emerging new world order. There are already the beginnings of an exchange and confrontation with recent European social movement theories, some of which have exposed some of the limitations of the dominant American approaches.[15]

This essay is one such product of an American–European confrontation. By not presuming that the American and European paradigms share social–theoretical frameworks, it has sought to uncover the assumptions researchers have worked with in the American context, and to account for their overwhelming influence in the social and historical sciences. European theories, still influenced by more or less explicit assumptions of a class-structured society and logics of material (re)production, assume that each new reproductive stage produces and is challenged by social movements that articulate historically changing social cleavages, if not the older variety of class antagonisms. This European attitude contrasts sharply with the view of society as an unstructured ensemble of groups, of ruling classes as a relatively homogeneous elite, of the state as structurally permeable or as institutionally biased against insurgency. These various elements of the American theoretical framework together produce the image of a static social arrangement that continually adapts, in the pluralist view, due to its permeability and openness or, in the social-democratic view, is only exceptionally perturbed.

Besides a caution against synthesizing theoretical approaches that are rooted in incompatible social–theoretical frameworks, this chapter has sought to account for the particularities of the American case. First, it brought to the foreground the assumptions made within classical and RM theories about the origin of social movements and about the polity within which they are located. Relating the concepts of society and politics to the patterns and qualities of social movements in American history, it showed that the themes, action repertoires, and organizational structures of these movements have been remarkably different from those in European history which were over determined by class movements. To account for the American case, the material basis of politics and a uniquely American political culture were examined, noting the open and decentralized structure of the American political system. The latter has prevented antagonistic polarization between movements and political the establishment. Utilitarian liberalism accounts for the repeated integration of insurgent innovative reform movements into the dominant social order. The close correspondence between movement activity and its social-science interpretations was illustrated by showing how liberal ideological assumptions that have shaped and guided American social movement practice have been incorporated into the premises and theories of American movement research.

Notes

1. This chapter cannot do justice to the rich variety, national specificities, and recent elaborations within European social movement theory. For this, cf. Rucht, 1991.
2. Besides the classical collective behavior and breakdown theories and the resource mobilization approach, other – not so dominant – theor-

etical models in the U.S. have included class-analytical approaches as well as populist-traditionalist interpretations. Cf. for an overview Mayer, 1991.
3. The variants were: the collective behavior approach (Turner and Killian, 1957; Blumer, 1951; Smelser, 1962) with its roots in the Chicago School (Park and Burgess, 1921); the mass society approach (Kornhauser, 1959); and the relative deprivation approach (Davies, 1963; Gurr, 1970).
4. See e.g. McCarthy and Zald, 1973; Oberschall, 1973; Shorter and Tilly, 1974; Gamson, 1975; Useem, 1975; Zald and McCarthy, 1979.
5. See e.g. McCarthy and Zald, 1977.
6. See Tilly, 1978; McAdam, 1982; Morris, 1984; Jenkins, 1985.
7. One might also argue that the more qualifications that are added, the more problematic becomes the integrity of the "theory". An effect of these "corrections" may be that the theory becomes instead a grab-bag full of too many disparate items, threatening to collapse it under the impulse of its upholders to keep it alive.
8. What observers have to note about these new types of movements is that their goals keep emerging and evolving in a process of internal and external communication and adaptation. They demonstrate particularly vividly what is probably the case for most social movements: that their unity is not given at the outset but is a precarious construct made up of different groups with different types of beliefs and different strategies for action. In the RM approach, however, "goals" and "claims" are treated as fixed, "interests" are not a variable to be explained but a given resource that the SMO can manipulate in order to attract supporters; the collective identity of a movement is assumed as given at the outset.
9. RM researchers employing these conceptual tools outside the US find out that the conclusions arrived at on the basis of the analysis of the dominant American type of movements are of limited usefulness in other contexts. Tarrow, researching social movements in Italy, soon stumbled over the fact that "the traits of professional movement entrepreneurs are hard to discern among Italian militants" (Tarrow 1983, pp. 50–51).
10. Cf. for a comparison between U.S. and European social movement research Klandermans and Tarrow, 1988; Tarrow, 1988; Kitschelt, 1985.
11. The traditional boundaries of political discourse dissolve when themes previously utterly non-political such as nature, weather, the forest, or those of gender relations or technology, have successfully been put on the political agenda by the new social movements.
12. A "movement sector" has emerged between the state and state-oriented intermediary institutions on the one hand, and a privatized civil society on the other; Some describe this as a repoliticized civil society with networks and infrastructures of its own. This new political sphere illustrates how these social movements are, at the same time, visible protest politics/political interventions *and* sociocultural alternatives seeking to redefine the social.

13. A notable exception is found in Tilly's work where "the operation of the polity" enters the calculations of the challengers with the categories "facilitation" and "repression." However, its limitations due to the strictly rational formulation of this model have been pointed out by Rule (1989).
14. A large body of political science literature is obviously concerned with processes of reform of political institutions and changes in public policy due to social movements. The effects of such innovation or reform on the movements themselves, however, are rarely raised.
15. Collaborative research between U.S. and Western European social movement scholars has been promoted by the Council for European Studies, which facilitated a series of workshops and conferences, the results of which have been edited by Klandermans, Kriesi and Tarrow, 1988. Cf. also Klandermans, 1989.

References

Bell, Daniel (1976) *The Cultural Contradictions of Capitalism* (New York: Basic Books).

Blumer, Herbert (1951) "The Field of Collective Behavior," in Alfred McClung Lee (ed.), *New Outline of the Principles of Sociology* (New York: Barnes & Noble), pp. 167–224.

Breines, Wini (1982) *The Great Refusal: Community Organization in the New Left* (New York: Praeger).

Davies, James C. (1963) *Human Nature in Politics: The Dynamics of Political Behavior* (New York: John Wiley).

Ferree, Myra Marx and F. D. Miller (1985) "Mobilization and Meaning: Toward an Integration of Social Psychological and Resource Mobilization Perspectives on Social Movements," *Sociological Inquiry*, vol. 55, pp. 38–51.

Freeman, Jo (1973) "The Origins of the Women's Liberation Movement," *American Journal of Sociology*, vol. 78, pp. 792–811.

Freeman, Jo (1975) *The Politics of Women's Liberation* (New York: Longman).

Freeman, Jo (1979) "Resource Mobilization and Strategy: A Model for Analyzing Social Movement Organization Actions," in M. N. Zald and J. M. McCarthy (eds.), *The Dynamics of Social Movements* (Cambridge, Ma: Winthrop).

Freeman, Jo (ed.) (1983) *Social Movements of the 60s and 70s* (New York: Longman).

Gamson, William A. (1975) *The Strategy of Social Protest* (Homewood, Ill.: Dorsey).

Gitlin, Todd (1980) *The Whole World is Watching* (Berkeley: University of California Press).

Goldstone, Jack A. (1980) "The Weakness of Organization: A New Look at Gamson's *The Strategy of Social Protest*," *American Journal of Sociology*, vol. 88, no. 5 (March), pp. 1017–42.

Gurr, Ted R. (1970) *Why Men Rebel* (Princeton University Press).

Margit Mayer 193

Gusfield, Joseph (1981) "Social Movements and Social Change. Perspectives of Linearity and Fluidity," *Research in Social Movements, Conflict, and Change*, vol. 3, pp. 317–39.

Huntington, Samuel P. (1981) *American Politics: the Promise of Disharmony* (Cambridge: Harvard University Press).

Jenkins, Craig J. (1983) "Resource Mobilization Theory and the Study of Social Movements," *American Review of Sociology*, vol. 9, pp. 527–53.

Jenkins, Craig J. (1985) *The Politics of Insurgency. The Farm Workers Movement in the 1960s* (New York: Columbia University Press).

Jenkins, Craig J. and Charles Perrow (1977) "Insurgency of the Powerless: Farm Workers Movements (1946–1972)," *American Sociological Review*, vol. 42 (April), pp. 249–268.

Kitschelt, Herbert (1985) "New Social Movements in West Germany and the United States," in M. Zeitlin (ed.), *Political Power and Social Theory*, vol. 5, Greenwich, Ct: JAI Press, pp. 273–324.

Klandermans, Bert (ed.) (1989) *Organizing for Change: Social Movement Organizations in Europe and the United States* (vol. 2 of International Social Movement Research) (Greenwich, Ct.: JAI Press).

Klandermans, Bert and Sidney Tarrow (1988) "Mobilization into Social Movements: Synthesizing European and American Approaches," in B. Klandermans, H. Kriesi and S. Tarrow (eds), *From Structure to Action* (Greenwich, Ct: JAI Press), pp. 1–38.

Klandermans, Bert, Hans Peter Kriesi and Sidney Tarrow (eds) (1988) *From Structure to Action* (vol. 1 of International Social Movement Research) (Greenwich, Ct: JAI Press).

Kornhauser, William (1959) *The Politics of Mass Society* (Glencoe, Ill.: Free Press).

Kriesi, Hans Peter (1988) "The Interdependence of Structure and Action: Some Reflections on the State of the Art," in B. Klandermans, H. Kriesi and S. Tarrow (eds), *From Structure to Action* (Greenwich, Ct: JAI Press).

Lipset, Seymour Martin (1977) "Why no Socialism in the United States?" in Severyn Bialer and Sophia Sluzar (eds), *Radicalism in the Contemporary Age* (Boulder, Co.: Westview Press).

Lipsky, Michael (1968) "Protest as a Political Resource," *American Political Science Review*, vol. 62, no. 4, pp. 1144–58.

Marx, Gary T. and James L. Wood (1975) "Strands of Theory and Research in Collective Behavior," *Annual Review of Sociology*, vol. I, pp. 363–428.

Mayer, Margit (1991) "Social Movement Research and Social Movement Practice: the U.S. Pattern," in Dieter Rucht (ed.) *Research on Social Movements* (Frankfurt/Boulder, Co: Campus/Westview Press).

McAdam, Doug (1982) *Political Process and the Development of Black Insurgency, 1930–1970* (University of Chicago Press).

McAdam, Doug (1983) "Tactical Innovation and the Pace of Insurgency," *American Sociological Review*, vol. 48, pp. 735–54.

McAdam, Doug (1986) "Recruitment to High-risk Activism: The Case of Freedom Summer," *American Journal of Sociology*, vol. 92, no. 1, pp. 64–90.

McAdam, Doug (1988a) "Micro-Mobilization Contexts and Recruitment to Activism," *International Social Movement Research*, vol. 1, pp. 125–54.

McAdam, Doug (1988b) *Freedom Summer* (New York: Oxford University Press).

McAdam, Doug, John McCarthy and Mayer N. Zald (1988) "Social Movements," in N. J. Smelser (ed.) *Handbook of Sociology* (Newbury Park: Sage).

McCarthy, John and Mayer N. Zald (1973) *The Trends of Social Movements in America: Professionalization and Resource Mobilization* (Morristown, NJ: General Learning Press).

McCarthy, John and Mayer N. Zald (1977) "Resource Mobilization and Social Movements: A Partial Theory," *American Journal of Sociology*, vol. 82, no. 6, pp. 1212–41.

McPhail, Clark (1971) "Civil Disorder Participation: A Critical Examination of Recent Research," *American Sociological Review*, vol. 36, pp. 1058–73.

McPhail, Clark and D. L. Miller (1973) "The Assembling Process: a Theoretical and Empirical Investigation," *American Sociological Review*, vol. 38, pp. 721–35.

McPhail, Clark and Ronald Wohlstein (1983) "Individual and Collective Behaviors within Gatherings, Demonstrations, and Riots," *Annual Review of Sociology*, vol. 9, pp. 579–600.

Morris, Aldon (1984) *The Origins of the Civil Rights Movement: Black Communities Organizing for Change* (New York: McMillan).

Oberschall, Anthony (1973) *Social Conflict and Social Movements* (Englewood Cliffs, NJ: Prentice Hall).

Park, Robert and Ernest W. Burgess (1921) *Introduction to the Science of Sociology* (Chicago: University of Chicago Press).

Parsons, Talcott (1964) *Social Systems* (Glencoe, Ill.: Free Press).

Piven, Frances Fox and Richard A. Cloward (1977) *Poor People's Movements: Why They Succeed, How They Fail,* (New York: Pantheon).

Rucht, Dieter (ed.) (1991) *Research on Social Movements: the State of the Art* (Frankfurt/Boulder: Campus/Westview Press).

Rule, James (1989) "Rationality and Non-Rationality in Militant Collective Action," *Sociological Theory*, vol. 7/2, pp. 145–60.

Shorter, Edward and Chalres Tilly (1974) *Strikes in France, 1830–1968.* London: Cambridge University Press.

Smelser, Neil J. (1962) *The Theory of Collective Behavior* (New York: Free Press).

Snow, David (1988) Review of Mayer N. Zald and John D. McCarthy (eds), *Social Movements in an Organizational Society: Collected Essays, Contemporary Sociology*, vol. 17, no. 5 (September).

Snow, David *et al.* (1986) "Frame Alignment Processes, Micromobilization, and Movement Participation," *American Sociological Review*, vol. 51, no. 4, pp. 464–81.

Snow, David and R. D. Benford (1988) "Ideology, Frame Resonance and Participant Mobilization," *International Social Movement Research*, vol. 1, pp. 197–217.

Snyder, S. and W. R. Kelly (1979) "Strategies for Investigating Violence and Social Change: Illustrations from Analyses of Racial disorders and Implications for Mobilization Research," in M. N. Zald and J. McCarthy (eds), *The Dynamics of Social Movements* (Cambridge, Ma.: Winthrop).

Tarrow, Sidney (1983) "Struggling to Reform: Social Movements and Policy Change during Cycles of Protest" (Ithaca, NY: Cornell University), Western Societies Program, occasional paper no. 15.

Tarrow, Sidney (1988) "National Politics and Collective Action: Recent Theory and Research in Western Europe and the United States," *Annual Review of Sociology*, vol. 14, pp. 421–40.

Tarrow, Sidney (1989) *Democracy and Disorder: Protest and Politics in Italy, 1965–1975* (New York: Oxford University Press).

Tarrow, Sidney (1991) "Comparing Social Movement participation in Western Europe and the United States: Problems, Uses, and a Proposal for Synthesis," in Dieter Rucht (ed.), *Research on Social Movements* (Frankfurt/Boulder, Co: Campus/Westview).

Tilly, Charles (1978) *From Mobilization to Revolution* (Reading, Ma.: Addison-Wesly).

Turner, Ralph and Lewis Killian (1957) *Collective Behavior* (Englewood Cliffs, NJ: Prentice Hall).

Useem, Michael (1975) *Protest Movements in America* (Indianapolis: Bobbs-Merrill).

West, Guida (1981) *The National Welfare Rights Movement* (New York: Praeger).

Zald, Mayer N. and John M. McCarthy (eds) (1979) *The Dynamics of Social Movements* (Cambridge, Ma.: Winthrop).

Zald, Mayer N. and John M. McCarthy (eds) (1987) *Social Movements in an Organizational Society* (New Brunswick, NJ: Transaction Books).

Part IV

Contemporary Studies

9 It Happened Here: Political Opportunity, the New Institutionalism, and the Townsend Movement*

Edwin Amenta and Yvonne Zylan

The Townsend movement, which sought pensions for the elderly in the Great Depression, was much larger in some states than others and its size fluctuated in the 1930s. Frustration or grievance theory predicts that the movement would be stronger when and where old people suffered more. The challenger perspective expects greater growth when and where indigenous organizations of the aged already existed. Political opportunity theories expect challenges to flourish when and where openings are provided by members of the polity or by related challenges. We supplement these theories by exploring the concept of political opportunity from an institutionalist perspective, assessing the model by comparing it with the other perspectives to account for longitudinal and cross-sectional differences in the movement's strength. Although some support for each perspective was found, the movement was spurred most by indigenous organizations and different forms of political opportunity. We suggest an expansion of Tilly's polity model, to recognize that the political party system can influence challenges and that the structure and policies of the state can aid challenges as well as hinder them.

The largest and most ambiguous American social movement of the Great Depression was led not by a menacing demagogue, but by a somewhat befuddled gray-haired doctor,

---

* Reprinted from *American Sociological Review*, vol. 56, no. 2 (April 1991), pp. 250–65.

Francis E. Townsend. The Townsend movement seems to fit conflicting views on social movements and thus presents a puzzle for social theorists.

The Townsend movement fits the imagery of "frustration" or "grievance" theories, which are based on anti-democratic movements of the 1930s (Cantril 1941). It was launched in hard times and propelled by a charismatic leader. A migrant to California, Townsend lost his job in the Depression and apparently suffered the rootlessness and despair imputed by grievance theorists to adherents of movements. He also sported a Hitler mustache. The movement reveled in the "hundred percent" Americanism that George Orwell felt might form the cultural basis of totalitarianism in the United States; club meetings often opened with a Pledge of Allegiance and closed with a corruption of the "Battle Hymn of the Republic" that equated the passing of the Townsend plan with the coming of the Lord. In 1936, Townsend allied with Father Charles E. Coughlin's National Union for Social Justice and the late Senator Huey P. Long's Share Our Wealth movement in a failed bid to unseat President Franklin D. Roosevelt (Brinkley 1982). If fascism were to "happen here," as Sinclair Lewis (1935, 1970) put it, men like Long and Coughlin might lead the way. Critics feared Townsend's followers would vote anti-democrats into power and ridiculed the Townsend plan, which demanded from the national government $200 per month for persons 60 years old and older. The utopianism of the plan – whose eschatology portrayed a this-worldly paradise without unemployment, crime, or alcohol – suggested that the Townsendites were a cult of personal salvation rather than a movement for social change.

Aspects of the movement also fit Tilly's (1978) "challenger" or "mobilization" model, which emphasizes the rationality of collective action and the influence of previous organization on social movements (see also McCarthy and Zald 1977). The bulk of the movement's resources came from dues and, later, sales of its newsletter, the *Townsend National Weekly*. The movement did not submit to the whims of some impulsive autocrat, but adhered to a program addressing both the insecurities of the aged and the Depression. It was not unthinkable that some version of it might pass, as its opponents feared well into the 1940s (Witte, 1943; Altmeyer, 1966).

The religiosity of the movement suggested that it used Protestant churches and recruited their members in blocs. Many contemporaries and scholars claim the movement provoked the passage of the Social Security Act and its amendments (Amenta, Zylan and Carruthers, 1989); maybe because the movement happened here the aged were better off than they otherwise would have been.

Finally, the movement may have flourished not because of the economic crisis or the movement's ability to mobilize resources, but because of new "political opportunities" for the aged and other challengers to the social order (Kitschelt, 1986). A pre-Townsend reform movement to provide compulsory pensions to the indigent aged had begun a string of successes in 1930. Many states passed pension laws, and pensions may have enabled aged volunteers to work for the Townsend cause. In 1933, Roosevelt took office and encouraged the organization of many relatively powerless groups. Economic orthodoxy was broken as the administration embarked on deficit spending for relief. Thus, a salubrious political climate may have enabled the movement to thrive when and where it did.

We extend the concept of political opportunity and Tilly's well known "polity" model (see below) by examining them from an institutionalist perspective, which focuses on the structure of political institutions and the state. We argue that the polity model typically represents political parties as electoral outcomes and the state as a tool of repression. However, the political party system may shape opportunities for challenges, and the state, through its structure and its policies, may aid challenges as well as repress them. We find support for these ideas by relating the strength of the movement across time and space to indicators based on our model and on other movement theories.

THE CHALLENGER AND POLITY MODELS

Following Tilly (1975, 1978), challenger or mobilization theorists see the roots of movements in institutionalized power arrangements. Power is distributed unequally, and movements enable the less powerful to seek redress. The challenger perspective focuses on large-scale social changes: the rise of the state and capitalism. Over time, collective action becomes "associational" rather than "communal," "proactive" rather than "reactive." Large "collective actors" demand new rights and resources, such as franchises or wage increases, rather than contest state-building and capitalism. Challenger theorists also usually subscribe to Tilly's polity model, which is a conceptual and definitional scheme rather than a causal framework. According to the polity model, a group that is a "member" of the polity has low-cost access to the resources of the "government," and "challengers" do not. The government controls the main means of coercion, and coalitions often form among contenders for power. From this point of view, movement activities are seen as rational responses to the costs and benefits of alternative lines of political action and the collective action of movement organizations is intended to win collective benefits. The mobilization or challenger model emphasizes the role of interests of group members, their previous organization, the mobilization of resources by movement organizations, collective action, and political opportunities for challenges in explaining the emergence and success of movements (Tilly, 1978; cf. Marwell and Oliver, 1984).

Common interests do not necessarily lead to the formation of movement organizations or to collective action. Challenger theorists typically agree, however, that strong and closely knit *indigeneous organizations* containing members of a subordinate group are crucial for generating challenges (Oberschall, 1973). A dense network of communication within such a group is likely to produce an organization with challenging goals (Freeman, 1973). In contrast, nonchallenging organizations do not have political or redistributive goals as their central mission and do not threaten or engage in disruptive activity. Once a movement organization forms, the resources it can mobilize are proportionate to the degree of previous organization within the group. For instance, the civil rights movement organizers relied on southern black churches (Morris, 1984; McAdam, 1982). Challenger researchers dodge the free-rider problem by arguing that organizers stage challenges from previously organized groups, but must decide which organizations are susceptible to being "co-opted."

POLITICAL OPPORTUNITY: THE POLITY MODEL AND
THE INSTITUTIONALIST CRITIQUE

In the challenger and polity models, political opportunities
to mobilize and take collective action also play a key role;
specific aspects of the political context may promote or discourage challenges. Opportunity is typically found in a
movement's organized allies and opponents. *Social movement
organizations* that demand the political or economic better-
ment of a disadvantaged group through disruption or threats
of it may aid one another (Tarrow, 1988) or merely demonstrate the possibility of change. A movement organization's fate may be influenced by opponents; for instance,
U.S. capitalist organizations dampened unionism (Griffin,
Wallace, and Rubin 1986). The standard polity model also
emphasizes opportunities based on *partisan politics*, notably
through realignments of the electoral system. Members of
the polity may ally with challengers when the polity is evenly
divided. If the coalition wins, challengers can more easily
pursue collective action. For instance, Jenkins (1985) argued
that U.S. social movements in the 1960s were aided by a
center-left Democratic coalition.

Focusing on the structure of political institutions, the "new
institutionalism" (March and Olsen 1984) suggests new types
of political helps and hindrances to social movements. The
political party system, reflecting the way members of the
polity are organized, may discourage challenges. Patronage-
oriented or *traditional parties*, to use Mayhew's (1986) term,
give benefits selectively and avoid programmatic principles.
Shefter (1983) argued that the mobilization of voters into
traditional parties prevents "third-party" and ideological
challenges, for people mobilized into traditional politics are
inoculated against challenger politics. Thus, in areas where
traditional Democratic and Republican parties in the late
19th century had mobilized voters, the Progressive party did
not challenge. Similarly, Valelly (1989) argued that a lack
of strong traditional parties permitted the organizational
breakthrough at the state level of radical "third parties" in
the 1930s. An institutionalist corollary to the polity model
suggests that left or center parties will aid challenges only
in nontraditional or *open party systems*.

The polity model is also limited in that it constrains the state to be a ready instrument of repression controlled by members of the polity. By contrast, the institutionalist perspective sees the state playing a key role in shaping political activity and in *aiding* social movements. First, movements may be aided if state political institutions promote and protect basic *democratic rights* and freedoms, such as voting rights and competing candidates. Such democratic institutional politics may activate noninstitutional challenges aimed at influencing elected politicians (Gamson 1975). They may also be necessary for the rise to power of regimes favorable to challengers.

Second, as Skocpol (1985) has argued, state bureaucrats have their own interests or pursue what they perceive to be the public interest. The greater their autonomy, the more likely that state actors will pursue their own agendas, including the support of like-minded challenges. As bureaucrats try to expand the powers of state institutions, they may encourage movements with similar goals. Moreover, challengers hoping to increase public spending for their members may coalesce if the state is fiscally strong to capitalize on such resources. Thus, movements may be aided or encouraged where state members have unencumbered *fiscal and bureaucratic capacities*.

Third, the state's *policies* may also shape challenges. Challenges may be spurred if state actors and politicians fashion specific policies to promote challenges and thereby increase the power of bureaus running such programs or the electoral prospects of the politician. Moreover, movements may also be encouraged when and where spending policies benefiting the members of a group are strong, even if the policy was not designed to encourage a challenge. Policies may unintentionally provoke challenges. Like the party system, the state, in the guarantees of its political institutions, in the autonomy of its bureaucracy, and in its policies, may shape the timing and course of social mobilization.

THE GRIEVANCE MODEL

In contrast, the frustration or grievance perspective typically sees social movements and collective behavior as responses to strains in the social structure, which lead individuals to become frustrated and discontended or to suffer "normative ambiguity" (Smelser, 1962). This discontent might include immiseration (Marx and Engels 1848, 1978), atomization (Kornhauser, 1959), relative deprivation (Merton and Rossi, 1968), status inconsistency (Hofstadter, 1952), or pecuniary setbacks (Davies, 1962). Discontent leads to aggression, which in turn is released in collective behavior – the collective action of movements is often viewed not as political action, but as a way to deal with personal discontent. Movements sometimes advance what are labeled "utopian" goals, and movement adherents are claimed to embrace irrational "generalized beliefs" (Smelser, 1962). The strong version of this model has had little empirical support. For instance, labor strikes usually occur during times of high employment (Tilly, 1978). American students (Perrow, 1979) and women (Freeman, 1973) were more active in the 1960s than in the 1950s, even though their circumstances were no worse. Little empirical backing is found in studies of right-wing movements, supposedly the "best" case for the model. Neither Hitler (Oberschall, 1973) nor McCarthy (Rogin, 1967) was sustained by the least attached members of society.

Recent researchers have incorporated insights from the grievance model into the challenger model. Walsh (1981) focused on the *intensification of grievances* in the generation of insurgencies, and Barnes (1984) argued that grievances shift the cost–benefit calculus of potential participants in movements. Dryzek and Goodin (1986) argued that crises and the uncertainties that accompany crises shift the interests of individuals. When individuals are unsure of their future economic status, it is in their interest to back social spending to aid the poor; the further a crisis reaches into the middle class, the more likely the middle class will support social spending. Although Dryzek and Goodin argued that World War II directly increased social spending, their model applies more readily to economic crises and the interests of individuals in supporting movements devoted to redistributive goals.

Crises may forge another potential link between grievance and challenger models by creating political opportunities for challenges. Large-scale challenges are aided when a regime loses a major war (Skocpol, 1979). Smaller challengers may succeed following crises, if the challenger was previously mobilized (Gamson, 1980). Piven and Cloward (1977) argued that crises promote electoral instability, which aids challenges. Thus, the influence of crises on challenges may be indirect.

Did the Townsend movement flourish when and where economic discontent was greatest? Was the strength of the movement related to the presence of "co-optible" organizations? Were some organizations more co-optible than others? Did the movement respond to political opportunities? If so, was the movement aided by likeminded movements or by polity members? Did the party system shape the movement? Did the configuration or strength of state institutions or their policies encourage the Townsendites?

THE RISE AND FALL OF THE TOWNSEND MOVEMENT

The Townsend movement centered on a plan that Dr. Townsend first made public in September, 1933: all Americans 60 years of age and older should be given $200 at the start of each month if they refrained from work and spent the $200 by the month's end. The plan, officially termed Old-Age Revolving Pensions, had a dual purpose: It would halt the pecuniary troubles of the aged, and the Depression would lift as the old stopped competing with the young for work and as spending stimulated the economy. In January, 1935, the plan was converted into a bill. To pay for the pensions, estimated initially at about $24 billion a year, the McGroarty bill called for a 2 per cent national tax on transactions, a kind of "multiple" sales tax. The bill was widely criticized. The left disliked the regressive tax, and the right objected to the amount of spending, fearing that high taxes might cut profits. Moderate policy advocates also disliked the plan – their insurance and assistance proposals were finally being backed by a president! Academic economists of all political persuasions thought it unworkable.

Simple as the plan was, its witnesses – Townsend especially – were unequal to defending it before Congress. Particularly damning were Townsend's admission that $200 per month was more than the tax would bear, that 75 years of age was a more viable retirement age, and that the transactions tax was merely a sales tax by a different name (U.S. Congress Senate Committee on Finances 1935, pp. 1019–23, 1126–7). Townsend's performance compared unfavorably with the well prepared depositions for the administration's Economic Security bill. The McGroarty bill was soon amended to pay only as much as its tax collected, but the House rejected it, mainly along partisan lines with Democrats opposed, 206 to 56; western Democrats feared going on record. The Social Security Act was passed in August, 1935. When a modified Townsend bill came before Congress in 1939, the results were similar: Townsend witnesses were flustered, the bill was amended, and the House rejected it even more decisively. Instead, Congress improved old-age insurance and assistance. Although the Townsend plan was introduced in Congress throughout the 1940s, it never again escaped committee.

The history of the organization is more complicated than that of the plan. In January, 1934, the not-for-profit Old-Age Revolving Pensions, Ltd (OARP) was incorporated. Its officers were Townsend, his brother Walter, and the real estate agent Robert E. "Earl" Clements. A former employer of Townsend, Clements led the organization and referred to himself as the "co-founder." The first Townsend club was founded in August, 1934 in Huntington, California. Local clubs were formed once local organizers, sometimes volunteers but often paid by commission, had amassed 100 members. In the late 1930s, this requirement was lowered to 30 members. The clubs had no official voice in OARP, but usually met weekly, heard speakers, and pressured the unconvinced. Initially a kind of tax-farming operation, OARP soon comprised four regional directors, one or two directors for each state, and many congressional-district and club organizers. The membership "contribution" was a quarter. From this, the national took a dime; the other three levels each took a nickel. OARP also solicited donations, organized fund-raising rallies, and sold paraphernalia.

The numbers of Townsendites are hard to ascertain because of a lack of data and exaggerations by movement leaders, but also because there is no easy way to define a movement member. In February, 1935, Townsend claimed 20 million adherents, that is, everyone who allegedly signed petitions calling for the enactment of the Townsend plan (U.S. Congress House of Representative Committee on Ways and Means, 1935, p. 752). However, these petitions were not presented to the bi-partisan House Select Committee Investigating Old-Age Pensions Organizations (U.S. Congress House of Representatives 1936, p. 584) until May 1936, and by then Townsend claimed only 10 million signatures, which were never counted. Most signers attended no club meetings or activities and were not aged, unlike almost all club members.

In February 1935 Townsend estimated that there were approximately 3,000 clubs with 150 members each – a total of 450,000 club members (U.S. Congress Senate Committee on Finances, 1935, pp. 1047–48). In April, 1936, during the Congressional investigation of the movement, Clements estimated membership at two million: approximately 7,000 clubs with 300 members (U.S. Congress House of Representatives, 1936, p. 208). In the same testimony, however, Clements admitted that membership might be as low as one million. He never revealed the bases for his estimates. Regional organizers prevented state organizers from cataloging members, presumably to prevent rival pension groups from raiding Townsendites (ibid., p. 431). Aged husbands and wives often joined together – the plan benefited both men and women – and would often enroll and pay for family members with no part in the movement. But who counted as a member in good standing? After the initial 25-cent "contribution," members were expected to pay the club 10 cents monthly – the "quota" as it was called for legal reasons – to be forwarded to the state office. Yet clubs and members not meeting quotas went unpunished. If members are defined as active "contributors" paying the "quota," membership was doubtless less than one million.

However membership is defined, the evidence indicates a leap in the movement's membership in the last quarter of 1935, *after* the initial failure of the Townsend plan. (See Table 1.) The movement did not spread beyond the West

Table 1   Paid membership and receipts of the Townsend
movement, 1934–53

Year	Paid membership (in 000s)	Gross receipts (in $1000s) y	Membership as percent of population 65 years and older
1934	NA	84	NA
1935	NA	905	NA
1936	NA	562	NA
1937	NA	NA	NA
1938	612.5	453	7.20
1939	761.6	622	8.69
1940	646.9	689	7.16
1941	468.7	636	5.05
1942	297.6	486	3.11
1943	271.8	424	2.75
1944	269.6	628	2.66
1945	234.8	512	2.23
1946	173.6	519	1.60
1947	134.3	418	1.20
1948	92.7	353	0.80
1949	52.8	328	0.44
1950	57.4*	391*	0.46
1951	56.7	407	0.44
1952	31.1	381	0.23
1953	22.1	306	0.16

* Data for 1950 are extrapolated to a yearly basis from data on
seven months.

Sources: Holtzman 1963, pp. 48–49. 172; U.S. Bureau of the Census,
1975, p. 10; U.S. Congress House of Representatives, 1936.

until the summer of 1935, when regional organizers were
chosen. The movement's finances, relying on dues, also took
off. OARP received only $84,000 in revenue in 1934 (ibid.,
p. 76), most of it in the last quarter of the year. OARP had
gathered approximately $555,000 in the first three quarters
of 1935, bringing the total revenue to approximately $640,000.
By April 1936, the total was more than $1,000,000, includ-
ing about $350,000 for the last quarter of 1935 and $180,000
for the first quarter of 1936 (ibid., pp. 65, 82). Because the

movement relied so heavily on dues, its membership probably peaked at the end of 1935.

In 1936, the movement was investigated by the House of Representatives. Although the only charges brought were for Townsend's contempt of Congress – he walked out while being questioned – the testimony proved disquieting. It was an unhappy revelation to many that the *Townsend National Weekly* was run by a for-profit concern, the unfortunately named Prosperity Publishing Company, which was owned by Townsend and Clements. Enormous commissions were pocketed by some state organizers and Clements, who cleared $70,000. Also, the northern California organizer had been indicted for bootlegging and pimping. In April, 1936, Clements resigned, membership drives stalled, and OARP's income plummeted (ibid., p. 445). By summer 1936, the cash on hand at OARP had dropped to about $30,000 from $130,000 in April.

Yet the movement soon rejuvenated, better records were kept, and membership reached a recorded maximum in 1939 when more than 750,000 people were affiliated with the renamed Townsend National Recovery Plan, Inc. The organization peaked in recorded revenues the next year at about $700,000, and the number of clubs increased to about 12,000. In the 1940s, however, the movement declined, and by 1942 membership had fallen below 300,000. After stabilizing during the war years, membership deteriorated after the war, dropping to 53,000 in 1949 and 22,000 in 1953; political purpose was lost (Messinger, 1955). The historical trajectory of the movement suggests a number of questions. Why did the movement arise when it did in 1934? Why did it take off in the latter part of 1935? Why did it decline in 1936, only to recover and gain until 1939 or 1940? Why did the movement degenerate in the 1940s, especially after 1945? Can grievance, challenger, or political opportunity theories answer these questions?

AN ANALYSIS OF THE TOWNSEND MOVEMENT ACROSS TIME

With respect to grievance theories, the evidence is mixed. The movement began after the Depression had passed its low point, in early 1933. Unemployment peaked at 25 per cent that year and gradually fell to 14 per cent in 1937 (Chandler 1970, p. 5). So the movement began during a period of slow, but steady growth, although unemployment was still extremely high in the middle of the 1930s. Moreover, the movement had a resurgence of strength in the late 1930s, perhaps in response to the "Roosevelt Depression" of 1938, when the economy went into recession and unemployment jumped to 19 per cent. It also fits the grievance perspective that when the onset of war ended the Depression – unemployment fell from about 15 per cent in 1939 to almost nothing in 1943 – the movement suffered losses. Perhaps declines in economic grievances in themselves did not prompt the decline of the movement, for movement adherents claimed that the plan would end the Depression and thus help everyone. In the 1940s, the movement shifted its discourse and claimed, doubtless unconvincingly, that the plan would end war. By comparison, the war did not dampen the labor movement, which continued to grow in the 1940s (Edwards 1981). Yet it is hard to deny a connection between Townsendism and the Depression; without it, the movement may not have happened.

That the movement did not spiral upward until the worst economic conditions were over fits the challenger perspective, which predicts that a movement's ability to challenge increases when the potential resources of a movement rise. The challenge got going only when people began going back to work. The Townsend movement may also have benefited from the fact that Long's Share Our Wealth movement suddenly found itself leaderless in the middle of 1935. Perhaps this helps to account for the tremendous gains the Townsend movement made later that year. In addition, the fortunes of the movement seemed to follow successes in its political endorsements. Against long odds, a Townsend candidate in Michigan, Verner Main, won an election in the fall of 1935 for a vacated House seat; movement gains followed. The third-party debacle of 1936, in which the movement contested the Roosevelt landslide, may have kept the movement in its post-investigation slump. After 147 victories by Townsend candidates in the 1938 congressional elections, the movement peaked in revenues.

The movement's main period of growth coincided with the improvement in political opportunities for challenges and the rise to power of the progressive wing of the Democratic Party. The Townsend movement did not emerge until after Roosevelt's victory in 1932 and did not take off until after the 1934 elections, which boosted left-wing Democrats. Indeed, the strongest left-wing Democratic coalition was in place from 1935 to 1939, the period of peak activity for the movement. During that time, the Democratic margin in the House was well over 200, and the Democratic margin in the Senate ranged from 44 to 60 seats (Congressional Quarterly, 1985). The administration did not encourage the Townsendites. Roosevelt refused to meet Townsend in December, 1934 when the Economic Security bill was being drafted, and Roosevelt had the Post Office investigate the movement in 1935. Though bipartisan, the House investigation was seen by Townsend as Roosevelt's attempt to discredit him. Thus opportunities for mobilization brought about by a new political coalition were partly offset by the administration's harassment of the movement.

Policies to aid the aged and to promote organizing in general also spurred the movement. Movement gains followed spending policies for the aged. The drive for compulsory old-age pensions had its biggest year in 1933 when 12 states passed legislation (Amenta and Carruthers, 1988; Quadagno, 1988), and the movement was inaugurated soon afterwards. The movement took off after the passage of the Social Security Act, with its benefits for the aged. As for policies to organize in general, the movement did not start until after the 1933 National Industrial Recovery Act, which encouraged workers to form collective bargaining units. The National Labor Relations Act of 1935, which guaranteed trade union organization coincided with the take-off phase of the movement. Thus, the policies of the coalition to incorporate new groups generally and the aged in particular fed the Townsend challenge.

Our examination of the movement's historical rhythm of growth and decline shows each perspective has some support. The Depression may have been necessary for the movement; it certainly would have been a vastly different movement without the Depression. But the movement's history did not

follow the patter of economic activity. Instead, short-term
surges in movement strength seemed to follow perceived
successes of the movement in Congressional endorsements. From a long-range viewpoint, the movement's success in organizing would have been unlikely without a new
political regime and its policies to encourage challenges and
the aged.
These theories aim to explain movement strength both
over time and across states. Each has some effectiveness in
explaining the key events in the historical trajectory of the
movement. Next we address the spatial strength of the
movement by examining state-level data with multiple
regression techniques, a methodology that allows one to
appraise the perspectives with greater rigor.

EXPLAINING THE STRENGTH OF THE TOWNSEND
MOVEMENT ACROSS THE COUNTRY

Early Explanations and Theories of Social Movements

To measure the strength of state-level Townsend organizations, we computed the per capita number of *Townsend clubs*
in existence from 1934 to 1950, using the only available
systematic state-level data on the movement (Holtzman, 1963,
pp. 50–1). (See Table 2). The total number of clubs over
this period was more than 12,000, and the vast majority of
these were in existence by 1939, when the recorded paid
membership reached its peak, or 1940, when the revenues
of the movement peaked. (See Table 1.) For these reasons,
we divide the number of clubs by the population of states
in 1940. Although we cannot determine precisely when clubs
came into existence, our search through the *Townsend National
Weekly* indicates that few clubs were begun in the 1940s, when
the movement declined. As a check, we averaged the percentage of a state's House of Representative candidates endorsed by the movement in five elections (*Townsend National
Weekly*, 1938, 1940, 1942, 1944, 1946). This measure is a further
indication of the movement's presence, for its political action
centered on endorsements. This measure correlates very
highly, (0.83) with the number of clubs per capita.

Table 2   Townsend clubs per 100 000 persons, by state

Rank	State	Clubs per 100,000 persons
Extremely strong presence:		
1.	Oregon	37.99
2.	Wyoming	31.11
3.	Colorado	29.91
4.	Washington	26.15
Very strong presence:		
5.	S. Dakota	23.80
6.	Montana	22.88
7.	Maine	22.07
8.	Idaho	21.91
9.	Florida	21.61
10.	New Hampshire	19.74
11.	Minnesota	19.16
Somewhat strong presence:		
12.	Indiana	17.62
13.	Kansas	17.32
14.	Vermont	16.70
15.	Michigan	16.44
16.	N. Dakota	16.36
17.	Arizona	16.02
18.	California	15.53
19.	Wisconsin	15.52
20.	Iowa	14.61
21.	Nebraska	14.52
22.	New Mexico	12.79
23.	Ohio	12.19
Somewhat weak presence:		
24.	Nevada	9.98
25.	Pennsylvania	9.56
26.	Missouri	8.83
27.	Utah	7.45
28.	W. Virginia	7.31
29.	Illinois	6.93
30.	Massachusetts	6.88
31.	Oklahoma	6.81
32.	New York	6.17
33.	Arkansas	5.95

Very weak presence:
34.	Maryland	5.05
35.	Connecticut	4.20
36.	Delaware	4.13
37.	Kentucky	3.83
38.	New Jersey	3.77
39.	Texas	2.96
40.	Alabama	1.98
41.	Georgia	1.95
42.	Tennessee	1.92

Extremely weak presence:
43.	Louisiana	1.10
44.	Mississippi	1.05
45.	N. Carolina	0.95
46.	Rhode Island	0.84
47.	Virginia	0.78
48.	S. Carolina	0.58

Note: For the construction of this measure, see text.

The Townsendites were strongest in the West, weakest in the South, and stronger in the Mid-west than in the Northeast. Oregon had the most clubs per 100,000 persons (38), whereas eight of the 11 former states of the Confederacy had less than two. Nevertheless, the movement reached out to the whole country. With 22 clubs per 100,000 residents, Florida ranked ninth, for instance, and the northeastern states of Maine and New Hampshire were more strongly represented than California, the birthplace of the movement. Early discussions about the movement's geographical spread sometimes had to do with each of the different theoretical perspectives we are considering.

In the most complete study of the Townsend movement, Holtzman (1963, pp. 53–5), offered several hypotheses for the regional dispersion of clubs. He speculated that the geographical pattern was due to regional differences in the severity of the Depression and asserted that rural areas and the South in particular escaped the worst effects. Thus, Holtzman seems to support the grievance perspective in his claim that the movement was weak where grievances were apparently lacking.

By contrast, Neuberger and Loe (1936, pp. 20, 258), early chroniclers of the movement, provided an explanation relying on indigenous organizations incorporating the aged. They noted that the Townsend membership included aged members of the Grand Army of the Republic (GAR), a Civil War veterans' organization that was successful in promoting pensions. Indeed, they labeled the movement *An Army of the Aged.* The GAR was almost nonexistent in the South, and its presence was stronger in the West than in the Northeast. Neuberger and Loe also noted that Protestant churches may have aided the movement; they refer to Townsendites as "Methodist picnic people." Townsend himself often emphasized that he was raised as a Methodist. Temperance societies may also have been co-opted by the movement, which shared their distaste for alcohol; a reporter at a Townsend convention referred to members as "WCTU types" (Bennett 1969, p. 175). Neuberger and Loe (1936, p. 77) also claimed the movement recruited leaders and followers from various religious cults. The movement's geographic spread may be due to configurations of voluntary organizations and churches that included large numbers of the aged and were susceptible to the multi-vocal appeals of the movement. Such organizations may have provided recruits and meeting places.

Holtzman also conjectured about political opportunities. He hypothesized that Republicans may have promoted the movement. The relative strength of the political parties, a measure of polity-based political opportunity, might explain where the movement prospered. The strength of Republicans in the West and Midwest and of Democrats in the South adds weight to this speculation. Yet Holtzman also argued, like Shefter (1983), that traditional political parties discourage challenges, noting that parties in the West were more open. Where patronage organizations were weaker, more people may have been drawn into movement politics.

Holtzman noted with considerable understatement that blacks in the South were prevented from exercising political rights. This was especially apparent in "rotten boroughs" dominated by plantation owners, whose profits might be threatened by the disincentives to menial labor inherent in generous old-age pensions or by other political activity. Democratic political institutions, a key element in the structure of the state, may have been necessary for sustained movement activity. Moreover, Townsend (1943) appealed to a statist political opportunity explanation in his autobiography. He claims that the movement relied on volunteers, who in turn often relied on "relief" payments for economic support. Compulsory old-age pensions may have encouraged the movement – a 1939 survey found that relief and pension recipients were more likely than others to favor the Townsend plan (Cantril, 1941, pp. 192–93). These observations suggest that the movement was influenced by the structure of political institutions and by state policies.

Finally, Holtzman argued that variations in the strength of the movement may be due to its pattern of organizing. Theories of social movements tend to assume that *organizers* are constant and focus on opportunities for organizers – grievances, previous organization, or politics. Yet the strength of American movements has depended on the presence and spread of organizers across states, notably in the case of the populist movement (Goodwyn, 1978, chap. 4). As Clements testified during the Congressional investigation, the Townsend movement was divided into four regions according to the timing of organizing efforts: the West region was created first, the Midwest second, the Northeast third, and the South last (U.S. Congress House of Representatives 1936, p. 17). An analysis of the movement's strength across states must consider organizers (McAdam, McCarthy and Zald, 1988, pp. 715–16).

Measuring the Grievance Approach

Four measures test the grievance approach. The measure *depression in manufacturing* operationalizes the degree of economic decline in industry and incorporates two components. The first is wage-earner employment in manufacturing at the Depression's low point (1933) as a proportion of employment in the last year of economic growth before the Depression (1929) (U.S. Bureau of Census, 1938, pp. 765–69); the second is the average rate of unemployment from 1930 to 1933 (U.S. Social Security Board, 1937, pp. 58–59). We use a scale based on the mean of these two measures, after both are normalized (i.e., a sum of "z-scores"). The measure

depression in farming is average gross farm income in 1932
through 1934 divided by the same measure from 1924 through
1928 (U.S. Bureau of the Census, 1932, p. 608; 1935,
p. 589). Data on farm income are more extensive than data
on manufacturing and total income (see Amenta and
Carruthers, 1988). Depressions in manufacturing and farming are treated separately because the aged may have been
affected differentially by them. The measures are not strongly
correlated (0.11). The grievance model predicts that the worse
the depression, the stronger the movement.

Movement activity may also correspond to long-term employment patterns among the aged; the measure *aged employed* is the percentage of those 65 and older gainfully
employed in 1930 (Conyngton, 1934, p. 6). The grievance
model predicts that the greater the employment among the
aged, the fewer the grievances, and the weaker the movement. Employing the strongest version of the theory, we
measured the prevalence of the group most implicated in
"status inconsistency" theories, the percentage of *native whites
of native parentage* in 1930 (U.S. Bureau of the Census, 1942,
p. 18). The theory predicts the greater the presence of native
whites, the stronger the movement.

Measuring Indigenous Organization

To measure the potential impact of indigenous organizations, we considered only organizations that were long-standing, that did not have political activity as their central mission,
or that did not threaten disruption in the 1930s. To be included they also had to include aged members and their
principal goals had to match appeals made by movement
organizers: temperance, Americanism, utopianism, pensions.
We estimate *Methodist Episcopal Church membership*, which was
often mentioned as a source of movement strength in historical studies of the movement (Neuberger and Loe 1936),
averaging per capita members in 1926 and 1936 (U.S. Bureau
of the Census, 1941, pp. 407, 415). The movement may also
have been aided by organized religious cults of personal
salvation. The largest such organization of this era and one
correlating closely with others was the Church of Christ,
Scientist (Stark and Bainbridge, 1985, chaps. 8, 11). We

average the per capita number of *Christian Scientists* in 1926 and 1936 (ibid., p. 383). In addition, we include the average per capita dues of state-level *Woman's Christian Temperance Unions* (WCTU) for 1926–29 (Woman's Christian Temperance Union, 1927, 1928, 1929). We also calculate the average per capita (1920 and 1930, *Grand Army of the Republic* (GAR) posts in the 1920s (Grand Army of the Republic, 1921, 1931); the GAR grew in the 1880s advocating veterans' pensions. These measures are expected to have positive effects on movement strength; the movement may have recruited members in blocs and employed their resources.

Measuring Political Opportunity

We first examine the positive influence of movements on one another. Social movement organizations are defined as those that have political or redistributive goals as their central mission, had begun in the 1930s or had changed in size or character during the 1930s, *and* threatened or engaged in disruptive activities. *Union density* is calculated as union members in 1939, the earliest data available, divided by the nonagriculturally employed (Troy and Sheflin 1985, p. 7–3; U.S. Bureau of Census, 1948, pp. 194, 196). We also computed the percentage *support for Huey Long* in public opinion polls taken by Emil Hurja (1935) for the Democratic National Committee (Brinkley, 1982, pp. 207–9; 284–86). Roosevelt was opposed by an unnamed Republican and Long. Roosevelt won easily, but Long captured about 11 percent. We use this measure as a proxy for Share Our Wealth clubs. Because unions and Share Our Wealth clubs were not in direct competition with pension movements, had similar general goals, and cooperated locally with the Townsend movement (Holtzman, 1963, chap. 8), these two measures are expected to have a positive effect.

We also examine opportunities provided by political parties. *Republican strength*–states traditionally controlled by the Republican party (states known as "one-party Republican") are scored 1, and zero otherwise (Hansen 1983, p. 158). Republicans may have encouraged the movement because Townsend frequently supported them.

The institutionalist critique suggests that electoral

partisanship is not all that matters. Many states were dominated by patronage-based political parties, a situation dating
from the late nineteenth century "third party system." Following Shefter, we expect movements to be discouraged by
the mobilization of voters into traditional parties. We use
Mayhew's (1986, p. 196) ranking system, based on his examination of nominating processes in all states. *Traditional party
organization* strength ranges from 5 in states where such
organizations monopolized nominations to a low of 1 in states
where they exerted little influence. The Roosevelt administration and its left-wing Democratic allies spurred challenges
of all kinds. Thus Townsend clubs may have been encouraged where *Democrats in open, competitive party systems* held
power during the 1930s. We use this measure rather than
Democratic voting because states dominated by one party
or by patronage parties may be immune from the ideology
of the presidential party. States with a competitive party system, without dominant traditional party organizations, and
where Democrats controlled the government for at least four
years in the 1930s, are scored 1, others 0 (see Hansen 1983,
p. 158).

One statist view of political opportunity concerns the construction of electoral institutions. We expect that democratic
political institutions and citizenship rights would aid the
development of movements. *Voting rights* are measured by
the natural logarithm of the percentage of eligible voters
voting in the 1932 presidential election (U.S. Bureau of the
Census, 1975, pp. 1071–72). We take the logarithm because
we expect a curvilinear effect. At high levels, differences in
voting indicate relative enthusiasm rather than rights; the
effects of differences in participation are expected to decline
in proportion to its level. Voting rights were lowest in the
South, where blacks and poor whites were systematically
disfranchised at the turn of the century (Key, 1949; Kousser,
1974).

A second statist view of opportunity focuses on state autonomy. Our measure of *state capacities* combines a fiscal component, per capita state revenues in 1932 (U.S. Bureau of
the Census, 1935, pp. 200–2), and a bureaucratic component that scores 1 for each year until 1929 that the state
labor commissioner had rule-making authority in the

Table 3   Standardized regression coefficients: per capita
Townsend clubs and selected independent variables for partial
models, 48 states

Independent measure	Model 1	Model 2	Model 3	Model 4
Frustration/grievance model:				
Depression in manufacturing	-0.148 (-1.19)	–	–	–
Challenger model:				
Indigenous organizations				
Per capita WCTU dues	–	0.304** (3.07)	–	–
Per capita Christian Scientists	–	0.687** (6.04)	–	–
Per capita Grand Army of the Republic posts	–	0.444** (3.16)	–	–
Political opportunity (Polity)				
Union density	–	–	0.256* (2.31)	–
Traditional party organization	–	–	0.338** (-2.75)	–
Democratic control in open, competitive system	–	–	0.126 (1.13)	–
Political opportunity (Statist)				
Voting rights	–	–	–	0.163 (1.05)
State capacities	–	–	–	0.196 (1.48)
Adoption of old-age pensions	–	–	–	0.334** (2.70)
Controls:				
Regional organization	0.541** (4.65)	0.271** (2.89)	0.309** (2.51)	0.380** (2.76)
Per cent aged, 1935	0.479** (3.88)	-0.323 (-1.83)	0.405** (3.62)	0.307* (2.35)
Per capita income, 1929	-0.342* (-2.55)	-0.401** (-4.00)	-0.115 (-0.85)	-0.576** (-3.92)

continued on p. 222

222   *It Happened Here*

Table 3   continued

Independent measure	Model 1	Model 2	Model 3	Model 4
Number of Cases	48.0	48.0	48.0	48.0
F-statistic	11.84	22.37	12.22	10.87
Adjusted R^2	0.480	0.732	0.589	0.558

* $p < 0.05$ ** $p < 0.01$
One-tailed tests, except for per capita income.

Note: Numbers in parentheses are t-ratios.

administration of safety laws (Brandeis, 1935, p. 654). These bureaus promoted social spending in the 1930s (Amenta and Carruthers, 1988). Scores for each component were standardized and summed. The result captures the capacities of state executive institutions and should be positively associated with movement strength, which should thrive in a state environment supportive of its goals.

The third statist measure is the timing of the *adoption of old-age pension* legislation. It scores 10 for California, which adopted the first compulsory old-age pension plan in 1929 and lower for others according to the number of years later such laws passed (Epstein, 1938, 1968, pp. 534–5; US Social Security Board 1937, pp. 161–62; U.S. Social Security Board, 1938). This measure correlates closely with average pension expenditures (Amenta and Carruthers, 1988) and provides a critical test: The frustration model holds that a lack of pensions would fuel grievances and promote the movement; the opportunity model predicts that the sooner pensions are adopted, the stronger the movement because pensions aid potential aged activists.

Control Measures

One key control measure concerns the strength of organizers across states. Although there are no data on the amount of time organizers spent organizing, the movement divided states into four regions defined by the timing of organization. Thus, the ordinal measure *regional organization* scores

4 for states in the West region, 3 for the Midwest, 2 for the Northeast, and 1 for the South. The West includes the 12 states that Clements testified were organized first (U.S. Congress House of Representatives, 1936, p. 31); other regions are defined as in Holtzman (1963, pp. 53–55). We also include the average of the percentage of *aged* people 65 years and older in 1930 and 1940 (U.S. Bureau of the Census, 1942, p. 43). This measure may indicate the human resources available for mobilization or potential discontent and is expected to have a positive effect. *Per capita income* in 1929 is a third control measure. A 1939 public opinion poll indicated that public support for the Townsend plan increased as one moved down the economic ladder, regardless of age (Cantril, 1941, pp. 192–93).

RESULTS AND DISCUSSION

We regress per capita Townsend clubs on independent measures from each of the four theoretical groups, separating statist from polity-based political opportunity, and including the three control measures. We eliminated measures that did not add to the overall explanatory power of the models and then fit models using the surviving measures and the control measures.

Initial regressions in which each perspective is examined alone show some support for each view (Models 1 through 4). Including the best independent measures from each group and the control measures, the indigenous organization model (Model 2) best explains the strength of the Townsend movement. This model explains about 73 percent of the variance in Townsend clubs per capita and coefficient for the organization measures are positive as expected. The measure of Methodist membership is highly correlated with that of WCTU dues (0.79), but does not perform as well as the latter measure and therefore is eliminated from Model 2.

The two political opportunity models (Models 3 and 4) are also well supported. For the polity-based opportunity measures (Model 3), our best fitting model explains about 59 percent of the variance. The measures for Republican

Table 4 Standardized regression coefficients: per capita Townsend clubs and selected independent measures for full models, 48 states

Independent measure	Model 1	Model 2	Model 3	Model 4
Grievance model:				
Depression in	0.038	–	–	–
manufacturing	(0.41)			
Challenge model:				
Indigenous organizations				
Per capita WCTU	0.163	0.172*	0.133	0.120
dues	(1.61)	(1.77)	(1.42)	(1.12)
Per capita	0.679**	0.668**	0.508**	0.426**
Christian	(4.78)	(4.85)	(4.56)	(3.19)
Scientists				
Per capita	0.539**	0.515**	0.275**	0.281**
Grand Army of	(3.41)	(3.57)	(2.99)	(2.55)
the Republic posts				
Political opportunity				
Union density	0.070	0.062	0.105	0.122
	(0.70)	(0.64)	(1.14)	(1.11)
Traditional party	0.170	0.159	–	–
organization	(1.13)	(1.09)		
Democratic	0.101	0.100	0.098	0.104
control in open,	(1.16)	(1.16)	(1.14)	(0.97)
competitive system				
Voting rights	0.089	0.091	0.095	–
	(0.70)	(0.72)	(0.76)	
State capacities	0.265*	0.261*	0.176*	0.172
	(2.10)	(2.10)	(1.76)	(1.44)
Adoption of	0.254**	0.248**	0.218*	0.256*
old-age pensions	(2.49)	(2.49)	(2.27)	(2.17)
Controls:				
Regional	0.075	0.070	0.111	0.159
organization	(0.65)	(0.62)	(0.96)	(1.16)
Per cent aged,	−0.354	−0.329	–	–
1935	(−1.98)	(−1.98)		
Per capita	−0.712**	−0.720**	−0.623**	0.598**
income, 1929	(−4.10)	(−4.23)	(−5.32)	(−4.65)
Number of cases	48.0	48.0	48.0	37.0
F-statistic	13.37	14.82	16.27	9.87
Adjusted R^2	0.774	0.779	0.765	0.689

*p < 0.05   **p < 0.01
(One-tailed tests, except for per capita income.)

Note: Numbers in parentheses are t-ratios.

strength and support for Long lowered the explained variance when the lost degree of freedom is taken into account, and therefore we omitted them from the model. Results for the statist model of opportunity are similar (Model 4). The three statist measures and the control measures explain about 56 percent of the variance, and all coefficients are in expected directions.

The best fitting grievance model (Model 1), which includes only the measure of depression in manufacturing and the controls, accounts for only about 48 percent of the variance in per capita Townsend clubs. When entered, the measures of the depression in farming, the aged employed and native whites lower the adjusted R^2, indicating that their inclusion does not justify the degrees of freedom lost. Because of the insignificance of the native white measure, the strong form of the frustration perspective finds no support. The coefficient for depression in manufacturing, though not significant, is in the expected direction, indicating some support for the grievance model.

To compare the performances of each of the models we enter all of the measures from the models in Table 3 (Model of Table 4). The model, with adjustments, explains approximately 77 percent of the variance in per capita Townsend clubs. Many coefficients, however, are not significant. Model 2 omits the measure of manufacturing depression from the grievance perspective, which adds little to the explanation provided by opportunity and organization measures.

Model 2 still includes measures not meeting the 0.10 level of significance. Following stepwise elimination procedures, we entered the nine social movement theory measures and the three control measures. Measures that added nothing to the adjusted explained variance and uninterpretable measures were eliminated, producing Model 3. Of the 10 measures in that model five are drawn from opportunity models: union density, open Democratic control, voting rights, state capacities, and the timing of adoption of old-age pensions all have coefficients in expected directions. Some of the coefficients are not significant, in part because the degrees of freedom are few. In addition, voting rights and regional organization are highly correlated (0.59), as the South was organized last and had the weakest democratic institutions. Perhaps few organizers were sent to or were supported in the South because movement leaders did not see it as fertile soil for Townsendism.

To check the robustness of the results, we ran a regression of Model 3 omitting the southern states (Model 4). Even without the South, Model 4 explains 69 percent of the variance. The main difference is that the coefficient for voting rights becomes negative, though not significant, and is eliminated from the model. This is not surprising because the missing states of the South were the states that denied voting rights. Relative voter enthusiasm had no influence on the strength of the movement. In short, the spread of the challenge was due mainly to political opportunities and like-minded indigenous organizations.

The grievance perspective is only mildly supported. The models and measures having to do with short-term grievances due to the Depression receive only minor backing in the regressions. Depression in manufacturing added nothing to the final 48-state models; other grievance indicators were eliminated in the initial trials. Perhaps the severity of the Depression induced the short-term political openings. But depression in manufacturing is only mildly, negatively correlated with the two short-term opportunity factors: Democratic control in open, competitive systems (0-.05), and the adoption of old-age pensions (0-.05). However, when Model 1 is calculated without these short-term opportunity measures, the depression in manufacturing measure still does not increase adjusted explained variance. Still, the fact that per capita income in 1929 has a strong negative effect provides some support for the grievance perspective.

CONCLUSION

These findings help to solve the theoretical paradox of the Townsend movement and have several important implications for social movement theory.

Grievances due to crises can augment challenger theories and require more consideration. These grievances are not constant and may influence the development of insurgencies consistent with the challenger perspective in at least two ways. Crises can breed uncertainty in people that may change their perceived long-term interests and the parameters of the free-rider problem. The Depression may have been necessary for the movement, and an economic crisis may activate people with pre-existing economic grievances. Moreover, crisis may shift political opportunities in favor of challenges, although we find no strong evidence of this.

A second implication concerns the range of indigenous organizations that might sustain a challenge. On the one hand, the Grand Army of the Republic, an organization whose main goal concerned economic security in old-age was positively associated with the Townsendites. The GAR mobilized to agitate for veterans' disability benefits, including old-age benefits. It may also have helped that by the middle of the 1930s the GAR had largely achieved its goals and lacked focus. On the other hand, groups more distantly related to the spending plans of the Townsend movements were still positively associated with it and perhaps provided considerable support. The WCTU was related to the movement only in that both groups denounced alcohol. The movement was also stronger where Christian Scientists were prominent. This suggests that the way that ideas of rights are embedded in a movement's rhetoric and the movement's use of symbolism may draw supporters from groups otherwise unrelated to the beneficiary group. Utopianism may purchase organizational advantages.

Our analysis shows that political opportunities play a positive role in promoting movements, as suggested by the polity model. The standard polity model emphasized aid from social movements and polity members, and we found that where the labor movement was strong, the Townsend movement also flourished.

However, the results support alterations of the standard polity model along the lines of the new institutionalism. Research must examine how members of the polity are organized, especially the structure of the party system. The patronage orientation of parties influenced whether or not partisanship would matter in supporting challenges. It was not merely where Democrats were strong that the Townsendites were aided, but where Democrats gained power in non traditional, competitive party systems. Where Democratic patronage organizations won office, the challenge was not aided.

Our analysis also suggests a recasting of the polity model in a more fundamental respect. The Townsend movement profited from a type of political opportunity not embraced by the polity framework: opportunities provided by state institutions, actors, and policies. Challenger theorists need to take a more sophisticated view that considers states as more than tools of repression. State structures, actors, and policies can shape movements both through restraints and encouragement.

States and policies can promote movements in two ways. First, the structure of state political institutions is important. The extension of democratic rights to citizens influenced where the movement mounted a challenge. Although movements work outside the bounds of institutional politics, the existence of such institutions promotes movements rather than discourages them. Second, executive bureaucratic and policy developments may drive challenges. State civil servants can be seen as members of the polity interested in expanding their own power as well as advancing their ideas of the public interest. To promote their goals, state actors may selectively spur challenges. The fiscal and administrative strength of the state promoted the Townsend challenge. The longer old-age pensions were in existence, the mightier the bureaucratic forces operating such programs. The financial aid such programs provided was important. In democratic polities, state structures and actors shape movements with inducements, as well as with repression.

Finally, the policy "successes" of a challenger may be due not to its collective action, but to the circumstances that made it possible for the group to challenge in the first place. The concept "political opportunity" can create a wedge, theoretically speaking, between the activities of a social movement and policies to benefit its constituents. The same opportunities that propel a movement may by themselves cause what are perceived to be victories won by the movement. Political developments may spur a challenge and may also lead to passage of laws favoring the group. Polity members may encourage the rise of a movement to gain a coalition partner – perhaps by introducing spending policies aiding the challenging group. The rise of a social movement may be epiphenomenal – indicating that policies may soon change rather than constituting the reason for changes. This possibility should not be ignored in studies of the purported "successes" of social movements.

The strength of political opportunity explanations begs the question of whether the Townsendites influenced spending policies. The Townsend movement happened when and where it did mainly because of indigenous organizations and political opportunities, but it may not have helped the aged.

Note

1. A version of this chapter was presented at the annual meeting of the American Sociological Association, August 1990, Washington, DC. For comments and criticisms, we thank Kimberly Blanton, Paul Burstein, Bruce G. Carruthers, Mark Chaves, James M. Jasper, Susan E. Marshall, Steven Mintz, Sunita Parikh, Richard R. Peterson, Paul Pierson, Harland Prechel, Theda Skocpol. Sheryl Tynes, the Workshop for Research on Politics and Social Organization at Harvard University, seven anonymous *ASR* reviewers, and especially, Robert Max Jackson. Edwin Amenta was supported in part by National Endowment for the Humanities grant #FT-33667-90 and a New York University Research Challenge Fund grant.

References

Altmeyer, Arthur (1966) *The Formative Years of Social Security* (Madison, WI.: University of Wisconsin Press).

Amenta, Edwin and Bruce G. Carruthers (1988) "The Formative Years of U.S. Social Spending Policies: Theories of the Welfare State and the American States During the Great Depression." *American Sociological Review*, vol. 53, pp. 661–78.

Amenta, Edwin, Yvonne Zylan and Bruce G. Carruthers (1989) "A Hero For the Aged? The Townsend Movement and Social Spending Policies For the Aged in America, 1934–1950," paper presented at the annual meeting of the American Sociological Association, San Francisco.

Barnes, Donna (1984) *Farmers in Rebellion: The Rise and Fall of the Southern Farmers' Alliance* (Austin: University of Texas Press).

Bennett, David H. (1969) *Demagogues in the Depression: American Radicals and the Union Party, 1932–1936* (New Brunswick, NJ: Rutgers University Press).

Brandeis, Elizabeth (1935) "Labor Legislation," in John R. Commons (ed.), *History of Labor in the United States, 1896–1932*, vol. III (New York: Macmillan), pp. 399–700.

Brinkley, Alan (1982) *Voices of Protest: Huey Long, Father Coughlin and the Great Depression* (New York: Random House).

Cantril, Hadley (1941) *The Psychology of Social Movements* (New York: John Wiley and Sons).

Chandler, Lester V. (1970) *America's Greatest Depression, 1929–1941* (New York: Harper & Row).

Congressional Quarterly (1985) *Guide to U.S. Elections*, 2nd edn (Washington, DC: Congressional Quarterly).

Conyngton, Mary (1934) "Extent and Distribution of Old-Age Dependency in the United States." *Monthly Labor Review*, vol. 38, pp. 1–10.

Davies, James C. (1962) "Toward a Theory of Revolution." *American Sociological Review*, vol. 27, pp. 5–19.

Dryzek, John and Robert E. Goodin (1986) "Risk-Sharing and Social Justice: The Motivational Foundations of the Post-War Welfare State," *British Journal of Political Science*, vol. 16, pp. 1–34.

Edwards, P. K. (1981) *Strikes in the United States, 1881–1974* (New York: St. Martin's Press).

Epstein, Abraham (1938, 1968) *Insecurity: A Challenge to America* (New York: Agathon Press).

Freeman, Jo (1973) "The Origins of the Women's Liberation Movement," *American Journal of Sociology*, vol. 78, pp. 792–811.

Gamson, William A. (1975) *The Strategy of Social Protest* (Homewood, Il: Dorsey).

Gamson, William A. (1980) "Understanding the Careers of Challenging Groups." *American Journal of Sociology*, vol. 85, pp. 1043–60.

Goodwyn, Lawrence (1978) *The Populist Moment: A Short History of the Agrarian Revolt in America* (New York: Oxford University Press).

Grand Army of the Republic (1921) *Journal of the 54th National Encampment of the Grand Army of the Republic* (Washington, DC: US Government Printing Office).

Grand Army of the Republic (1931) *Journal of the 64th National Encampment of the Grand Army of the Republic* (Washington, DC: US Government Printing Office).

Griffin, Larry J., Michael E. Wallace and Beth A. Rubin (1986) "Capitalist Resistance to the Organization of Labor Before the New Deal: How? Why? Success?" *American Sociological Review*, vol. 51, pp. 147–67.

Hansen, Susan B. (1983) *The Politics of Taxation: Revenue Without Representation* (New York: Praeger).

Hofstadter, Richard (1952) *The Age of Reform* (New York: Vintage).

Holtzman, Abraham (1963) *The Townsend Movement: A Political Study* (New York: Bookman).

Hurja, Emil (1935) materials Relating to the "National Inquirer," presidential preference polls, FDR Library: Hurja Papers, Box 72.

Jenkins, J. Craig (1985) *The Politics of Insurgency: The Farm Worker Movement in the 1960s* (New York: Columbia University Press).

Key, V. O. (1949) *Southern Politics in State and Nation* (New York: Knopf).

Kitschelt, Herbert P. (1986) "Political Opportunity Structures and Political Protest: Anti-Nuclear Movements in Four Democracies." *British Journal of Political Science*, vol. 16, pp. 57–85.

Kornhauser, William (1959) *The Politics of Mass Society* (New York: Free Press).

Kousser, J. Morgan (1974) *The Shaping of Southern Politics: Suffrage Restriction and the Establishment of the One-Party South, 1880–1910* (New Haven, CT: Yale University Press).

Lewis, Sinclair (1935, 1970) *It Can't Happen Here* (New York: New American Library).

March, James and Johan P. Olsen (1984) "The New Institutionalism: Organizational Factors in Political Life," *American Political Science Review*, vol. 78, pp. 734–49.

Marwell, Gerald and Pamela Oliver (1984) "Collective Action Theory and Social Movements Research." *Research in Social Movements, Conflicts and Change*, vol. 7, pp. 1–27.

Marx-Karl and Friedrich Engels (1848, 1978) "Manifesto of the Communist Party," by Robert C. Tucker (ed.), *The Marx Engels Reader* (New York: W. W. Norton), pp. 499–500.

Mayhew, David R. (1986) *Placing Parties in American Politics* (Princeton University Press).

McAdam, Doug (1982) *Political Process and the Development of Black Insurgency* (University of Chicago Press).

McAdam, Doug, John D. McCarthy and Mayer N. Zald (1988) "Social Movements," in Neil J. Smelser (ed.), *The Handbook of Sociology* (Beverly Hills, CA: Sage), pp. 695–737.

McCarthy, John D. and Mayer Zald (1977) "Resource Mobilization in Social Movements: a Partial Theory," *American Journal of Sociology*, vol. 82, pp. 1212–39.

Merton, Robert K. and Alice S. Rossi (1968) "Contributions to the Theory of Reference Group Behavior," in Robert K. Merton (ed.), *Social Theory and Social Structure* (New York: The Free Press), pp. 279–334.

Messinger, Sheldon L. (1955) "Organizational Transformation: A Case Study of a Declining Movement." *American Sociological Review*, vol. 20, pp. 3–10.

Morris, Aldon D. (1984) *The Origins of the Civil Rights Movement: Black Communities Organizing for Change* (New York: The Free Press).

Neuberger, Richard L. and Kelley Loe (1936) *An Army of the Aged: A History and Analysis of the Townsend Old Age Pension Plan* (Caldwell, ID: The Caxton Printers).

Oberschall, Anthony (1973) *Social Conflict and Social Movements* (Englewood Cliffs, NJ: Prentice-Hall).

Perrow, Charles (1979) "The Sixties Observed," in Mayer N. Zald and John D. McCarthy (eds), *The Dynamics of Social Movements* (Cambridge, MA: Winthrop Publishers), pp. 192–211.

Piven, Frances Fox and Richard A. Cloward (1977) *Poor People's Movements* (New York: Random House).

Quadagno, Jill S. (1988) *The Transformation of Old-Age Security: Class and Politics in the American Welfare State* (University of Chicago Press).

Rogin, Michael Paul (1967) *The Intellectuals and McCarthy: The Radical Specter* (Cambridge, MA: Massachusetts Institute of Technology Press).

Shefter, Martin (1983) "Regional Receptivity to Reform: the Legacy of the Progressive Era." *Political Science Quarterly*, vol. 98, pp. 459–83.

Skocpol, Theda (1979) *States and Social Revolutions* (Cambridge University Press).

Skocpol, Theda (1985) "Bringing the State Back In: Strategies of Analysis in Current Research," in Peter B. Evans, Dietrich Rueschmeyer and Theda Skocpol (eds), *Bringing the State Back In* (Cambridge University Press), pp. 3–37.

Smelser, Neil (1962) *Theory of Collective Behavior* (New York Free Press).

Stark, Rodney and William Sims Bainbridge (1985) *The Future of Religion* (Berkeley: University of California Press).

Tarrow, Sidney (1988) "National Politics and Collective Action: Recent Theory and Research in Western Europe and the United States," *Annual Review of Sociology*, vol. 14, pp. 421–40.

Tilly, Charles (1975) "Revolutions and Collective Violence," in Fred I. Greenstein and Nelson W. Polsby (eds), *The Handbook of Political Science* (Reading, MA: Addison-Wesley), pp. 483–555.

Tilly, Charles (1978) *From Mobilization to Revolution* (Reading, MA: Addison-Wesley).

Townsend, Francis E. (1943) *New Horizons: An Autobiography*, edited by Jesse George Murray (Chicago: J. L. Stewart).

Townsend National Weekly (1938–1950) (Chicago: Townsend National Weekly).

Troy, Leo and Neil Sheflin (1985) *U.S. Union Sourcebook* (West Orange, NJ: Industrial Relations Data and Information Services).

US Bureau of the Census (1932) *Statistical Abstract of the United States, 1931* (Washington, DC: US Government Printing Office).

US Bureau of the Census (1935) *Statistical Abstract of the United States, 1935* (Washington, DC: US Government Printing Office).

US Bureau of the Census (1938) *Statistical Abstract of the United States, 1938* (Washington, DC: US Government Printing Office).

US Bureau of the Census (1941) *Religious Bodies, 1936*, Vol. I (Washington, DC: US Government Printing Office).

US Bureau of the Census (1942) *Statistical Abstract of the United States, 1942* (Washington, DC: US Government Printing Office).

US Bureau of the Census (1948) *Statistical Abstract of the United States, 1948* (Washington, DC: US Government Printing Office).

US Bureau of the Census (1975) *Historical Statistics of the United States: From Colonial Times to 1970* (Washington, DC: US Government Printing Office).

US Congress House of Representatives Committee on Ways and Means (1935) *Hearings on the Economic Security Act* (Washington, DC: US Government Printing Office).

US Congress House of Representatives (1936) *Hearings Before the Select Committee Investigating Old-Age Pension Organizations*, seventy-fourth congress, second session, vols. 1 and 2 (Washington, DC: US Government Printing Office).

US Congress Senate Committee on Finances (1935) *Hearings on the Economic Security Act* (Washington, DC: US Government Printing Office).

US Social Security Board (1937) *Social Security in America: The Factual Background of the Social Security Act as Summarized From Staff Reports to* the *Committee on Economic Security* (Washington, DC: US Government Printing Office).

US Social Security Board (1938) "Special Types of Public Assistance." *Social Security Bulletin*, vol. 1, pp. 44–50.

Valelly, Richard M. (1989) *Radicalism in the States: The Minnesota Farmer-Labor Party and the American Political Economy* (University of Chicago Press).

Walsh, Edward J. (1981) "Resource Mobilization and Citizen Protest in Communities Around Three-Mile Island." *Social Problems*, vol. 29, pp. 1–21.

Witte, Edwin E. (1943) "American Post-War Social Security Proposals." *American Economic Review*, vol. 33, pp. 825–38.

Woman's Christian Temperance Union (WCTU) (1927–1929) *Report of the Annual Convention of the National WCTU* (Minneapolis: Woman's Christian Temperance Union).

10 Ideology as Episodic Discourse: The Case of the Iranian Revolution*

Mansoor Moaddel[1]

Sociological research on ideology and revolution has been guided by three models: the subjectivist model, which proposes that ideology re-orients disoriented and discontented individuals in situations of social strain; the organizational model, which analyzes ideology in terms of organized contention for power and emphasizes the organizational context in which ideological producers respond to challenges to their authority; and the Marxian model, which attributes causal primacy to class conflict in its analysis of ideological dynamics. I argue for a fourth model, one that treats ideology as an episodic discourse, consisting of general principles, concepts, symbols, and rituals that shape human actions in a particular historical period, and considers a revolutionary phenomenon as a particular mode of historical action constituted by revolutionary ideology. The Iranian Revolution is examined to demonstrate the fruitfulness of the episodic discourse model.

Characterizing Iran as "an Island of peace and tranquility," the Shah had every reason to believe in the political stability of his kingdom. Except for the religious disturbances of 1963, the country's political climate had remained exceptionally calm since the early 1950s. The quadrupling of oil prices in 1974 had substantially increased the state's revenues, enabling the state to finance its ambitious modernization program and military growth. But the Shah was wrong. Minor and isolated antigovernment demonstrations in 1977 soon developed into mass mobilization against the Shah. By the end of 1978, virtually all political experts on Iran felt that

* Reprinted from *American Sociological Review*, vol. 57, no. 3 (June 1992), pp. 353–79.

the Shah's downfall was imminent. The revolution proceeded so quickly that it took foreign observers and even the revolutionaries themselves by surprise.

For students of revolution, the Iranian Revolution is a particularly interesting case. The rapidity with which the revolutionary movement proceeded, the unanimity of the public demand for the overthrow of the Shah through mass demonstrations that crippled one of the strongest repressive regimes in the Third World, the decline of secular politics, and the increasing importance of religious ideology in the revolutionary movement – all become particularly intriguing given that Iran had not experienced a major economic or political crisis. Many scholars have interpreted this revolution in terms of the major current theoretical perspectives. I discuss the shortcomings inherent in these approaches and develop an alternative approach, one that focuses on ideology and changes in the nature of *discourse* before, during, and after the Revolution. I then extend the lessons of the empirical case of the Iranian Revolution to theories of revolution in general.

The distinctive feature of the Iranian Revolution was the all-encompassing role played by the imageries and symbolism of Shi'i Islam[2] in initiating and sustaining the revolutionary movement. The importance of Shi'i Islam brings ideology to the center of debates on theories of revolution. To incorporate ideology into the explanation of the causes and process of revolution, I make an analytical distinction between revolution as a *content* – a series of specific institutional changes in a relatively short period of time – and revolution as a particular *mode* of historical action shaped by revolutionary ideology (Furet, 1981). In a revolution, ideology takes over politics and transcends social differences among participants, moving them in a communitarian relation and orienting them to act directly against the state. It is ideology that distinguishes revolution from routine contentions for power.

THEORIES OF REVOLUTION AND THE IRANIAN CASE

Despite recent advances in sociological theories of revolution, the status of ideology in these theories remains obscure.

In these theories, ideology is either reduced to its psychological function in re-orienting disoriented individuals to the dynamic of organized contentions for power, or to class conflict. Current theories also tend to over emphasize the notion that human action is guided by abstract values or rational interests. Finally, existing theories fail to capture the revolutionary phenomenon in its entirety – as a mode of action, not simply a content produced by contention for power or class conflict. In this chapter, I re-examine the role of culture in guiding human action, reformulate the concept of revolution, and develop a nonreductionist conception of ideology by viewing ideology as episodic discourse.

Subjectivist Models

The connection between individual psychology and the outbreak of revolution is most explicitly modelled in social-psychological and structural-functional theories of revolution, which treat revolution and rebellion as "an individual act intimately dependent on a certain attitude – rebellious attitude – toward some or all authorities" (Tilly, 1975, p. 487). According to this view, revolutions occur when rapid structural changes build up unresolved tensions that burst into disorder if restraints are weak. Tensions are produced in several ways: (1) by a disequilibrated system that produces disoriented individuals whose social ties are broken (Johnson, 1964, 1966); (2) by the breakdown of intermediate social and political organizations, which produces a mass society (Arendt, 1958, Kornhauser 1959); (3) by the gap between rising expectations and needs gratification (Davies, 1962, Gurr, 1970); and (4) by rapid modernization that outpaces institutionalization (Huntington 1968).

Disorientation and discontent alone cannot cause individual revolutionary action. They are aspects of "critical situations" furnishing the psychological predispositions "that make individuals suggestible" (Cantril, 1941, p. 64; Toch 1965, p. 12) and "vulnerable to the appeal of mass movement" (Kornhauser, 1959, p. 112). Individuals begin to act when an ideology is available that offers an alternative value structure (Johnson, 1966, pp. 82–83), explains the loss of community, politicizes some of their most basic needs – "identity,

belonging, worthiness, efficacy" (Schwartz, 1971, p. 123) –
and presents "a 'cafeteria' of appeals, catering to a diversity
of needs" (Toch, 1965, p. 17). Ideology is portrayed as a
hierarchy of values and beliefs whose effectiveness in guiding human action is contingent on the degree to which it is
internalized by individuals. Concepts such as "generalized
beliefs" (Smelser, 1963, pp. 79–84), "framework of consciousness" (Apter, 1964), and "cultural and mental complex" (Dion,
1959, p. 49) are suggested to explain how ideology functions to bind the community together, define ultimate purpose, and ensure social consensus (ibid., p. 52; Apter, 1964,
p. 18).

The connecting link between ideology and human action
in subjectivist models is fundamentally psychological. This
poses a serious problem for testing its validity because the
subjectivist link is difficult to operationalize using historical
materials (Wuthnow, 1985, p. 816). Scholars in this tradition never directly measure individual psychological conditions, or demonstrate how ideology shapes the mental
conditions of individuals. Their methodology generally involves demonstrating that certain proxy measures of independent variables (such as systemic disequilibrium, relative
deprivation, critical situations, unbearable and dead-end situations, social isolation, or socioeconomic crisis) precede the
occurrence of protest movements or revolution (Cantril, 1941;
Davies, 1962; Kornhauser, 1959; Toch, 1965). For example,
Johnson (1966, pp. 119–34) used rising suicide rates, heightened ideological activity, rising military participation, and
increased rates of crime, especially political crime, as indicators
of the normative disturbances produced by social change.

Various scholars have applied subjectivist interpretations
to the role of religion in Iranian politics. If ideology is seen
as a hierarchy of values, then the argument that Shi'i opposition to the state is rooted in its political theory falls within
the subjectivist model. For example, Algar (1969, p. 2), following Watt (1960), derived the oppositional role of Shi'ism
from its political theory and primordial political values. Shi'ism
believes in the *Imamate*, a succession of charismatic figures
who are believed to be the dispensers of true guidance after
the death of Prophet Mohammad. Since the twelfth *Imam* is
in occultation, no worldly legitimate authority remains on

earth. Similarly, Savory (1979, p. 10) claimed that "there is no theological basis in Twelver Shi'i state for an accommodation between the *mujtahids*... and any form of polity". This ideological precedent, which renders all temporal rulers illegitimate, is alleged to underlie the oppositional role of Shi'ism in Iran's politics. This interpretation, however, is not supported by historical facts. The Shi'i movement in Iran has always been diverse and the ulama (theologians) have been politically heterogeneous. On many historically significant issues in Iranian politics in the last 200 years, one group of the ulama has tended to support the monarchy while another has supported the opposition. It is difficult to explain such a politically diverse movement by a constant of Shi'i political theory. Ulama political unity against the state was a post-1963 phenomenon (Moaddel, 1986). Furthermore, ulama unity against the late Shah does not adequately explain the popularization and politicization of religion in the post-coup (1953) period. Lay intellectuals played a crucial role in advancing the Islamic alternative to the Pahlavi monarchy.

Another way of framing the problem of a subjectivist interpretation is to argue that the 1960s and 1970s rapid economic growth was followed by an economic crisis intensive enough to produce a mental state among the people that made them highly susceptible to Khomeini's fundamentalist appeal. But this argument is also problematic: Although Iran's prerevolutionary economic growth was unprecedented, the economic problems of the late 1970s can hardly be labelled a crisis. Some economic difficulties existed, such as infrastructural bottlenecks (Graham, 1979), inflation and scarcity of basic necessities (Brun and Dumont, 1978), and a budget deficit caused by a sudden drop in international demand for Iranian oil, but inflation was not severe by Third World standards. Retail prices fluctuated between 11 and 25 percent in the 1973–7 period, and the drop in the demand for oil was about 11 percent (Bank Markazi Iran, 1976). While economic difficulties contributed to general discontent, these difficulties do not seem to have produced an intolerable gap between expectations and achievement, or had disorienting effect on individual psychology. Thus, this line of reasoning cannot account for the change in people's perceptions about the regime that caused them to follow the religious opposition.

A third, and final, line of defense of the subjectivist interpretation was advanced by Arjomand, who argued that Iran's rapid social change resulted in social dislocation and normative disturbance. With the state's failure to reintegrate dislocated groups and individuals, Shi'i Islam arose as a rival integrative movement (Arjomand, 1988, pp. 4–5). Unfortunately, Arjomand brought little empirical data to bear on his thesis: he only provided the example of one particular dislocated group – recent migrants to towns – who turned to religion because "the Shah did not integrate this group into his political system" (ibid., p. 107). However, Arjomand acknowledged that "the extent of participation of recent migrants in the revolutionary movement is not clear" (ibid., p. 236, fn. 12). Furthermore, evidence indicates that the urban poor living in shanty towns did not participate in the revolution to any significant degree (Kazemi, 1980; Parsa, 1989). In fact, analysis of the occupational background of over 500 people who were arrested or killed in protest demonstrations against the Shah in 1963 indicated that core support for Ayatollah Khomeini came from those with petty bourgeois backgrounds (Moaddel 1986). The available evidence strongly suggests that marginal and isolated individuals and groups played a minor role in the revolutionary movement. Some of Arjomand's historical assertions run contrary to his theoretical claim. For example, although he emphasized the alliance between the ulama and the bazaaris against the state and against foreign penetration (Arjomand 1988, pp. 15, 106), the ulama and the bazaaris were not marginal or isolated groups produced by social change.

Thus Shi'i primordial political values that question the legitimacy of temporal rulers cannot explain the diversity of the Shi'i movement in contemporary Iran. Furthermore, factors like war and social and economic crises, which are often presented in the literature as proximate measures of individual disorientation, were absent in prerevolutionary Iran. Finally, the Iranian case provides little support for the integrative/value-consensus argument because marginal and isolated groups played a minor role in the Revolution.

Organization Models

What is taken for granted in subjectivist models becomes problematic in organizational theories of revolution: How do dissatisfied individuals accept a revolutionary ideology and organize to act collectively against the state? To play a significant role in revolution, ideology must first be presented to interested audiences. Books and articles must be written, pamphlets and newspapers published, audiences provided, speeches prepared and delivered effectively. In short, ideas must be produced and disseminated, a requirement that is contingent on the availability of resources. Resource mobilization is a collective endeavor that requires organization to coordinate individual dissatisfactions and formulate strategies and tactics in a revolutionary situation. Ideology is therefore modeled in terms of organized contention for political power. Ideas are molded by organized power contenders in order to justify their "exclusive alternative claims to the control over the government" (Tilly, 1978, p. 200). Revolutionary ideologies are thus "self-conscious political arguments by identifiable political actors" (Skocpol, 1985, p. 91). They provide power contenders with a revolutionary agenda that justifies their presence and mission in society, outlines their responsibilities, and indicates the action necessary for seizure of power.

In the subjectivist model, individual mental states provide the context for the growth of a revolutionary ideology. In the organizational model, ideological change is analyzed in terms of the organizational context within which "ideological producers respond to the problem of contested authority" (Zaret, 1989, p. 234). Political groups develop or use a revolutionary ideology when they "lose their position in the polity and . . . are refused access to power" (Tilly, 1978, p. 203). The context varies from situation to situation. For example, Fulbrook analyzed the varying political responses of Puritanism and Pietism to absolutist rule in England, Wurttemberg, and Prussia in terms of the obstacles these movements faced "in pursuit of their specifically religious goals" (Fulbrook, 1983, p. 16). Similarly, Zaret explained the significance of the Puritan idea of the heavenly contract in sixteenth and seventeenth century England in terms of "the organizational *pressures* the Puritan clerics faced in their dual role as ordained ministers and as pastoral leaders of a popular social movement" (Zaret, 1985, p. 5). In these and other studies (e.g., Wuthnow, 1985; Stepan, 1985; Neuhouser, 1989) ideological change is determined by the interaction between the organizational context of ideological producers and broad environmental conditions.

To support the organizational model, the rise of revolutionary Shi'ism must be explained in terms of the interaction between the organization of Shi'i religion and Iran's prerevolutionary social conditions. Considering the first factor, some analysts have emphasized new developments among the Shi'i ulama that made them autonomous from the state. A leading proponent of this interpretation, Keddie (1972), related the change in Shi'i doctrine in the late eighteenth century – the rise of the *Usuli* school and the decline of the *Akhbari* – to the growth in ulama power. The *Usuli* assigned the ulama the key role in the interpretation of law and demanded that all believers follow a living *mujtahid* and abide by his judgments. The *Akhbari* school, on the other hand, rejected the idea that religious scholars should use their reasons to enact judgment. Keddie stated that *Usuli* doctrine "gave the living mujtahids a power beyond anything claimed by the Sunni ulama, and gave to their rulings a sanction beyond anything merely decreed by the state" (Keddie, 1972, p. 223). *Usuli* doctrine thus eliminated confusion among the ulama regarding their role in society and provided a strong organizational ideology justifying their intervention in politics. The ulama's independent sources of income, derived from religious endowments and religious taxes, furthered their institutional autonomy and political power for they did not have to rely on the state for financial support.

The growth of the Islamic alternative to the Shah's rule is thus explained within the context of the interaction between the ulama and the state. The state's modernization policies in the 1960s and 1970s stripped the ulama of their traditional socioeconomic and political privileges. The rise of Khomeini's political ideology is seen as a response to the state's challenge to ulama authority and justifies ulama participation in the Revolution (Akhavi, 1980). In short, ulama

242   *Ideology as Episodic Discourse*

institutional autonomy – the organizational context – and
the state's modernization policies – the environmental condition – interacted to set in motion the production and growth
of the Islamic alternative to the ideology of the monarchy.
This argument, although interesting and plausible, has
serious problems. First, the state's anticlerical policies began
under Reza Shah (1925–41), the first Shah of Pahlavi. From
virtually every perspective – economic, political, and cultural
– the entire ecclesiastical establishment came under Reza
Shah's bold attack. The ulama gradually lost control over
educational and judicial institutions and lost their seats in
Parliament as well. The importance of Islam was downplayed
while the Shah's ideologues glorified pre-Islamic Iranian
kingship and culture. While the ulama did not like these
policies, they did not unite in opposition. The organizational
model also has difficulty with the fact that the grand Ayatollah
of the time, Burujirdi, maintained a friendly relationship
with the Pahlavis throughout his career. Even after the forced
abdication of the Shah by the Allies in 1941 and the emergence of a strong democratic-nationalist movement in the
country, ulama orientation toward the state was not
oppositional. On the contrary, an ulama–state alignment was
forged that lasted until 1959. Ayatollah Burujirdi, in a large
conference he organized in Qum in 1949, even prohibited
the ulama from joining parties and trafficking in politics
(Akhavi, 1980, p. 63). Muslim apologists have argued that
Burujirdi was attempting to protect the religious establishment by depoliticizing it. But the politics of the ulama in
this period run against Tilly's (1978, p. 203) assertion because
they show that when power-holders lose their position in
the polity they do not necessarily join the opposition. Organizational structure and environmental change, although
important, were not sufficient to transform the Shi'i ulama
into full-time revolutionaries.
    A second problem pertains to the availability of audiences.
A strict organizational analysis cannot explain why a significant number of people would participate in an ulama-led
religious opposition movement against the state, for without
devout followers any attempt by the ulama to oppose the
state would be doomed – as happened when a small faction
of the ulama resisted Reza Shah's modernization policies.

Marxian Models

The Marxian model of ideology assigns a central role to audiences. Changes in the economy and the emergence of new class positions are key historical processes that produce revolutionary actors. In a revolutionary situation, class struggle intensifies, the repressive apparatus of the ruling class collapses, the ruling ideological superstructure loses its validity, and the revolutionary consciousness associated with the ascending mode of production negates the existing social order and provides an alternative vision of society. While revolutionary ideology claims to represent the general interests of society, its existence "in a particular period presupposes the existence of a revolutionary class" (Marx and Engels 1976, p. 60), because "the '*idea*' always disgraced itself insofar as it differed from the "'*interest*'" (Marx and Engels, 1975, p. 81).

To be sure, the question of what constitutes the central conception of ideology within Marxism has been the subject of debate among Marxists. Ideology first appeared in Marx's works as a negative concept – ideology distorted and misrepresented the contradiction between the forces and relations of production. Later ideology was portrayed as the totality of forms of social consciousness and was expressed by the concept of ideological superstructure. Finally, ideology assumed a positive connotation in the works of Lenin, Lukacs, and Gramsci, in which it represented the set of political ideas connected with the interests of a class (Larrain, 1983). These theorists underscored the significance of ideology in class mobilization as expressed in Lenin's (1977) famous dictum, that "without a revolutionary theory there can be no revolutionary movement" (Lenin, 1977, p. 369). Thus, a determinate relationship between ideology and class practice was established (Larrain, 1983, p. 22).

Nevertheless, Marxists continue to differ regarding the mechanism connecting ideology to class action. In earlier interpretations, the emphasis was on class consciousness, so that a Marxian conception of ideology was basically a variant of the subjectivist model. In recent decades, Marxists have argued that ideology is a social/material practice institutionalized in apparatuses (Althusser, 1971; Therborn, 1980). Against the subjectivist conception of political crisis, they have stressed the material-based character of ideologies and the role of organizational structures (Therborn, 1980, p. 115). Drawing on Gramsci's theory of hegemony, Przeworski (1980) argued that the workers' consent to capitalist relations, rather than reflecting false consciousness, mass delusion, and hoax, is a chosen strategy that has a material basis. Similarly, Burawoy argued that "consent . . . is not a subjectivist state of mind, but rather is expressed through choosing among alternative activities" (Burawoy, 1980, p. 282). Workers consent to their exploitation because the labor process is organized in a way that produces consent. These analyses pointed to the significance of historical conjunctions and contingencies that articulate ideological dynamics with class politics. New subjectivities, new matrices of affirmation/sanction, and a new discursive order emerge as a result of struggles waged by social forces at times of crisis and contradiction. However, "the decisive aspect of these struggles in class societies is class struggle, and the resulting discursive order is class order, articulated with existential- and historical-inclusive discourses" (Therborn, 1980, p. 82).

The Iranian experience, however, provides little support for the argument that ideology reflects class consciousness and interests. The connection between capitalist development of the 1960s and 1970s and the growth of revolutionary Islam was too complex to support a simplistic correspondence between revolutionary ideology and the ascending mode of production. Prerevolutionary Iran was based on a capitalist mode of production and the state was the principal agent for capitalist expansion. Nevertheless, the case of Iran does provide some support for a neo-Marxist interpretation. Within Iran's historical context, there has been an enduring articulation between class politics and the oppositional role of Shi'i Islam that may account for the problem of audiences and may also explain the changes and variations in the politics of the ulama. The class politics in question were those of the bazaaris (those engaged in trade and industry in the bazaar, the traditional sector of the economy) and the landed interests. The bazaar was the most important source of support for the religious institutions, and the ulama and bazaaris were often related through family ties (Thaiss, 1971, pp. 193–94).

The bazaaris' oppositional activities have typically been a response to foreign economic penetration and the state's failure to protect domestic industrial and commercial interests (Issawi, 1971). The merchant-led tobacco protest of 1890–2 best reflects the connection between the bazaaris' interests and religious opposition and was the first of many such protest activities to occur in the following decades. The movement was a rebellion against a concession granted to a British citizen by the Shah of Qajar in 1890 for a 50-year monopoly of the tobacco trade in the Kingdom of Iran (*Correspondence*, 1892, pp. 210–211). In their mobilizing efforts against the Shah and the British company, the merchants used religion effectively and persuaded the ulama to participate in the movement (Adami'yat, 1981). Ulama attitudes toward the concession, however, were contradictory – some ulama played an important role in mobilizing the public against the British company, while others refused to join the movement and in some cities even supported the concession (Nateq, 1983).

Similarly, Shi'i ideology tended to correlate with class politics in the Constitutional Revolution of 1905 to 1911. The bazaaris and the religious establishments fought for a strong and well-organized government under the protection of which merchants and craft guilds could run their businesses in peace, domestic industry and trade could be encouraged, and foreign penetrations could be terminated. Again, the ulama were not united. Anti-constitutionalist and royalist ulama were led by Shaykh Fazlullah Nuri, whereas the modernist ulama attempted to reconcile Islam with constitutionalism (Hairi, 1977).

The connection between religious opposition and class politics under the Pahlavis provides some support for a Marxian model. Religious opposition to the Reza Shah's early anticlerical policies was quite weak, possibly because his absolutism rested on the bourgeoisie (including large merchants) and a landed aristocracy (Tabari, 1977, pp. 70–75; Abrahamian, 1982, p. 149). Thus, even though some ulama resisted the Shah's modernization policies, they gained little support from the merchants and landowners. Under the second Shah, however, class politics began to change. The state's economic policies, which favored large, modern

commercial and industrial establishments, which were tied
to and dominated by international capital, undermined the
bazaar. The licensing system, the expansion of banks and
other state credit institutions, and the growth of a modern
commercial sector contributed to the decline of the merchants' economic power (Keddie, 1981). Moreover, the Shah
even endorsed the physical destruction of the bazaar and
the establishment of new shopping centers outside the bazaar (Graham, 1979, p. 221). The Shah later admitted his
contempt for the bazaaris, stating that they are "a fanatic
lot. . . . Moving against the bazaar was typical of the political and social risks I had to take in my drive for modernization" (Pahlavi, 1980, p. 156). The Shah's land reform and
agricultural policies, which favored the unpopular farm
corporations and agribusiness, antagonized the landowners.
For these reasons, the bazaaris and landowners joined the
opposition movement and provided extensive resources as
well as audiences for the Islamic alternative to the monarchy. Thus, there was a historical correlation between the dynamic of religious opposition to the state and the dynamic
of class politics.

A more powerful explanation of the role of Shi'ism in
the Iranian Revolution emerges when the organizational
model supplements the Marxian model. Together, these
theories would argue that as a result of complex historical
factors, the ulama came to enjoy considerable institutional
autonomy. The institutionalization of the *Usuli* doctrine in
the early nineteenth century equipped the ulama with a
powerful ideological justification for their intervention in
worldly affairs and a leadership role in society. However,
because of their conflicting interests in society, which arose
from their historical relations with the state, landed interests,
and the bazaar, the ulama seldom had a unified basis for
political action. When the late Shah's economic policies
antagonized the bazaaris and landowners, a strong basis for
ulama unity against the Shah was created. Therefore, the
production of the Islamic alternative was a response to the
obstacles faced by the ulama as a result of the Shah's modernization policies, and its growth was made possible by the
convergence of the politics of the classes constituting their
historical basis against the state.

Still, crucial problems of interpretation remain. Clearly the ulama, the bazaaris, and landowners were antagonized by the Shah's policies and therefore supported the Islamic alternative to his rule. However, the emergence of coordinated action among the members of diverse classes and their fascinating harmony in demanding the overthrow of the monarchy and the establishment of an Islamic government cannot be adequately explained by class and organizational analyses. The working class was numerically small and organizationally weak, while the bazaaris, who enjoyed some degree of organization, faced a strong centralized state with a proven repressive capacity. The bazaaris were not organized nationally and it was highly unlikely that they could organize without the knowledge of SAVAK, the extensive secret police network. Furthermore, the Marxian and organizational models cannot explain why Shi'ism became the dominant ideology of the Iranian Revolution while other ideologies like Marxism, nationalism, and liberalism failed to arouse more than a minimal interest among the various classes and groups involved in the Revolution. After all, not all of the participating classes and groups had adhered to Islam in past political struggles. Most puzzling is the question of why many secular intellectuals resorted to Islam in their critiques of the postcoup (1953) socioeconomic and political order. These intellectuals played a crucial role in the popularization of Islam in society, for without their efforts, Khomeini's political theory was too restrictive to attract educated groups to Islam in the 1960s and 1970s.

An important ingredient was required to transform Iran's economic and political problems into a revolutionary crisis, to produce coordination among the masses, to establish channels of effective communication between the masses and their leaders in the absence of a strong nationwide organization, and to account for the collapse of the Shah's repressive machine in a nonmilitary confrontation. That ingredient was ideology. A serious remodeling of the role of ideology in revolution is required to capture the ways in which ideology autonomously contributed to the emergence of the revolutionary crisis, the collapse of the state, and the formation of postrevolutionary society.

Revolutionary Ideology as Episodic Discourse

The above models tend toward reductionism – ideology is reduced to its psychological functions for the disoriented and discontented individuals, to organized contentions for power, or to class conflict. These models, therefore, overlook the autonomy of ideology in the revolutionary process. They also over-emphasize the notion that people act "piece by piece" according to their interests or values. In reality, action is necessarily integrated into larger assemblages or strategies of action (Marwell and Oliver, 1984); ideology plays an independent causal role because it "shapes the capacity from which such strategies of action are constructed" (Swidler, 1986, p. 277). Ideology is not simply a set of ideas in people's minds or in an accomplished text. Ideology can be observed in people's attempts to formulate their strategies of action and in the activities and artifacts of its producers (Wuthnow, 1989, p. 16). Ideology operates through discursive practices inscribed in matrices of nondiscursive practices (Therborn, 1980, p. 81). Therefore, ideology is best conceptualized as a *discourse* consisting of a set of general principles, concepts, symbols, and rituals used by actors to address problems in a particular historical episode.

Discourse is the method by which people construct their strategies of action. It permits certain questions to be raised and others be ignored. It influences what coalitions are permissible and structures the opportunities available for building intellectual justifications for actions. "Discourse subsumes the written as well as the verbal, the formal as well as the informal, the gestural or ritual as well as the conceptual" (Wuthnow, 1989, p. 16). The autonomous process of symbolic formulation connects social structure to human action (Geertz, 1973, p. 207). Symbolic behavior and ritual performances are phases in broad social processes that transform the obligatory and constraining into something desirable. "The irksomeness of moral constraint is transformed into the 'love of virtue'" (Turner, 1967, p. 30). Rituals, however, do not always play an integrative function. "Ritual's primary purpose is social change in the direction of communitarian relations. . . . The primary motivation behind ritual is the desire to break free temporarily of social structure in order to transcend its existential limitations and reconfigure it along communitarian lines" (Alexander, 1991, p. 27).

The construction, maintenance, and domination of a particular ideology must be understood within its specific episodic context. Macro structural changes are treated as a succession of episodes. An episode in the history of a society comprises a sequence of historically significant events that stand out in their relationship with each other as well as their differences with the preceding and following events. The broad socioeconomic, political, and cultural conditions that characterize an episode can cause changes in the worldview of ideological producers and determine the domination of a particular discourse in society. Hence, ideology is an episodic discourse.

Finally, the major theories of revolution fail to distinguish between two principal aspects of the revolutionary process. One is revolution as a content, the other is revolution as a mode (Furet, 1981). Emphasis on the content of revolutionary change characterizes virtually all theories of revolution. In Marxism, revolution resolves the contradiction between the forces and relations of production by destroying the bureaucratic and military institutions of the old regime, overthrowing the exploiting classes, and removing all social and cultural obstacles to the objective process of historical development. In organizational theories, revolutionary change begins with multiple sovereignty and ends with the replacement of one group of powerholders by another. Huntington defined revolution as "the rapid and violent destruction of existing political institutions, the mobilization of new groups into politics, and the creation of new political institutions" (Huntington, 1968, p. 266). Revolutionary change is then explained in terms of the interaction between a set of variables at a particular historical juncture. In Skocpol's (1979) model, for instance, the emergence of a revolutionary situation, the breakdown of state power, and the accomplishments of revolutionary leadership are analyzed in terms of the existing international structure, the exigencies of the world historical development, and class conflict. Revolution as a distinct historical phenomenon above and beyond a series of institutional changes in a relatively short period of time is not considered the object of explanation.

The content of revolutionary change is important, but what makes revolution a historically distinctive phenomenon is that it "is a specific mode of historical action; it is a dynamic that one may call political, ideological or cultural, for its enhanced power to activate men [and women] and to shape events arose from the fact that it meant many things to many people" (Furet, 1981, p. 22). Revolutionary action is shaped by revolutionary discourse. It differs from ordinary oppositional political discourse in a democratic election in that it negates both the powerholders and the routine means of negation. Revolution therefore denotes "the appearance on the stage of history of a practical and ideological mode of social action totally unrelated to anything that came before" (ibid., p. 23). The notion of discontinuity between revolutionary and routine contentions for power advanced in social psychological and structural–functional theories of revolution is insightful.

A revolutionary situation is not simply a condition of dual sovereignty. It is a dual sovereignty constituted by two mutually negating ideological universes – the state ideology and the ideology of the opposition. Revolutionary discourse contradicts the discourse of the state and advances an alternative way of viewing and solving the problems of social life, an outcome that can be achieved only through direct, unmediated revolutionary actions of the masses. The term "discourse" denotes a back-and-forth argument between two parties. Revolutionary discourse is generated within the context of the interaction and propaganda warfare between the state and its opposition – the state structures the arguments its opponents are likely to advance against it and vice versa. Ideological mobilization does not occur simply through the internalization of the alternative value system by individuals or through the organizational effectiveness of the revolutionary movement, it occurs through the discursive field, i.e., "a symbolic space or structure within the ideology itself" (Wuthnow, 1989, p. 13). In Marxist–Leninist terms, it is a "breathing space" that structures discourse by determining what arguments make sense, who may speak, and what issues are relevant. A revolutionary discursive field systematically shrinks the discursive field of the state and narrows its breathing space. In a revolutionary situation, ideology takes precedence, subjecting human action to its internal logic and dynamics. It transforms the individual subjectivity of the committed and subordinates their suffering and possible death to a meaning-of-life as defined by the ideology (Therborn, 1980, p. 117).

These theoretical considerations determine my strategy for explaining the role of Shi'i Islam in the Iranian Revolution. I begin by describing the episodic context within which Shi'i Islam became the dominant ideology of the opposition. Next, I describe the rise of Islamic discourse in the context of the state versus opposition dialectic. Then, I explain the role of Shi'i discourse in the revolutionary mobilization of 1977–9. Finally, I consider how the internal dynamic of Shi'i discourse contributed to the shaping of post-revolutionary events and structured the opportunities available to power contenders for justifying their interests.

EPISODE AND DISCOURSE IN THE IRANIAN REVOLUTION

The connection between religion and the political concerns of various groups and social classes in nineteenth and twentieth century Iran has been noted by most historians and area specialists. The bazaaris often used religious rituals and symbols in their mobilization efforts to change or resist unpopular policies initiated by the state. In its turn, the state resorted to religion to justify its actions. On some occasions ulama theological hair-splitting also paralleled mundane political conflicts in society. The rise of Islam as the dominant discourse of the opposition, however, is a phenomenon of the 1960s and 1970s. The episodic context commences with the coup of 1953, which resulted in the defeat of the nationalist-democratic movement and the regaining of power by the Shah. The broad environmental conditions causing the growth of revolutionary Islam were characterized by the decline of secular discourse, the ideology of the Pahlavi state, and the antistate alliance between classes constituting the historical bases of the ulama in Iran. On one hand, the decline of international support for liberalism and communism, combined with the Shah's effective repression of these ideological movements, helped channel oppositional activities into the religious medium. On the other hand, the ideology of the state, which glorified Iranian kingship and ancient history while overlooking the Islamic period, helped define the identity of the opposition and promote the rise of revolutionary Islamic discourse.

Of course, ideological discourse in Iran was never separate from discourse in the larger Islamic world. Three major ideological discourses have emerged in the Islamic world in the contemporary period. The first is Islamic modernism, which became dominant in the late nineteenth and early twentieth centuries. Prominent Islamic intellectuals and theologians like Sayyid Jamal ud-Din "al-Afghani," Sayyid Ahmad Khan, Muhammad 'Abduh, Amir Ali, and Muhammnad Iqbal argued that Islam as a world religion, by reason of its inner spiritual force, could adapt to the changing conditions of every age (Adams, 1968; Ahmad, 1967). Because law and reason are hallmarks of the perfect Muslim community. Abduh argued that the true rejector of Islam, the true *kafir* (infidel) was one who refused to accept the proof of rational argument. Thus, Muslims could accept the results of scientific and rational inquiry (Turner, 1974, p. 147). These intellectuals rejected the claim that the only truth of interest to believers comes from Islamic sources. They considered it appropriate for Muslim scholars to conduct their own investigations using the best available tools, including books written by authors unaware of the Islamic revelation (Butterworth, 1982).

In Egypt, Islamic modernism took the form of a movement under the leadership of the Grand Mufti, Shaykh Muhammad 'Abduh, and was dedicated to an ambitious program of social, religious, and economic reform (Adams, 1968, pp. 175–81). During the Constitutional Revolution (1905–11) in Iran, some ulama, deeply influenced by modern liberal thought and constitutional ideas, began to reconcile Shi'i political theory with the idea of constitutional government (Adami'yat, 1976). Liberal interpretations of Islam were also common among Muslim activists in India in the period surrounding the formation of the state of Pakistan (Ahmad, 1967).

The second relevant discourse is the ebb of Islam and the rise of secular ideologies like nationalism and liberalism in the early to mid-twentieth century. In Egypt, under the impact of the nationalist revolution of 1919–22, the first modern mass party, the *Wafd*, emerged and the country entered more than two decades of liberal politics (Marsot, 1977). Iran's first liberal nationalist experience began with the breakdown of Reza Shah's rule in 1941, but was abruptly ended by the American- and British-backed coup in 1953. Syria also enjoyed short periods of liberal politics (1946–9, 1954–8) as well as a nationalist movement that emerged in opposition to Ottoman rule and continued against the French mandate between the two world wars (Rabinovich, 1972; Seale, 1965).

The third discourse is the growth of Islamic fundamentalism in many Middle Eastern countries. Men like Hasan al-Banna and Sayyid Qutb in Egypt, Mustafa as-Siba'i in Syria, Abul Ala Maududi in Pakistan, and Ayatollah Khomeini in Iran insisted on unconditional fealty to Islam and sought to undermine the validity of any learning that was not rooted in Divine Law (Butterworth, 1982, p. 87). Clearly ideological movements are transnational phenomena that are not reducible to the interests of any particular group or class and that tend to rise and decline in episodic fashion.

The Rise and Decline of Nationalist-Liberal Ideology

The causal linkage between ideology and its broad episodic context is demonstrated by the rise of the nationalist-liberal discourse in the period ushered in with the Allies' invasion of Iran in 1941 and its decline in the post-coup (1953) period. Following World War II, nationalist-liberal ideology was espoused by the National Front led by a Swiss-educated lawyer, Mohammad Mosaddeq. The main objectives of nationalist groups were democracy and independence for Iran within the framework of the existing semiconstitutional monarchy. The Front's democratic objectives were to check the arbitrary power of the monarch, strengthen the democratic process, and eliminate voting fraud in the country's parliamentary elections (Abrahamian, 1982, pp. 251–52). Its nationalist objective was to eliminate British control over the Iranian oil industry. Both objectives were achieved with Mosaddeq's election as Prime Minister by a large margin in the spring of 1951.

Several factors account for the rise of national-liberalism

to ideological prominence in the 1941–53 period. On the national level, the breakdown of Reza Shah's despotic rule encouraged pluralist politics. Furthermore, the secular trend unleashed by the Constitutional Revolution (1905–11) continued unabated under Reza Shah. The country's leading intellectuals and social critics continued to attack Iran's traditional culture, which rested on various religious practices. Kasravi (1348/1969), a famous Iranian social critic and iconoclastic historian, considered tribal, linguistic, and sectarian divisions as major causes of Iran's backwardness. He was particularly critical of various religious rituals commemorating the martyrdom of Imam Hosein on the grounds that they reflected superstitions and were incompatible with a modern lifestyle. The dominant cultural trend supported the formation of a centralized state with an emphasis on pre-Islamic kingship and culture, expansion of secular education, spread of the Persian language among non-Persians, adoption of Western philosophy and technology, and destruction of clerical power (Abrahamian, 1982, pp. 123–7). On the international level, the Allies' military confrontation with fascism and Nazism under the banner of democracy along with the anticolonial and liberal internationalist ideology of the United States, which was well-articulated under the Wilson administration (Levin, 1970), further reinforced the rise of democratic ideology in Iran. The popularity of the United States among nationalist-liberal groups was also helped by the favorable posture of America toward Iran at the initial stage of the Iranian-British oil dispute (Moaddel, 1989). In fact, the Front's leaders counted heavily on U.S. support for the realization of their democratic and nationalist objectives. The most radical members of the Front even eulogized the U.S. government in characteristically Persian romantic terms:

> From the other side of the Atlantic Ocean, from the State of Liberty and the Land of George Washington, these days we hear the message of affection. The United States of America that, with its invaluable material and moral assistance, have saved many nations of the world from death and starvation, and the hungry and destroyed Europe from embracing Communism, today is going to assume a much heavier responsibility.

The United States must help us at the mouth of the volcano [implying the Soviet Union].... We do not interpret the United States' assistance but as a reflection of humanitarianism and feeling of love for the humanity (cited in Dshawanshir, 1980, p. 72).

The 1953 coup, which destroyed the organizational network of the Front and other opposition collectivities including the Tudeh (Communist) party, marked a new episode in Iran's contemporary history. State repression of the National Front, however, was only one factor in the decline of liberal politics. U.S. support of the Shah became a serious anomaly for liberal thinking. Before the coup, the democratic and anticolonial expressions of U.S. politicians reinforced liberal discourse in Iran, whereas in the post-coup period, persistent attempts by the Front's leaders to gain U.S. support became counterproductive for attracting political activists to their ranks (Jazani, 1978, pp. 91–92). Likewise, the influence of communist ideology was undermined by the Soviet Union's tacit approval of the Shah's policies as well as by the intensification of Sino-Soviet disputes, which resulted in a split in the Tudeh party in 1965.

The Ideology of the State

The state's ideology broadly set the agenda for the opposition and defined its identity. For the opposition, which aimed to transform the state, any ideology that was the ideology of the state was not right. The state's ideology revolved around a monarchy-centered nationalist discourse. Following the coup, the state's discourse rebutted the ideologies of the opposition – liberalism and communism – and appropriated the ideas of nationalism from the National Front and revolution from communism. But the state's discourse became increasingly anti-Islamic and drifted toward totalitarianism. In response to Mosaddeq's ideology of negative nationalism, the Shah portrayed his nationalism as "positive" and "constructive," whereas Mosaddeq's nationalism was labelled "destructive," and "pro-Communist" (Pahlavi, 1961, p. 127). Nevertheless, the idea of "positive nationalism" failed to provide a strong defense of the monarchy vis-à-vis the critiques of the National Front's leaders, the Communists, and the ulama, particularly in light of the fact that the Shah had regained power with foreign assistance. However, land reform and other social policies in the early 1960s changed the course of the ideological struggle to the Shah's advantage. These initiatives placed the Communists and nationalists on the defensive (Halliday, 1979, p. 27) and created a strong reaction among the ulama. The Shah, however, portrayed himself as the champion of revolutionary change:

> Iran needed a deep and fundamental revolution that could, at the same time, put an end to all the social inequality and all the factors which caused injustice, tyranny and exploitation, and all aspects of reaction which impeded progress and kept our society backward (Pahlavi, 1967, p. 15).

Referring to the ulama-led disturbances against the reforms in 1963, the Shah labelled the ulama the "black reaction" and the Communists the "the red forces of destruction" who combined to paralyze his action (Pahlavi, 1967, p. 12). The Shah's ideologues claimed that the ship of state was steering a proper course, navigated by an experienced captain capable of guiding it through the stormy waters of social change to the threshold of a "Great Civilization" (Zabih, 1979, p. 3).

The totalitarian tendency of the state's ideology was further reflected in its attempt to glorify the Iranian kingship and exclude Islam. The Islamic calendar was changed to a civil calendar, and then into a monarchical calendar that began with a vaguely specified date of the establishment of the first monarchy in Iran and in 1971 the Shah celebrated the 2,500th anniversary of continuous monarchy. The importance of religious holidays was played down, while new holidays were added including the Shah's and his son's birthdays and the date of implementation of land reform. The state's discourse became truly totalitarian in 1975 when the Shah abruptly dissolved all "official" political parties and declared a one-party system. The Shah demanded total ideological commitment to his rule:

> Iranians had the choice of supporting or rejecting the three basic principles of Monarchy, Constitutionalism, and

the White Revolution. Supporters now would join the Rastakhiz party to consolidate and promote these objectives. Opponents could either remain apathetic and be non-participants, (in which case they would be denied the fruits of Iran's prosperity); or if they wished to actively oppose these principles, they would be allowed to leave the country (Zabih 1979, p. 9).

In crucial respects, the Reza Shah's ideology resembled that of his son, but there was one major difference. The dominant cultural trend in civil society during Reza Shah's time and the Reza Shah's cultural policies belonged, in principle, to the same ideological universe. Reza Shah was successful in daringly outlawing traditional clothes, including the veil that covered women from head to toe, obliging the people to wear Western-style dress, expelling the powerful ulama from the state bureaucracy, and initiating many other secular reforms, not simply because of his leadership ability and military might. Rather, the dominance of secular discourse facilitated Reza Shah's modernization policies, and at the same time made it difficult for conservative groups to develop a strong ideological argument against modernization. The secular discourse was adhered to by members of the polity and by intellectuals who were excluded from the polity. It informed the flatterers of the monarchy as well as its critics. Although the Reza Shah's critics supported these measures, they were ambivalent about his rule. Under his son, however, the ideology of the opposition began to change, and post coup social critics and ideologues began to resort to Islam in their attempts to address Iran's problems. The more the Shah insisted on his secular antireligious ideology, the less he was applauded by his critics; the more the Shah's discourse excluded civil society, the more explicit became his regime's domination over society.

Revolutionary Islamic Discourse

Political repression, the economic policies of the state, and a highly uneven distribution of resources were problems facing the Shah's opposition. While revolutionary Islamic ideologues were inspired by these practical problems, they were constrained by Islamic concepts as well as state ideology. Islamic opposition discourse was formed in response to the monarchy-centered nationalist discourse. Although the resulting Islamic movement was heterogeneous, consisting of various Islamic ideologues with diverse backgrounds, interests, and political agendas, it appeared to be a single movement by virtue of its focus on a common enemy, the Shah.

The ulama's call for the overthrow of the Shah emerged gradually. In the early 1970s, only a faction of the ulama, under the leadership of Ayatollah Khomeini, called for the establishment of an Islamic government under the exclusive control of a supreme religious leader. The growth of this ideology among the ulama seems to have resulted from changes in the triadic relationship between the state, class, and the ulama in the 1960s and 1970s. The state not only broke with the ulama, but also antagonized the bazaaris and landowners, classes with historically close ties with the ulama. In this context, Khomeini's political theory for the establishment of an Islamic government gained increasing attention.

Khomeini's arguments for the establishment of an Islamic government based on *velayat-i faqih* (governance by the juris-prudent) were geared toward the antistate and anti-foreign orientation of the bazaaris and landowners. Khomeini presented his view of the crisis and blamed "imperialists" and their "agents" for the imposition of an "unjust economic order" on the Muslim people that divided them "into two groups: oppressors and oppressed" (Khomeini, 1981, p. 49). Throughout the world, said Khomeini, "hundreds of millions of Muslims are hungry and deprived of all forms of health care and education, while minorities comprised of all the wealthy and powerful live a life of indulgence, licentious-ness, and corruption" (ibid.) Khomeini resolved that "it is the duty of Islamic scholars and all Muslims to put an end to this system of oppression and, for the sake of the well-being of hundreds of millions of human beings, to over-throw these oppressive governments and form an Islamic government" (ibid., pp. 50–1).

The ulama are central in Khomeini's political theory be-cause accepting the authority of the ulama was a precondi-tion for being a true Muslim. Khomeini argued that Islam gives, in the Quran and Tradition (*Sunnat*), "all the laws and principles needed by man for his happiness and perfection" (Richard, 1981, p. 207). But, "their execution and implementation depend upon the formation of a government" (Khomeini, 1981, p. 44). The ulama's governance would be "an institution for ensuring the rigorous application of Shari'a to Muslim society" (Rose, 1983, p. 180). Therefore, the jurisprudent, i.e., *faqih*, "has the same authority that the Most Noble Messenger and the Imams had," except that his authority does not extend to other jurisprudents (ibid., p. 177).

Khomeini's political project, however, was only one version of the discourse of the Islamic opposition. Many secular intellectuals in the post-coup period also resorted to Islamic discourse to address Iran's problems. In particular, two lay intellectuals played prominent played prominent roles popularizing revolutionary Islam among the educated people. Jalal Ale-Ahmad, an ex-Communist, re-examined the causes of the defeat of the nationalist and democratic movement and sought to understand the roots of Iran's underdevelopment and its domination by imperialism and to rethink the ideological resolutions offered by Iranian intellectuals. At the outset, he argued that Iranians have been forced to be servile consumers of the products of western industry and to reshape themselves, their government, culture, and everyday lives to resemble a machine (Ale-Ahmad, 1982, p. 6). The root of the problem, in his view, lay in the contradiction between Islam and Western culture:

> The West, in its dealing with us, not only struggled against . . . Islamic totality . . ., but it also tried to as quickly as possible tear apart that unity which was fragmented from within and which only appeared whole on the surface. . . . The stopping of Ottoman artillery outside of the gates of Vienna in the nineteenth [sic] century was the end of a prolonged event which had begun in 732 in Spain (Andalus). How can we view these twelve centuries of struggle and competition between East and West as anything but a struggle between Islam and Christianity? (Ale-Ahmad, 1982, p. 9).

Ale-Ahmad's solution was the emancipation of Iranian culture from Western domination, which involved a relentless attack on intellectuals who were the bearers of Western culture in Iran. Those who translated the French constitution for Iran and those who sacrificed Iran's national interests for the Communist International were equally responsible for the decline of Iran's historical and cultural identity (Ale-Ahmad, n.d., p. 355). Ale-Ahmad argued that the antireligious orientation of Iranian intellectuals was simply an imitation of their European counterparts and was not rooted in Iranian culture or history (ibid., pp. 261–72). Since the conflict between Islam and the West constituted the fundamental contradiction, a defense of Islam was the only path to national liberation and development.

Shari'ati began where Ale-Ahmad left off and criticized the intellectuals' critique of religion. He sympathetically quoted 'Abduh who had said, "Europe abandoned religion and made progress, we abandoned religion and went backward" (Shari'ati, 1969, p. 23). Shari'ati argued that "the opposition of Iranian intellectuals to religion is rather based on a blind mimicking of the Europeans" (ibid.). For Shari'ati, religion was the most effective weapon against imperialism and Western cultural domination (Shari'ati, 1985, p. 19). Islam was also a superior ideology to liberalism and Marxism:

> Humanity arrived at liberalism, and took democracy in place of theocracy as its key to liberation. It was snared by a crude capitalism, in which democracy proved as much a delusion as theocracy . . .
>
> The desire for equality, for liberation from this dizzying whirl of personal avarice, so horrifyingly accelerated by the machine, led humanity into a revolt that resulted in communism. This communism, however, simply represents the same fanatical and frightening power as the Medieval Church, only without God. It has its popes, but they rule not in the name of the Lord but in the name of the proletariat (Shari'ati, 1980, p. 92).

Shari'ati's criticism of Marxism was evidently in line with the Shah's policy of anti-Communism. Between February and March of 1976, the regime began publishing Shari'ati's works on this topic in the daily *Kayhan* in a series of articles entitled

"Man, Marxism, and Islam," an act that probably helped the cause of the religious opposition.

Thus, revolutionary Islamic discourse was produced and shaped, as it were, as a result of the propaganda warfare and back-and-forth argument between the state and the opposition occurring within the changing conditions of the post-coup period. When secular-nationalist discourse was the dominant ideology, Iran's economic problems were attributed to clerical influence, tribalism, communal sectarianism, and the undemocratic nature of the monarchy, and the solution was the separation of religion from politics, the strengthening of democratic institutions, and national integration. Western democracy was envied and emulated. Secular ideology also left its mark on religion, e.g., one group of ulama attempted to reconcile Islam with the idea of constitutionalism during the Constitutional Revolution, and then to depoliticize Islam altogether in the late 1940s. With changes in the socioeconomic and political climates of the post-coup period, revolutionary Islam became the dominant discourse of the opposition, and different themes gained significance: (1) underdevelopment and economic inequality were connected to Western cultural domination; (2) religion and politics were considered inseparable and Islam was a revolutionary and anti-imperialist ideology; (3) the monarchy was an anti-Islamic institution; and (4) the political systems of both West and East were rejected.

The Shi'i Discursive Field and Ideological Mobilization

In the 1960s and 1970s, the Shah did not need to worry about the possibility of a serious revolutionary challenge to his rule. The Left and the National Front had been undermined, and the religious opposition was unable to organize another massive protest after the suppression of the Khomeini-led rebellion in 1963. It was a period of remarkable economic growth and industrialization with no noticeable economic problems. As a result, the monarchy-centered nationalist ideology had some degree of efficacy. However, when the country began to experience economic difficulty, the association of the monarchy with progress, economic development, and prosperity weakened. The monarchy became ideologically vulnerable, and the state's policies to resolve the economic problems, such as an antiprofiteering campaign and cuts in social spending, backfired and contributed to the general social discontent. The inauguration of the Carter administration and increasing international pressure on the Shah to ease political control led the opposition leadership to believe that the time was ripe for open political activities (Ashraf and Banuazizi, 1985).

Although these were problems for the Shah, it cannot be argued that prerevolutionary Iran was experiencing economic and political *crises*. Rather, the Shah's regime was thrown into crisis, and social discontent was transformed into revolutionary movement by and through Islamic discourse. The revolutionary crisis erupted when revolutionary ideology began to take over the protest movements because the monarchy's ideology and that of the Islamic opposition were mutually exclusive. Thus, when the public became dissatisfied with the Shah and gradually joined the Islamic opposition, their dissatisfaction was transcended and expressed in terms of Islamic discourse. Given that revolutionary Islam negated the ideology of the monarchy, the actions of the discontented took a revolutionary direction. By posing the problem in terms of a conflict between Islam and the infidels, Islamic revolutionary discourse transcended class differences and social divisions in a communitarian relation, that is, the *ummat* (Islamic community) was pictured as fighting the *taghut* (boundless tyrant).

The discursive field of revolutionary Islam was expanded and ideological mobilization took place in several ways. First was the transformation of the politics of the clerical establishment and its reconstitution in terms of Islamic revolutionary discourse. This was important because alternative courses of action were available to the ulama in pursuing their occupational and religious goals. The idea of revolutionary overthrow of the state and the establishment of an Islamic government were Khomeini's invention (Rose, 1983, p. 188) – there was no ideological precedent to justify ulama direct rule in society. Indeed, many grand ayatollahs disagreed with Khomeini's political views. In particular, Ayatollah Abol-Qasem Kho'i argued that no direct ulama governance existed. Khomeini's first crucial revolutionary task therefore was to convince his colleagues of the necessity of establishing such a rule. In his response to Ayatollah Kho'i, Khomeini instructed his followers:

Present Islam to the people in its true form so that our youth do not picture the *akhunds* as sitting in some corner in Najaf or Qum, studying the questions of menstruation and parturition instead of concerning themselves with politics, and draw the conclusion that religion must be separate from politics. This slogan of the separation of religion and politics and the demand that Islamic scholars not intervene in social and political affairs have been formulated and propagated by the Imperialist; it is only the irreligious who repeats them (Khomeini, 1981, p. 44).

Even in the initial stage of the revolution, the first priority for Khomeini and his followers was the radicalization of the ulama, pressuring them to take an active part in the revolution (Ashraf and Banuazizi, 1985, pp. 27–28).

Second, the discursive field generated by revolutionary Islam – its symbolic structure, religious rituals, calendar, and theme of martyrdom – began to provide an effective channel of communication between the leaders and the led, and to maintain a continuity in the people's mobilization against the Shah. The chain of events that triggered and perpetuated the revolutionary crisis began when the Shah ordered publication of an article in a daily newspaper, *Ittila'at* (17 Dey 1356/1978, p. 7), that accused Khomeini of being a foreign agent. In response, several thousand followers of Khomeini staged antigovernment demonstrations in Qum on 9 January 1978, and clashed with police. Several people were killed and many more injured. The article and the violent repression of Khomeini's supporters provided an occasion around which various religious and secular opposition groups mobilized against the Shah. The leading ulama in Tehran and other major cities expressed outrage at the regime's violent behavior as did the Society of Merchants and Guild of Tehran Bazaar, the Isfahani and Tabrizi bazaaris in Tehran, the National Front, the Toilers' party, and the Left. Just as the ideology of the monarchy shaped the ideology of the opposition, the state's repressive policy helped make Khomeini the leader of the Revolution.

This event strengthened the alliance between secular and religious opposition forces and helped Khomeini and his followers establish hegemony over the movement. Secular groups, including the Left, had often used religious tactics to mobilize the people against the Shah. One example of the ideological compromise made by many secular groups was their acceptance of the idea that women should wear the veil while participating in street demonstrations. Whether the veil was a symbol of resistance to the Shah's Westernization policies or simply represented the patriarchal nature of the Islamic opposition is a matter of interpretation (Tabari and Yeganeh, 1982; Nashat, 1983), but the tactic epitomized the total invasion of Islamic revolutionary ideology into secular discourse. However, the enhanced power of Shi'i revolutionary discourse did not system solely from the tactical necessity of the struggle against the Shah. It activated people to action precisely because it meant different things to different contenders. As became clear after the Revolution, there were as many interpretations of the teachings of Shi'i Islam on practical issues as there were Islamic groups. Highly educated women, who had proudly worn the veil for the sake of the Revolution, probably had no idea what Khomeini and his followers would do to women's liberty in the postrevolutionary period. Likewise, the Tudeh and other groups of the Left accepted Khomeini's hegemony because they believed that he was a revolutionary democrat or petty bourgeois anti-imperialist and overlooked the fact that he was equally anti-Communist. Finally, the liberals do not seem to have contemplated the incompatibility of their democratic ideals with ideals prescribed by revolutionary Islam.

The Qum incident unleashed a chain of ideologically constituted events that prolonged and intensified the revolutionary crisis. These events were produced by the Islamic ritual for the dead, which includes memorial services and commemoration of the deceased on the fortieth day after death. During this ritual for those killed in the anti-Shah demonstrations, some of the participants were killed, providing another occasion for performing memorial services 40 days later, and so on. Major anti-Shah demonstrations occurred in several cities on 18 February – that is, 40 days after the Qum incident on 9 January. In Tabriz, in particular, the occasion sparked serious riots and violent clashes between troops and demonstrators that left a dozen dead and twice as many injured. Forty days later, on 29 March, during the commemoration for those killed in Tabriz, scattered riots erupted in several major urban centers, again leading to a number of deaths (particularly in Yazd). Forty days later (8–9 May), disturbances occurred in some 34 towns. This cycle continued until 1979 (Fischer, 1980, pp. 195–96). Hence, there was no need for revolutionary leaders to "schedule" demonstrations against the Shah – the cycle of these religious rituals provided the dates and rationale for protest.

Third, the Islamic calendar not only negated the ideology of the monarchy, it also provided periodic occasions to mobilize people against the Shah. By observing the rituals and ceremonial practices associated with religious holidays and disregarding the state-specified civil holidays, the opposition undermined the ideology of the monarchy. In fact, the Shah's first retreat vis-à-vis the opposition was to reinstate the Islamic calendar in the summer of 1978. Furthermore, major demonstrations against the Shah often transpired in the holy months and were initiated in the mosques. August 1978 was the lunar month of Ramadan (the month of fasting), a time when religious activities and evening sermons were paramount. The religious opposition used these occasions to attack the Shah and to prepare the first massive demonstration to occur on the day following the end of Ramadan – *Id-i Fitr* (a religious holiday). Following the prayers and sermons, mass demonstrations occurred during which people handed out flowers to the soldiers (Bazargan, 1984, pp. 33–34). The month of Moharram provided an even more effective context for mass mobilization against the Shah. In Shi'i tradition, Moharram is a month of mourning and ceremonial practices commemorating the martyrdom of Imam Hosein, the third Shi'i Imam. In their mobilization efforts, the religious opposition invoked the theme of martyrdom and vowed to make Moharram "the month of victory of blood over sword." In defiance of the dusk-to-dawn curfew imposed by the military government, men in white shrouds signifying their readiness to be martyred, went into the streets. Another ideologically inspired mobilization tactic was that, again in defiance of the curfew, millions of people in the cities went to the roofs of their houses in the evening and shouted repeatedly *Allah-o Akbar* (God is Great) (Davani, 1980, pp. 6–46). On the ninth and tenth of Moharram (10 and 11 December 1978), large demonstrations took place in Tehran and other major cities in which several million people participated. The resolutions passed during these demonstrations designated Ayatollah Khomeini the leader of the nation and demanded the overthrow of the monarchy and the establishment of an Islamic government (ibid., 1980, pp. 72–75). The resolution of the ideological conflict between the state and the opposition ended the first stage of the Iranian Revolution. Islamic discourse set the framework for the resolution of political and economic conflicts in the postrevolutionary period.

IDEOLOGY AND POSTREVOLUTIONARY CONFLICTS

11 February 1979 is celebrated as the date of the Iranian Revolution. A number of significant events stand out in the postrevolutionary period: the seizure of the U.S. embassy in Tehran in the fall of 1979; public endorsement of the Constitution of the Islamic Republic in late 1979; the cultural revolution that began in the spring of 1980; political conflict in the Islamic Republic that developed into a reign of terror in the summer of 1981; the resolution of class-related issues in favor of merchants and landowners; and the outbreak of the Iran–Iraq war.

The revolutionary dynamic set by the Shi'i discourse continued unabated for several years after the overthrow of the monarchy. As long as the Shah, i.e., the common enemy, was present diverse Islamic groups were united and the Islamic alternative to the ideology of the monarchy seemed uniform and consistent. But when concrete plans emerged for building the postrevolutionary "Islamic" order, disputes replaced harmony. Of notable significance were three rival groups: (1) liberal Muslims, headed by Mehdi Bazargan, who predominantly controlled the provisional government, and was succeeded by Bani-Sadr and his supporters; (2) the ulama followers of Ayatollah Khomeini; and (3) the Mojahedin, a radical Islamic political organization. To liberals, a form of

parliamentary democracy within the existing capitalist relationship guided by the moral values of Islam was all that
was achievable or even suitable for Iran. For Khomeini and
his followers the overthrow of the Shah was only the first
stage of the Revolution – several decades of secularization
had to be stopped and reversed. Liberalism, Marxism, and
other ideologies belonged to the West or the East and had
no place among the Muslim people – society needed reorganization and purification according to the teachings of
Islam. In short, the central objective of Ayatollah Khomeini
and his followers, who were now largely organized in the
Islamic Republican Party (IRP), was the establishment of
the governance of Islamic jurisprudence (*velayat-i faqih*).
Finally, the Mojahedin advanced a sort of Islamic socialism.
The presence of these ideological variants, however, does
not indicate that Shi'i ideology as a whole became a tool in
the contention for power. On the contrary, Shi'i discourse
contributed to the shaping of postrevolutionary events, structured the opportunities available to the diverse social classes
and contenders for power and determined the legitimacy
of their claims.

Ideological disputes in the postrevolutionary period drifted
increasingly in an extremist direction. This extremism was
not a simple outcome of contentions for power or class
conflict, but emanated from the internal logic of Shi'i discourse itself. A foremost function of Shi'i revolutionary discourse was the signification of the idea of counterrevolution.
In a real sense, the Iranian Revolution had no counterrevolution. In a referendum, the public overwhelmingly
endorsed the establishment of the Islamic Republic. The
United States and its allies, who were the prime supporters
of the Shah, reluctantly accepted the Revolution. To be sure,
the U.S. government was apprehensive about the nature of
the postrevolutionary regime and the Left had every reason
to see this apprehension as counterrevolutionary. But for
the Revolution as a whole, there were no organized interests inside or outside the country that aimed to overthrow
the new Islamic Republic. Therefore, the idea that the Revolution was under attack and being undermined by the dia-
bolical machinations of the United States was primarily the
product of Islamic revolutionary discourse. And the seizure

of the U.S. embassy in the fall of 1979 was dictated by this ideological prophecy. Suggestions that the ruling clerics supported the embassy takeover because they wanted to expel liberals from government and that the takeover was triggered by the Shah's admission to the United States are inadequate. The provisional government had already decided to resign before the embassy takeover and the ruling ulama knew this (Bazargan, 1984, p. 95, fn. 1). Furthermore, the plan to seize the embassy was contemplated well before the Shah entered the United States. None of these reasons prompted the seizure of the embassy. Rather, the Shah's admission to the United States was a circumstance that the revolutionary ideology fed upon and saw as part of a counterrevolutionary conspiracy by the United States. When Ayatollah Khomeini proclaimed that the seizure of the embassy was tantamount to a "second Islamic Revolution" and demanded that the counterrevolutionary, the "Great Satan," be exposed and disarmed in its "spy nest," he was acting as the spokesperson for the Revolution.

The embassy seizure, however, did contribute to ulama success in realizing their revolutionary ambition – the passage of a Constitution in which the doctrine of *velayat-i faqih* was central. Using mass mobilization resulting from the seizure of the embassy, the ulama quickly set up a referendum on the new Constitution, which received mass endorsement in December 1979. The Constitution gave the ulama unprecedented power: Besides the doctrine of the *velayat-i faqih*, which extended the Shi'i "juristic norm of authority from the religious to the political sphere" (Arjomand, 1988, p. 151), the Council of Constitutional Guardians was empowered to interpret and determine the conformity with Islam of any law passed by Parliament, to supervise presidential and parliamentary elections, and to hold referenda (Islamic Republic, 1979). The Constitution effected an unprecedented change in the clerical establishment in the direction of formally centralizing religious authority.

Islamic revolutionary discourse also conditioned the *form* of political conflict. The intermeshing of ideological disputes with contentions for power was reflected in the course of conflicts over control of the state bureaucracy. The election of Bani-Sadr as the country's first President was a serious defeat for the IRP and a resounding success for the liberals. Soon, however, the revolutionary ideology helped tip the balance of forces in the government in the IRP's favor. The contradiction between Islam and the West (a major theme of Islamic revolutionary discourse) was the ideological dynamic underlying the cultural revolution launched in April 1980. Although one of the initial objectives of the cultural revolution was to expel the Left from university campuses (*Jomhouriye Islami*, 30 Farvardin 1359/1980, p. 1), the influence of the Left in academia was additional ammunition for the revolutionary ideology. When the IRP leaders and the liberals agreed to the idea of a cultural revolution, they were acting in accordance with revolutionary ideology to eradicate all vestiges of the anti-Islamic policies implemented by the Pahlavis. The cultural revolution was a further expansion of the discursive field of revolutionary Islam toward the Islamization of all social relationships.

The cultural revolution, however, meant different things to its diverse executioners and worked to the advantage of the IRP vis-à-vis the liberals. For liberals, it was a means to get rid of leftist agitators in public institutions, factories, and rural areas so that economic and political stability could be restored. The IRP, on the other hand, wanted to eliminate liberals as well. They mobilized gangs of *Hezbullah* (the Party of God) to invade the universities, injure or kill members of the opposition, and burn books and papers thought to be un-Islamic. The IRP then accused those who opposed the cultural revolution of being the agents of the West or the East (*Jomhouriye Islami*, 1 Urdibihisht 1359/1980, p. 9).

In the parliamentary elections during the cultural revolution, the IRP won a majority. With Bani-Sadr as President and the IRP dominating Parliament, selection of the Prime Minister and the members of his cabinet became the subject of intense dispute. Ideological disputes revolved around the criteria for selection of members of the state bureaucracy – Bani-Sadr emphasized technical competence and specialization whereas the IRP emphasized religiosity and commitment to the *Maktab-i Islam* (school of Islam). Reja'ie, the Prime Minister, stated that the Revolution was for the sake of Islam and not for material things such as "the availability of, say, oranges and grapes" (cited in *Kar*, 8 Mehr

1359/1980, p. 8). IRP leaders further argued that "morality" took precedence over "science," and "value" took precedence over "knowledge," and that only by hiring devout Muslims could Iran gain true independence and self-sufficiency (*Kar,* 6 Azar 1359/1980, p. 15). These disputes were accompanied by *Hezbullah's* attacks on Bani-Sadr's supporters. Pressures on Bani-Sadr prompted him to forge an alliance with the *Mojahedin.*

Bani-Sadr and the *Mojahedin* defined freedom and democracy as their prime issues. The Mojahedin's critique of the ulama and the IRP, however, went beyond their anti-democratic activities – they called the ulama the petty bourgeois, and argued that they had distorted and ridiculed Islam (*Mojahedin,* 1981, p. 3). The Mojahedin claimed there was only one true Islam – "all other kinds of Islam . . . are the slogan of the declining forces and classes" (ibid., p. 1). The Mojahedin criticized the petty bourgeois understanding of Islam as "defending private property and exploitation" (ibid., p. 17), having a "dogmatic and narrow-minded understanding of the social laws of Islam" (ibid., p. 19), "overlooking or ignoring the realities and the objective economic bases of society and social development" (ibid., p. 33), and "negating social orientation of Islam in the direction of eliminating classes" (ibid., p. 74). Therefore, "the petty bourgeois understanding of Islam, from a 'socioeconomic' viewpoint, requires the acceptance of exploitation and social duality, and is thus a manifestation of *shirk* (the assignment of partners to God), invalid and empty of *towhidi* (pertaining to divine unity) content" (ibid., p. 38). In response, an IRP ideologue argued that the Islam of the *Mojahedin* was eclectic and influenced by Marxism. He claimed that, in the *Mojahedin* eclectic philosophy, history had replaced God; and social groups and movements were evaluated in terms of concepts like "reactionary" or "progressive" instead of "right" or "wrong" (*Jomhouri-ye Islami* 22 Urdibihisht 1360/1981, p. 1).

These charges and counter-charges concerning ideological "correctness" were not resolved through ideological debate. The IRP called for the arrest and prosecution of the leaders of the Mojahedin, while the Mojahedin, in turn, launched an armed attack on IRP leaders and cadres. In their mobilization efforts, the ulama and the IRP used popular idioms and rhetoric to condemn Bani-Sadr and the Mojahedin. However, the bombing of the IRP headquarters in June 1981, which resulted in the death of Ayatollah Beheshti, the IRP chairman, and other leaders and cadres of the IRP, provided the ulama with an excuse to unleash a reign of terror unheard of in Iran's contemporary history. To excite the faithful against Bani-Sadr and the Mojahedin, the ulama claimed there were 72 casualties, which was also the number of legendary Hosein and his followers killed in Karbala (*Jomhouri-ye Islami*, 10 Tir 1360/1981, p. 1). The armed confrontation resulted in the defeat of Bani-Sadr and the Mojahedin. Thousands of members of the Mojahedin were either killed during armed clashes with the regime or executed in captivity (*Mojahed*, 1364/1985).

Clearly, coercive power played a crucial role in shaping events as rival contenders manipulated ideology to fit their goals. Nevertheless, these events took place within the context of Shi'i revolutionary discourse that structured the form of political conflict. Shi'i discourse dictated political change through revolutionary action and glorified martyrdom and self-sacrifice. It emphasized unity within the Islamic community and warned of the presence of the counterrevolution. Any disagreement was considered a sign of danger, and an indication of the infiltration of the counterrevolution and U.S. agents into the ranks of the Muslim people that must be effectively suppressed. Each side in the dispute questioned the Islamic nature of its opponent, meaning that "deviants" not only lost the right to be members of the polity, but also the right to exist. The victor had no difficulty accusing the defeated of being the *Mof-sid-i fil Arz* (corrupt on earth), a crime punishable by death. If national-democratic ideology had been the dominant discourse, as it was under Mosaddeq, competition among political groups clearly would have taken quite a different form.

Class Conflict

Class struggle in the postrevolutionary period revolved around three major issues: land reform; labor law, including labor control of production through newly formed labor councils; and nationalization of foreign trade. Islamic revolutionary discourse helped resolve these issues in favor of landowners and merchants.

Peasant–Landlord Struggle
The land reform law formulated by the Islamic Republic was an outcome of extensive peasant struggles prompted by the breakdown of the old regime's central authority. Peasant self-assertion was initially directed toward the seizure of land in large estates—especially those belonging to members and associates of the Shah's regime—and then expanded to include smaller holdings (Nik-A'een, 1359/1980, pp. 96–117). Rural turbulence, however, was not initiated by peasants. In parts of Khorasan and in areas where semitribal forms of social organization persisted such as Kurdistan, Fars, and Baluchistan, khans and landlords sought to reclaim lands they had lost under the land reforms of the 1960s. Elsewhere, landlords laid claim to disputed properties or pasturelands in the public domain (Bakhash, 1984, p. 197).

The provisional government opposed the land seizures and launched military attacks on the peasants and even armed the landlords and khans in some areas (*Ummat*, 10 Bahman 1358/1980, p. 5). However, the government's actions to calm the anxious climate were hampered by the "pro-poor" rhetoric of Ayatollah Khomeini and other radical clerics. Khomeini proclaimed that "the country belongs to the slum dwellers" (*Jomhouri-ye Islami*, 9 Aban 1358/1979, pp. 1–2). Ayatollah Beheshti stated that "the line of the revolution is anti-imperialism, anti-capitalism, and anti-feudalism" (*Jomhouri-ye Islami*, 11 Khurdad 1359/1980, pp. 1, 4). Finally, Ayatollah Dastghaib encouraged the peasants to seize lands from the landowners and cultivate these lands "behind the banner of Islam" (*Kayhan*, 6 Shahrivar 1362/1983).

With the fall of the provisional government, many liberal politicians were replaced by men committed to radical economic change. A radical Muslim, Reza Isfahani, the new Undersecretary for Land Affairs in the Ministry of Agriculture, announced that revolutionary land reform begins with the seizure of land from large landowners and its distribution among landless and small peasants (Ashraf, 1361/1982, p. 31). By mid-April 1980, the Revolutionary Council had passed a land reform bill that "provided for a sweeping land distribution" (Bakhash, 1984, p. 202). However, landowners, merchants, and the conservative ulama continued to oppose the reform (*Ummat*, 24 Dey 1359/1981, p. 11), and the outbreak of the Iran–Iraq war prompted Ayatollah Khomeini to halt implementation of the land reform. Subsequently, the land reform law was reviewed and revised by Parliament, which retreated from the original objectives of the law passed by the Revolutionary Council. The revised law was still rejected by the Council of Constitutional Guardians.

The Labor Movement
Although they were latecomers to the Revolution, industrial workers played an important role in the downfall of the monarchy. Strike committees were major coordinators of the workers' movement during the Revolution and formed the nucleus of the subsequent workers' councils in different industrial units. These councils assumed the management of factories. In many cases, workers were able to reduce working hours, obtain a more favorable job evaluation and classification, fire corrupt managers, hire additional workers, obtain across-the-board pay raises, lower managers' salaries, and receive regular health examinations (Azad, 1980, pp. 17, 21).

The upsurge of the workers' movement in the summer of 1979 continued into the fall. In Khuzistan and Azarbayjan, workers concentrated on establishing a minimum wage, a 40-hour working week, and councils and syndicates. They also took steps toward forming regional unions. By March 1980, 31 factory councils in Gilan had formed a coordinating council that incorporated 20,000 workers. A coordinating council was also formed by eight factory councils in Tabriz (ibid., pp. 20–22). In Fars, the Islamic councils of workers formed their first Congress (*Ummat*, 5 Isfand 1358/1980, p. 5).

However, the workers' movement, like the peasant movement, was also undermined. The provisional government opposed workers' councils. Bazargan assailed radical political groups who "say that the army must be destroyed and councils run the affairs of the nation, and that people must be in a state of revolution all the time. If this goes on we will have no alternative but to resign" (cited in Azad, 1980,

p. 19). In the same vein, the Minister of labor expressed his opposition to the councils by threatening that "the Ministry of Labor is either my place of work or the councils" (cited in Fedai'yan, 1982, p. 10). Although Khomeini called workers the pillar of the revolution, in practice the Islamic Republic did not tolerate the autonomy of the labor councils.

The Merchants and Foreign Trade

Prerevolutionary economic difficulties worsened after the Revolution. Skyrocketing inflation and scarcity of basic commodities expedited the government's intervention in the distribution of commodities. The provisional government was not interested in nationalizing foreign trade and simply suggested the establishment of centers for the provision and distribution of commodities with the direct participation of the private sector, in particular the merchants (*Ittila'at*, 7 Farvardin 1359/1980, p. 9). With the fall of the provisional government, the nationalization of foreign trade and its relationship to domestic distribution of commodities were subjects of acrimonious debate in and outside the government. Parliamentary debates on the nationalization of foreign trade began in early fall 1980, and Parliament overwhelmingly passed the nationalization bill in April 1982 (*Ittila'at*, 23 Urdibihisht 1361/1982, p. 7). However, the bill was rejected by the Council of Constitutional Guardians in late fall 1982 on the grounds that it was incompatible with Islam (*Ittila'at*, 6 Azar 1361/1982, pp. 15–16).

Islamic Discourse and Class Capacity

The demise of the social revolutionary movement cannot be adequately explained in terms of political conflict or the exigencies of state-building. The dominated classes failed despite the fall of the provisional government, Bani-Sadr and Quotbzadeh, who had supported the bazaaris and landowners. The Marxian model also faces difficulty explaining the failure of peasants and workers. Although the organizational power and class capacity of the warring classes were crucial variables that determined the social outcomes of the Revolution, class organization and capacity were not primarily rooted in the structure of class relations or pre-existing class organizations. The ideological context of the class conflict tipped the balance of forces in favor of the dominant classes. By structuring the legitimacy of the claims advanced by diverse classes and promoting selected organized activities, Islamic revolutionary discourse operated in favor of merchants and landowners vis-à-vis workers and peasants. Industrial workers were weak because of limited industrial development in Iran. According to 1981 statistics, nationwide, there were 7,531 industrial enterprises with 10 or more employees. Of this total, 6,738 (89 percent) had between 10 and 100 employees, and 4,628 (61 percent) had 10 to 19 employees. Of 793 enterprises with more than 100 employees, only 233 employed more than 500 workers. The predominance of small enterprises hindered the development of an organized workers' movement. Workers had some latitude for effective collective action because of the oil industry's strategic location in the economy and because industrial units were concentrated in a few major cities (Markaz-i Amar-i Iran, 1983, pp. 7, 13, 37). Although a prolonged national strike could shut down the economy, in the absence of a nationwide union, such a unified class action was unlikely. The peasants' capacity for collective action was no better than the workers'. Historically, the geographical dispersal of villages, the persistent threats of raiding nomads, and the absence of a middle peasantry hindered the peasants' collective power (Halliday, 1979, pp. 108–109; Kazemi and Abrahamian, 1978). Furthermore, the state's policies in the 1960s added to the peasants' political weakness by destroying traditional farming organizations and undermining the newly emerged nationwide cooperative movement.

Organizational problems in the other camp were no less important. Landowners as a class were effectively undermined by the land reforms of the 1960s, and there was no nationwide network in the postrevolutionary period through which landowners could mobilize support against the land reform movement. To be sure, landowners took advantage of the law concerning the establishment of agricultural councils passed by the Revolutionary Council in April 1979. This law was a response to pressures from the Left for the formation of councils of peasants and agricultural workers to supervise production. However, with the aid of the provisional government, councils of landowners were formed for the defense of their common interests. With the fall of the provisional government, landowners lost an important ally, and by themselves these councils were too weak to defeat the land reform movement. Similarly, merchants had no nationwide union in the prerevolutionary period. During the oil nationalization movement, the Society of Merchants and Guilds, which was tied to the National Front, was formed. It was outlawed after the coup but was re-established in the late 1970s as the Society of Merchants and Guilds of the Tehran Bazaar (SMGTB). But, in the postrevolutionary period, the bazaar was represented by politically diverse organizations. SMGTB was tied to the liberals, the Committee on Guild Affairs was tied to the IRP, and the Traders' Towhidi Guild was connected with the Mojahedin. During the conflict between the IRP and the Bani-Sadr/Mojahedin coalition, a group of bazaar activists and organizers was executed or fled the country (Parsa, 1989, p. 282). To be sure, following the Revolution, merchants accumulated substantial wealth (*Ittila'at*, 7, 10 and 11 Aban 1360/1981), and lobbied the government against nationalization of foreign trade. Nonetheless, the profiteering of the merchants had reached the point where it outraged the public as well as Parliament and reinforced the move for nationalization of foreign trade (*Ittila'at*, 20 and 31 Farvardin 1362/1983).

Therefore, the key to understanding the landowners' and merchants' ability to protect their interests despite popular support for the social revolutionary movement lies in the ideological context in which class conflict took place. Merchants and landowners were successful because of the built-in bias of Islamic discourse toward the property owning classes. Furthermore, the Islamization of the country produced by Shi'i revolutionary discourse encouraged the re-establishment of the traditional organizations of the bazaar that had been undermined under the Pahlavis. There were ideological and historical precedents for the establishment of various bazaar-based organizations, while no such precedents existed for the formation of workers' and peasants' unions.

When a leading governmental official began to support land reform, landowners reacted strongly and accused him of being a Communist and labelled his land reform bill part of a Communist conspiracy. The conservative ulama also mobilized against the bill. Ayatollah Ruhani in Qum and Ayatollah Qumi in Mashhad voiced their opposition (*Ittila'at*, 20 Farvardin 1359/1980), Ayatollah Ruhani argued that the bill was contrary to the law of Islam (*Ittila'at*, 2 Urdibihisht 1359/1980, p. 4). Landowners also secured *fatva* (an authoritative statement) from the conservative ulama against land reform. Ayatollah Golpayegani issued a statement declaring the law to be in violation of Islamic tenets, and Ayatollahs Ruhani, Mahallati, Qumi, and Shirazi also criticized the measure. The Society of the Seminary Teachers at Qum, a group close to Khomeini, issued a declaration warning against bills "damaging to the interests of the oppressed . . . which appear in the dress of Islam," and said that the land reform measure would lead to "the ruin of the cultivated lands" (Bakhash, 1984, p. 204).

Given that religious opposition was partly a reaction to the Shah's land reform program of the 1960s, landowners and the conservative ulama could easily invoke past arguments against the reform, while there was no ideological precedent in Islam favoring land redistribution among peasants. For example, in Hamadan, landlords circulated an old *fatva* by Khomeini that prohibited the usurpation of land. Even Ayatollah Taliqani, who was considered the most radical and socially conscious cleric, in his book *Islam va Malikiyyat* (Islam and Private Property), never questioned the legitimacy of private ownership of land. Thus, when the Council of Constitutional Guardians pronounced the land reform bill to be contrary to the law of Islam, there was little the social revolutionary forces could do short of questioning the legitimacy of the Council itself. However, for pro-land-reform activists who believed in the Islamic Republic, this option was not acceptable, and the land reform debate could not be taken out of the Islamic discourse. Those who opposed the government did not have the right to speak.

Likewise, merchants effectively used religion to question the legitimacy of the bill for the nationalization of foreign trade. When the Reja'ie government began drawing up a plan for nationalizing foreign trade, merchants questioned his competence for running the government. Addressing Prime Minister Reja'ie, a pro-merchant placard read "for the sake of Islam, we demand that you resign from the job; you are incapable of handling its responsibilities and should vacate the position for a devout Muslim" (cited in *Ummat* 22 Dey 1359/1981). The merchants mobilized the conservative ulama, who objected to the nationalization of foreign trade on the grounds that it was contrary to the law of Islam. A chief opponent of the measure was Ayatollah Hasan Qumi of Mashhad, who condemned the arbitrary nationalization and expropriation of private property (Bakhash, 1984, p. 194). Pro-merchant politicians and the ulama proclaimed that "the *Shari'a* (holy law of Islam) does not allow anyone to point a finger at the merchants. From the beginning of Islam, the bazaar has been operating in this manner, and any deviation from it is *kufr* (the rejection of Islam) and Communism" (*Ittila'at*, 6 Aban 1360/1981, p. 5). In a series of editorials published in *Jomhouri-ye Islami*, Asgar-Owladi— the Minister of Commerce and an influential member of the IRP—outlined the tasks of the "devout Muslim of the bazaar" by encouraging the bazaaris "to strengthen the Islamic Societies of the Bazaar and the formation of such Societies where there is none" (*Jomhouri-ye Islami*, 7 Urdibihisht 1360/1981, pp. 1, 3). Asgar-Owladi charged that the "counter-revolution and the hypocrites were spreading rumors aimed at the exclusion of the bazaar and for that matter the whole private sector from domestic and foreign trade, the exclusion of 'distribution cooperatives,' and the nationalization of all commercial transactions, domestic and foreign, whole-sale and retail" (*Jomhouri-ye Islami*, 15 Urdibihisht 1360/1981, p. 1). Finally, although the Islamic Republic disrupted some bazaar-based political organizations like SMGTB and Traders' Towhidi Guild, the process of the Islamization of society provided a favorable ideological context for the bazaaris to re-establish and revitalize their traditional organizations. In addition to the Committee on Guild Affairs, which was highly influential, the merchants set up other organizations like the Organization of Islamic Economy and the Interest Free Loan Fund, which allowed merchants to mobilize support against the foreign trade nationalization bill (*Rah-i Tudeh*, 27 Jan. 1984, p. 9).

The Iran–Iraq War

Shi'i revolutionary discourse contributed to the resolution of contention for power and class conflict in favor of the followers of Ayatollah Khomeini and the dominant classes. In turn, the victors channeled ideological discourse in a direction consonant with their interests. The Iran–Iraq War mediated this process by directing ideological debate away from the class and political issues raised by contenders for power, thereby influencing the outcomes of political and class conflict. While Shi'i revolutionary discourse was a factor in the outbreak of the war, it also mediated the war's influence on the reconstruction of the state and shaped the attitudes of the leaders of the Islamic Republic toward the war.

Historically, tension between Iraq and Iran revolved around two basic issues: (1) control over the Shatt-ul Arab waterway and (2) control over three strategic Gulf islands of Abu-Mousa and Greater and Lesser Tunbs. These disputes had never led to full-scale war. Indeed, political arrangements in the prerevolutionary period favored peaceful coexistence. The Iraqi regime did not have the military capability to confront the Shah's army, and, even if it had, the Gulf States would not have supported a war between the two countries: Saudi Arabia and Iran were partners in curbing revolutionary movements in the region; Kuwait preferred Iran over Iraq because of Iraq's territorial claim to Kuwait; the Sultan of Oman needed the Shah for his own protection; and Iran and Iraq needed each other's cooperation to control and suppress Kurdish demands for autonomy in both countries.

The Iranian Revolution suddenly changed the balance of forces in the region as the Shi'i revolutionary ideology began to affect neighboring states. In Saudi Arabia, about 200,000 Muslims of the Shi'i sect rioted, carrying signs hailing Ayatollah Khomeini. In Oman, it was reported that political dissent was growing in the northern provinces distinct from the struggle that had been going on in the Dhoffar province for many years (MERIP Reports, 1980; Abdulghani, 1984, pp. 193–200). Iraqi leaders viewed the Iranian Revolution with mounting anxiety. To make the matters worse, Ayatollah Baqir Sadr, Khomeini's counterpart in Najaf (Iraq) sent a congratulatory message to Khomeini, saying that "other tyrants have yet to see their day of reckoning," an apparent reference to Iraqi leaders (Hiro, 1985, p. 106). Khomeini then called upon Iraqis to overthrow the Baath regime. Because the Baathist Party was dominated by secular-minded Sunnis while 55 percent of the Iraqi population was Shi'i, the threat of a Shi'i uprising in Iraq was real. The threat of the Iranian Revolution and Iraq's desire for a leadership position in the Middle East, combined with Iran's military disorganization, prompted Iraq to seek to end the rule of the Ayatollah by military invasion (Falk, 1980; *U.S. News and World Report*, 1980, 6 Oct., pp. 24–29).

Preparation for the war, and the urgent need to defend Iran and the Revolution against the invading forces changed national priorities. It shifted attention away from the issues of democracy and freedom. Furthermore, on the grounds of maintaining unity among the people, Ayatollah Khomeini ordered the halt of land reform "temporarily." The war also provided an occasion to usurp the workers' right to strike. In February 1989, using the justification that the "citadel of Islam" was in danger because of "the war imposed by the United States and Iraq" and that there was an urgent need to increase production, the ruling clerics organized a gathering of the "representatives" of 170 Islamic associations of factories to condemn any form of labor strike (*Jomhouri-ye Islami*, 6 Isfand 1359/1981, p. 5). Finally, the war led to a further consolidation of IRP political power. The Revolutionary Guards (the armed wing of the IRP), previously under pressure to be dismantled or incorporated into the military, were demanding heavy weapons to fight the war, a demand that was gaining increasing support in the government because of the military's inability to resist the invading forces. The army was portrayed as an organ inherited from the old regime that could not be trusted. Although the ouster of Bani-Sadr and the subsequent purges of military personnel left no significant rival in the army, the Guards were trusted by the ulama and favored over the armed forces (Rose, 1984; Hickman, 1982). Most of the leaders of the Revolutionary Guards were related to the ulama, and their rank-and-file were mostly ethnic Persians. To mobilize volunteers to join the Revolutionary Guards, the IRP utilized the "Islamic fervor and Iranian nationalism" provoked by the invasion (MERI, 1985, pp. 20, 33). At the same time, the ulama set up the Ideological and Political Bureau of the Armed Forces to monitor the activities of military personnel. Soon the ulama were promoting their own men in the army. Indeed, "the military officers chosen for command positions were young, ambitious, motivated, and dedicated to Islam" (Hickman, 1982, p. 30).

Therefore, while the war expedited the concentration and centralization of power, supporting Skocpol's (1979) theory of postrevolutionary reconstruction of the state, the preparation for war by the leaders of the Islamic Republic, and the continuation of the war for nearly a decade cannot be fully understood without considering the role of Shi'i revolutionary discourse. The revolution was to go beyond Iran's borders to fight "world imperialism" (*istikbar-i jahani*), and Iraq's invasion of Iran produced another circumstance that the revolutionary ideology fed on. In Iran, the war was perceived as a plot engineered by the United States and executed by the Iraqi regime to destroy the Islamic Revolution. The leaders of the Islamic Republic were quick to pronounce that the war was a gift from the West that they had been expecting, and that given their historic revolutionary mission, they were proud to welcome it and meet the challenge of the counterrevolution. The leaders of the Islamic Republic pursued their objectives of overthrowing the Iraqi regime and establishing an Islamic Republic in Iraq, conquering Jerusalem and destroying Israel, and beating "the Great Satan" overseas. Because Saddam Hosein was portrayed as an infidel (*kafir*) and the agent of imperialism, any peace negotiation with him was tantamount to the betrayal of Iran and Islam (Bazargan, 1984, pp. 154–58). The self-fulfilling prophecy that a contradiction existed between Islam and the West was confirmed.

CONCLUSION

I began by questioning the adequacy of the major existing models to explain the role of Shi'i ideology in the Iranian Revolution. As an alternative model, I conceptualized ideology as episodic discourse: a set of general principles, concepts, symbols, and rituals that humans use to address the problems of a particular historical period. This conception of ideology differs from conceptions that treat ideology as a set of ideas internalized by actors or connected to interests. To specify the connection between ideology and revolution, I distinguished two principle aspects of the revolutionary process: revolution as content and revolution as a mode. While emphasizing the significance of the content of revolutionary change, I argued that the dominant role of revolutionary ideology in shaping human action makes revolution an historically distinctive phenomenon. Above and beyond its content, revolution is a unique mode of social action that differs from routine social actions.

Islamic revolutionary discourse was not simply a pre-existing ideology resting on the political theory of Shi'ism or ulama institutional development, ready to be used by discontented groups and classes against the Shah. Rather, it was produced by diverse ideologues as a result of the dialectic between the state and its opponents in a broad episodic context. To demonstrate this, I contrasted the post-coup (1953) period with the national-democratic episode ushered in with the Allies' invasion of Iran in 1941. The coup ended the national-democratic episode and the subsequent events undermined secular ideologies and promoted the production and growth of Islamic revolutionary discourse within the opposition. Therefore, although the ideology of the state under Reza Shah and under his son, Mohammad Reza Shah. was similar, Reza Shah's secular and anticlerical policies did not lead to the rise of Islamic opposition because the Shah's cultural policies and the dominant cultural trend in society belonged to the same ideological universe. Under his son, in contrast, the state ideology and the dominant ideological movement within the opposition began to diverge and by the late 1970s the ideology of the monarchy and Islamic opposition were two mutually negating discourses. Revolutionary Islam autonomously contributed to the Iranian Revolution by transforming the economic difficulties of the 1970s into a revolutionary crisis. This role was significant because prerevolutionary Iran did not experience serious economic and political crises. During the revolutionary mobilization of 1977–9 the religious calendar, rituals, and symbols facilitated communication among participants and provided occasions for demonstrations against the Shah. Finally, in the postrevolutionary period, Islamic discourse affected the outcome of contention for power and class conflict. Shi'i discourse was a factor in the outbreak of the war and mediated the effect of the war on the reconstruction of the state. The war, in turn, directed the course of ideological debate away from class issues and the issues of democracy and individual freedom raised by the rival groups.

The Iranian case has implications for sociological theories of revolution. The social psychological and structural–functional theories of revolution rest on the notion of a discontinuity between a revolutionary and a routine contention for power. In contrast, organizational and conflict theories of revolution reject such a notion and emphasize that revolutionary action is a form of resource mobilization similar in logic to routine contention for power. However, my analysis modifies this claim. Because revolution is a mode, there is an important difference between revolutionary and routine contentions for power. Revolutionary action is dictated by a revolutionary ideology, and economic and political considerations play a secondary role. The availability of resources in a revolution is important, but, as the Iranian case demonstrates, groups that succeed are often those whose actions are consistent with the dynamic of ideology. It is not simply that ideology contributes to the resources of certain groups vis-à-vis others, but rather the resources themselves are constituted through discourse.

The contribution of ideology to the cause of revolution may vary from case to case. For future research, analysis of the rise of revolutionary ideology should consider the broad episodic context in which it emerges, including changes in the economy and class relations; the international context, including not only the world economy and interstate system but also the nature of international ideological relations; and the relationships between the state and civil society. Because revolutionary ideology arises within the context of a dialectic between the state and its opposition, the ideology of the state is an important clue to understanding the kind of ideology most likely to become the ideology of the opposition. The probability of the emergence of a revolutionary ideology is enhanced if the state ideology and the dominant cultural trends in civil society belong to different ideological universes. Finally, consideration should be given to the basic themes, ritual performances, and symbolic structures of the revolutionary ideology. These parameters determine the internal dynamics of ideology as they shape human actions and limit the options available to diverse actors.

Notes

1. I am grateful to Ervand Abrahamian, Joseph Elder, Richard Lachmann, Karen Sacks, Stuart Karabenick, and Milton Yinger for their comments and criticisms. Comments by the nine anonymous reviewers for the *American Sociological Review* is also gratefully appreciated. A shorter version of this essay was presented at the 1991 annual meeting of the American Sociological Association in Cincinnati, Ohio. This research was partially supported by a fellowship from the National Endowment for the Humanities.
2. Shi'ism is a religious sect in Islam, predominantly the Twelver Shi'i, which recognizes twelve religious leaders (*Imam*), after Prophet Mohammad. The first is Imam Ali Ebn-i Abi Talib, the Prophet's cousin and son-in-law, who is believed to be the true successor of Mohammad, and the last is Imam Mohammad al-Mehdi, the messiah, who is believed to be in Occultation, absented from the physical plane but will reappear someday to solve humanity's problems. In this essay, revolutionary Shi'ism and revolutionary Islam are used interchangeably.

References

Abdulghani, Jasim M. (1984) *Iraq and Iran: The Years of Crisis* (Baltimore, MD: John Hopkins University Press).
Abrahamian, Ervand (1982) *Iran: Between Two Revolutions* (Princeton University Press).
Adami'yat, Fereydoun (1976) *Idi'olozhi-ye Nahzat-i Mashrutiyat-i Iran* (The Ideology of the Constitutional Movement in Iran) (Tehran, Iran: Payam Publications).
Adami'yat, Fereydoun (1981) *Shourish bar Imtiyaz' name-ye Rizhi* (Rebellion Against the Regie Concession) (Tehran, Iran: Payam Publications).
Adams, Charles C. (1968) *Islam and Modernism in Egypt* (New York: Russell & Russell).
Ahmad, Aziz (1967) *Islamic Modernism in India and Pakistan: 1857–1964* (London: Oxford University Press).

Akhavi, Shahrough (1980) *Religion and Politics in Contemporary Iran* (Albany: State University of New York Press).

Ale-Ahmad, Jalal (n.d.) *Dar Khedmat va Khianat-i Rowshanfikran* (Concerning the Service and Betrayal of the Intellectuals) (Tehran, Iran: Ravaq Publications).

Ale-Ahmad, Jalal (1982) *Plagued by the West* (*Gharbzadegi*), translated by Paul Sprachman (New York: Columbia University Press).

Alexander, Bobby C. (1991) "Correcting Misinterpretations of Turner's Theory: An African-American Pentecostal Illustration," *Journal for the Scientific Study of Religion*, vol. 30, pp. 26–44.

Algar, Hamid (1969) *Religion and State in Modern Iran* (Berkeley: University of California Press).

Althusser, Louis (1971) *Lenin and Philosophy* (London: New Left Books).

Apter, David (ed.) (1964) *Ideology and Discontent* (New York: Free Press).

Arendt, Hannah (1958) *The Origins of Totalitarianism* (Cleveland: Meridian Books).

Arjomand, Said Amir (1988) *The Turban for the Crown: The Islamic Revolution in Iran* (Oxford University Press).

Ashraf, Ahmad (1361/1982) "Dihqanan, Zamin va Inqilab" (Peasants, Land and Revolution), in *Masael-i Arzi va Dihqani* (Agrarian and Peasant Problems) (Tehran, Iran: Agah Publications).

Ashraf, Ahmad and Ali Banuazizi (1985) "The State, Classes and Modes of Mobilization in the Iranian Revolution," *State, Culture, and Society*, vol. 1, pp. 3–40.

Azad, Shahrzad (1980) "Workers' and Peasants' Councils in Iran," *Monthly Review*, vol. 32, no. 5, pp. 14–29.

Bakhash, Shaul (1984) *The Reign of the Ayatollahs: Iran and the Islamic Revolution* (New York: Basic Books).

Bank Markazi Iran (1976) *Annual Report and Balance Sheet* (Tehran, Iran).

Bazargan, Mehdi (1984) *Inqilab-i Iran dar Du Harakat* (The Iranian Revolution in Two Stages) (Tehran, Iran: Mehdi Bazargan).

Brun, Thiery and Rene Dumont (1978) "Iran: Imperial Pretensions and Agricultural Dependence," *Middle East Research and Information Project Reports*, vol. 8, no. 8, pp. 15–20.

Burawoy, Michael (1980) "The Politics of Production and Production of Politics: A Comparative Analysis of Piecework Machine Shops in the United States and Hungary," in M. Zeitlin (ed.), *Political Power and Social Theory* (Greenwich, CT: JAI Press).

Butterworth, Charles E. (1982) "Prudence Versus Legitimacy: The Persistent Theme in Islamic Political Thought," in A. E. Hillal Dessouki (ed.), *Islamic Resurgence in the Arab World* (New York: Praeger).

Cantril, Hadley (1941) *The Psychology of Social Movements* (New York: John Wiley & Sons).

Correspondence (1982) "Correspondence Respecting the Persian Tobacco Concession," *Sessional Papers*, vol. 79 (London: British Government).

Davani, Ali (1980) *Nahzat-i Rohaniyun-i Iran* (The Movement of the Clergy in Iran), vol. 9 (Tehran, Iran: Imam Reza).

Davies, James C. (1962) "Toward a Theory of Revolution," *American Sociological Review*, vol. 27, pp. 5–18.

Dion, Leon (1959) "Political Ideology as a Tool of Functional Analysis in Socio-Political Dynamics: An Hypothesis," *Canadian Journal of Economics and Political Science*, vol. 25, pp. 47–59.

Dshawanshir, Farajullah M. (1980) *Tajrebeh-ye Bistto Hasht-i Mordad* (The Experience of Twenty Eight of Mordad) (Tehran, Iran: Tuden).

Falk, Richard (1980) "America's Pro-Iraqi Neutrality," *The Nation*, vol. 231 (25 Oct.), pp. 398–401.

Fedai'yan (1982) *Tahlili az Hoqouq-i Senfi va Shurai-ye Kargaran va Zahmatkashan dar Jomhouri-ye Islami-ye Iran* (An Analysis of the Conditions of Workers and Toilers under the Islamic Republic of Iran). Released by the Organization of the Iranian People's Fedai'yan, Tehran, Iran.

Fischer, Michael M. J. (1980) *Iran: From Religious Dispute to Revolution* (Cambridge, MA: Harvard University Press).

Fulbrook, Mary (1983) *Piety and Politics: Religion and the Rise of Absolutism in England, Wurttemberg and Prussia* (Cambridge University Press).

Furet, François (1981) *Interpreting the French Revolution* (Cambridge University Press).

Geertz, Clifford (1973) *The Interpretation of Culture.* (New York: Basic Books).

Graham, Robert (1979) *Iran: The Illusion of Power* (New York: St. Martin's Press).

Gurr, Tedd R. (1970) *Why Men Rebel* (Princeton University Press).

Hairi, Abdul Hadi (1977) *Shi'ism and Constitutionalism in Iran* (Leiden, Netherlands: E. J. Brill).

Halliday, Fred (1979) *Iran: Dictatorship and Development* (Harmondsworth: Penguin).

Hickman, William F. (1982) *Ravaged and Reborn: The Iranian Army* (Washington, DC: The Brookings Institution).

Hiro, Dilip (1985) *Iran Under the Ayatollahs* (London: Routledge and Kegan Paul).

Huntington, Samuel (1968) *Political Order in Changing Societies* (New Haven, CT: Yale University Press).

Islamic Republic (1979) *Qanoun-i Asasi-ye Jombouri-ye Islami* (The Constitution of the Islamic Republic) (Tehran, Iran: Government of the Islamic Republic).

Issawi, Charles (1971) *The Economic History of Iran, 1800–1914* (Chicago: University of Chicago Press).

Ittila'at (Information) (1356/1978), 17 Dey.

Ittila'at (1359/1980) 7 and 20 Farvardin.

Ittila'at (1359/1980) 2 Urdibihisht.

Ittila'at (1360/1981) 6, 7, 10 and 11 Aban.

Ittila'at (1361/1982) 23 Urdibihisht.

Ittila'at (1361/1982) 6 Azar.

Ittila'at (1362/1983) 20 and 31 Farvardin.

Jazani, Bijan (1978) *Tarh-i Jame-eh Shenasi va Estratejik-i Enqilabi-ye Iran* (A Sociological and Strategic Scheme for the Revolutionary Movement in Iran) (Tehran, Iran: The Organization of the Iranian People's Fedai'yan Guerilla).

Johnson, Chalmers (1964) *Revolution and the Social System* (Palo Alto, CA: The Hoover Institution, Stanford University).
Johnson, Chalmers (1966) *Revolutionary Change* (Boston: Little Brown).
Jomhouri-ye Islami (Islamic Republic) (1358/1979) 9 Aban.
Jomhouri-ye Islami (1359/1980) 30 Farvardin.
Jomhouri-ye Islami (1359/1980) 11 Khurdad.
Jomhouri-ye Islami (1359/1980) 1 Urdibihisht.
Jomhouri-ye Islami (1359/1981) 6 Isfand.
Jomhouri-ye Islami (1360/1981) 7, 15 and 22 Urdibihisht.
Jomhouri-ye Islami (1360/1981) 10 Tir.
Kar (Labor) (1359/1980) 8 Mehr (Tehran, Iran: Organization of the Iranian People's Fedai'yan Guerilla).
Kar (1359/1980) 6 Azar (Tehran, Iran: The Organization of the Iranian People's Fedai'yan Guerilla).
Kasravi, Ahmad (1348/1969) *Din Va Siyasat* (Religion and Politics), 2nd edn (Tehran, Iran).
Kayhan (The World) (1362/1983) 6 Shahrivar.
Kazemi, Farhad (1980) *Poverty and Revolution in Iran* (New York: New York University Press).
Kazemi, Farhad and Ervand Abrahamian (1978) "The Non-Revolutionary Peasantry of Modern Iran," *Iranian Studies*, vol. 11, pp. 259–304.
Keddie, Nikkie R. (1972) "The Roots of Ulama Power in Modern Iran," in N. R. Keddie (ed.), *Scholars, Saints and Sufis* (Los Angeles: University of California Press).
Keddie, Nikkie R. (1981) *Roots of Revolution: An Interpretive History of Modern Iran* (New Haven, CT: Yale University Press).
Khomeini, Ruholla (1981) *Islam and Revolution: Writing and Declaration of Imam Khomeini*, translated and annotated by H. Algar (Berkeley, CA: Mizan Press).
Kornhauser, William (1959) *The Politics of Mass Society* (Glencoe, IL: Free Press).
Larrain, Jorge (1983) *Marxism and Ideology* (London: Macmillan).
Lenin, V. I. (1977) "What Is to Be Done? Burning Questions of Our Movement," in V. Jerome (ed.), *Collected Works*, vol. 5, translated by J. Fineberg and G. Hanna (New York: International Publishers).
Levin, N. Gordon, Jr (1970) *Woodrow Wilson and World Politics* (New York: Oxford University Press).
Markaz-i Amar-i Iran (1983) *Amar-i Kargah'ha-ye Buzurg-i San'ati-ye Sal-i 1360* (Statistics for Large Industrial Establishments in 1981) (Tehran, Iran: Islamic Republic of Iran).
Marsot, Afaf Lutfi (1977) *Egypt's Liberal Experiment: 1922–1936* (Los Angeles: University of California Press).
Marwell, Gerald and Pamela Oliver (1984) "Collective Action Theory and Social Movement Research," in Louis Kriesberg (ed.), *Research in Social Movements, Conflicts and Change* (Greenwich, CT: JAI).
Marx, Karl and Frederick Engels (1975) "The Holy Family," in *Collected Works*, vol. 4. (New York: International Publishers).
Marx, Karl and Frederick Engels (1976) "The German Ideology," in *Collected Works*, vol. 5 (New York: International Publishers).

Middle East Research and Information Project (MERIP Reports) (1980) vol. 10 (November).

Middle East Research Institute (MERI) (1985) University of Pennsylvania, *Report, Iran* (London: Croom Helm).

Moaddel, Mansoor (1986) "The Shi'i Ulama and the State in Iran," *Theory and Society*, vol. 15, pp. 519–56.

Moaddel, Mansoor (1989) "State-Centered versus Class-Centered Perspectives in International Politics: The Case of U.S. and British Participation in the 1953 Coup Against Premier Mosaddeq in Iran," *Studies in Comparative International Development*, vol. 24, pp. 3–22.

Mojahed (1364/1985) no. 219 (Paris: The Organization of the Iranian People's Mojahedin).

Mojahedin (1981) *Varshekastegy-ye Tarikhi-ye Darki Khordeh Bourgeoisie Az Islam* (The Historical Bankruptcy of the Petty Bourgeois Understanding of Islam) (Long Beach, CA: The Muslim Student Society).

Nashat, Guity (1983) *Women and Revolution in Iran* (Boulder, CO: Westview Press).

Nateq, Homa (1983) "Sar Aghaz-i Eqtedar-i Eqtesadi va Siasi-ye Mollayan" (The Beginning of the Political and Economic Dominance of the Clergy), *Alefba*, vol. 2, pp. 40–57.

Neuhouser, Kevin (1989) "The Radicalization of the Brazilian Catholic Church in Comparative Perspective," *American Sociological Review*, vol. 54, pp. 233–44.

Nik-A'een (1359/1980) *Dar Bareh-ye Mas'aleh-ye Arzi va Jonbesh-i Dihghani dar Iran* (On the Problem of Land and Peasant Movement in Iran) (Tehran, Iran: Organization of Democratic Youth and Students of Iran).

Pahlavi, Mohammad Reza (1961) *Mission for My Country* (New York: McGraw Hill).

Pahlavi, Mohammad Reza (1967) *The White Revolution*, 2nd edn (Tehran, Iran: Imperial Pahlavi Library).

Pahlavi, Mohammad Reza (1980) *Answer to History* (New York: Stein and Day).

Parsa, Misagh (1989) *Social Origins of the Iranian Revolution* (New Brunswick, NJ: Rutgers University Press).

Przeworski, Adam (1980) "Material Bases of Consent: Economics and Politics in a Hegemonic System," in M. Zeitlin (ed.), *Political Power and Social Theory* (Greenwich, CT: JAI Press).

Rabinovich, Itmar (1972) *Syria Under the Ba'th: 1963–66* (Jerusalem: Israel University Press).

Rah-i Tudeh (The People's Way) (1984) 27 January.

Richard, Yann (1981) "Contemporary Shi'i Thought," in N. R. Keddie (ed.), *Roots of Revolution: An Interpretive History of Modern Iran* (New Haven, CT: Yale University Press).

Rose, Gregory (1983) "Velayat-e Faqih and the Recovery of Islamic Identity in the Thought of Ayatollah Khomeini," in N. R. Keddie (ed.), *Religion and Politics in Iran: Shi'ism from Quietism to Revolution* (New Haven, CT: Yale University Press).

Rose, Gregory (1984) "The Post-Revolutionary Purge of Iran's Armed Forces: A Revisionist Assessment," *Iranian Studies*, vol. 17, pp. 153–94.

Savory, Roger M. (1979) "The Problem of Sovereignty in an Ithna Ashari ('Twelver') Shi'i State," *Middle East Review*, vol. 11, no. 4, pp. 5–11.

Schwartz, David C. (1971) "A Theory Revolutionary Behavior," in J. C. Davies (ed.), *When Men Revolt and Why* (New York: Free Press).

Seale, Patrick (1965) *The Struggle for Syria: A Study of Post War Arab Politics: 1945–58* (New York: Oxford University Press).

Shari'ati, Ali' (1969) *Eslamshenasi* (Islamology), (Mashhad, Iran: Tous).

Shari'ati, Ali' (1980) *Marxism and Other Western Fallacies: An Islamic Critique*, translated by R. Campbell (Berkeley, CA: Mizan Press).

Shari'ati, Ali' (1986) *What Is To Be Done*, translated by A. Alidust and F. Rajaee (Houston, TX: Institute for Research on Islamic Studies).

Skocpol, Theda (1979) *States and Social Revolutions: A Comparative Analysis of France, Russia, and China* (New York: Cambridge University Press).

Skocpol, Theda (1985) "Cultural Idioms and Political Ideologies in the Revolutionary Reconstruction of State Power: A Rejoinder to Sewell," *Journal of Modern History*, vol. 57, pp. 86–96.

Smelser, Neil J. (1963) *Theory of Collective Behavior* (New York: Free Press).

Stepan, Alfred (1985) "State Power and the Strength of Civil Society in the Southern Cone of Latin America," in P. B. Evans, D. Rueschemeyer and T. Skocpol (eds), *Bringing the State Back In* (New York: Cambridge University Press).

Swidler, Ann (1986) "Culture in Action: Symbols and Strategies," *American Sociological Review*, vol. 51, pp. 273–86.

Tabari, Azar and Nahid Yeganeh (1982) *In the Shadow of Islam: The Women's Movement in Iran* (London: Zed Press).

Tabari, Ehsan (1977) *Jame'eh-i Iran dar Douran-i Reza Shah* (The Iranian Society Under Reza Shah) (Iran: Tudeh).

Thaiss, Gustav (1971) "The Bazaar as a Case Study of Religion and Social Change," in E. Yarshater (ed.), *Iran Faces the Seventies* (New York: Praeger).

Therborn, Goran (1980) *The Ideology of Power and the Power of Ideology* (London: Verso).

Tilly, Charles (1975) "Revolution and Collective Violence," in F. I. Greenstein and N. W. Polsby (eds), *Handbook of Political Science* (Reading, MA: Addison-Wesley).

Tilly, Charles (1978) *From Mobilization to Revolution* (Reading, MA: Addison-Wesley).

Toch, Hans (1965) *The Social Psychology of Social Movements* (New York: Bobbs-Merrill).

Turner, Bryan S. (1974) *Weber and Islam* (Boston: Routledge & Kegan Paul).

Turner, Victor (1967) *The Forest of Symbols: Aspects of Ndembu Ritual* (Ithaca, NY: Cornell University Press).

Ummat (Islamic Community) (1358/1980) 5 Isfand.

Ummat (1358/1980) 10 Bahman.

Ummat (1359/1981) 22 Dey.

Ummat (1359/1981) 24 Dey.

U.S. News and World Report (1980) "U.S. Stake in Mideast War," 6 Oct., pp. 24–9.

Watt, Montgomery (1960) "Shi'ism Under the Umayyads," *Journal of the Royal Asiatic Society*, parts 3 and 4, pp. 158–72.

Wuthnow, Robert (1985) "State Structures and Ideological Outcomes," *American Sociological Review*, vol. 50, pp. 799–821.

Wuthnow, Robert (1989) *Communities of Discourse: Ideology and Social Structure in the Reformation, the Enlightenment, and European Socialism* (Cambridge, MA: Harvard University Press).

Zabih, Sepehr (1979) *Iran's Revolutionary Upheaval: An Interpretive Essay* (San Francisco, CA: Alchemy Books).

Zaret, David (1985) *The Heavenly Contract: Ideology and Organization in Pre-Revolutionary Puritanism* (Chicago: University of Chicago Press).

Zaret, David (1989) "Religion and the Rise of Liberal-Democratic Ideology in 17th-Century England," *American Sociological Review*, vol. 54, pp. 163–79.

11 AIDS, the Politically Correct and Social Theory*

Daniel Harris

"PC": DILEMMAS AND CONTRADICTIONS

When the San Francisco AIDS Foundation launched a refreshingly brash safe-sex campaign targeted at young gay men, they received as much flak from the left as from the right for a series of posters, displayed at bus stops around the city, featuring two androgynous men, draped in an American flag, who smiled directly out at us, naked, life-size and in sensuous color. While most of those who were disturbed by these innocuous, if blatantly homoerotic, images objected to the desecration of the flag by "pervert[s] ... [who] do not deserve the great privilege of being Americans," as one irate San Francisco resident put it, an entirely unexpected criticism arose from within the gay community itself, as excerpts from the following letter, published in the local gay newspaper, *The Bay Area Reporter*, suggest:

> My outrage does not arise from the moralistic sensibilities of Jesse Helms, but from the disenfranchisement I feel and been [sic] subjected to as a woman, an Asian American and a lesbian. I am no longer willing to be the 'silent majority' in any of these categories nor am I willing to be silent when I see other peoples being subjected to the same racism and sexism I have experienced ... the [San Francisco AIDS Foundation] uses the American flag and two stereotypical White All-American looking males ... The Asian gay man, Black gay man, Hispanic gay man,

* Retitled essay combining two essays by Daniel Harris: "What Is the Politically Correct?," *Salmagundi*, no. 90–91 (Spring–Summer, 1991), pp. 45–55; and "AIDS and Theory," *Lingua Franca: The Review of Academic Life* (June 1991), pp. 1, 16–19.

substance user of any color and heterosexual female of any color are also at risk. . . . Where are the Black men wrapped in an American flag? Where are the Hispanic men wrapped in an American flag? Where are the Asian men wrapped in the American flag? Where is the heterosexual couple wrapped in the American flag? This new safe-sex campaign is dangerous to gay men of color, substance users of any color, and to heterosexual couples of any color.

In the flurry of vitriolic responses printed in the issue of the following week (which referred to the author of the above as everything from a "moralistic pig" to just plain "scum"), the photographer of the series himself wrote in to lambaste her for an unforgivable racial oversight on *her* part: that one of the men included was actually a light-skinned Hispanic. Another respondent diligently beat her at her own game when he excoriated her for sexism and homophobia directed against a disenfranchised minority that she herself neglected, "gay white males," who, as he pointed out, still comprise 90 percent of the cases in San Francisco. To complicate the racial and sexual dynamics of the controversy even further, his attack fell short of its mark when one of the models in the poster, presumably aghast at the disquieting possibility that the AIDS Foundation's campaign could inflict irreparable damage on future modeling prospects, leaked to the press that, even though he looked gay in the photograph, he was in actuality a heterosexual. If there's a lesson to be learned from this troubling instance of in-house skirmishing, it's that no one group will ever prevail in its attempt to claim exclusive squatter's rights on prime property in the treacherous and ever-shifting terrain of the politically correct until we call a truce in the fashionable game of minority one-upmanship.

Although the politically correct is almost impossible to avoid, it is difficult to define, perhaps because we are somewhat unfairly predisposed against it from the outset. In a society that is not only apolitical but vigorously antipolitical, activism as a whole is often denigrated as a ridiculous charade performed by a self-serving group of purists who, like the Princess Casamassima, are in it for the illicit thrill of self-negation. Our contempt for the reigning political orthodoxies is so strong that the suspicion even arises that what we detest in this righteous bickering about the oppressed is in fact something intrinsically ridiculous in ourselves – our ineffectuality and our inability to take political initiative in a world in which we have relinquished power to a special class of bureaucrats. Before I go on to examine the purpose and utility of this relatively recent strain of censoriousness, I offer for the sake of clarity one further example of what it is, of its occasionally alarming zealotry, and then two contrasting examples of what it is not.

First, an instance of the way the activism inspired by unquestioning allegiance to the "pc," as it is often derisively abbreviated, leads to extremism. Several years ago an upscale San Francisco card shop called "Does Your Mother Know" stocked a birthday card that represented a group of barefoot, antebellum black children above a caption reading "If You Get Somethin' for Your Birthday, Can I Have It?" Posters of this image, with a text accusing the store of racism, began appearing around town on lamp posts. If the card was indeed racist (and certainly it tacitly exploited the iconography of the pickaninny), its use of these children, with their beseeching faces, raggedy clothes and gangly, prepubescent bodies, was probably intended to be more endearing than satiric or patronizing. But however virulent and offensive the bigotry it unconsciously betrayed, it surely didn't merit the boycotting, leafletting and, ultimately, picketing held outside the shop until the bewildered owner and his disgusted black clerk, who scoffed at the protests as shameless grandstanding, relented, apologized and, within a week, removed the offending card from the racks.

Two instances of the politically *in*correct provide an illuminating foil to these examples of the pedantry and priggishness that often link both the tactics and objectives of various sectors of the left with fanatics on the right, Andrea Dworkin with Phyllis Schlafly, the Reverend Al Sharpton with Jesse Helms. Deliberately organized as a vicious broadside against the perceived humorlessness of the pc, the student-curated "Straight White Male Show", held at the San Francisco Art Institute, elicited a barrage of angry criticism from the "Coalition of Degenerate Artists," which denounced it with hilarious solemnity for its jeering disrespect for "multi-cultural, gay, lesbian and women's concerns." The sole criterion for admission into the harmless burlesque of exclusionary politics (which the right wing is constantly reviling as an unconscionable form of racism in reverse) was that the artist had to be a Caucasian heterosexual male – in the eyes of many, the consummate martyr of the contemporary art agenda.

Virtually at the same time this controversy flared up (and then just as quickly fizzled out), "Saturday Night Live," the popular late-night television show of 'hip' comedy and satire, threw itself into a much more disturbing fray when it announced that it had invited the scurrilous stand-up comedian Andrew Dice Clay to host one of its forthcoming shows. Like Eddie Murphy's savage and gratuitously sadistic humor, Clay's truly objectionable taunting of homosexuals, women, fat people and the handicapped is fixated on the pc, whose linguistic taboos he dismantles with as much sacrilegious carnage as he can. In the course of his routine we are forced to watch a kind of ideological cannibalism, as if he were chewing with his mouth open all of the forbidden words and prejudices that only a licensed buffoon can utter with impunity. Disaffected members of the cast refused to appear on the show and many others protested (with good reason in this instance), but that evening's ratings soared so high that they surpassed the best that the program had ever received.

Why are these sudden eruptions of the politically incorrect (which are usually seen in an off-color remark but which occasionally seize an entire community such as Bensonhurst or Howard Beach) in one sense inevitable and, in another, necessary? At least part of the answer lies in the inadequate ways in which the majority of Americans, including the left, have dealt psychologically with integration. Glossing over, rather than confronting, social complexities, the pc is rooted in a typically middle-class response to the disorienting phenomenon of ethnic diversity: the innocuous panacea of reducing the relations between various antagonistic groups to a simple matter of etiquette, to saying, rather than thinking, the right thing and thinking, rather than doing, the wrong. If the examples I have given of how outraged we can be about a poster and a birthday card are any indication, all that feminism, gay liberation and the civil-rights movement have taught us is to watch what we say, to curb our tongues and to cringe before a new and distinctly menacing sense of decorum, of what we are permitted to air in public without trampling on the feelings of the minorities we welcome among us, not with genuine acceptance, but with a frozen smile that masks a discomfort with racial differences that we must never openly reveal.

In a culture that substitutes politeness for tolerance, silence and repression are our answer to the stress of ethnic pluralism. Our daily lives have become so constrained with anxieties about potential faux pas that it has become almost impolite to mention someone's color or sexual orientation in his or her presence, with the result that the only political achievement we have made at the most fundamental level of American consciousness is the institutionalization of distrust and caution. The discussion of ethnic issues has thus been fractured between the public forum (which we have painstakingly depoliticized in order to avoid insulting others) and the private forum of our own homes (in which we escape the stranglehold of these new social prohibitions in the presence of members of our race and class). In other words, the contemporary focus on semantics and protocol guarantees the introversion as opposed to the control and eventual elimination of bigotry. We internalize and quarantine our prejudices in the private circle in which they are acceptable, and in the process we create the ideologically antiseptic no-man's land of the business world, an eerie, intellectually inert neutral zone in which the races coexist in a fragile détente that we have achieved through etiquette rather than understanding, through silence rather than debate, through repression rather than dialogue.

And thus the necessity for these cathartic purges in which the politically incorrect is released amidst all of the brittle taboos that we have introduced into public discourse. Even if unconsciously, we despise the hair shirt of timidity and reticence that we are forced to wear as part of a new, disingenuous social code, the retrograde and superficial accommodation we have made to three decades of minority-rights movements – an accommodation that serves only to heighten, not diminish, our resentment of cultural differences. Just as obsessive dieting makes us hate our bodies so that we are constantly in danger of binging, so excessive sensitivity about offending minorities creates not respect or understanding, but the hostility and bitterness that culminate in bigoted scatologists such as Andrew Dice Clay rushing into the depoliticized public forum to shriek out all of the bad words upon which we have imposed such an inhibiting moratorium. In that incendiary moment when the satirist heaves all of our prejudices onto the pyre he has raised in a forum in which they have been previously outlawed, we delight in gutting the artificial divisions we make between our public personas and our private beliefs. In this sense the politically correct provokes and unleashes, rather than monitors or contains, the politically incorrect.

An entire subculture, the pc itself, has grown up around this rigidly enforced closeting of racial and sexual phobias, this rictus grin of anxiously conciliatory professionalism. The extraordinary irony about run-of-the-mill liberal attitudes towards minorities is that, far from being an expression of an advanced and forward-looking counterculture, they rise out of, and are nourished by, the culture of repression that they ostensibly oppose. The pedantic politics implicit in the more exotic antics of contemporary activists are the concentrated essence of the new etiquette we have instituted out of our fear and intolerance of social differences. The pc is best understood as the body of rules and civilities that one small faction of the left has codified into Holy Writ and then implemented with the proselytizing fervor of an evangelical sect for the sake of minimizing (or at least camouflaging) conflict and achieving specious harmony with various destabilizing components of the population by scrupulously adhering to a "correct" and socially inoffensive form of behavior. Just as etiquette teaches us to use the "correct" fork, so the pc teaches us to use the "correct" phraseology – "Asian" rather than "Oriental," "Afro-American" rather than "black."

In an era that has taken the easy way out and driven inward our insecurities about diversity, the duties of the pc are essentially janitorial and cosmetic in that its whole purpose is to sanitize discourse and to sweep under the carpet all visible traces of racism, sexism and homophobia. Not coincidentally, of the four examples noted above, three of them involved controversies about images: a poster, a birthday card and an art show. This compulsive and at times implacable caviling about what we are permitted to see – and occasionally, as in the case of Andrew Dice Clay, to hear – in public often reduces the efforts of even the most well-intentioned liberal groups to a trivialized form of pictorial and linguistic activism mired in the token politics of words and images. Although the radical posturing of members of the pc would lead us to believe that they are part of a visionary movement, a dissident underground that subverts the bigotries of the status quo, they actually march in lockstep with most Americans, whose concerns they share and interests they ultimately promote as the unwitting agents of a conservative ethnic agenda. As a self-appointed brigade of samaritans who follow after us disinfecting our terminology and tidying up our images, these ecologists of verbal and visual euphemisms serve a vital function as the custodians of a new and stifling sense of propriety.

That the pc is a manifestation of the dominant response of mainstream culture to ethnic tensions, as opposed to a manifestation of the irrelevant extremism of a subversive counterculture, is also apparent in the way that its adherents glamorize oppression. For many middle-class Americans, ethnic culture has become a colorful vacation spot in which the political tourist engages in diverting ideological sprees of self-negation. The politics of the pc are essentially the politics of the "other" in that they aestheticize, sentimentalize and, by necessity, *trivialize* the plight of disenfranchised groups by converting it into a form of chic. Only a member of the educated bourgeoisie can take such a radically external and nonimplicated view of oppression that it turns it into the opposite – a form of privilege and emancipation, as if quaint and bucolic minorities grazed peacefully in a pastoral idyll, at one with themselves, free of the burden of affluence and guilt whose onus their captivated admirers seek to relieve by exalting, and thus exploiting, ethnicity as an antidote to their own sense of culpability. For many of us the minority represents freedom from ourselves, a means of pacifying our shame about our economic and social good fortune (without, nonetheless, requiring us to relinquish the

298   *AIDS, the Politically Correct and Social Theory*

opportunities, luxuries and mobility our class affords). Given
that marginality and oppression are never glamorous for those
who are indeed marginal and oppressed, our romance of
life at the fringes of American society is by definition a fiction
that the majoritarian outsider, tormented by his own self-
incriminations, has created at the expense of the politically
and economically disadvantaged.

At their most doctrinaire the excited attempts of the radical
chic to deify the downtrodden often take us on a kind of
safari in which members of the white majority hunt down
the sacred cow of the most marginalized person, the ethnic
group with most strikes against it – the ultimate minority:
the "vertically-challenged" Jewish lesbian of color; the hear-
ing-impaired, bisexual, substance-abusing native American;
the handicapped Asian gay indigent cross-dresser. Oppression has become so glamorous and such an enviable condition (at least for those who are immune to its direct effects)
that a spirit of competition even prevails among educated
members of minorities who scrimmage acrimoniously to rack
up points on the "oppression count," that conversational
tournament held so frequently among members of the left
for the undisputed title of the most victimized minority of
all – the heterosexual woman vs the gay man, the gay man
vs the lesbian, the lesbian vs the Afro-American, the Afro-
American vs the native American, and on and on with one
group jousting with another for the privilege of being the
most pitiably subjugated and "disempowered."

We have aestheticized marginality to such an extent that
the whole concept of the minority has been robbed of its
specificity and become an engulfing and inclusive paradigm
that is now applied to groups of peoples whose misfortunes
have no social or political ramifications whatsoever: fat people,
alcoholics, the uncircumcised, smokers, incest victims, love
addicts. In our minoritizing of the world we have essentially
become ethnic lepidopterists in that we chase after minorities like butterflies, which we add to our collections as a
tangible confirmation of our own righteousness. Yet another
irony thus emerges from the pride we take in our vast port-
folio of oppressions. Just as the censoriousness of the pc
derives from a conservative response to social tensions, so
the sentimentalizing of ethnic disadvantages also shows that

the politically correct is directly related to the politically incorrect: the bigot's desire to legislate segregation emerges from the same culture that glamorizes exclusion. In other words, in a way similar to that in which prejudice dehumanizes the group towards which its antipathy is directed, so the pc dehumanizes the object of its idolatry.

What psychological need does the aestheticizing of oppression fulfill for the majority of Americans and what is the reason for this anxious, almost imperialistic search to colonize new minorities, new groups that have been persecuted in new unsuspected ways? As mentioned above, the transformation of social disadvantage into a form of chic alleviates guilt among the middle class by changing oppression into a privilege, an enviable condition with its own peculiar cachet. But perhaps the most important function that the cult of the minority serves for the mainstream is self-flattery. Since the 1960s we have cast ourselves over and over again in the heroic role of the rescuer of the downtrodden in order to play out a self-adulating fantasy that we are knights in shining armor swooping down through the classes for the dramatic deliverance of the minority in distress. We have become so infatuated with this alluringly narcissistic scenario, this basic Rapunzel myth of scaling up the tower in order to emancipate the imprisoned ethnic damsel, that we have actually begun to invent minorities for the sole purpose of rescuing them. In light of our quixotic attempts to stake out, define and then rehabilitate new forms of ethnicity, it often seems that we build these dilapidated social hovels to enkennel the latest disenfranchised group in order to set them ablaze for the sheer pleasure of putting out the fire.

Although it is often difficult to say exactly what it is, the pc is clearly not just an agenda. Instead it is an encompassing life-style that is far more than just the sum of its issues but rather a way of living and consuming that has built up an entire economy that sustains a number of flourishing cottage industries. We deride the pc not only because its members are puritanical, humorless, doctrinaire, censorious and predictable, but also because they wear the same Birkenstocks, eat the same granola, go to the same Shiatsu masseur, buy the same organically grown produce, read the same leftist magazines, boycott the same products, wash their clothes with the same nonphosphate detergents and pursue the same kinds of liberating relationships. As a fully contained and protective ideological ghetto that offers its cloistered denizens the amenities of a complete social life, the pc at once creates the conditions for its own insularity and ensures minimum contact with the mainstream culture that it has demonized. Residing in the hermetic isolation of the internal squabbles of their own leadership, its adherents retreat further and further into their test-tube utopianism – their divisive, academic politics that seem so irrelevant to the racial and ethnic issues plaguing society at large.

Given that the pc smothers its proponents in edicts about everything from food to clothing, there is something distinctly problematic about the incessant attempts of activist groups to achieve in their own ranks the inclusiveness, democracy and parity of power that society at large has failed to achieve on such a demoralizingly grand scale. Are activist groups themselves as pluralistic and tolerant of cultural differences as their stated goals of diversity would suggest? Certainly the comprehensive life-style that has grown up around contemporary politics is anything but heterogeneous but rather is far more uniform and monolithic than mainstream capitalist culture itself. Moreover the actual membership of the pc, while often multicultural in a superficial sense (in that it includes educated members of many races and ethnic groups), is based on a fundamentally flawed and illusory kind of pluralism: a pluralism of sameness that flourishes on the affinities shared only by the educated and articulate representatives of minorities who are unified by the most leveling force of all in our culture – education. The composition of the pc is thus a paradox, an ethnic mirage, because it is essentially a coalition of unanimity, of the ideologically synonymous.

Despite this fact the pc persists in believing in its own respect for social differences, when in fact it would be truly pluralistic only if it included in its membership the poor and the uneducated, who by necessity it excludes: the crack dealer from the inner-city ghetto, the Hispanic gang member, the ancient Chinese street vendor who speaks no English or the Filipino drag-queen prostitute (none of whom could ever be classified – nor would they ever think of classifying themselves – as politically correct). In the confines of their own culturally monotonous vacuum, the tightly serried ranks of the educated elite have the luxury of nitpicking over minute technicalities of racial politesse (such as the absence of Hispanics and heterosexuals from a safe-sex poster for gay men or the presence of patronizing stereotypes in a birthday card sold in a chichi boutique), while out there in the real world we see the resurgence of widescale ethnic tensions in Bensonhurst, Boston and Howard Beach.

Which brings me to my final concern about a fashion in politics whose tactics I repudiate but whose social positions I subscribe to. As a writer and gay activist, my contact with the pc over the years has led me again and again to the disturbing realization, not only that its cliquishness demands rigid, totalitarian conformity of opinion, but that it is fundamentally *disrespectful* of cultural differences within society at large. It is a mistake to take literally its claims for pluralism and rainbow-coalition building, its anxious and often outlandish attempts to be uncompromisingly inclusive, swallowing up new minorities as fast as it can invent them, when it is clear how prescriptive the conditions for being admitted into its fold of the sanctimoniously like-minded really are. In fact, given the oppressive completeness of its life-style, the process of becoming politically correct for the member of an ethnic group essentially involves minority suicide, an act of obliteration and submersion in a culture so intolerant of differences of opinion and education that one is forced to slough off the habits one has been accustomed to since childhood in order to pledge allegiance to the established political orthodoxies. What's more, the kind of assimilation involved in a minority entering the radical chic is in every way as strict and self-annihilating as the assimilation that racial and ethnic groups are understandably afraid of experiencing as they are integrated into society at large. For all of its championing of the underdog, its punctilious taxonomy of the myriad flora and fauna of oppression, the pc is an undifferentiatedly monolithic political group that mandates, not the preservation, but the wholesale cooptation of minorities. In the very act of testifying to the value and, in some extreme instances, the hallowedness of ethnic diversity, the pc wipes it out among its own ranks. The defenders and apologists of social disparities themselves thus inadvertently offer appalling proof of how intolerant American culture is of heterogeneity and "otherness": the self-appointed guardians of ethnic differences, who have adopted multicultural politics as their platform, insist on creating for themselves a social enclave that is irreducibly, irretrievably uniform.

Although the preceding remarks were written nearly a year before the controversy arose over the disruptive effects of the politically correct on college campuses, they were published several months after two simultaneous cover stories on speech codes and and quotas in *Time* and *Newsweek* had elevated the issue to national attention. When the essay was published I had a feeling that, through an unfortunate accident of bad timing, it was anticlimactic. Because the debate has proven to be less ephemeral than it first appeared, however, I have had the opportunity to revisit many of the same questions in an essay entitled "AIDS and Theory." Reprinted below as a continuation of my commentary on the subject, it shows how the politically correct has dovetailed disastrously with postmodern literary theory to form an intellectual alliance that intensifies tenfold the cliquishness, insularity and linguistic priggishness of the pc movement.

AIDS AND PC: THE POSTMODERN ALLIANCE

Although critical theorists are so isolated from mainstream American culture that they have long been under what amounts to house arrest in English and comparative-literature departments, they have recently begun to branch out into subjects that have little to do with their specific training in literature. Their unconventional preoccupations and methodologies are proving to be infinitely applicable to society at large. In fact postmodern academic theorists have become ruthlessly appropriative, trying their hand at everything from nuclear disarmament to the beating of Rodney King, from physics to MTV.

Although the university has traditionally played host to political activists ranging from the rank and file of the antiapartheid movement to protesters against the Vietnam War, it is seldom that a school of thought originating within this increasingly marginalized institution has had a determinative effect on the very mechanism of social dissent – on the tactics and procedures by which change is sought. The flamboyant and controversial strategies of ACT UP, however, may be the first examples in history of the direct influence of academic theory on the actual policies of grassroots activists, whose intellectual obsessions have not only set the tenor of the organization's propaganda but have helped select both the specific sites and the occasions of its often ingenious *coups de théâtre*. From the rhetoric of critics such as Cindy Patton, who says that ACT UP (AIDS Coalition to Unleash Power) "provides an interesting example of emerging postmodern political praxis using deconstructionist analyses and tactics," to the methodology described by ACT UP spokesman Douglas Crimp, who maintains that the organization's graphic art addresses "questions of identity, authorship, and audience – and the ways in which all three are constructed through representation," the fight against AIDS is tainted with the faddish argot of postmodernism – linguistic evidence of the considerable leakage of esoteric theory out of the ivory tower into the public sphere. This unlikely mélange of politics and sloganeering, however, has not so much checked the ghettoization of the American university from mainstream though as it has extended this ghettoization to some of the most worthwhile aspects of the AIDS movement, serving to insulate vitally important forms of left-wing activism from the general public.

Take, for example, Lee Edelman's analysis of the ACT UP logo, a pink triangle resting above the equation "Silence = Death," the neat, algebraic epitaph that effectively serves as the crack-and-peel coat of arms of the splashiest and most cerebral form of AIDS activism. In "Politics, Literary Theory, and AIDS,"[1] Edelman claims that the analytical techniques of critical theorists give them a crucial edge over other experts in exposing the tendentious schemes of homophobic ideologues because their literary training enables them to plumb the depths of an epidemic rich in unsavory

connotations and destitute of plain, unembellished facts. He
writes:

> Precisely because the defensive appeal to literality in a
> slogan like Silence = Death must produce the literal *as a*
> *figure* of the need and desire for the shelter of certain
> knowledge, such a discourse is always necessarily a dan-
> gerously contaminated defense – contaminated by the
> Derridean logic of metaphor so that its attempt to achieve
> a natural or literal discourse beyond rhetoricity must re-
> produce the suspect ideology of reified (and threatened)
> identity marking the reactionary medical and political
> discourse it would counteract.

All of the mannerisms of recent trends in critical theory
are present in this passage: the Pinteresque circularity, the
zany periphrasis of words such as "literality" and "rhetoricity,"
the brief splash of italics intended to evoke the impression
of heated debate, and the leaden nominalism that saturates
this sentence with pompous generalities.

The addled abstractions of Edelman's often unintelligible
prose raise questions about how postmodernism could ever
contribute anything to the work of left-wing activists, who
are by and large impervious to its flirtatious overtures and
to its desperate forays into the public sphere in its theorists'
restless search for validation outside of academia.

One of the most concrete influences of academic discussions of AIDS on the procedures of urban activists lies in
the postmodern emphasis on the so-called construction of
the epidemic; that is, the ways in which a meaningless bio-
logical catastrophe has been invested with the various agendas and biases of the right wing or the medical establishment,
to name just two of the special-interest groups that have
exploited AIDS as a vehicle for their own moral and economic concerns. For theorists such as Paula Treichler, who
is particularly sensitive, and rightly so, to the techniques by
which the mass media have packaged the disease for the
American public, AIDS is less of an objective, epidemiologi-
cal phenomenon than a "social construction" comprising
"representational icons and discursive strategies" that mask
homophobia.[2] Similarly, for Douglas Crimp,[3] who asserts that
there is no empirically verifiable reality behind AIDS at all,

the only standard of truth in a world dominated by the spurious half-truths of conflicting "representations" is power – namely the success with which any one group appropriates the means of construction and thus foists its sectarian view on mainstream America.

For AIDS activists, this deconstructive skepticism manifests itself in the new interest not so much in circumventing as in manipulating the media, in seizing hold of the actual apparatus by which various moral interpretations of the disease are conveyed to the average consumer. The Media Committee of ACT UP, for example, has taken its cue from the White House and has gone so far as to prepare press kits, which it distributed, prior to several of its demonstrations, to eager reporters and television crews, who dutifully plagiarized this material, ultimately reporting what was "sold" to them in advance, "almost like a Hollywood movie."[4]

Although this cagey ability to outflank the media has served ACT UP well in forcing the hand of criminally negligent institutions such as the FDA, academic theory has, in my view, hobbled the organization intellectually. Rather than simply inspiring legitimate efforts to undermine the misogyny, racism and homophobia of the monolithic media establishment, it has fomented a totalitarian zeal to "wrest control of the public discussion of AIDS,"[5] to grandstand, to dominate, rather than to reform. The outcome of the relativism of deconstruction is a media fascism that equates truth with power over representation (the ultimate and most disingenuous realization of this principle being that everyone else's construction is written off as a racist chimera, whereas one's own is elevated to the status of The Truth). Postmodernism has placed the policing of speech acts at the very top of ACT UP's agenda, at time even relegating much more compelling concerns such as drug release to a subordinate status. Theories about the ways in which the public discussion of the epidemic needs to be sanitized and reformed have thus given ACT UP members carte blanche for the reckless censoriousness embodied in their signature acts of electronic terrorism and their cavalier attempts to muzzle alternative points of view by unplugging microphones, jamming fax machines, chaining themselves to news desks, hurling themselves in front of cameras and heckling public speakers into silence.

While it is true that ACT UP has infused the flagging political momentum of the 1960s with camp and theatricality, there is a sense in which the intellectual underpinnings of the organization have made activism, not more radically interventionist, but more passively theoretical. In the last few years university theorists have tended to redefine activism in such a way that the sedentary activities they themselves perform in the course of fulfilling the normal requirements of their profession, such as reading, interpreting, decoding and deconstructing, are exalted as subversive acts in a new kind of guerrilla movement. In effect they have cunningly redefined as intrinsically political the work they already perform as literary critics.

A case in point is the summer 1984 issue of *Diacritics*, which was assembled in the astonishing naïve belief that critical theory can make an "important contribution to the public discussion of nuclear issues."[6] In "No Apocalypse, Not Now," Jacques Derrida claims that literary theorists can propose solutions to the dicey business of disarmament far beyond the ken of their less sophisticated diplomatic counterparts on the ground that the former, with their training in the analysis of literature, can "read" nuclear war because it hasn't happened yet and therefore is a "fiction," that is, a "text" – the bread and butter of the profession. This sweepingly inclusive definition of activism can also be found in academic discussions of AIDS in which the inert activity of image ecology – the exegesis of texts, the cracking of codes and the deciphering of social hieroglyphs – is now considered a form of activism in itself.

The facile self-apotheosis implicit in the image of the warrior hermeneuticist hacking through the insidious ideologies present in the media's handling of the disease could be easily dismissed as the harmless vanity of deluded academics if it were not for the fact that it has had a direct impact on AIDS activism. By reordering the priorities of AIDS visually and linguistically so that the janitorial duties of cleaning up the public discussion of the disease often take precedence over things such as the availability of hospital beds and experimental drugs, academics have repositioned themselves vis-à-vis the epidemic so that their peculiar expertise as explicators of images and texts is endowed with more glamor and importance than even the activities of those lobbying for increased federal funding. As postmodernists redefine an entire medical crisis so that they can be its central players, its arbiters, its experts, academic theory becomes the narcotic that promotes the illusion that politically disenfranchised and utterly insular groups such as American intellectuals are engaged with social issues without really requiring engagement; in fact, without effecting any change in their behavior at all. Instead, in the emphasis in AIDS activist literature on theoretical hair-splitting over such issues as the "epidemiology of signification," as Paula Treichler calls it,[7] or the "inevitable inscriptions of the literary that mark the discourse on AIDS,"[8] we are witnessing the careerist imperialism of a profession desperately in need of confirmation from the outside world of its own social utility.

One practical consequence of exaggerating the role academics can play in AIDS activism is an entirely new style of political protest, which, while brash, is often impotently theoretical. A good example is a demonstration held by the New York chapter of ACT UP in 1988 in which a group of demonstrators marched to City Hall wearing T-shirts silk-screened with a photograph of Cher. When asked what the image meant, the protesters told the uninitiated onlookers that it was an acronym for "Commie Homos Engaged in Revolution," "Cathy Has Extra Rollers," or any other non sequitur improvised on the spot for no apparent reason other than to make a cryptic joke advancing a certain privileged esprit de corps – an example of what Douglas Crimp meant when he said that "sometimes [ACT UP's] graphics signify only internally."[9] Such a deliberate obfuscation of the organization's propaganda in this opaque, semiotic pun serves only to shore up the group's own sense of intellectual elitism, a smug self-referentiality that bears all the linguistic hallmarks of academic theory, which has proven to be so damaging to effective activism.

Finally, it must be mentioned that one of the most seductive and overlooked attractions of the AIDS epidemic for postmodern theorists is that it uniquely engages an academic anxiety that has undermined the self-esteem of liberal-arts faculties for decades – namely their belittling awareness of the greater prestige of their scientific colleagues. The utter inability of the latter to find a cure, a vaccine or even an effective treatment for the disease has created a kind of power vacuum in the university, a temporary eclipse of authority that affords a perfect opportunity for nonscientists to rush forward into an arena from which they have been previously excluded. In fact academic AIDS theorists malign the presumed "objectivity" of science every step of the way, as Donna Haraway does in her essay "The Biopolitics of Postmodern Bodies," in which she jeers at our society's veneration for science, for the "univocal language" of empiricism, which in fact conceals "a barely contained and inharmonious heterogeneity."[10] AIDS has thus come as a blessing in disguise for the liberal arts in that it has enabled academics not only to ape the mannerisms of science, as postmodern theorists have long been doing, but also to obtain temporary hegemony as crusading social reformers over a scientific establishment that has suffered a withering loss of credibility in the course of tackling this most demoralizing of epidemics.

Notes

1. Lee Edelman, "The Plague of Discourse: Politics, Literary Theory, and AIDS," *South Atlantic Quarterly*, vol. 88, no. 1 (Winter 1989), p. 313.
2. Paula Treichler, "Seduced and Terrorized," *Art Forum* (October 1989), p. 149.
3. Douglas Crimp with Adam Rolston, *AIDS Demo Graphics* (Seattle: Bay Press, 1990), p. 78.
4. Gregg Bordowitz, "Picture a Coalitions," *October: Cultural Analysis, Cultural Activism* (Winter 1987), p. 184.
5. Ibid.
6. Quoted in "Academagogues," by John Dark (pseudonym for Daniel R. Harris), *The Boston Review* (December 1985), p. 11.
7. Paula Treichler, op. cit.
8. Quoted in Lee Edelman, op. cit.
9. Douglas Crimp with Adam Rolston, op. cit.
10. Donna Haraway, "The Biopolitics of Postmodern Bodies," *Differences: Life and Death in Sexuality; Reproductive Technologies and AIDS* (Winter 1989), p. 4.

12 Environmentalism and Human Emancipation*
Robert J. Brulle[1]

The spirit of the time, growing slowly and quietly ripe for the new form it is to assume, disintegrates one fragment after another of the structure of its previous world. That it is tottering to its fall in indicated only by symptoms here and there. Frivolity, and again ennui, which are spreading in the established order of things, the undefined foreboding of something unknown – all of these betoken that there is something else approaching.

G.W.F. Hegel[2]

Hegel's characterization of the cultural situation as standing on the verge of a major transformation is now a widely shared image of our current world. In this cultural world, a world in which the old is not yet dead and the new has not yet been born, intellectuals bear both a special task and a responsibility. As creators of new realities, we must actively foster a new social image of society that can better address the conditions our society now faces. In fulfilling this task, however, we must meet our moral responsibility to critically evaluate the social and political consequences of the alternative realities advocated in our work.

This essay focuses on the environmental movement as one of the major political and cultural actors that is now originating and acting to enable an alternative social order. Because of the critical nature of environmental problems, and the collapse of the old dogmas of modernity, I argue that some form of environmentalist discourse has an enhanced possibility of achieving dominance in our society.

To evaluate these discourses I nominate three initial criteria that I feel constitute the minimum requirements that

---

* Reprinted from Robert J. Brulle, 'Environmentalism and Human Emancipation', paper presented at 6th meeting of the Society for Human Ecology (October 1992), Snowbird, Utah.

an adequate environmentalist discourse will have to meet. Through a discussion of rhetoric and critical theory, I detail a theoretical position that defines a critical environmentalist position. I maintain that the development of an adequate environmentalist discourse can only be accomplished if the insights provided by a critical perspective are integrated into the formation of the alternative world views. The role of social-movement organizations in realizing this type of practice is described. Based on these theoretical perspectives, a research project is defined by which a critical evaluation of these discourses and the associated social-movement organizations can be initiated.

How we go about solving environmental problems will have significant impacts on the future structure of our society. In developing these alternative world views, we have to evaluate their ability to develop solutions to our environmental problems. In addition we have to critically evaluate the type of social and political relations they engender. These tasks are required of us to meet our responsibilities as both intellectual and moral actors. As Brown notes:

> Only when we have trained ourselves to articulate the congruencies between individual thought and social structures, and between personal values and political conduct, can we say we are truly human, for only then can we foresee both the origins and the outcomes of our acts and so be masters of ourselves.[3]

THE TASKS OF ENVIRONMENTAL DISCOURSE

My argument starts with two key premises. The first is that the current culture is best characterized as postmodern. Postmodernism, as defined by Lyotard, means that the dominant cultural belief is an "incredulity toward metanarratives."[4] A metanarrative is a master world view that serves as the uncontested organizing dogma of a social order. It takes form in the story of a society's origins, destiny and purpose. It establishes and legitimates a set of pragmatic rules through which the social bond is formed.[5]

The previous, or modern, culture was characterized by a generalized belief in two metanarratives. The first was the notion that "science will make us free". This metanarrative envisioned that humanity would be able to master the physical world through the growth and development of scientific knowledge, thereby allowing creation of a rational scientific world in which all human wants could be fulfilled. On this vision of the social order, the Comtean project of a technical–rational world order was built.[6] The second master narrative was the enlightenment myth. This projected that a just social order would emerge from a consensus reached through democratic deliberation of individual citizens. This metanarrative provided the basis for the formation of the democratic nation state.

Lyotard maintains that the taken-for-granted nature of these metanarratives was shattered by both the historical outcomes of these metanarratives in practice, and their philosophical delegitimation, which originated in the work of Wittgenstein. Now, the only taken-for-granted world views are small localized language games that govern our everyday interactions. With the fall of the master narratives from their previous position of unquestioned dominance, a discursive space in which new alternative realities can be considered has opened up. Since every "reality" is now subject to questioning, the old master narratives have become part of the many unrelated language games that make up the polysemous world we exist in today. The most prevalent attitude toward these still dominant, but no longer unquestioned master narratives is one of cynicism.[7]

With the decline of the master narratives, numerous, alternative world views are competing to establish intellectual hegemony. Included in this competition are feminism, various forms of environmentalism, assertion of historical culture and the reemergence of traditional religions.[8] So although the old metanarratives are not yet dead, the burial arrangements are now being made. Concurrently the present is pregnant with new alternatives that are now in gestation.

Lyotard's propositions have been subjected to much debate, and these objections will be considered later in this essay. However, by bracketing these objections for the time being, the value of his arguments regarding our current situation can be appreciated. His characterization of our current cultural situation as being both one of cynicism and questioning of the previously dominant Western metanarratives, and one of a proliferation of multiple, local language games seems to capture some vital aspects of our current lived experience.

My second premise is that environmental problems will force a serious consideration of the alternative world views now being constructed and debated within the environmental movement. Because the growing environmental crisis will drive rapid and dramatic shifts in productive capacities of the world economy,[9] increasing emphasis will be focused on meeting these problems in the next century. This focus on environmental problems will enhance the prospects for the environmental alternative world views to compete for ideological hegemony. Thus in comparison with the other alternative world views now being developed by other social movements, I believe that some form of environmentalism occupies an enhanced possibility of being seriously considered as the new social metanarrative.[10] Hence I believe that the forthcoming century could be the beginning of a critical historical period of social change to an ecologically sustainable society. After a growing number of ecological catastrophes, and great suffering by all living creatures, we may have the opportunity to initiate fundamental changes in our society. This can lead to the origination of a new ecological metanarrative. If we develop and act to create a new world, a long period of societal readjustment based on this new metanarrative could follow. We have the opportunity to affect the future structure of our society. In this situation intellectuals can serve as a midwives to the birth of a new social reality. We have a responsibility to foster the birth of a discourse that can guarantee both human survival and dignity, while at the same time preserving the natural environment.

To accomplish this task it seems to me that an adequate environmentalist discourse must be capable of accomplishing three social and political tasks. First, it must enhance the learning capability of society. To construct a sustainable society that is in harmony with our natural environment, the creative energies of many different lifeworlds have to be mobilized to create alternative visions of how we can better live within our natural environment. Then, these alternative ways of life need to be tested in practice. Currently these alternative practices are blocked by the institutions of the capitalist world economy and the nation-state system. The hegemony of these systems delegitimizes alternative social arrangements and discourages their implementation.[11] An adequate environmentalist discourse must enable and legitimate a political practice that is capable of both effectively challenging the hegemony of these institutions and expanding the range of effective practices beyond the current limits established by these structures.

Second, an adequate environmentalist discourse must provide an ethics for worldwide social action. An effective solution to our most pressing environmental problems, such as global warming, ozone depletion and deforestation, will require cooperative human efforts on a global scale. As noted by Apel:

> Scientific–technical civilization has confronted all nations, races, and cultures, regardless of their group-specific, culturally relative moral traditions, with a common ethical problem. For the first time in the history of the human species, human beings are faced with the task of accepting collective responsibility for the consequences of their actions on a world-wide scale.[12]

Yet there is currently no global discourse capable of legitimating this type of effort across the innumerable cultures of our globe. In fact one of the major barriers to effective action by the environmentalist social movement is factionalism.[13] Part of this factionalism is based on a tendency by the creators and advocates of alternative discourses to describe their positions as given, rather than constructed, realities. This leads to struggles for intellectual hegemony within the social movement itself. As noted by Frey:

> The need to clearly differentiate from the other faction may lead to internal demands for ideological purity that alienate members and produce still more internal divisions. This cycle continues to alienate members and supporters, and diverts each organization from efforts to achieve broader goals.[14]

This tendency toward factionalism must be overcome and a global political practice initiated. An adequate environmentalist discourse must acknowledge the wide range of cultural viewpoints, including conflicting notions of what is sacred and profane, what constitutes truth and heresy, and even basic notions regarding what it means to be human. In addition it must form a global ethic that allows these different cultural and political systems to work toward a common goal. Finally, an adequate environmentalist discourse must preserve human dignity and autonomy. If one accepts the humanist definition of human dignity and autonomy as being capable of acting morally, this implies that the individual must be empowered to participate in the creation and change of the social order. As Brown argues,

> One moment of its [that is, humanism's] meaning remains the person as a conscious and intending actor capable of exercising *virtus* – a moral courage in life that combines virtuosity with virtue. In such a view, moral agency is understood as the capacity to create culture.[15]

To maintain the dignity and autonomy of humanity, the political practice engendered by this discourse must enable democratic participation for all members of the society. Consequently the process by which environmental problems would be solved must be a process of democratic will formation.

These three criteria provide an initial basis from which to critique the adequacy of the different environmentalist discourses. In creating alternative solutions to our environmental problems, the authors must consciously take these criteria into account. Hence a critical and self-reflexive perspective on the political and cultural implications must be included in our discussions of alternative environmentalist discourses.

TOWARD A CRITICAL ENVIRONMENTALISM

To create a self-reflexive environmentalist world view, an intellectual position must be defined from which a critical perspective is enabled. To undertake this task two intellectual approaches provide essential views on the links between language, social order and rationality. They are rhetoric and critical theory.

Rhetoric

Over the past 20 years rhetorical studies have emerged as a major intellectual movement. Initially based in studies of English and communications, this school of thought has developed a series of powerful techniques that connect language and social order. Rhetorical studies focus on the process of mutual influence through communication.[16]

In meeting existence, the human community forms symbolic expressions of meaning that constitute a world view. This common language creates a horizon of understanding within which consciousness exists, and the world is constituted as a comprehensible phenomenon.[17] The creation of meaning requires intersubjective agreement on the symbolic structures that organize experience. Intersubjective agreement is arrived at through dialogue among the participants. This means that "truth is a matter of collective opinion gained through persuasive argumentation".[18] Rhetoric constitutes individuals in a given lifeworld[19] and constructs a knowable world. Thus the construction of a world view is a rhetorical act of creative human agency, and a practical accomplishment of a human community over time.

The creation of social knowledge and power are intimately linked. To act together, a human community must come to some agreement on what version of reality will be used. Establishment of a bounded world view creates an operative 'definition of the situation'. Thus achieving linguistic closure defines the establishment of a social order.[20] This 'stable definition of the situation' takes the form of a discourse. A discourse is a series of rules by which meaningful statements can be formed. Foucault argues that society is constituted through the formation of a dominant discourse, or a "regime of truth" within which society exists:

Each society has its regime of truth, its 'general politics' of truth: that is, the types of discourse which it accepts and makes function as true; the mechanisms and instances which enable one to distinguish true and false statements, the means by which each is sanctioned; the techniques and procedures accorded value in the acquisition of truth; the status of those who are charged with saying what counts as true.[21]

A discourse enables some statements to be made, and excludes others from consideration. Certain aspects of reality are highlighted, while others are obscured. Consequently it limits what constitutes a world and what types of practices can be pursued. Thus the nature of the dominant discourse limits the range of human activities. This "definition of the situation" by the dominant discourse enables the consistent reproduction of stable patterns of human interaction; in other words it enables the creation of a stable social order. It also excludes other types of practices from consideration. Hence the key to the realization of a stable social order is the ability to define what constitutes the common-sense reality that applies to a field of practice.

Maintaining social order requires the operation of power to continue the operation of this definition of what constitutes common-sense reality. The maintenance and change of symbolic discourse is the locus of political struggle. Changes in social structures are brought about through a redefinition of what constitutes the common sense embodied in the everyday practices of society. From this viewpoint, political struggles in the form of social movements are attempts to alter social structures through the promotion of an alternative discourse.[22]

From a rhetorical viewpoint, then, social order is a hierarchy legitimated by a dominant definition of reality. Coexisting within a social order are other, subjugated definitions of reality. This contention over the definitions of reality breaks up the naturalness and taken-for-granted nature of the dominant discourse. In doing so a symbolic space is created in which contending versions of reality can appear. The alternative reality takes the appearance of heterodoxy. Orthodoxy also appears as an attempt to restore the reign of doxa in the face of disputed belief. Thus social order is seen as both a practical historic accomplishment, brought about through everyday communicative practice, and as the result of political struggles over the nature of reality.

Rhetorical analysis allows us to view the strategies implicit in the creation of different discourses and shows the links between a particular world view, how it is constructed and how it can function to establish a group's political power. By examining their structure we can examine the political practices that these discourses engender and exclude. *Hence to study rhetoric is to study the process of how social order is created and maintained.*[23] Viewing society as a linguistic creation, this perspective provides an important insight into the creation and change of social order. It also shows the socially constructed nature of *all* discourse. In doing so it encourages the author to adopt a self-awareness regarding his/her intellectual productions.

Critical Theory

The second perspective necessary to undertake a critical discussion of environmental world views is the critical theory of Jürgen Habermas. This perspective provides a moral position from which alternative world views can be evaluated. In addition it provides an overall perspective on the social process linked to the expansion of the global capitalist economy and the nation-state system.

Habermas provides a moral position for evaluating alternative world views by linking reason to an 'ideal speech situation'.[24] His "theory of communicative action" provides this argument for the linkage between reason, justice and ethics. In this theory Habermas defines rationality as "a disposition of speaking and acting subjects that is expressed in modes of behavior for which there are good reasons or grounds".[25] Rationality is thus tied to intersubjective communication carried on in the conduct of life. Habermas maintains that language games and forms of life can be compared and evaluated in terms of their rationality. This claim is based upon an analysis of the communication process through which insersubjective agreement is reached.

Rational intersubjective agreement requires satisfaction of three validity claims: truth, normative rightness and sincerity. In addition the speech must satisfy the validity claim of comprehensibility. The process of fulfilling the validity requirements of speech defines an "ethics of logic". In engaging in intersubjective discourse in a human community, the validity claims must be fully validated for the discourse to be rational. The process of validation requires an open-speech community. Once one asks a question and enters into discourse to seek an answer, the ethics of logic are implicitly accepted. Based on this premise Habermas has proposed the following condition under which normative statements can be evaluated:

> All affected can accept the consequences and the side effects its general observance can be anticipated to have for the satisfaction of everyone's interests.[26]

Habermas argues that a commitment to rational argumentation also implies a commitment to developing the material conditions of life in which an open communication system can exist. Thus the communicative ethic applies to social action. Based on this ethic, Habermas seeks to provide the moral grounding for a rational society.

Apel expands Habermas' argument by maintaining that the ideal-speech situation presupposes its realization in a real human community. Because of this Apel maintains that the attempts to create the ideal-speech situation in reality provides a legitimation for the survival of humanity.

> I believe that two *fundamental regulative principles* for the long term moral strategy of action for every human being can be derived from this (implicit) demand on the part of all philosophical argumentation. First, in all actions, it should be a matter of ensuring the *survival* of the human species qua real communication community. Second, it should be a matter of realizing the *ideal* communication in the real one. The first goal is the necessary condition for the second, and the second goal provides the first with its meaning – the meaning that is already anticipated with every argument.[27]

Thus, human survival and the humanist goal of a self-creative human community are given moral legitimation through their mutual support of one another.

Habermas uses his characterization of rational communication to describe the process of social evolution as a cultural learning process. The development of learning potential involves creating intersubjective agreements based upon rational discourse instead of uncritical adherence to tradition. Habermas' term for this is the linguistification of the sacred. Modernity is viewed by Habermas as a shift from tradition to intersubjective agreements as the basis for social order. This process allows for the implementation of increased learning potential as more social arrangements are subjected to validity testing through discourse. The modern social order becomes differentiated as the processes of learning becomes specialized and develop as separate institutions based upon the different types of knowledge claims.

As noted above, rational intersubjective agreement requires satisfaction of three validity claims: truth, normative rightness and sincerity. These three validity claims are correlated with three types of action and corresponding knowledge claims. The first type of action is teleological. In teleological action the actor aims to bring about some end in the physical world. This action employs empirical–theoretical knowledge, which corresponds to the validity claim of truth. This type of action is institutionalized in the market and state administrative agencies. The second type is normatively regulated action. In this type the actor seeks to orient her/his action to common values with the social world. This action is based on moral–practical knowledge. This corresponds to the validity claim of normative rightness. This action is institutionalized in the legal system. The third is dramaturgical action, in which the actor presents his/her subjective (or inner) self to an audience. This action is created through conscious self-monitoring based on aesthetic knowledge. This corresponds to the validity claim of sincerity. Aesthetic rationality is institutionalized in the artistic institutions of society.

Habermas traces the pathologies of modern life, including environmental destruction, to the rationalization of society along technical–rational lines. Modernity is seen as a one-sided development of technocratic society based on instrumental reason. It lacks the concurrent development of independent normative and aesthetic institutions capable of directing the technical–rational institutions. Instead our society's technical institutions (the multinational corporation and the state administrative agencies) dominate the normative and aesthetic institutions, resulting in our society's one-sided and limited learning capacity.

Without any effective controls the market and state expand into areas that were previously controlled by normative or aesthetic logics. As this process expands, the ability of society to create and maintain meaning becomes diminished.[28]

Since, as Habermas says, "meaning can neither be bought nor coerced"[29] neither the market nor the state can perform the tasks of cultural reproduction. This translates into a series of crises in culture, politics and the sustainability of our cultural and personal world.[30] In general this results in the failure to develop and transmit valid cultural knowledge throughout society, a lack of solidarity among societal members and a failure to develop responsible adult personalities capable of acting as moral agents.

With the atrophy of the lifeworld, the development of human interactions based upon a shared version of morality becomes more difficult to form and sustain. This means the gradual decay of relations of mutual trust, reciprocity and a genuine identification with the other. Instead the modern personality develops around two key values – hedonistic consumerism and possessive individualism.[31] Hedonistic consumerism creates a personality easily manipulated by advertisements promising "the good life". This leads to an unending quest for consumption in an anxious search for social status. Possessive individualism manifests itself in narcissistic personalities, and leads to a life divorced from civil involvement and a single-minded careerism that exalts the satisfaction of personal ambition as the preeminent value.

The technical institutions encounter at two level limitations to their continued expansion in the natural environment. First, at the global level, the expansion of the market and state administrative apparatus runs up against the limits of the ecosystem. In addition the destructive environmental effects of meeting systems requirements for more resource utilization enters into the lifeworld and begins to destroy the organic foundations of human life. This destruction of the basis of the lifeworld generates local resistance movements.

The intervention of large-scale industry into ecological balances, the growing scarcity of nonrenewable natural resources, as well as demographic developments present industrially developed societies with major problems; but these challenges are abstract at first and call for technical and economic solutions, which must in turn be globally planned and implemented by administrative means. What sets off the protest is rather the tangible destruction of

the urban environment; the despoliation of the country-
side through housing developments, industrialization, and
pollution; the impairment of health through the ravages
of civilization, pharmaceutical side effects, and the like –
that is, developments that noticeably affect the organic
foundations of the lifeworld and makes us drastically aware
of standards of livability, of inflexible limits to the deprivation of sensual–aesthetic background needs.[32]

Habermas maintains that the resolution of the problems of
modernity require a reconstruction of the social order by
subordinating technical–rational organizations to normative
and aesthetic values. In everyday terms, this means that to
solve our social and ecological problems we must come to a
consensus about what norms we want to have enacted, and
then impose controls over the market and state administrative agencies to ensure their realization. To subordinate these
technical systems to normative and aesthetic values requires
democratic participation in society's economic and administrative organizations.[33] This task is defined by Habermas
as follows:

> We are faced with the problem of how capabilities for
> self-organization can be developed to such an extent within
> autonomous public spheres that radical–democratic process
> of will-formation can come to have a decisive impact on
> the regulatory mechanisms and marginal conditions of me-
> dia-steered subsystems in a lifeworld oriented toward uses
> values, toward ends in general. This task involves holding
> the systemic imperatives of an interventionist state appa-
> ratus and those of an economic system in check, and is
> formulated in defensive terms. Yet this defensive resteering
> will not be able to succeed without a radical and broadly
> effective democratization.[34]

In his analysis of the requirements for a situation in which
such a moral competence in social actors can be developed,
Offe notes that associative relations in the form of social-
movement organizations serve as a "beachhead" for the
development of lifeworld direction over the steering media
of the state administrative apparatus and the market.[35] Since
the learning ability of our society is hindered by the

dominance of decision-making criteria based on the institutions of the market and state administrative agencies, social movements must take actions that will enable and legitimate a political practice that is capable of both effectively challenging the hegemony of these institutions and expanding the range of effective practices beyond the current limits established by these structures.

The public sphere's recreation requires effective action by social-movement organizations. These organizations would be able to translate the impulses of the lifeworld into the political discourse of the system, thereby restoring democratic control over the political and economic systems.

> The counterinstitutions are intended to dedifferentiate some parts of the normally organized domains of action, remove them from the clutches of the steering media (money and political power), and return these 'liberated areas' to the action-coordinating mechanism of reaching understanding.[36]

By developing a practice in this manner, the imperatives of he lifeworld would be conveyed into the public sphere, and a legitimate and moral course of action could be developed. An effective public sphere would restore democratic control to areas currently controlled by the criteria of political power and economic profitability. The actions in corporations and the administrative bureaucracies of the state would be decided through open, public discourse.

To enact the type of cultural and political changes necessary to ensure a sustainable society in the future, a consensus developed and legitimated in the public sphere seems likely to be the only way in which such a fundamental change could possible come about in a peaceful manner. Hence Habermas concluded that the public sphere could:

> only be realized today, on an altered basis, as a rational reorganization of social and political power under the mutual control of rival organizations committed to the public sphere in their internal structure as well as in their relations with the state and each other.[37]

Both critical theory and rhetoric form a critical perspective from which existing environmentalist discourses and the associated organizations can be evaluated. They also provide a criterion of aesthetic adequacy by showing the relationships between social order and discourse. This perspective enhances the self-awareness and responsibility of both the author and the social movements that are acting to bring alternative realities into being. Because the intellectual product and the political actions are seen as conscious human action, a self-reflexive position is developed. This makes the author and political actor responsible for the social and political consequences of their actions. Second, it provides a moral perspective that justifies both human survival and dignity. This criterion provides a basis from which the normative rightness of an environmentalist discourse can be judged. Finally, it provides an overall perspective on the current situation and suggests ways in which an alternative social order can be created. This perspective can provide valuable information upon which strategic action can be constructed. What this perspective does not do is to prescribe what should be done. Rather it attempts to put the social actors themselves in the position of deciding what should be done.

This analysis forms the basis of Habermas' objections to Lyotard's analysis. Rather than seeing the source of our problems as resulting from the application of scientific and emancipatory metanarratives, Habermas offers a more historically and sociologically cogent explanation. Habermas maintains that Lyotard's analysis does not lead to developing a political practice capable of addressing these problems. Rather it serves as an intellectual block in the development of alternative world views. In this sense it is a conservative ideology of the status quo. Accordingly Habermas rejects Foucault's explanation of the source of our current dilemmas. Referring to Lyotard's work, Habermas maintains:

> This significance is obscured, both in the self-understanding of those involved and in the ideological imputations of their opponents, if the communicative rationality of cultural modernity is rashly equated with the functionalist rationality of self-maintaining economic and administrative action system. . . . This confusion explains the fronts – which are out of place and obscure the real political opposition – between the antimodernism of the Young Conservatives

and the neoconservative defense of postmodernity that robs a modernity at variance with itself of its rational content and its perspectives on the future.[38]

EMANCIPATION AND THE ENVIRONMENTAL MOVEMENT

The development of an adequate environmentalist discourse can only be accomplished if the insights provided by a critical perspective are integrated into the formation of the alternative world views. As noted earlier, this discourse must first enhance the learning ability of society. As shown by Habermas, the learning ability of our society is hindered by the dominance of decision-making criteria based on the institutions of the market and state administrative agencies. Hence one key to developing a solution to our environmental problems is to create environmental organizations that strive to create and enact an adequate environmentalist practice. Such a practice must be open and self-reflexive, and created and changed through an open communicative process. It must also enable and legitimate a political practice that is capable of both effectively challenging the hegemony of these institutions and expanding the range of effective practices beyond the current limits established by these structures.

Second, it must provide an ethics for worldwide social action across multiple cultural worlds. Because the only moral criterion for the communicative ethics is that *all* affected are able to participate; no group, regardless of cultural position, is eliminated from the conversation. In addition, by seeing all world views as the result of communicative processes within the human community, the ideological rigidity of the different environmentalist discourses is reduced. This can create a more open and dialogical relationship between the various environmentalist discourses, reduce factionalism and, perhaps, lead to more effective political action. Finally, an adequate environmentalist discourse must preserve human dignity and autonomy by enabling democratic participation for all members of society. Here critical theory provides an overall strategic viewpoint from which such a practice could be oriented.

The research questions for social science become not which
environmentalist discourse is right, but rather, what type of
political practice these discourses engender. Since these
discourses are enacted by environmental groups, this type
of analysis must focus on existing social-movement organizations. Habermas' theory of modernity provides a series of
criteria from which an evaluation of these organizations can
proceed. The strength of this approach is that it specifies
the requirements for an emancipatory political practice, and
thus "opens up the possibility of linking normative considerations to empirical sociological ones".[39] In expanding the
ideas of Habermas, Offe suggests the need for empirical inquiry into this area. The question that he raises for this
evaluation is an examination of which of these associative
relations best fits the requirements of creating and sustaining an emancipatory practice.

A closer look at concrete institutions of interest mediation and political will-formation may thus render the perspective of discourse ethics fruitful for a differential
diagnosis showing which institutional arrangements, under
the prevailing structures and conditions of the social division of labor, help agents to bear the burden of mceting
the criteria of fairness, justice, and solidarity better than
other arrangements, and why. The question of which associative contexts are more conducive to the development
of a decontextualized capacity for moral judgement than
others may sound paradoxical, but without this kind of
evaluation of associative relations, it seems, the critical
potential of discourse ethics will not be fully utilized.[40]

The discourse ethic of Habermas provides a positive ethic
for the formation of a democratic and rational social order.
To recreate the public sphere requires opening up the dominant economic and administrative organizations to the democratic will-formation process. This would allow for currently
suppressed definitions of reality to be considered through a
process of public discourse. The end result would be a more
open and democratic society. In addition the problem-solv-
ing ability of society would be enhanced. Just as a scientific
community progresses through vigorous debate and the
generation and testing of alternative theories, a more open

social order would allow for more social experimentation in the form of alternative life practices.

This perspective defines a research project that evaluates the links between environmentalist discourses and their social and political consequences. This research would evaluate the ability of social movements to effectively communicate moral and aesthetic values from our everyday worlds into effective political action. This evaluation would be done in the hope of encouraging self-examination by social movements, and to assist these organizations in developing more effective and morally responsible actions. Serious intellectual and political efforts are now ongoing to realize these values of a just, democratic and sustainable society. Much further theoretical and practical creative work and experimentation is necessary to develop a fuller repertoire of critical social-research practices. As this repertoire expands, the ability to create a rational society will also expand. By creating an open and self-reflexive political discourse, a more rational and just social order can be created that can resolve the structural conflicts that threaten human survival, and at the same time preserve and expand human agency and dignity.

The restructuring of our society to harmonize with the natural environment is, at best, an almost impossible task. However we can take heart from historical changes of this magnitude. In just the past 100 years the worldwide practice of slavery has been abolished. Just recently the seemingly impregnable communist bloc has disintegrated. Where there is action there is hope. By advocating an open and self-reflexive environmentalist discourse, intellectuals can attempt to foster a more rational and just social order that can resolve the conflicts that threaten human survival.

Notes

1. An earlier version of this chapter was presented at the Society for Human Ecology's annual meeting at Snowbird, Utah, on 2–4 October 1992.
2. G. W. F. Hegel, *The Phenomenology of Mind* (New York: Harper, 1967), p. 75.
3. R. H. Brown, *Society as Text* (Chicago: University of Chicago Press, 1987), p. 63.

4. J.-F. Lyotard, *The Postmodern Condition: A Report on Knowledge* (Minneapolis: University of Minnesota Press, 1979), p. xxiv.
5. Ibid., p. 21.
6. See R. J. Brulle, "Power, Discourse, and Social Problems: Social Problems from a Rhetorical Perspective," forthcoming in G. Miller (ed.), *Current Perspectives in Social Problems, Volume 5* (Greenwich, CT: JAI Press, 1993) for a fuller discussion of the Comtean project.
7. See J. Goldfarb, *The Cynical Society* (Chicago: University of Chicago Press, 1991) for an excellent discussion of the dominance of cynicism in our society.
8. H. S. Hughes, *Sophisticated Rebels* (Cambridge MA: Harvard University Press, 1988).
9. See Paul Stern, C. Young, R. Oran and D. Druckman (eds), *Global Environmental Change: Understanding the Human Dimension* (Washington DC: National Academy Press, 1992), Carlo C. Jaeger, "Regional Approaches to Global Climatic Risks", paper presented at symposium on "Current Developments in Environmental Sociology", Amsterdam, June 1992, and Clive Ponting, *A Green History of the World* (New York: St. Martin's Press) for a discussion of this point.
10. In fact this process has already begun. Senator Al Gore, in his book *Earth in the Balance* (New York: Houghton Mifflin, 1992), called for "adopting environmental concerns as the core organizing principle for our society" (p. 231).
11. See J. Habermas, "Modernity: An Incomplete Project", in Hal Foster, *The Anti-aesthetic: Essays on Postmodern Culture* (Port Townsend, WA: Bay Press, 1981).
12. K. O. Apel, *Toward a Transformation of Philosophy* (Boston: Routledge & Kegan Paul, 1980), p. 228.
13. See B. G. Norton, *Toward Unity Among Environmentalists* (New York: Oxford Univ. Press, 1991), pp. 3–13, for a description of this problem.
14. S. Frey, T. Dietz and L. Kayloff, "Gamson's Strategy of Social Protest and Successful U. S. Protest", *American Journal of Sociology*. vol. 98, no. 2 (September 1992), p. 384.
15. R. H. Brown, *Society as Text*, op. cit., p. 141.
16. B. Brummett, "Some Implications of Process Or Intersubjectivity: Postmodern Rhetoric," *Philosophy and Rhetoric*, vol. 9, no. 1 (Winter 1976), pp. 21–51.
17. See A. J. Greimas, *On Meaning: Selected Writings in Semiotic Theory* (Minneapolis: University of Minnesota Press, 1987), and J. Bruner, "Life as Narrative", *Social Research*, vol. 54, no. 1, pp. 11–32.
18. R. H. Brown, "Theories of Rhetoric and the Rhetoric of Theory: Toward a Political Phenomenology of Sociological Truth", *Social Research*, vol. 50, no. 1 (1983), pp. 126–57.
19. J. M. Hermans, H. Kempen and R. van Loon, "The Dialogical Self", *American Psychologist*, Jan. 1992, pp. 23–33.
20. M. Foucault, *Power/Knowledge* (New York: Pantheon books, 1972), p. 131.
21. Ibid., p. 131.

22. Klaus Eder, "The New Social Movements: Moral Crusades, Political Pressure Groups or Social Movements?, *Social Research*, vol. 52, no. 4, pp. 873–4.
23. A useful analysis of this type is provided by Thomas Lessel in his article, "The Priestly Voice", in the *Quarterly Journal of Speech*, vol. 75 (1989), pp. 183–97. In this article he examines the links between the use of the organic root metaphor in creating a world view, and its political implications. This is performed through an analysis of the rhetorical structure and ideological function of the discourse of the Planetary Society.
24. See Robert J. Brulle, "Jürgen Habermas: An Exegesis for Human Ecologists", *Human Ecology Bulletin*, no. 8 (spring/summer 1992), pp. 29–38.
25. J. Habermas, *The Theory of Communicative Action*, vol. 1 (Boston: MIT Press, 1985), p. 11.
26. J. Habermas, *Moral Consciousness and Communicative Action* (Boston: MIT Press, 1990), p. 65.
27. K. O. Apel, *Towards a Transformation of Philosophy* (Boston: Routledge and Kegan Paul, 1973), p. 282.
28. J. Habermas, *The Theory of Communicative Action Vol II* (Boston: MIT Press, 1987), p. 330.
29. J. Habermas, "A Reply" in A. Honneth and Hans Joas, *Communicative Action* (Boston: MIT Press, 1991), p. 259.
30. J. Habermas, *The Theory of Communicative Action, Vol. II*, op. cit., p. 386.
31. Ibid., p. 325.
32. Ibid., p. 394.
33. J. Habermas, "Modernity, An Incomplete Project", op. cit., p. 13.
34. J. Habermas, "A Reply", op. cit., p. 261.
35. K. Offe, "Bindings, Shackles, Brakes: On Self-Limitation Strategies", in Axe Honneth, Thomas McCarthy, Klaus Offe and Albrecht Wellmer (eds), *Cultural–Political Interventions in the Unfinished Project of Enlightenment* (Cambridge MA: MIT Press, 1992), p. 76.
36. J. Habermas, *The Theory of Communicative Action, Volume II*, op. cit., p. 396.
37. J. Habermas, "The Public Sphere: An Encyclopedia Article", in S. Bonner and D. Kellner, *Critical Theory and Society* (New York: Routledge, 1980), p. 142.
38. J. Habermas, *The Theory of Communicative Action, Volume II*, op. cit., p. 396.
39. J. Habermas, "Further Reflections on the Public Sphere", in Craig Calhoun (ed.), *Habermas and the Public Sphere* (Boston: MIT Press, 1992), p. 448.
40. C. Offe, "Bindings, Shackles, Brakes: On Self-Limitation Strategies", op. cit., p. 90.

Part V

The Future of Social Movements

13 Rethinking the Sixties Legacy: From New Left to New Social Movements*

Carl Boggs

In contrast with the "total break" thesis characteristic of most New Left literature, which posits a collapse of 1960s radicalism in the period of 1968–70 and therefore a gulf separating it from the future, this essay argues for a continuity from the 1960s to the contemporary phase of new social movements and the appearance of political formations such as the Greens. The themes that permeated and galvanized the New Left – participatory democracy, community, cultural renewal, collective consumption, and the restoration of nature – have been typically carried forward into the modern ecology, feminist, peace and urban protest movements that have proliferated since the early 1970s. At the same time, whereas the New Left failed to establish durable organization, constituencies or even a theory of its own development, the new movements represent a far more mature and stable representation of local democratic struggles that grew out of the earlier period. The immense diversity of new social movements, which increasingly shapes progressive politics today, suggests an obsolescence of those global solutions and strategies that the left has historically embellished.

As we enter the 1990s, that now-distant era of 1960s radicalism appears to be strangely alive and worthy of renewed attention. After nearly two decades of scorn or neglect, the New Left has reentered the American conscience, this time in a spirit of nostalgia and even celebration. Twenty years

* Reprinted from Michael Peter Smith (ed.), *Breaking Chains: Social Movements and Collective Action* (New Brunswick: Transaction Publishers, 1991), pp. 50–68.

after the explosive upheavals of 1968–70, more than a dozen books on 1960s politics and culture have been published, most of them offering "fresh" insights into the peculiar energy and rhythms of that period.[1] The general thrust of such books, as well as the scores of magazine articles, musical tributes and films on the same topic, contrasts sharply with the hostile attitude toward the 1960s previously adopted by most academic and popular writers. The New Left was typically viewed as at best utopian, irrational and reckless; at worst crude, willfully destructive and violent. Most agreed that it was little more than a temporary childish phase of rebellion; an impetuous acting out of immature youths who, saturated with drugs, sex, rock music and mysticism, were destined to self-destruct in a frenzy of rage, hedonism and fanaticism.[2]

Participants in New Left politics and the counterculture were often described as self-righteous, dogmatic and narcissistic. Harsh verdicts of this sort permeated the observations not only of such mainstream writers as Lewis Feuer, Seymour Martin Lipset, Daniel Bell, Christopher Lasch and, more recently, Allan Bloom, but also of academic Marxists and traditional leftists who saw the 1960s as an infantile distraction from the "real world" of class struggle, economic crisis and contestation for state power.

The recent wave of contributions shows, if nothing else, just how truly mythological these verdicts were. Employing a combination of sociological, biographical and journalistic insights, they demonstrate that the familiar negative stereotypes, often constructed from a remote vantage point, do not hold up under close scrutiny. With rare exceptions, it has become clear that previous efforts to analyze New left radicalism ultimately failed to grasp the complex interplay among cultural and political forces that shaped the deep currents of popular revolt.

This revisionist history of the New Left, however, has been marred by the so-called "total break" thesis: the notion that the popular struggles associated with the 1960s came to an explosive and sudden halt somewhere between 1968 and 1970, when the more apocalyptic visions held by activists were presumably dashed once and for all by an out-of-control drug culture, rampant street fighting and Marxist–Leninist sectarianism. This perspective is extremely distorted, confusing the collapse of the SDS (Students for a Democratic Society) with the broader legacy of both the New Left and the counterculture rooted in some enduring oppositional processes at work in American society. This legacy, so poorly understood by progressive and mainstream analysts alike, gave rise to a vigorous (if still limited), independent radicalism throughout the 1970s, as well as to that historically significant phenomenon commonly subsumed under the label "new social movements."

The conventional notion that the various 1960s movements were fashioned from more or less the same ideological cloth does not really bear up under close scrutiny. Revisionist interpretations suggest that, on the contrary, the New Left was defined by only one overarching political theme from beginning to end, from the civil rights movement to the early SDS years to the Columbia University uprising to the Yippie phase: the commitment to participatory democracy. What galvanized all social forces was a passionately anti-authoritarian ethos, a preoccupation with direct action, community and self-activity that carried into virtually every arena of struggle. The period was shaped by a certain utopian revival of democratic, populist and even anarchist traditions that, despite their vagueness, appealed especially to youth, students and intellectuals. There was a consensus that democratic ideals could be established on a foundation of abundance and technological innovation. As Miller (1987) shows in his carefully developed study, the early SDS was the repository of two broad impulses: a grass-roots populism that would test the limits of liberalism and a dedication to civil-rights empowerment in the South. The *Port Huron Statement*, the founding document of the SDS, thus embraced a Rousseauian fascination with the virtues of direct democracy and social solidarity that, from the standpoint of its very optimistic authors, could be realized without confronting the power structure itself. (In Western Europe, on the other hand, this theme took on a more clearly institutional expression in the form of such concepts as "autogestion" and "self-management.")

If democratic empowerment was the prime mover of SDS activism from 1962 to 1968, the reality was that the SDS was only a small part of the 1960s panorama, contrary to much New Left historiography (see, for example, Sale, 1973). There was, of course, the counterculture, with its diffuse amalgam of cultural, political and even spiritual influences that unfolded on an altogether different terrain: Yippies, Diggers, communards, street people and other marginalized elements of a youth scene that championed alternative lifestyles, a theatrical politics and a revolt against leaders, heroes and organizers. For many, cultural insurgency was directed toward the realization of "collective peak experiences" (Stevens, 1987, p. 293). The Berkeley People's Park episode of May 1969 expressed these accumulated visions and sensibilities and more, including an embellishment of "nature" and a revival of public space consonant with the concerns of the later ecology movement.

Todd Gitlin's far-ranging account reveals in great detail how the New Left was in reality an uneasy agglomeration of crosscutting groups, interests and ideologies. Youth culture overlapped with, but was separate from, the student movement and its struggle for educational reform, academic freedom and a greater share of power within the university. The civil rights movement itself was divided between the liberal-reform outlook of groups such as CORE, the SCLC and the NAACP and the militant strategy of groups such as the SNCC and, later, the Black Panthers. Of course, there were the early voices of feminism associated with the Redstockings, the Women's Liberation Front, and scattered protests by women against male domination within the SDS and other New Left groups. The sometimes catalyzing role played by independent socialist organizations such as IS, SWP and YSA is generally overlooked; theirs was typically a "third-camp" socialism that rejected the Cold-War politics of both Western capitalist powers and Soviet-bloc Communism. By the end of the 1960s, as is well known, rival Marxist currents surfaced along with the appearance of various movements, hero-figures such as Ché Guevara, Regis Debray, Fidel Castro, Rosa Luxemburg, Wilhelm Reich, Herbert Marcuse and, of course, Lenin and Mao.

The turn toward Marxism (and Marxism–Leninism) after 1969, identified with the rise of the Progressive Labor and Weather politics that doomed the SDS, is usually characterized as nothing more than a misguided sectarian exercise or a reckless vanguardism. There is much truth to such depictions. At the same time, there was another dimension to this shift that has been overlooked by most observers: the discovery of issues related to class, power and the Third World that in fact opened up new avenues of theorizing about social change even as the framework within which such issues were posed – generally Third Worldist, often self-righteous – commonly sapped political energy. Many Marxist currents (often inspired by "Western" Marxist thinkers) that appeared within and around university campuses, and within a variety of grass-roots movements, moreover, were complex enough to resist facile characterizations of them as outdated, vanguardist sects. (In Western Europe, where Marxist groups enjoyed considerably greater popular support as well as theoretical influence, a dismissive attitude was even harder to sustain.)

The 1960s political reality, therefore, was a fragmentary, pluralistic and sometimes chaotic mosaic of rebellious impulses and currents that could never be incorporated into the rubric of a single, overarching "movement." This complexity is magnified even further once the global nature of the period is taken into account. Thus, in Western Europe, as both Fraser (1988) and Caute (1988) stress, the political complexities allowed for a rather different trajectory: an entrenched socialist tradition, where strong Social Democratic and Communist parties had long been fixtures of the system, meant that a far more coherent "extraparliamentary" opposition could emerge, making possible the coexistence (for a brief time) of old and New Lefts within the same orbit.

Given such social and ideological diversity, the New Left as a whole could not have been afflicted with the degree of anti-intellectualism (sometimes referred to as "hostility to theory") that the conventional wisdom assumes. Activists in 1960s movements have been characterized as antidemocratic nihilists with no regard for the pursuit of knowledge, whether in the university or in the arena of social change itself. A disrespect for authority, rife within the counterculture, carried over into all intellectual, political and cultural pursuits. Most of the New Left turned its back on the pretentious, arid theorizing of both academic social scientists and traditional Marxists; they were, understandably in the context of the Vietnam War, anxious to stress the primacy of action. Still, the period was undeniably one of acute intellectual ferment. The SDS, the student movement and the youth culture were born of a deep alienation from technocratic education, cultural boredom and inherited political beliefs. The very notion of a "Great Refusal" that defined an entire decade of rebellion implied, more than anything, a widespread sense of critical and reflective opposition to the status quo; one that was abundantly articulated in books, magazines, music, poetry, films and underground newspapers.

According to Miller (1987), the final draft of the *Port Huron Statement* was woven together after many long and difficult exchanges among the authors, many of whom viewed the manifesto as the first salvo of a new American radicalism. In it one could detect the influence of a wide range of thinkers: C. Wright Mills, Paul Goodman, Albert Camus, Erich Fromm, Allen Ginsberg, Jack Kerouac and John Dewey. That the early SDS sought to transcend, however awkwardly, the confines of both liberalism and Marxism indicates a critical probing, an openness and a willingness to experiment with new ideas. Such an enterprise demanded a restless, eclectic intellectual style, that is, anything but the ritual acceptance of established beliefs or correct ideological lines.

Despite a tendency to glorify spontaneity, most activists within the SDS and elsewhere (e.g., SNCC) respected intellectual work that was removed from the academic milieu; they hoped to reconstitute the educational process on a different, more critical basis that linked campus life to the larger imperatives of social change. Moreover the SDS had, from the outset, assigned a vital if not decisive role in the popular struggles of the time to students and intellectuals.[3] The *Port Huron Statement* is very clear about this (Miller, 1987, chapter 9). In Western Europe, a school of radical theorists (Andre Gorz, Alain Touraine, Serge Mallet and others) insisted that the university was destined to be one of the dynamic centers of "new working-class" initiatives in an increasingly complex, advanced, capitalist order. Wedded to corporate and military priorities, yet home to a new generation of radicals, the university was seen as more a locus of ideological conflict and social transformation than a hostile institution to be smashed.

At the same time, the abiding emphasis on participatory democracy meant that intellectuals would not be assigned any sort of historically decisive (or "Jacobian") role; that tenet was too closely identified with the old left, with the Marxist tradition and, especially, with Leninist regimes. Thus, intellectual energy was absorbed into a broader totality of processes. As Gitlin observes, the New Left was fueled by a cycle of energy that was simultaneously intellectual and moral, political and sexual. The SDS itself originated out of a sense of historical urgency and existential will that set in motion a series of explosive actions and events that, by the late 1960s, took on what Miller (1987, p. 141) calls a nearly "mythic stature". The year 1968 alone was more turbulent than any since the Second World War; from France to Mexico to Japan, from Berkeley to Chicago to Columbia, assaults on politics-as-usual rekindled the long-dormant radical tradition in the West. At the height of the May events in France, activists upheld the dictum that only the imagination could impose limits on what was possible. French sociologist Raymond Aron observed that "almost everyone was in the grip of a kind of delirium. The French people, and certainly the people of Paris, felt that the state had disappeared, that there was no more government and that once more anything was possible" (Caute, 1988, p. 239). Throughout the industrialized world, the proliferation of insurgent movements, however amorphous they were, signalled a legitimation crisis that was profoundly political and cultural as well as economic in origin. The 1960s, despite its many well known failures, did offer a glimpse of a truly radical opposition.

Of course, the New Left as such never developed into such a radical opposition, in the U.S. or elsewhere. There were several reasons for this: the inability to create durable forms of local organization, the absence of a coherent ideology that could link together the disparate groups and movements, a focus on momentary, demonstrative actions at the expense of building alternative forms, a fetishism of Third World liberation movements and their theories and a base of support largely confined to university campuses and college towns. The eclipse of the New Left came down to the collapse of its three main components: the SDS as a national organization, the vision of revolutionary apocalypse and the idea of a youth culture (Flacks, 1989, pp. 96–7). Thus, even to suggest that the turbulence of the 1960s posed the theme of "revolution" or challenged bourgeois hegemony seems farfetched, especially from the vantage point of the 1990s.

Given this context, it should hardly be surprising that, as Miller, Gitlin and others have noted, the New Left scarcely attempted to develop a social theory appropriate to its own experience. (The Marxist–Leninist currents did offer a "theory," but one derived from external models.) Underlying the fiery rhetoric was a spontaneity so strong that strategic thinking about social change (as opposed to mere tactical maneuvering) was impossible. Nor did an imputed "global" solidarity furnish real answers: from issue to issue, from locale to locale, from country to country, each popular struggle essentially went its own way.

BEYOND THE "TOTAL BREAK" SCENARIO

A full historical account of the 1960s legacy, however, cannot stop here; while some parts of the New Left died or were left to atrophy, others continued and even gained strength over time, although often in new guises. Most writers, sympathetic or not, agree that the New Left fell apart sometime between 1968 and 1970. Amid the chaos of left sectarianism, organizational impasse and a wildly self-indulgent counterculture, the "movement" is said to have disintegrated virtually overnight, giving way to cooptation, privatized escape, religious cults, novel therapies and, for some, the return to traditional lifestyles. The historical break was seen as abrupt and total.

In its cover story on the 1960s in January 1988, *Time* magazine wrote that "1968 was a knife blade that severed past from future," an epochal year that "stepped outside of time" (*Time*, 1988, p. 19). In his memoir of the period, Richard Goodwin laments the passing of "the heady days when we thought we were going to change the whole world." Such idealism, he says, was ultimately killed by greed and self-interest.[4] Most would agree with the proposition that the 1960s was a time that embodied great visions of change but which turned into a nightmare of adventurous violence, dogmatic posturing and a decaying drug culture. In 1968 the May events in France, Columbia, Chicago and Mexico City took place; 1968 was also the year of the Martin Luther King and Robert Kennedy assassinations and Richard Nixon's ascendancy to the White House. In David Farber's (1988, p. 263) view, it was the Chicago events outside the Democratic Convention that framed the "breakdown of political discourse," after which the movement became a victim of its own distorted media image. George Katsiaficas (1987, p. 81), whose understanding of events is far less apocalyptic than most, nonetheless wrote that "a whole epoch ended in 1968," For Gitlin, 1968 was the time in which violence and fantasy finally triumphed over rational political discourse and action. "For the rest of the decade," he writes," there was a lingering sense of playing in overtime, wondering when the game was going to end in sudden death." Chicago became the "Gotterdammerung" of the period because "all the protagonists thought polarization served their larger purposes" (Gitlin, 1987, pp. 317–19). Reflecting on the wreckage of SDS in June 1969, Gitlin (ibid., p. 408), in a candid personal statement, confesses that "[a]nxiety and despair were most of what I knew. My world had exploded, ten years of the movement. I had lost the ground I walked on."

For Caute, too, the end came in the wake of the SDS collapse, when the ultraradicalism of Progressive Labor and the Weathermen had destroyed political initiative just as popular mobilization against the war was reaching its peak. The Marxist–Leninist groups turned their wrath on everything from the campuses to the Yippies to the counterculture, resulting in alienation, burnout and, eventually, demobilization. Thus, "the campus insurrection that began at Berkeley in 1964 faded and was replaced by the reassuring contours of normality" (Caute, 1988, p. 449). According to Miller (1987, p. 317), the decade ended with the Weathermen's "Days of Rage" in Chicago in October 1969, when the original democratic spirit of Port Huron was lost in an orgy of random violence. What remained were little more than small oases of "cultural space" along with a "congeries of smaller single-issue movements." In this context the search for democratic renewal could only "swim against the tide of history" (ibid., p. 326).

By 1970, judging from Tom Hayden's personal account, the generation of idealists who, in the context of the anti-war movement, stood for life and against death, was haunted by the specter of hatred, egomania and death. The political culture of the 1960s degenerated into a kind of "radical claustrophobia" that in the end forced many activists out of the movement entirely. Hayden (1988, p. 415) writes that "[a]fter the Chicago trial ended in 1970, everything around me continued to decay, our lives spiralling toward some personal and political abyss." But Hayden, who eventually made the transition from grass-roots activist to California state legislator, came to revise his view both of the New Left and of the political order it sought to call into question: "It took me a long time to accept that, far from being a police state, the system had worked" (ibid., p. xvi).

Gitlin, too, found that with the passing of nationwide campus upheavals in May 1970 an "exhausted movement had lost its moral edge" (Gitlin, 1987, p. 415). Government repression against the student, antiwar and black movements hurt, but the left had collaborated in its own demise; the dialectic of defeat was largely internal, an "implosion." Above all the SDS failed to supply the organization and leadership needed to keep centrifugal tendencies under control. Thus, "the riptide of the Revolution went out with the same force it had surged in with, the ferocious undertow proportionate to the onetime hopes" (ibid., p. 420). Breakdown gave way to an incoherent" grab-bag of movements," a penchant for conventional lifestyles and the ubiquitous "transcendence industry" (ibid., p. 425).

This "implosion" of the New Left, though clearly exaggerated by many observers, did reflect a building tension between the participatory impulse of the early SDS and the emergent vanguardism of Marxist–Leninist currents. For one thing, the Marxist–Leninist contempt for "petty bourgeois" values, individualism and formal democracy – not to mention the university setting itself – amounted to a dismissal of New Left experience *tour court*. The bankruptcy of 1960s radicalism meant that it would be necessary to undertake a new start, inspired perhaps by Cuba, China or, most likely,

Vietnam. In fact, vanguardism represented a facile solution to the chronic 1960s impasse rooted in spontaneity and lack of strategic direction. The Marxist–Leninist response was to substitute organized cadres, party building and "scientific" theory for the frustrating amorphousness of local struggles that seemed to lack political focus. This desperate search for political certainty in a chaotic world, however, turned out to be illusory.

What Gitlin refers to as "pseudo-Leninism" was in reality a caricature of radicalism, indeed a flight from politics, insofar as it rested on a foundation of class guilt, name calling and prefabricated phrases borrowed from other contexts that served as a substitute for genuine theory and analysis. More than that, the Marxist–Leninist style of "desperado politics" was simply another expression of the elitist arrogance toward the common person that typifies vanguardist behavior.

Interestingly, the revisionist literature illuminates the extent to which virtually every 1960s current (e.g., Yippies, the SDS, Marxist–Leninist groups, Weather underground) were afflicted with the same problems. In different ways they shared a romantic fascination with heroic vanguards, an organization dilettantism and a social rootlessness that gave rise to a roving style of politics, a detachment from local constituencies, a male-aggressive leadership and the use of ritual phrases strung randomly together in place of theoretical discourse.

It was therefore easy for activists to gravitate toward simplistic formulas readily available in orthodox Marxism, Leninism and Maoism, a temptation heightened by the weakness of American Marxism and the vast gulf separating the "old" and "new" lefts. At the same time, one is struck by the degree to which both 1960s radicalism and its Marxist–Leninist antithesis adopted a common political language ("smash the state," "smash monogamy," "off the pigs," etc.) and the inevitable self-righteous posturing that accompanied it. In each case, when it came to hard and precise questions about long-term strategy there were surprisingly few statements or manifestos that could furnish viable answers. What were the main features of a rapidly changing social structure in advanced capitalism? What was the character of state power? What were the main forms of ideological control? How could a truly New Left build a politically effective bloc of forces around distinctly radical objectives? Indeed, what were the radical objectives? Of course, theorizing along these lines could never have progressed very far in such a limited time span. The point, however, is that the New Left responded to such pressing questions with silence, whereas the Marxist–Leninist groups were content to apply formulas from another period (nineteenth century capitalism) or another geopolitical setting (Cuba, China or Vietnam).

Meanwhile, the ideology of Black Power advanced by the Panthers and kindred was likewise lacking in strategic potential. As a seductive myth and mobilizing tool, Black Power could be highly cathartic; as a framework for long-term political struggle, however, it was destined to bring only frustration, resting as it did on the charismatic appeal of leaders such as Bobby Seale and Eldridge Cleaver and the specter of ongoing violent conflict between black militants and local police. While the earlier civil rights movement, much like the SDS, sought to incorporate its demands within the orbit of liberal democracy, the Panthers' own version of vanguardism turned out to be just as mechanistic and illusory as that of the white, Marxist–Leninist currents.

It follows that the unravelling of the New Left as a cohesive force was a process that went much deeper than the disintegration of the SDS alone. What needs to be emphasized and what even the revisionist literature fails to recognize, is that the SDS was but a small, distorted part of the entire 1960s scene, a kind of "young boys' network" increasingly cut off from the larger flow of energy and the pressing concerns of students, youth, blacks and women. The internal conflict within the SDS was symptomatic of certain divisions within the New Left, but it was only a single act within the whole drama. Thus, any analysis that seeks to explain the demise of 1960s radicalism as a failure of SDS organizational resolve is highly misleading.[5] As Wini Breines (1988, p. 543) argues, critiques of the New Left that attribute everything to the failure of the SDS have often come from former SDS leaders, typically male, who felt cut off from the growing militancy of local movements. More significantly, such critiques obscure the very rich multiplicity of realities that shaped insurgent activity during the 1960s and later. Breines points out that "[t]here were many centers of action in the movement, many actions, many interpretations, many visions, many experiences. There was no unity because each group, region, campus, commune, collective and demonstration developed differently, but all shared in a spontaneous opposition to racism and inequality, the war in Vietnam and the repressiveness of American social norms and culture, including centralization and hierarchy" (ibid).

Such rebellious energy, moreover, did not disappear with the death of the SDS, nor with the Chicago events or any other apocalyptic moment. Those obituaries that locate the end of 1960s radicalism in the 1968–70 period ignore the fact that peak expressions of militancy actually occurred between 1968 and 1972 rather than 1967–9. Thus it is often forgotten that the protests over the U.S. mining of Haiphong harbor in spring 1972 were quite massive, surpassed only by the May 1970 outbursts that followed President Nixon's bombing of Cambodia and the events at Kent State and Jackson State. Even leaving this aside, it is clear that the broader meaning of the New Left, including its failures and successes, cannot be grasped by the mechanistic "total break" thesis which insists that the "rebellious" 1960s was immediately followed by the "passive" 1970s, and that the failure of organizational resolve was at the center of this presumed collapse. This thesis obscures a sense of history as process rooted in the unfolding of social forces, where past is connected to future, the 1960s to the period that followed.

Despite the popular energy they were able to mobilize, 1960s movements were ultimately unable to consolidate anything resembling local power bases; the dynamics of spontaneity were far too powerful. A potential radical bloc existed, but lacking any clear political translation, ideologically or organizationally, it inexorably dissipated. The problem, however, was not lack of centralized organization or leadership, nor was disruptive sectarianism the critical obstacle. In the context of a New Left that glorified participatory democracy and local community, no centralized structure and no vanguard leadership could have salvaged the radical initiatives of the moment since the very effort to do so would have negated the essence of such initiatives. The disintegration of the New Left, if one can characterize it as that, was a function of much deeper problems at the level of theory and strategy: there was no overall sense of direction, in part because of the persistence of romantic fantasies and revolutionary visions unrelated to the actual forces at work.

ELEMENTS OF CONTINUITY

It would be a mistake to allow preoccupation with the themes of "collapse" and "decline" to obliterate our understanding of the historical legacy of New Left politics. It is impossible to read this new wave of literature on the 1960s without becoming persuaded of the immense novelty of what was going on. In a relatively brief decade, popular struggles ignited a phase of rebellion that touched the lives of millions in the U.S. alone.

What then were the novel and enduring features of 1960s politics? Beyond immediate achievements – helping to force the U.S. military out of Indochina, pressing for social reforms and affirmative action, democratizing many institutions – what was truly original and significant about the New Left? Hayden (1988) suggests that the period was unique precisely in its call for a politics of identity and authenticity that could no longer be realized within either the liberal or socialist traditions. Gitlin (1987) argues that the peculiar blend of politics and culture, especially the music but also the life styles, gave the New Left a distinct, nearly messianic, sense of mission. Miller (1987) and others stress the recurrent theme of participatory democracy. The most visionary account is probably that of Katsiaficas (1968), who situates the 1960s within the European radical traditions of 1848, 1905 and 1917, with 1968 symbolizing another phase of the universal struggle against domination. These and other accounts point toward an understanding of the New Left as the initial expression of explosive new social forces based in the knowledge industry, the new middle strata and marginal groups that are likely to reshape the contours of social change in the West.

To affirm the novelty of the New Left is also to stress the immense gulf that separated the old from New Lefts, the

1930s from the 1960s generation. While Maurice Isserman may be correct in stating that traditional socialist groups sometimes played a creative role in the formation of the New Left (especially the SDS), this connection was always tenuous and strained at best. At least before the celebrated turn toward Marxism, the differences were sharp. The traditional left extolled the primacy of parties, unions, manifestos and programs; a search for ideological certainty cloaked in the garb of "scientific" theory; faith in social progress through economic growth fueled by science and technology; and attachment to conventional social and cultural norms. In contrast, the New Left was anarchistic in its quasi-existential desire for free self-expression and creativity, in its attack on elitism, personality cults and bureaucracy, in its passion for alternative life styles and in its willingness to break with established patterns and experiment with new social arrangements. The short-lived triumph of New Left ideology guaranteed a basic shift away from previous definitions of radical politics, at least those associated with the Marxist tradition.

From this viewpoint, it seems unlikely that such a novel phase of radicalism could have disappeared as abruptly as the conventional (and revisionist) wisdom assumes. Could the "mythic" struggles of the 1960s have come crashing down to earth so quickly, with so little trace of their historical influence? Put another way, was the break between the 1960s and 1970s really so total, so cataclysmic?

The "total-break" argument rests on a myopic view of how the 1960s generated enormous currents of social change that flowed into the subsequent two decades, beneath the conservative hegemony of national politics. A nostalgia for the specific drama of New Left forms – huge, unruly demonstrations, marches, sit-ins, street confrontations and dramatic cultural events – can easily obscure those elements of historical continuity that outlive such forms. An identifiable 1960s legacy has persisted and in some ways even expanded since the epochal events of 1968–70.

The legacy was one less of structural or policy changes than of shifts in popular consciousness, in the "rules" governing most facets of everyday life. Participants in New Left politics and the counterculture typically experienced, or at least anticipated, a sense of cultural renewal. What was the long-term impact of such renewal? The total break scenario assumes that the vast majority of activists either turned away from this conversion (akin to the "God is Dead" thesis) or simply renounced their progressive commitments in favor of careers, consumerism and privatized lifestyles. The general thrust of both conventional and revisionist literature notwithstanding, it now seems clear that the main trajectory from 1960s to 1980s does not fit either pattern. Ronald Fraser, for example, interviewed a large number of New Leftists from several countries and found that most are still politically active; while few could be defined as "socialists," most remain dedicated to some vision of social change while many are described as "independent leftists" (Fraser, 1988, p. 367). Most ex-activists, especially in the U.S., continue to adhere to broadly libertarian values, even where ideological self-understanding may be lacking.[6] The exhaustive study conducted by Daniel Yankelovich (1982) and associates found that many 1960s beliefs, most notably a distrust of authority, persisted in large sectors of the American population throughout the 1970s.

More revealing insights into the post-1960s dynamics abound in an important study by Jack Whalen and Richard Flacks (1989). They undertook the difficult task of analyzing shifts in ideology and life styles among a leading group of student radicals who were involved in the burning of the Bank of America building in Santa Barbara, California in February 1970. Comparing activists with nonactivists from the same milieu, the authors found a surprising continuity in both sets of respondents: the militants, for their part, were able to sustain the idealism that had inspired the commitment of their student years through their adult working lives.

In dozens of interviews, Whalen and Flacks construct fascinating portraits of young people who were consumed by "revolutionary" identities in 1970 and who, when faced with the erosion of the student movement and its various supports, had to search for a new world of meaning. Despite often severe dislocation, most ex-activists somehow managed to integrate New Left themes (participation, autonomy, creativity) into their work, careers, family and community lives

(Whalen and Flacks, 1989, chapter 6). Fifteen years after the bank burning, former participants still viewed themselves as "progressives" or "left liberals"; in contrast, nonactivists were more likely to be "conservatives" with comfortable, suburban lifestyles tied to the nuclear family, career mobility and material affluence. Ex-activists typically worked in the public sector or in social service occupations, while most non-activists had well paying jobs in the corporate sector.

The 1960s militants, of course, were no longer involved in the demonstrative politics of their youths. They were either active in the more routine world of popular movements and community service, or they had become "disengaged." Many were what Whalen and Flacks call "passive radicals." Here the response of one former activist is worth repeating at length:

> I don't think my political beliefs that I had and was acting on in 1970 have changed. I'm not suddenly ready to register with the Republican Party and I'm not into the idea of getting a job at the top of a corporation. I think that capitalism is collapsing right before our eyes. . . . And Ronald Reagan – it's a living nightmare. And I'm against the death penalty. I don't want to put up a new parking lot across the street. [But] I'm not doing anything to make those things happen. I know my life is very insular, but it's the one I'm living" (Whalen and Flacks, 1989, pp. 210–12).

Whalen and Flacks demonstrate, against all received wisdom, that the 1960s legacy has had a durable impact on the consciousness of those who were most engaged. Their findings might have been even more suggestive had they chosen to interview participants outside the inner circle, so that ideological impact could be measured according to levels of involvement. Their study has put to rest the myth that New Leftists were simply affluent students whose "alienation" soon gave way to high-powered careers, large incomes and conservative beliefs. What emerges instead is a continuity, however partial and uneven, of ideas and even commitments, despite a profound change of political milieu. Most ex-activists still distrust authority, reject conventional lifestyles and question materialistic values. The contours of progressive politics in the 1980s were thus probably shaped less by the limits of personal conviction than by various contextual factors that, at least during the Reagan years, encouraged more low-key forms of activity. It might even be argued that the continuity described by Whalen and Flacks reflects a political maturing insofar as a sense of "realism" – despite its overall reformist implications – has replaced the earlier New Left eschatology with its naïve faith in total, imminent change, its glorification of marginalized strata and its romantic attachment to "armed struggle."

POST-1960s RADICALISM

The implications of the Whalen–Flacks study can be carried a step further: ideological continuity of the sort identified here may suggest other, more concrete and structural, linkages between the 1960s and what followed later. Like most other observers of the period, the authors never fully explore the intricate connection between New Left radicalism and the proliferation of new social movements in the 1970s and 1980s. The rhythm of grass-roots feminist, gay, peace, ecology and urban protest movements that have mobilized millions of people *since* 1970 clearly has this pulse in the 1960s. In the most global sense, as Katsiaficas (1968) argues, the New Left and the new movements have roots in the assault against the same general conditions: bureaucratization of authority relations, industrial and urban decay, the ecology crisis, the arms race, widespread social anomie and so forth. Surely the collective forms of action that have evolved mainly outside the sphere of production, and that have certainly grown in numbers since the 1960s, would seem to affirm the validity of this argument.

As is shown elsewhere, the new movements embrace themes that were already present, in less developed form, in 1960s radicalism: a popular, grass-roots insurgency centered primarily outside the existing (pluralist) public sphere; an emphasis on qualitative goals, cultural radicalism, collective and consumption-oriented demands and nonclass-based identities (Boggs, 1986, chapter 2). At the same time, while such thematic commonality lends historical meaning to the period, the very modalities of popular struggles have shifted dramatically. The 1960s phase was characterized by a diffuse, rapidly shifting, more or less rootless politics with apocalyptic ideologies and exhibitionist style. The later appearance of social movements, however, signalled more durable, stable patterns of activity that were grounded in concrete, ongoing work in patient efforts to build coherent organization. With the new movements there is less attachment to externally derived ideologies, and also less reliance on the campuses as sources of mobilization. (Indeed, the very idea of "mobilization" seems far less appropriate to the new phase of activism.)

During the 1970s and 1980s, contrary to prevailing opinion, local movements actually became more numerous and differentiated; thus the feminist, ecology and peace movements each gave expression to a diverse range of groups, ideologies and strategies. There is uniformity, however, that seems irrepressible; new social movements are located at the core of social contradictions (class, bureaucratic, patriarchal, ecological and racial) that permeate advanced capitalist societies. The New Left was perhaps the first, and clearly the most explosive, glimpse of cumulative struggles around these contradictions, which were not anticipated by liberalism or Marxism.

New movements expanded at a time when the growth of centralized power and the bureaucratization of public life led to a closure of political discourse, to a massive gap between a remote, national state and a more dynamic, local life. In this context an independent radicalism implied more than anything the struggle for empowerment, though one confined essentially to civil society (Bookchin, 1989, chapter 4). The feminist and ecology movements take on particular significance here, insofar as they both represent, in different ways, efforts to overcome alienation, a sense of imbalance and domination. These movements ideally embellish not only democratization but a recovery of the self in a world in which politics has been deformed. Not coincidentally, both feminist and ecological sensibilities intersect with, and are reinforced by, the progressive side of the holistic revolution in therapy, healing and health care stemming from the counterculture. As Bookchin (1989, p. 157) stresses, both feminism and ecology demystify the role of power in all spheres of life; both carry forward the strong anti-authoritarian impulses of the 1960s and both cut across class lines, status issues and parochial interests. Further, there is within feminism and ecology alike a prefigurative dimension that rejects a purely instrumental approach to politics typical of liberal pluralism and the productivism inherent in Marxism.

New social movements in the U.S. have survived into the 1980s, often even extending their local presence at a time when the right has had a strangle-hold on the national agenda. Surely this phenomenon owes much to the absence of left-ist parties and the relative closure of the two-party system, the partial inroads of the Rainbow Coalition notwithstanding. New movements have been at the center of public protests around an infinite variety of concerns: apartheid in South Africa, nuclear reactors, the arms race, violence against women, abortion rights, gay rights, homelessness, U.S. intervention in Central America, affirmative action, animal rights, oil drilling, toxic wastes and tenants' rights, to name only the most visible. In this context, new movements have catalyzed the formation of alternative institutions (cooperatives, alternative media, bookstores, clinics, etc.); they have helped sustain electoral coalitions with progressive agendas; they have given rise to a new critical discourse and a radical intelligentsia both within and outside the universities, and they have stimulated the rebirth of student activism in the late 1980s (Vellela, 1988).

The growth of a radical, intellectual subculture is the sometimes forgotten legacy of the 1960s. Many elements of this subculture – feminism, Western Marxism, post-structuralism, social ecology, critical political economy – converge with the themes of the new movements, which permeate not only the universities but also the high schools, media, art world, trade unions and even some municipal governments.

In higher education, the discovery of neo-Marxism and the various offshoots of critical social theory by a generation of students and scholars, a process that did not really begin until the late 1960s, was inspired by the New Left preoccupation with ideology and consciousness, culture, social relations and the larger problem of domination that extends not only to institutions but also into the very interstices of civil society and the natural habitat. Creative theorizing, while often dull and abstruse, has, on the whole, transcended the limits of mainstream academic work, the New Left and traditional Marxism. As for the stale formulas of Marxist–Leninist thinking, they seem increasingly archaic in the dynamic, pluralistic world of postmodernity and the new social movements, not to mention the disintegration of the Communist world itself. The presence of a sizeable critical intelligentsia alongside the popular movements underpins the renewal of student political involvement. Beneath the surface manifestations of social conservatism and careerism on most campuses has unfolded a surprising amount of ferment and protest. Student mobilization at dozens of schools has been fueled by some familiar issues (such as racism, affirmative action, CIA recruiting, U.S. intervention abroad), along with newer priorities such as gay rights, toxic waste and animal experimentation. Vellela (1988, pp. 249–56) lists hundreds of progressive organizations, programs and protest actions on major American campuses, most of which (in 1987) achieved expression through nine umbrella student groups.

The immense diversity of social movements makes it difficult to generalize about their bases of support, organizational styles, strategies or trajectories: some look to direct action, others are more inwardly focused, and still others are content to pursue moderate reforms. During relatively quiet periods, as in the 1980s, movements, regardless of their ultimate goals, commonly lose their subversive energy. At the same time, Katsiaficas (1987) is correct in emphasizing the radical potential of new movements insofar as they can be located within emergent global forces of social transformation. Thus, while the New Left was more explosive and was guided by greater revolutionary pretensions, the new social movements have probably carried forward a more deeply oppositional theory and practice. This is especially true in Western Europe where, for example, the Greens movement achieved a dramatic breakthrough of sorts in the mid-1980s, laying the basis of a radical strategy that had always eluded the New Left (and the diffusion of movements that followed). Constructed on a unique convergence of citizens' initiatives and local movements, the Greens movement has sought to incorporate essentially New Left themes within a coherent party structure and electoral framework.

As post-war capitalism moved to stabilize itself on a foundation of centralized state power, Keynesian social policies, a militarized economy and the institutionalization of class conflict, the new social movements made their own indelible imprint on the political landscape. Like similar movements in an earlier era, these modern incarnations of popular struggle have run up against the immense power of national and multinational economic and political institutions; power that has restricted their autonomy and, in many cases, absorbed, isolated or marginalized them. For most movements, however, some form of insurgency persisted throughout the 1970s and 1980s, shaped more often than not by the historic concerns set in motion by the 1960s: the recovery of community, direct action, personal politics and consciousness transformation. As Bookchin writes: "No radical movement of any importance in the future could ignore the ethical, aesthetic and anti-authoritarian legacy created by the New Left and the communalist experiments that emerged in the counterculture" (Bookchin, 1989, p. 151).

CONCLUSION

The historical lineage connecting the New Left and new social movements has been obscured, if not completely ignored, in the bulk of writing on the period, which has adhered to the total-break scenario. The notion that the New Left came to a sudden, convulsive ending around 1970 or earlier blurs not only this connection but also obliterates the historical meaning of the 1960s as such. To postulate two distinctly separate moments in time – the turbulent 1960s vs the quiescent 1970s and beyond – not only ignores the remarkable diffusion of new movements but, perhaps more significantly, over-idealizes the New Left. Thus, of the post-1960s period, Gitlin concedes the "formidable success of popular movements, local projects and reform efforts," but quickly adds that it would be naïve to believe that history has moved forward and upward when, in fact, "left victories" really dwindled over time (Gitlin, 1987, p. 433). As we have seen, Miller (1987) views with contempt the "congeries of movements" that followed the disintegration of the

SDS. Whether seen in a positive light or not, scattered references to New Left residues in whatever form do not amount to a serious analysis of the 1960s legacy.

As for the New Left itself, Katsiaficas conjures an image of "revolutionary politics" that may be only slightly more exaggerated than the revisionist norm. For him, the 1960s was an historical watershed of a "synchronized world-historical movement" directed against far-flung networks of domination (Katsiaficas 1987, p. 27). He argues that the New Left brought a renovated idea of revolution to the industrialized countries through the "praxis of millions" tied to an "insurgent culture" that is not limited to material concerns (ibid., p. 22). Moreover, "As the practice of the New Left went beyond the existing categories of experience, so its theory transcended the established forms of social thought" (ibid., p. 220). Such sentiments agree with the apocalyptic visions trumpeted by a good many 1960s activists, but after two decades one can only ask, "What theory? What transcendence?" The implications of such an overdrawn picture should be obvious: in claiming too much for the New Left it winds up claiming too little for what followed.

This is not to denigrate the immensely powerful and enduring radical legacy that grew out of the New Left. The point is that the 1960s were merely a beginning. As an embryonic and youthful movement, if often affirmed the drama of the spectacle and a discourse of inflated rhetoric over political substance; the idea that the turbulence of the 1960s was somehow "revolutionary" could be entertained only as fiction. Despite its often grandiose self-conception, New Left politics was never more than a series of disparate, chaotic revolts against authority; there was no transformative project, no systematic challenge to bourgeois hegemony. Probably the most that can be established is that it anticipated, in multiple ways, the likely future shape of political opposition in the West. If the later social movements have become more routine and less attractive to the mass media, they also embody a theoretical depth and practical grounding that was rarely visible in the 1960s. Perhaps for this reason, feminism alone has, since the early 1970s, shaped popular consciousness, daily life and public policy to a greater extent than all New Left struggles combined.

Notes

1. See, for example, Caute (1988); Farber (1988); Fraser (1988); Gitlin (1987); Hayden (1988); Isserman (1987); Katsiaficas (1987); Miller (1987); Goodwin (1988); Stevens (1987); Vellela (1988); and Whalen and Flacks (1989).
2. A notable exception to this dismissive attitude toward the New Left is Breines (1982).
3. On the role of students and intellectuals as agencies of change in New Left ideology, see Breines (1982, chapter 6).
4. Goodwin expressed these ideas in an interview with the *Los Angeles Times* (1988).
5. Sale (1973) was the first of many to argue for the decisive role of SDS organizational collapse in the decline of the New Left.
6. The response of Black Panther co-founder Bobby Seale, based on a 1988 interview, may not be typical but is nonetheless suggestive. Seale, who works at Temple University in Philadelphia, has been working to help build grass-roots movements around the issues of racism and literacy. "I'm still a political revolutionary," said Seale. "The fire never went out of me, but perceptions and realizations change" (*New York Times*, 1988).

References

Boggs, Carl (1986) *Social Movements and Political Power* (Philadelphia: Temple University Press).

Bookchin, Murray (1989) *Remaking Society* (Montreal: Black Rose Books).

Breines, Wini (1982) *The Great Refusal: Community and Organization in the New Left, 1962–68* (New York: Praeger).

Breines, Wini (1988) "Whose new left?", *Journal of American History* (September).

Caute, David (1988) *The Year of the Barricades: A Journey Through 1968* (New York: Harper and Row).

Farber, David (1988) *Chicago '68* (Chicago: University of Chicago Press).

Flacks, Richard (1989) "What happened to the new left?", *Socialist Review* (January-March).

Fraser, Ronald (ed.) (1988) *A Student Generation in Revolt* (New York: Pantheon).

Gitlin, Todd (1987) *The Sixties: Years of Hope, Days of Rage* (New York: Bantam).

Goodwin, Richard (1988) "A Different View of the Sixties," *Los Angeles Times* (14 September), section C, p. 1.

Goodwin, Richard (1988) *Remembering America: A Voice from the Sixties* (Boston: Little, Brown).

Hayden, Tom (1988) *Reunion: A Memoir* (New York: Random House).

Isserman, Maurice (1987) *If I Had a Hammer: The Death of the Old Left and the Birth of the New Left* (New York: Basic Books).

Katsiaficas, George (1987) *The Imagination of the New Left: A Global Analysis of 1968* (Boston: South End Press).

Miller, James (1987) *Democracy is in the Streets* (New York: Simon and Schuster).

New York Times (1988) "Bobby Seale: Legacy of a Revolutionary Revisited," 20 August, p. 19.

Sale, Kirkpatrick (1973) *SDS* (New York: Basic Books).

Stevens, Jay (1987) *Storming Heaven* (New York: Harper and Row).

Time (1988) "1968: The Year that Shaped a Generation," Special Issue, vol. 11, no. 19 (January), p. 19.

Vellela, Tony (1988) *New Voices: Student Political Activism in the '80s and '90s* (Boston: South End Press).

Whalen, Jack and Richard Flacks (1989) *Beyond the Barricades: The Sixties Generation Grows Up* (Philadelphia: Temple Univeristy Press).

Yankelovich, Daniel (1982) *New Rules* (New York: Bantam).

14 The Left as the Counterculture of Modernity *

Zygmunt Bauman

> At the end of this development the intellectuals of the opposition asked themselves in all seriousness: is there still a proletariat? Is there still a ruling class? Whereas they would have been more justified in asking: is there still an intellectual opposition?
>
> Short-term hopes are futile. Long-term resignation is suicidal.
>
> Hans Magnus Enzenberger

The Left is characterized by its lack of humor. This has set it apart from other forms of opposition to capitalism, e.g., avant-garde art. The latter's irony, self-mockery, and playfulness was a *lèse-majesté* to the Left as much as it was to the priests of the establishment. *Épater-le-bourgeois* has never been a Left strategy, because the Left has treated *le bourgeois* seriously as the author of a project the Left thought worth fulfilling and as the hindrance to its fulfilment at the same time.

The left was and remained until recently the counter-culture of capitalism. Etiologically it could only come into being once capitalist culture launched a program geared towards achieving a rational society. Logically, it made sense only by "taking capitalism at its word" – a demand to deliver on the capitalist promise. Liberty, Equality, and Brotherhood were capitalist passwords. The Left had nothing to add. It only took the capitalist program seriously and asked everyone else to do the same.

The Left was indebted to capitalism in a number of ways. First, that one can change the world by relying solely on

* Reprinted from *Telos*, no. 70 (Winter, 1986–7), pp. 81–93.

human resources. Second, that the world can be improved by rational human intervention. Third, that to do this it is sufficient to increase the material wealth at mankind's disposal, and to make nature useful, first by learning its secrets, and then relating it to human needs and ignoring the rest. Fourth, that as material wealth grows, so do the possibilities for happiness, understood as the lack of want, but also as freedom from natural necessity. Fifth, that this freedom will promote liberty, equality and brotherhood among people and, given the possibility of this rational choice, people will select a way of life best suited to their needs. Sixth, that the value of "really existing" societies can be measured by the degree to which liberty, equality and brotherhood have been attained, and the chances for their further growth.

Because it had borrowed all these capitalist ideas and treated them seriously, the Left had become a critic of capitalist practice. Eager to successfully complete the process, the Left questioned the qualifications of its current managers. Capitalist practice had to be rejected because it could not fulfill the capitalist promise, and it threatened to waste the opportunities opened up by the capitalist revolution.

The critique of capitalist practice had to be on two grounds – moral and rational ones. The newly attained material wealth had not been used wisely, i.e., it had not been used to promote liberty, equality and brotherhood. Capitalist administration of production generated far less wealth than could be achieved, and in sufficient quantities to put an end to poverty.

Thus, the Left critique of capitalist practice pointed out that the reproduction of economic inequality limits liberty (or allows only for pseudo-liberty) and as long as the profit motive determined the production of wealth, the use of resources and technological opportunities would remain erratic, wasteful, and irrational. In other words, the Left critique claimed that the capitalist administration of social production did not live up to the standards set by the capitalist revolution.

Disenchanted with the capitalist administration of social production, the Left looked for a more appropriate historical agent, better suited for the tasks on the historical agenda.

For most of the Left, the industrial working class seemed the natural option. A number of reasons spoke in favor of this – at least at the time. (1) As an historical agent, the propertyless working class had no track record and thus was not discredited. (2) The working class was rapidly growing to the point of eventually encompassing the nation as a whole. (3) Unlike other disaffected classes, industrial workers were subject to uniform rhythm and discipline, technically trained and organically tied to rational production. (4) They showed proclivities to militancy. Their often violent rebellion against the rise of capitalism easily could be misread as resistance to capitalist administration. (5) For reasons of militancy, industrial workers had already been defined as the "dangerous classes" and a threat to capitalist order. Here the Left only accepted the dominant view. (6) Industrial workers were a particularly tempting choice, as they clearly needed the guidance of the educated elite, of which most Left critics were a part. Workers could be raised to the level of historical agency only by engaging intellectuals as supervisors of the historical process.

All these considerations have now turned into their opposites. Industrial workers are now the most rapidly shrinking part of the population. It is projected that within a generation they will be reduced to the size of agricultural labor at the beginning of this century. Employees who have displaced traditional industrial workers are transient, unorganized, scattered and unskilled – unlikely candidates to rule a rational society. Organized labor's militancy is now defensive in nature and particularistic in vision. Far from being a "dangerous class," organized labor has become the staunchest defender of law and order. Rather than listening to the spokesmen of reason, it has been seeking illumination from the entertainment industry.

The changes in the nature of industrial labor have not made today's capitalist society more rational or just. If anything, poverty and suffering are still increasing. But poverty is no longer associated with organized labor. It has become much less romantic and politically interesting. It is now a suffering that does not entail redemption but calls for more bureaucracy and – if heeded – this call would only strengthen the oppressive grip of the capitalist state. In addition, this new kind of poverty, the poverty of flawed consumers, sees the rich and powerful not as enemies, but as role models and as the measure of their own inadequacy. Thus, it is difficult to see the new poor as agents of historical transformation. The Left is reluctant to throw in its lot with this particular form of suffering. There can be pity and compassion, but no political identification.

To the extent that the Left seeks to retain its identity as the counterculture of capitalism, it finds itself without any historical agent to complete the capitalist project. This absence of a plausible agent creates an unprecedented situation. It is at the root of the present "disenchantment" and "loss of direction" or, more simply, the contemporary crisis of the Left.

There are two common reactions to this sense of crisis. The first is to dismiss this loss of direction as another case of middle-class intellectuals getting cold feet when confronted with successive spells of misfortune. Thus, it is claimed that organized labor's revolutionary potential is far from exhausted and that it must remain the benchmark of Left politics. Such a reaction is reinforced by the Left's collective memory. But even the most powerful collective memory is bound to weaken under the pressure of a prolonged input of negative experience, and difficult to explain away by readjusting old ways of thinking. It is unlikely, therefore, that this reaction, with its limited life-expectancy, will provide a firm foundation for a Left capable of engaging effectively with the crucial disabilities of contemporary Western Society.

The first reaction doesn't produce a unified politics. One possible politics is to translate loyalty to the working class as the historical agent to loyalty to organized labor. In practice, this means uncritically supporting organized labor, whatever its interests and demands may be, as "by definition" anticapitalist. This may occasionally re-establish credibility during brief periods of trade-union militancy. In the long run, however, it is likely to reinforce the divisive "policy of closure" pursued by a class in retreat. Rather than contributing to solving social ills, this policy intensifies them. Whatever the value of this policy, its Left credentials are, for these reasons, in doubt.

Another offshoot of this reaction is a politics privileging an orthodox philosophy of history. If "really existing" workers do not behave according to the pattern this philosophy suggests, all the worse for "really existing" workers. Their deviation from the projected pattern may be easily explained in terms of ideological state apparatuses, police repression, consumerism, social democratic betrayals, bribes, or the weakening of Left intellectuals. As a temporary abnormality, the behavior of "really existing" workers is dismissed as a possible refutation of a policy grounded in the philosophy of history. In practice, this is a sectarian policy of retreat into ever smaller groups of faithful, who reinforce their collective legitimacy by imputing to workers (as they should be and not as they are) their own middle-class spiritual tribulations.

Since life is short, and waiting for workers to change "in the long run" from "really existing" into "existentially real" has limited appeal for anyone but the most patient (and in revolutionary politics patience is suspect: it smells of treason), this politics leads to demands for shortcuts. Ever since the Russian populists – who, having found among the "people" more appreciation for the Tsar than for revolution, resorted to revolution "for the people" but not "by the people" – the politics under discussion occasionally ends up in terrorism. Unlike the Russian populists, the new terrorism is not necessarily aimed at emperors. Thanks to the modern media and the "global village" it has created, any act of spectacular cruelty now attracts the attention that only plots against kings once commanded. Apart from its more repulsiveness, the trouble with terrorism as a "Left" policy is, of course, that however many personal problems it may solve, it can hardly promote traditional Left goals. If anything, it allows the capitalist state to mobilize popular cravings for law and order to reinvigorate the fading popularity of the interests its policy defends.

The second reaction is the very opposite of the first: it proclaims the "end of modernity" and the coming of "postmodernity." Accordingly, the times of "universal projects," of a world that made such projects plausible, are over. From this point on, however, the theorists of postmodernity split. Some dwell on the growing plurality of the contemporary world, on the autonomy of "language games," "communi-

ties of meaning," or "cultural traditions" that are impervious to objective evaluation since they themselves individually provide the ground of all authority that any evaluation
may claim. Others do not feel obliged to refer to the changing
world to justify a plurality of ideas. The difference between
postmodernity and modernity appears to them as another
chapter in the history of thought. They abandon the futile
search for universal standards of truth, justice and taste, and
modestly claim that there is nothing but our own conviction to justify our decision to pursue values we claim worth
pursuing. The steadfastness with which we stick to our decision is all the more powerful for our realization that "history is not on our side," and others are unlikely to adopt
values we cherish. We have neither material force nor arguments to make them change their mind.

In varying degrees, both forms of postmodernist theory
are philosophies of surrender. Both resign themselves to the
impossibility, or unlikelihood, of improving the world, aware
of the powerlessness of critique in influencing other communities.[1] Occasionally, in the past, despair led to courage.
This particular despair does not. The only courage that may
be born of resignation is one feeding on resilience in self-
preservation.

As a philosophy of resignation and futility, postmodernism
can hardly serve as the foundation for the Left's new self-
identity. The Left-intellectuals' current flirtation with
postmodernity can be accounted for by the desperation with
which new inspirations are sought within a context that
appears increasingly as a theoretical void. This romance of
the Left with postmodernity, however, is bound to prove
another case of unrequited love. Indeed, while condemn-
ing as futile the hopes that bourgeois values can ever be
universalized, postmodern theory at the same time declares
the futility of the Left. There is no conceivable way a realistic Left program could be patched together out of postmodernist theory. There can be no Left as a counter-culture,
i.e., a positive and effective critique of neglects, drawbacks,
and mismanagements in implementing the cultural promise of a better society, without the conviction that this cultural promise is viable and in principle realizable. There
can be no Left without the belief that society can be improved

and history brought to our side. There can be no Left without the idea that among different things, some are good and some are wrong, and that the first can be made more numerous than the latter. Postmodern theory is an invitation to intellectuals to make the best of their freedom bought at the price of irrelevance. Whatever else the Left can be, it cannot, by definition, be irrelevant.

This does not mean that postmodernist theory, in its acceptance of contemporary society as irreparably plural and exclusive of any "foundation" or "meta-narrative," cannot breed a radical critique. It does mean, however, that not all radicalism is Left. The radicalism inspired by the postmodernity debate is an aesthetic radicalism: a radicalism of self-expression and self-affirmation, dictated by the awareness that all constraints have been removed from action, now subject solely to decisionist logic. Left radicalism is, first and foremost, a moral radicalism. It is addressed to objective reality and is conscious of its needs. It is subject to a goal-directed logic based on values. This action is self-monitored by its ability to promote objectively viable values. The Left's moral radicalism cannot be rebuilt using the postmodernity debate as a foundation.

If these two responses are either backward-looking or unpromising, it may be advisable to look for a third one. This third response is the reconstitution of the Left critique as the counter-culture of modernism and may avoid the drawbacks of the other two, while inserting the Left in the most crucial moral issues of Western society today.

A "counter-culture of modernism" differs from a "counter-culture of capitalism" in several respects. The counter-culture of capitalism was predicated on the possibility of the emancipation of labor from capital. It saw present and future society the way capitalism did: as a society whose members were primarily engaged in labor, in a society organized around the task of replenishing the labor supply (productive relations proving their rationality by promoting the proliferation of productive forces). This task, the counter-culture of capitalism maintained, was ill-served by capital. Realizing the first task introduced an auxiliary task: removing capital from the administration of the productive process and replacing it with another version of the self-administration of labor.

The unanticipated effect of Left pressure and of the politics of industrial labor it generated, turned out to be the very opposite of what had been expected. Instead of the emancipation of labor from capital, what happened was the emancipation of capital from labor. Today capital depends less and less on labor for its reproduction and growth. Increased investment means less labor, and greater profits are achieved through less labor. Instead of engaging the rest of society as producers or servants of the productive process, capital today engages society as consumers or servants of consumption. The most obvious consequence of the changed mechanism of the reproduction of capital, and of the new form of systemic domination is the obsolescence of the self-management of producers as a valid alternative to the present system. There are, however, other less self-evident consequences.

For the revelation of those other consequences, the Left is indebted, as so often in the past, to the system's political administrators. They were the first to draw practical conclusions from the newly acquired freedom of capital from labor and the newly acquired freedom of politics from the task of recommodification of labor. The present upsurge of neo-conservative politics, the reappearance of notions that the previous network of class-based checks and balances rendered unmentionable for many a decade, indicates that such conclusions have been drawn. In pursuing these new policies without fear of imminent backlash, neo-conservative administrators assume the irreversibility of the process leading possibly to a complete emancipation of capital and marginalization of that labor that capital may need, residually, for its reproduction. In assuming this they may feel again that history "is on their side." This feeling generates an otherwise difficult to obtain political boldness that the ruling classes have not exhibited in a long time.

The Left should be indebted to neo-conservatism for exposing values in urgent need of protection – values with which the Left has been hardly concerned with, until the new dangers have made them visible. There is no need to ask what the hammer is, Heidegger used to say, until it is broken. Some vital facets of that society brought about by the bourgeois revolution remained invisible to the Left as long as they remained "unproblematically given," and taken for granted. Under the neo-conservative threat, they have been made problematic. What are these new problems?

To start with, the poor are less and less important to the reproduction of capital in their traditional role as the "reserve army of labor." They are no longer the object of concern for the twofold political task of recommodification of labor and limitation of working class militancy. The previously taken-for-granted principle of social responsibility for the survival – and, indeed, the well-being – of that part of society not directly engaged by capital as producers (a principle resulting from an encounter of Left moral pressures and capital's instrumental needs), has suddenly come under attack. In view of the progressive emancipation of capital from labor, the reaffirmation of the principle cannot be left to the rationality of the productive process. The logic of economics cannot be viewed as an ally. It has to be re-negotiated and re-imposed by appeal to those aspects of the counter-culture that capitalism tended to underemphasize: political democracy as distinct from the self-management of producers.

Without this new anchorage, today's poor are under a threat worse than the misery of the early capitalist workhouses. Those were at least institutions of "social rehabilitation" in terms of the requirements of rising capital in acute need of a rising labor force. Today, the rehabilitation rhetoric in which welfare transfers are wrapped may only be used, in view of its phoniness, as a device to confirm the inadequacy of the poor and their ineligibility for social assistance. The same Social Darwinist rhetoric that once served to reforge small producers into disciplined industrial laborers, today firmly and irreversibly stamps the poor as stigmatized, permanent outcasts of the consumer society, underserving of citizen status. It is unlikely that welfare transfers will be eliminated. The obsessive public ritual of counting "the costs of welfare" immediately translated as the "taxpayer's sacrifice" is a tool used to raise a wall of incomprehension and estrangements between the "fit" and the "unfit," and deepen the stigma attached to poverty. Quite real, however, is another threat: that of welfare transfers becoming instruments of disenfranchisement and the withdrawal of citizenship rights for that rising minority of the consumer society who cannot prove their citizenship in the only way a consumer market admits. The reality of such a threat has been documented by the legally enforced interference of welfare agencies with the private and family life of their "clients": an imposed "infantilization" of welfare recipients through denial of their rights to autonomous decision-making, and the dense network of surveillance that consumes an ever growing slice of welfare funds. Thus the poor are not just growing poorer. They are being made into a deviant category: a section of the population defined as a separate entity by the withdrawal, or at least suspension, of political and personal rights that were thought to be the lasting and universal achievement of modernity.

The poor are the first to experience the threat to democracy and citizenship rights – and to experience it in the most tangible form. But they are not the only ones under threat. The political arena is in the process of acquiring a new role in the reproduction of the social system. Its function in systemic reproduction was, throughout most of the modern era, confined to guaranteeing the general conditions for the smooth reproduction of capital–labor relations. With this function performed, the perpetuation of the structure of domination could be entrusted to the mechanisms built into the capitalist relations of production. Capital, engaging the bulk of the population as producers and servants of production, could be relied upon as the major drilling and disciplining force. Emancipated from labor, capital cannot and need not carry on this function. The reproduction of the structure of domination becomes directly the matter of law and order, rather than indirectly the matter of the "work ethic." Systemic reproduction, in other words, has become more than ever before the responsibility of the political state.

Under these circumstances new pressures come to bear on political democracy and the modern form of public life in general. Indeed, with the new and enhanced function of the state, the political game cannot be left to "democratic" politicians. Considerable freedom of political opinion and organization, which virtually all interests enjoyed through a better part of modern history (the quality of modernity that the Left came to see – or rather not see – as unproblematic), was more than tangentially related to the relative innocuousness of political conflict in a system where domination was guaranteed primarily through non-political means. Too much hangs on political conflict today to expect this situation to last. Two kinds of assaults on political democracy as we know it are to be expected and, indeed, signs of both are already discernable.

First, there will be attempts to preserve the facade of political democracy while draining the substance of politics from public forms of democratic life. This can be seen in the shifting of real decision-making from ostensible democratic institutions to government bureaucracies unaccountable to democratic control. The growing hysteria around "state secrets" is instrumentalized to remove the daily work of the state from control by its subjects. This is facilitated by technological means presently at the government's disposal, which allow the most seminal decisions affecting the citizen's survival to be taken and implemented before democratic institutions have a chance to intervene. For example, modern warfare no longer requires the mobilization of popular emotions for waging wars. Indeed, it does not even require informing the population that they are in a state of war. Especially in the case of great powers, the leverage provided to state secrecy by the "external threat" and the procedural patterns it breeds, is exaggerated by relegating all but the most trivial political decisions to state security.

Second, the range of issues open to discussion within the democratic process is shrinking. This is brought about by proclaiming a growing number of radical attitudes out of the bounds of democracy; by lowering the threshold of opinions considered subversive;[2] privatization of a growing number of functions previously performed by the state;[3] and problematizing of the visible side of the democratic process by reducing it, with the help of technological media, to popularity contests where issues evaporate in public-relations exercises.

One of the consequences of the emancipation of capital from labor may be, therefore, the even more crucial emancipation of political power from democratic institutions. This is all the more important given the state's enhanced destructive powers and the deeper penetration by state bureaucracies within spheres hitherto relegated to private life.

The severity of the first factor cannot be overestimated. We live under the shadow of mass destruction. This has rendered possible the end of history and the human race. As such, it goes beyond the scope of a traditional politics meant to deal with everyday problems of human welfare. But the existence of weapons of mass destruction is also crucial for internal politics. As the ultimate weapons permitting the total annihilation of "external enemies," they also allow the state to become emancipated from control by its own society. This is the decisive link in the chain of factors that threaten the survival of the democratic achievements of modernity. No definite progress can be made by the Left without the destruction of the weapons of mass destruction. This is not merely another concern of the Left, but the key to the viability of its identity as the counter-culture of modernity.

The second factor that renders particularly sinister the emancipation of political bureaucracies from democratic control is the growing penetration of the "private" sphere (Habermas' "life-world") by the state. This penetration, of course, further strengthens the autonomy of the state: the deeper the penetration, the less realistic are the chances for democratic institutions to recapture those areas of control from which they have been evicted. Thus, in addition to having an instrumental political relevance, this penetration also has moral ramifications and has to be resisted on both accounts.

Resistance to these developments is unlikely to generate a mass movement because the encroachment on individual autonomy and subjective freedom by state bureaucracies has its counterpart in solutions to the problem of autonomy provided by the market. In the same way that early capitalist conflicts about control over the producers' body and spirit were redirected and neutralized as conflicts over the distribution of surplus value, today the energy generated by the drive towards individual autonomy and political subjectivity is redirected and neutralized as a need to construct individual uniqueness and authenticity out of mass-produced commodities supplied, in ever growing variety, by the market. In early capitalist societies organized around production, every call for autonomy tended to be translated immediately into increased pressure on the redistribution of surplus value, while in the present consumer society calls for autonomy tend to be translated into intensified preoccupation with the opportunities offered by the market. This circumstance renders the Left critique of individual autonomy as self-defeating today as it was in the past. Contrary to its intention, it ends up contributing to the retrenchment of the system it wished to reform.

What ultimately feeds the intense preoccupation with market varieties of autonomy is the politically induced limitation on individual freedom. Because of this, members of the consumer society seek redress in the market. Thus, enhancement of individual autonomy may be better attained by attacking the sources rather than their effects. Rolling back the bureaucratic invasion of the life-world may relieve the pressure to seek the kind of autonomy that the market can provide.

All of today's critical issues point to the same central problem: the threat of emancipation of the political state from democratic control, and the resulting freedom of state bureaucracies to colonize the everyday world, thereby rendering their own domination permanent. This central problem defines the Left today.

Focusing the Left critique on the political state is not exactly a new idea. Indeed, before the emancipation of capital from labor reached its present proportions, this strategy was largely misdirected and rightly criticized by Gramsci as "statolatry." Gramsci's critique pointed out that the domination of capital was grounded in a "civil society" colonized by capital by relegating civil society to, first and foremost, the reproduction of labor. Now, however, civil society is increasingly colonized by the state as the sphere of reproduction of consumers, i.e., men and women whose interests in autonomy are permanently redirected to fit the needs of the market.

This new situation necessitates the redefinition of the Left as the counter-culture of modernity. With the emancipation of capital from labor, the gap between the potential and the reality of the bourgeois revolution can no longer be located in the exploitative role of capital. The material wealth made available by capitalism does not lead to the expected expansion of democracy and personal autonomy because of the parallel, but not inevitable, emancipation of the political state from public control, and the weakening of local sources of resistance. If the Left as the counter-culture of capitalism located the causes of the failure to realize the promises of the capitalist revolution in capital's control over production, the Left as the counter-culture of modernity should seek such cases in the failings of political democracy and personal autonomy.

The emphasis shifts following seminal transformations in the social system. When it engaged society in the role of producers, capital was the very force seeking the expansion of both political democracy and individual autonomy. Today capital is, at best, indifferent to both; it may well consider them costly nuisances. Thus, today democracy and autonomy cannot be taken for granted. They must be consciously and stubbornly defended.

The Left as the counter-culture of modernity must take democracy and autonomy seriously – not as useful but dispensable instruments in the reproduction of a certain structure of domination, but as values in their own right; not as means to safeguard the reproduction of capital to boost economic efficiency (at same point, the interests of democracy and autonomy may came into conflict with the requirements of efficiency), but as indispensable conditions of the emancipation that brought the bourgeois revolution described as Liberty, Equality, and Brotherhood.

Unlike the counter-culture of capitalism, the program of the counter-culture of modernity does not unequivocally privilege any particular social group as its primary or "natural," target. In this sense, it is a program without an easily identifiable "historical carrier." As the counter-culture of capitalism, the Left has long lived in the shadow of an historical agent. An artifact of the program, this agent lulled the Left into forgetting its origins and legitimation. More often than not, the conclusion turned into the premise and the Left identified itself as a collective spokesman for the class to which it imputed its own concerns. Memory of those long years make today's Left uneasy. It has yet to learn to live without an historical agent. It must see through what today may be only a delusion, straight into the only firm foundation of its purpose: the conviction that the values

promoted by the bourgeois revolution need to be defended
and can be defended only by exposing the mechanisms that
prevent their fulfillment.
Living without an historical agent has its discomfiting aspects. It also has its virtues. Making shortcuts unattractive is
one of them, maybe the main one. Revolution is a shortcut
in its purest form: an attempt to force history where the
agent is not ready to take it (if it was, revolution would not
be needed). Revolution is hence an act of violence on history and on its assumed agent. This is what makes the shortcut
morally odious and ineffective as the means to bring history
where it was intended to be brought. In history, most shortcuts
appear to be *cul-de-sacs*.
Living without a hope for a shortcut is another thing today's
Left has to learn. Indeed, to repeat Enzensberger's motto:
short-term hopes are futile and long-term resignation is
suicidal. But the virtue of living without an historical agent
is that the futility of short-term hopes does not lead to long-
term resignation. Resigning short-term hopes saves long-term
ones from futility.

Notes

1. "Communities" here are left deliberately vague; they may mean other
   parts of the globe, other regimes, other states – but much of this
   pessimism regarding the prospects of the global proselytism can be
   traced back to the experience of this irrelevance at home, which is
   the price one pays for intellectual and cultural freedom from dis-
   dainfully indifferent powers-that-be. Political freedom is fast devalued,
   let us add, by the new dependence on market forces.
2. This strategem is particularly attractive as it becomes a self-fulfilling
   prophecy unable to obtain democratic representation. These opinions
   tend to become "subversive," as any attempt to express them can
   only take "extra-democratic" forms.
3. Ostensibly justified as efforts to strengthen competition and mini-
   mize waste, the trend clearly has an antidemocratic edge, as it effectively removes vital aspects of social life from control by political-
   democratic means.

15 Beyond Social Movements?*

Alain Touraine

INTRODUCTION

All of us employ the term 'social movements' in such different
ways that our debates are often artificial. Even more clearly,
historical analyses of the current situation of any given country
and of factors favourable or unfavourable to the formation
of social movements are almost meaningless. One must therefore replace this exceedingly vague expression by a precise
representation of social dynamics. Without in any way attempting to impose one conception over against others, I
wish to examine the historical context of that conception
of social life that views it as simultaneously collective action,
operation of society on itself, and organized around a central social conflict, opposing those who direct the self-production and transformation of society and those who are
subjected to its effects. This conception cannot be identified with a particular current of thought. Rather, Marxist
and post-Marxist thought has long been one of the most
widespread expressions of this representation. One encounters this representation every time that the notion of social
class is employed (at least as this notion is customarily used
in Europe), but also every time that society is defined as
industrial – that is, by a mode of production. This is the
case even when these expressions are in no way associated
with a Marxist form of thought. The question that arises
with respect to countries that have been considerably influenced by socialist, communist or anti-imperialist forms of
thought, is: can the idea of a central social conflict – which
I here identify with the recognition of social movements –

* Reprinted from *Theory, Culture and Society*, vol. 9 (1992), pp. 125–45.

survive what now appears as the irremediable decline of historicist thought, that is, of a form of thought that defined the social actor by his position in a social progress opposed by the forces of conservatism and reaction? This is the essential point: it is surely impossible to dissociate the concept of social movement, thus defined, from the representation of social life as, simultaneously, a set of cultural representations through which society produces itself and all the aspects and consequences of a central social conflict. Thus, the notion of social movement, as used here, designates a general representation of social life rather than a particular type of phenomenon. This representation differs both from the liberal image of society as a marketplace and from the identification of society with a central power or a set of mechanisms implacably bent on maintaining the established social order. One can, of course, reject this representation of social life at the outset. But one cannot deny that it has been very influential, especially in the twentieth century, which has been largely dominated, at the international level, by the association of Marxist parties and movements of social and, especially, national, liberation. Our thought is dominated by the crumbling of communist and nationalist regimes that claimed to be the heirs and representatives of these social and nationalist, anti-capitalist and anti-imperialist, movements. This collapse has rapidly attained almost all regions of the world: Central and Eastern Europe first and foremost, but also the Soviet Union and China (though the latter remains subject to a repressive regime), and the greater part of Latin America. It has attained yet other regions, including especially the Islamic world, where Marxist-inspired revolutionary parties, formerly so powerful in Syria, Egypt, Turkey and even Iran, have been destroyed or greatly weakened. In many countries, including especially those of Western Europe, references to Marxism have disappeared over a period of a few years. These references had been extremely frequent and formed a kind of catechism, usually an intolerable one. Yet suddenly, any serious consideration of the thought of Marx and his successors, and even of the traditions of the workers' movements and socialism, seems to take place in a vacuum. Fukuyama's article (1989) merits its success, because the question it poses is formulated in the very terms of historicism and, more precisely, of Hegelian thought. Doesn't historicism lead to its logical conclusion, the end of history? Put more simply, is it not striking that the collapse of communist and nationalist regimes appears not as the victory of one camp over the other, but rather as the triumph of reality over artifice, of social life itself over the authoritarian discourses that claimed not only to control it but to define it? Shouldn't the crisis of these political voluntarisms, of these modernizing, voluntarist and authoritarian states, intellectually imply the elimination of a whole set of notions, including those of social class, modes of production, historical phases and social movement in the sense indicated above (actor in a central social conflict through which the major orientations of a culture are transformed into social, political and economic organization).

This question should not be rejected or discarded through overhasty answers. One must study the principal forms assumed by the decomposition of this historicist representation of social life prior to deciding whether nothing of it should survive, or whether, on the contrary, the concept of social movement can be separated from or even reinforced and deepened by, the crisis of historicism.

TRIUMPHAL INTEGRATION

The most obvious form taken by the crisis of the notion of social movement is the replacement of a bipolar image of society by that of a system maintained and reinforced by integrative mechanisms and the corresponding mechanisms of marginalization and social exclusion.

At the most readily observable level, many social analysts have long indicated that an organization of labour based on a direct conflict between the logic of managers and the logic of workers defending their individual and collective autonomy has been replaced by a system based on the circulation of information, so that work has increasingly become a position in a system of communication rather than a principle of autonomy and subjectivity. The world of employees is not that of workers. In particular, it is markedly different from that of qualified workers of the classic period of industry. Occupation was a fundamental principle of the autonomy of those workers in business enterprises where the various types of salary based on productivity placed workers in direct conflict with executives and management, as the thought and activity of Taylor himself very clearly indicate.

The transformation is even more apparent in the field of consumption. Our societies are decreasingly pyramidal, and one can no longer speak of a workers' or proletarian culture, as Maurice Halbwachs did, in a non-Marxist sense, shortly after the Second World War. We live in industrialized countries, in societies dominated by a feebly differentiated middle class, bounded on top by the world of the rich and extremely rich (who define themselves by their position in a market rather than by their professional roles), and below by the world of the temporarily or permanently excluded – the unemployed, sick or handicapped, isolated old people, ethnic and other minorities, etc.

More generally, isn't it obvious that the American concept of 'minority' has by and large replaced the European concept of social class? For example, in France, a country where Marxist-inspired discourse has been frequent, attention focuses not on socioeconomically deprived minorities, but on the rejection of ethnic minorities (including many immigrant workers) by a significant fraction of the population. It is remarkable that in France, attempts to develop a workers' movement claiming the 'right to be different' were very rapidly brushed aside in favour of anti-racialist campaigns aimed at better integration of the newcomers in the nation, rather than concentrating on their differences and conflicts with socially and culturally more privileged categories. From a purely descriptive point of view, one observes that in many countries, including France, manual workers are increasingly unlikely to identify themselves with the working class. Thus, one encounters in France a situation that took place much earlier in the United States.

One should emphasize that the vision of society as a social body or as a mass society appears – with very different connotations – among both conservative and radical thinkers. Is not the opposition to both social democratic and communist themes – and thus denial of the capacity for collective action of the exploited masses – the very definition of leftism? This naturally leads to rejection of the notion of social movement and even that of class. The form of leftism that has had the greatest impact is the Castroist and Guevarist theory of *foco* and guerrilla struggle. These are based on the idea that a country defined by its dependence on foreign imperialism cannot develop mass action, nor even an avant-garde party. It must therefore rely on the action of mobile guerrillas, who will ultimately topple the corrupt power and then transform themselves into a Leninist-type party leading to mass mobilization. This hyper-Leninism results, tragically, in a complete break with mass movements and in adventures like those of Guevara in Bolivia. Of coure, leftist thought may lead to support for political regimes utterly dedicated to the pursuit of integration and the rejection of deviant minorities, where internal social conflicts and, more broadly, social movements, are not recognized. In a less politicized form, limited to an ideological representation, structural-Marxist thought (as it has sometimes been labelled) has analysed society as a discourse of domination and unveiled the mechanisms by which the system imposes its own interests on its members and prevents conflict formation. Reference to conflicts is purely artificial, because the actors are necessarily submissive and only marginals can be aroused to revolt, as Marcuse and, a generation later, Foucault attempted. In the West, including Latin America, it is the theme of social integration that has dealt the heaviest blows to the theme of social struggle and social movements. It is as if the nineteenth century believed that the oppressed could liberate themselves, whereas twentieth-century thinkers are primarily impressed by the weakness of particular actors vis-à-vis the capacities for domination and manipulation of both absolute power and mass culture. It seems that today we think more readily in terms of social contradictions, exclusion and minorities than in terms of conflict, domination and social movements.

LIBERAL FRAGMENTATION

The classical image of social movements, as developed in European thought since the nineteenth century, is linked to the image of social life as a society of production. We have not yet – at least in this part of the world – become aware of the profound transformation of our analytical tools implied by the transition from a society of production to one of consumption. The worker is defined, first and foremost, by his place in the division of labour and the social relations of production. The consumer can surely be defined, as we have just recalled, by the type and degree of his participation in what some call values and others systems of social control, but this image is almost worthless, as it cannot explain the real operation of consumer society. Consumer society is based on demands that are also needs, and these cannot be reduced to the quest for status, as some superficial critics and commentators have claimed. These needs are centred on the individual himself, on his desire to affirm himself, to please or be attractive to others, to develop his experience of time and space, to ensure his health and the education of his children, etc. Consumption leads to the introduction into social life of demands that are by no means always social, and are sometimes even antisocial, inasmuch as the eroticization of numerous consumer goods suggests the pertinence of Freudian analyses. Therefore, consumer identity is no longer fully defined by social relations. Consequently, the demands or requests of the consumer are no longer organized around a central principle. In contrast, at the beginning of this century, one could still believe that workers' claims found specific expression in the domains of lodging, education and culture as well as in the political order and in unions. How could the patient, the parent of a schoolchild, the tourist, the TV viewer, and the automobile buyer have the same interests, and why should they find themselves in the same camp, facing the same adversaries?

The business enterprise – from the workshop to the entire system of capitalist production – was the natural and obvious adversary of popular movements. Yet, we everywhere observe a remarkably rapid and profound transformation of the image of the business enterprise. In the United States, the captains of industry have long been the heroes of popular imagination. However, this has not been the case in Europe nor in many other parts of the world, since business was defined above all as a social actor whose interests were assumed to be opposed to those of the workers. But today, in numerous countries, businesses have ceased to be social actors and have become purely economic actors, defined by their position in the national and, especially, international market, rather than by their role in relations of social production. Business is not the basic cell of post-industrial society; modern businesses are like the regiments that protect the frontiers of society from foreign invasion and provide their country with a strong position in the international marketplace. Here too, we have difficulty in adjusting our representations to such fundamental transformations. One still hears, on all sides, that business is the place where workers and, especially, managers, must invest their efforts. Yet, the principal characteristic of the present situation is the dissociation of the world of business, the professional world in general, and the world of culture. The success of business no longer depends on its ethic, Protestant or otherwise, but on its ability to develop strategy and to mobilize its financial, and also its technical and human, resources.

Thus, a great gulf is created between the two actors of industrial society – business and the worker – previously so close that they were almost entirely defined by their mutual relations and conflicts. The worker has been transformed into a consumer, and what was an organization in the sociological sense of the word has truly become a business, defined by its position in the capital, goods and services markets.

Daniel Bell (1976), in a well-known book, *The Cultural Contradictions of Capitalism*, stressed the dissociation of norms and values concerning production, consumption and politics in American society. How can we fail to see that he was right? We have just examined this dissociation in the spheres of production and consumption. This dissociation is equally striking in the realm of politics. Traditions inherited from the nineteeth century have defined democracy as – above all – representative. Yet, as the twentieth century draws to a close, the notion of representative democracy is in deep crisis almost everywhere. It is losing ground not to participatory democracy – which negatively evokes revolutionary and populist engines – but to the more modest conception of a democracy defined by institutional rules. This kind of democracy does not guarantee power-sharing by all, but at least it safeguards against its illegitimate appropriation by a man, a governing apparatus or a privileged social category. In other words, the main problem facing democracy is no longer its struggle against the ruling classes, nor the opposition of an all-powerful elite and a dependent mass, but its struggle against the various types of totalitarianism that have so brutally dominated the twentieth century. The nineteenth century was characterized by a great increase in power sharing. The late twentieth century is primarily preoccupied with the attempt to create limits to power, which so often tends to become absolute and to speak in the name of the society it devours. Hannah Arendt was surely the great initiator of this reversal in our thinking about democracy, of the affirmation that the problems of order and political liberty are more fundamental than social problems and, in any case, are not dominated by them. This non-social, nonrepresentative concept of democracy, which was so strongly held by Isaiah Berlin and Karl Popper, but also – in a very different spirit – by Claude Lefort, no longer sees the political order as the stake in what are ultimately work conflicts. Thus, the vast domain of political analysis is separated, by a single stroke, from the study of conflicts and social movements.

Should this new form of thought be labelled liberal? To me, this term seems adequate, since the essence of liberal thought does not consist in a positive affirmation nor in the definition of a central goal, but rather in the refusal of any central principle of analysis and action. According to liberals, such principles inevitably transform themselves into a central power – a power that is more ideological than political or economic, and therefore constitutes an insurmountable obstacle to the respect and development of freedoms.

Even if we do not feel satisfied with this critical vision, how can we fail to see that we have entered – probably for a long time – what may be labelled a liberal climate? This, after having lived – for a very long time and in the great majority of the word's countries – in a social-democratic or socialist climate; that is, with the idea that the intervention of a central power, based on the increasing political participation of the masses, would reinforce freedoms and help them penetrate the sphere of work. Today, all forms of state intervention are called into question, not only in the countries formerly labelled socialist – who strive to rid themselves of this appellation as a sick person seeks to rid himself of infectious disease – but also in the democratic countries, where the Welfare State – the principal political invention of the nineteenth-century West – is accused of impotence, and even of the maintenance and reinforcement of social inequalities. How can one fail to recognize – whatever our political positions – that the theme of social movements (as I defined it at the outset) was closely associated with the theme of the necessity of state intervention? As if the ultimate justification of social movements, which may initially be violent, is the progress of social security programmes, which always depend on the state and efficiently limit the risks and inequalities that strike most dramatically the feeblest and the poorest. The interest in social movements would not have been as great, had it not always been linked to the desire for reform. Conversely, even the partisans of the most moderate forms of industrial democracy, such as the English Fabians or the German theorists of the Weimar Republic, or even the yet more moderate defenders of *Sozialmarktwirtschaft*, have always kept in mind that behind these policies, however moderate, there lurks the profile of the workers' movement and its class organizations.

How can we fail to conclude that in a newly liberal world, the very idea of a social movement becomes meaningless, because social movements are not conceivable without the recognition that social relations of production have a central role in determining political choices and relations? Once again, the debates about social movements would be of very little significance if they did not call into question not only particular phenomena but a general representation of social life.

THE DESTRUCTIVE EFFECT OF THE STATE ON SOCIAL MOVEMENTS

It has been very frequently observed that the idea of 'social movement' is more appropriate to countries that have experienced genuine capitalist development than to others.

This observation is of critical importance. It reminds us that social movements oppose the actors of civil society, and thus presuppose not only that civil society is distinct from the state, but also – and this goes much further – that modernization processes are subordinate to the functioning of an already modern society; or – to cite the simplest and most extreme formulation – that modernization is endogenous. Is not this the very definition of Western rationalism, for which modernization is nothing other than the triumph of reason over tradition, of instrumental thought over religious belief, of achievement over ascription? It is only insofar as the modernization effort *is* the functioning of modernity that there appears sufficient space for social movements. On the contrary, wherever development has been exogenous rather than endogenous, wherever modernity has been imposed and primitive accumulation (to use Marx's term) clearly dissociated from capitalist accumulation properly speaking – in brief, wherever the inception of the modernization process has been due to war, conquest or the expropriation of significant social, regional or national categories, the state and the relationships of dominance, alliance and protection created by it replace the civil space of social movements.

Whereas the nineteenth century was marked by the development of capitalist economic centres, especially those of the Victorian economy, the twentieth century has been marked by the entry of non-modern countries into the modernization process. These countries were non-modern both because they had maintained social, religious or economic organizations that opposed the formation of endogenous actors of modernization, and because colonization had maintained or even re-established structures of command and control that favoured the subordination of local society to the colonial order, rather than colonial society's capacity for self-modernization. If the central figure of the nineteenth century was the bourgeoisie, then the central figure of the twentieth century was the state, whether revolutionary, nationalist, socialist or communal. In the central countries, growth in wealth and the actions undertaken by the workers' movement, in all its forms, led to the rapid institutionalization of labour conflicts and therefore to a normal decline in the social movements that accompanied the first industrialization. In the rest of the world, however, the state replaced social movements and generally considered them its principal enemies. It is no accident that the most important revolution of the twentieth century, the Soviet revolution, was led by the Bolsheviks, who, on the eve of the revolution, still constituted a small minority among Russian labour movements, then in full development, and that the first victims of the new Soviet power came from what was then called the workers' opposition. In communist regimes, unions are the part of the political system most strictly subordinated to the central power. This allows us to appreciate the extraordinary newness of the Polish Solidarity movement, which appeared in 1980, for it is simultaneously a labour, democratic and nationalist movement.

How could the social movements have survived the tentacular development of the totalitarian state? And, now that the totalitarian power is crumbling or called into question, how can the opposition speak in the name of social movements? It is evident that the idea of democracy is the only direct and efficient antidote to totalitarian power.

It is perhaps too early to propose analyses of post-communist societies, and of what will happen in post-nationalist societies. But we already know enough to realize that these regimes do not box in or crush social movements or, more generally, social actors. Rather, they pervert them, or even destroy or dissolve them. The horses do not race the day the barriers are raised, because they have been locked up for too long. They lacked oxygen, many have died, and others do not have the strength to run or are afraid of the whippings they used to receive. True, when totalitarian regimes crumble, persons, groups and organizations that have struggled for a long time, at the cost of great sacrifices, seem ready to occupy the place of the collapsed powers; but the testimony of these individuals and groups shows us that we must be prudent in assessing the capacity of the new regimes to produce new actors and new social movements. In most cases, the chief factor is the desire to be completely rid of the old system, and therefore, to adopt a clearly liberal position, giving priority to political liberty and the market economy, considered as the only efficient means of eliminating nomenklatura and totalitarianism. In both cases, chaos is the dominant note: the decomposition of the old system does not automatically lead to the formation of a new system. In a third set of cases – this is especially true of ones characterized by deep political and economic crises – the actors formed are defensive, populist and nationalist rather than offensive. They are incapable of directing social relations (particularly those involved in production) and become absurdly irrational. These are not statements of extreme pessimism, but of realism. They recognize the testimony of the most incontrovertible witnesses, who have declared the extraordinary difficulty of the renaissance and recreation of social actors in regimes whose very essence was the destruction of these actors – whose policy was to let the state bureaucracy devour, pervert or reduce them to slavery. In writing these lines, I in no way give up hope that actors and social movements will be recreated: that would contradict the hopes of so many of the participants in liberation struggles around the world. But one cannot accept a superficial image of social movements as a quasi-mechanical phenomenon. The same holds true of the study of the conditions of return to a market economy. To cite two, particularly clear, examples: neither in the Soviet Union nor in Poland do we witness the rise of a new generation of entrepreneurs. The ruins of an administered economy lead more easily to disorder, a black market and speculation than to investment efforts and the reconstitution of a price system, that is, to the rational allocation of a market economy.

How can we fail to conclude that the grandiose image of a society that results from conflicts and negotiations among social movements, adversaries and yet partners in the social construction of the same cultural orientations and actors in the same civil society, has been dealt a severe, most would say a deadly, blow? On the one hand, the liberal explosion has suppressed every central principle of regulation of social life. On the other hand, the totalitarian or post-totalitarian systems have destroyed the plurality of actors and refused to allow any autonomy to negotiations, social conflicts and political debates. Caught between these two extremes, the idea of social movement is lost. In this respect, it is similar to the various forms of social and industrial democracy, which increasingly tend to forget their origins in struggle and transform themselves into corporatisms, that is, integrate themselves into the reductive apparatus of the state.

THE RETURN OF SOCIAL MOVEMENTS?

Can civil society, defined as the social space of production of social life by work and the creation of cultural values, reconstitute the two fronts that, as we have just described, have been destroyed? Can civil society free itself from the control of the state on the one hand and, on the other, can it reconstruct itself beyond the increasing diversity of demands on the market? This question is of interest not only to those who seek to defend analysis in terms of social movements. One may well consider that the question raised is that of the very existence of sociology. The manifest decline of sociological thought is due to invasion of its field of study by two intellectual approaches very different from its own. It cannot be sufficiently stressed that the response to totalitarianism is, neither theoretically nor practically, a social one. The response to totalitarianism can only be a political one, based on reflection about the concept of democracy. Thus, the field of sociology is invaded by political philosophy, which is making a remarkable intellectual comeback. The other aspect of the situation is more complex because, as we have seen, criticism of the notion of 'social movement' comes from two seemingly unrelated perspectives, whose attacks are in fact co-ordinated and complementary. On the one hand, a strictly liberal form of thought attempts to reduce sociological analysis to economic analysis, that is to rational – which is not to say transparent – choices in the marketplace. According to the other point of view, society is an organized apparatus of self-control, and social behaviours are merely effects of the system – false consciousness. This radical separation of meaning and consciousness occults not only the idea of social movement but also that of social actor, and more generally, the whole field of sociology, especially as defined by Weber. Put more simply, whether one believes in the implacable logic of systems or, on the contrary, seeks to liberate oneself from such logics, one no longer formulates one's analysis or one's action in social terms. One refers either to institutional rules or to properly individualistic demands. Social space tends to fragment or disappear, and the most pessimistic are convinced that public space – *öffentlichkeit* – dissolves under the blows of mass politics, and especially mass culture. The mass media are merely the most visible aspects and the best-organized power centres of mass culture.

It would be an exaggeration to claim that one can only save sociological analysis by reconstructing thinking about social movements. Many would prefer to stop half-way, and not to accept the most demanding and critical proposition of a sociology of social movements: the idea that we must always think of social systems as organized around a central conflict. But in reality, tomorrow as well as yesterday, it is probably the most radical thought, the one that does not fear the introduction of the most exacting hypothesis – that of a principle of integration and centering of social conflicts, which has the best chances of playing a central role in the reconstruction of sociological analysis. If such an awakening does not take place, sociological analysis may disintegrate completely, to be absorbed partly by economic analysis and partly by political philosophy.

Let us successively examine the three fronts on which sociological analysis is attacked. Does each of them show signs of the reconstruction of an analysis in terms of social movements?

Current historical circumstances oblige us to give priority to the theme of the totalitarian state or, more precisely, to the downfall of modernizing, authoritarian, voluntarist states. Our prudent, critical remarks should not make us lose sight of the nature of the upheavals we are observing. More concretely, is not the appeal to a Western democratic model the most striking characteristic of post-communist societies? Are not these countries, which so ardently wish to move to democracy, capable of rediscovering the sources of representative democracy, even though there exists today the danger of a more or less brutal break between an extreme economic liberalism and a fairly aggressive nationalist populism? Is not democratization the specific characteristic of the political transformation process in these countries; that is, democratization in the sense of the reconstruction of institutional forms of political liberty, is the initial condition for the renaissance of social actors and the debates among them, debates that, in the first instance, concern ways of avoiding a negative break between extreme economic liberalism and a populism that cannot achieve the economic reconstruction of the country. Is not this power game, which we have so often considered a degeneration of the democratic process when observing Western character, also a phase of democratization in countries emerging from totalitarian regimes? The democratic game can only develop completely if it combines and opposes forces that consider themselves responsible for the economic life of the country, its national existence and the defence of specific social interests. Let us note that democracy's institutional framework has reconstituted itself, without major difficulties, in Czechoslovakia, Hungary, Poland and East Germany, that it has partially reconstituted itself in the Soviet Union and even in Bulgaria. At the time of writing Romania is the only country of the region where it is not yet possible to speak of the re-establishment of a democratic regime. Whatever its limits, the functional differentiation of social actors is progressing: the intellectuals and managers are freeing themselves from the administrative and ideological logic of the state, unions are reconstituting themselves, enterprises are being created, cultural life is admirably enriched. Would it be anticipating observable reality too much to say that the political and social life of these countries is organized around the choice – both political and social in character – between the dissociation of political and economic liberalism, on the one hand, and the reconstruction of socio-economic actors, on the other? These developments are not the harbingers of social movements, but they are signs of the transition from purely institutional democracy to the formation of choices that could make this democracy representative.

What is already manifest in post-communist Central Europe is a tendency in other parts of the world. The situation in the new Latin American democracies is assuredly confused. Nevertheless, it is clear to all that the present conjuncture, which exacerbates populist-type demands on the state, renders a populist policy absolutely impossible. If this contradiction is not recognized, it quickly leads to an increase in social demands that cannot be satisfied, and thus to hyper-inflation.

Beyond Social Movements?

But although this is the image that first meets the eye, it is far from realistic. On the contrary, one cay say that the major countries of Latin America are already engaged in the chaotic, because extremely difficult, but tenacious, search for different ways of combining an open economic policy with the struggle against the growing menace of internal social dualism. In many countries, this orientation is labelled social democracy. But in fact, this term can be applied to situations as different as those of Mexico, Argentina, Brazil, Chile and Costa Rica – to mention only the clearest-cut. In other words, the current development of Latin America is dominated by the formation of opposed and complementary social actors: exporters and the urban masses. These social actors can certainly engage in civil war, as they did for such a long time in Argentina, leading it to disaster. But they may also, often in a similarly excessive manner, strive not to choose between equally catastrophic unilateral solutions. Sociologists cannot be satisfied with aggressively superficial images that reduce the history of Latin America to an irrational tumult. The smallest effort at observation allows us to see the operation of the difficult process – always at risk of failure – of the formation of new social actors, or even of new social movements, and therefore of a political process having a certain representative character.

It is much easier to answer those who consider that industrialized democratic societies are systems of integration that eliminate any possibility of movement of social actors. First, because this image, which had so much success in the 1970s, has been largely eroded by the neo-liberal vision we have already evoked, and to which we shall soon return. Is it not paradoxical to view societies in accelerated transformation, whose economic, social and political systems are assuredly more flexible and open than any others, as self-controlled systems for the transmission of inheritances, for the reproduction of inequalities and privileges? Is it not irresponsible to say, with Marcuse, that societies of pure tolerance exercise a self-control as tight as that of totalitarian state societies? But these remarks are insufficient, since they address only the most excessive, exaggeratedly critical theories of social integration. It is more important to underline, for those who insist on the end of social bipolarity and the increasing integration of mass society, that this integration is much more limited than they claim. In fact, our societies are engaged in a race for change and, as in any running team, the stiffer the competition, the more numerous the obstacles to be overcome, the greater also the distances separating the runners. Today, we realize that equality of opportunity has made far less progress than expected, that most of the professions in which women have acquired an important role are ones in decline and that the decision centers remain overwhelmingly masculine; that the equalizing effects of schools, even when free and secular, are feeble or nil; that the redistribution of revenues effected by social security systems is much weaker than one could hope and sometimes non-existent. The theme of inequality thus again becomes the basis of an analysis in terms not only of social distance but of social conflicts. On condition, however, that this observation is strictly limited to the domain to which it applies: the management of change. This is what distinguishes the present analysis from earlier analyses, which dealt with the whole of social structure, and more particularly with the production system.

This leads us to the final field of debates and to the most critical interrogation, that concerning the renaissance – possible or improbable – of social movements. Is our consumer society one in which individuals throw their demands at a market that, for all its rigidities and deviations, attempts to respond to them, or is it still a society based on production, with social relations of production at its core? It has been quite some time since Toffler (1980) made an important contribution to this discussion by creating the term *prosumer*, which encountered considerable success. What he meant by this is that the production system we are, by and large, embarked upon makes us into not only consumers of goods, but also – as consumers – operators of the system. Clearly, the patient is not merely a consumer of the hospital, the pupil or student a mere consumer of education, and – must one add – the TV viewer a mere consumer of television programmes, even if a certain logic tends to reduce him to this role. To take the most dramatically obvious example, the patient is placed in a hospital to which he both brings and opposes his will to autonomy, liberty and identity, though he also accepts and positively values the technical logic of health care. Sociologists and other observers, but also politicians and labour leaders, have come late to the recognition of the extreme importance of political opinion in post-industrial countries, of tensions, conflicts and compromises between the logic of health care and that of the patient. Some superficial minds have contrasted qualified scientific medicine and 'natural' medicine. This reaction is fully analogous to that of the Luddites at the beginning of the industrial revolution. But, just as the workers' movement could only constitute itself once industry was accepted (which allowed contestation of relations of property and social control), so it is that genuine social conflict among administrative, technical and corporative logics only appears when the positive functions of science applied to medicine are recognized. This development has created a new political arena. So far, this arena has not found a specific form of expression, but it is extremely important to public opinion, as indicated by the success of certain television programmes and, in some countries, by the extreme development of juridical conflicts among patients, hospitals and doctors.

We are even less advanced in the realm of other cultural industries, such as schools and universities on the one hand, and the mass media on the other. Nevertheless, numerous sociological studies have already shown that we must replace the weak theme of socialization by a much richer and more readily observable one: the growing distance between the socializing and educative function of schools and universities and the psychological and cultural universe of pupils and students. This dissociation, which found such dramatic expression in the student movements of the 1960s, seems to have been forgotten, despite the fact that it is continuously reinforced and creates a world of misunderstandings and psychological crises to which teachers generally are extremely sensitive. It is more difficult to find clear formulations of conflicts of interest and orientation in the mass media, as the public is dispersed and has little means of influencing the centres that create the programmes.

In these three cases, how can we fail to recognize the competition and conflict between two logics? As so many critics have pointed out, one logic is that of reinforcement of the system, of maximization of the production of goods of general value, such as money, power and information. The other logic is the increasing reference, in the cultural industries, to the effort made by each individual to construct and defend his individuality. Let us call 'subject' the individual's effort to construct him or herself as an individual, rather than as a subordinate in a logic of order, whatever that order may be. We know only too well that this appeal to the individual can autodestruct if the individual defines himself as devoid of content, or may on the contrary nourish a new populism, or even new forms of cultural, national or other fundamentalisms. But already, in the post-industrial societies, that is, the ones where the cultural industries have acquired a dominant role, public opinion is structured by the debate between what may be labelled a logic of the marketplace – which is also a logic of power and accumulation – and a logic of individual liberty, which cannot be reduced to the affirmation of a self-destructive narcissism, nor to the return to cultural and ethnic roots in which the individual is suppressed in favour of a return to religions and theocracies.

These social movements, which develop in the cultural industries, may combine with the policies of struggle against exclusion and for equality evoked above. However, they are of a different nature, which shows the degree to which political action and social movement remain separated. A social movement does not speak in the name of a collectivity, it speaks either in the name of a ruling category or in that of a directed category, that is, in all cases, in the name of a category defined by dominance and power relations. All these movements present themselves as representatives and defenders of cultural movements recognized by all. Those who direct the great cultural industries speak in the name of individualism, because they put science into the service of medical care, education and information. They speak of creativity, liberation and liberty of choice, while constructing health, education and information systems aimed at maximizing 'output', i.e., developing as much as possible the quantity of medical, pedagogical and general information in circulation. In the other camp, one also speaks of individualism, of liberty and of movement, but in a more defensive and more 'utopian' manner, for here one speaks not merely for the individual, but in the name of his or her ability and desire to defend his or her individuality, his or her subjectivity. The essential point I wish to stress here is that these new movements differ from earlier, better-known ones not only in their nature, but above all in the break they establish between the social sphere, become increasingly moral, and the sphere of the state and strictly political action. The workers' movement in its central aspect – that is, the labour unions – was always a political actor and had a vision of reality well expressed by the term 'socialism'. In fact, union action was almost always subordinated to political action because, as we have seen, the working class was defined not as a subjectivity but as an agent in the implementation of an historical necessity. This mixture of subjectivity and objectivity, of voluntarist action and historical necessity, is disappearing. Simultaneously, social movements free themselves from the tutelage of a political party. This situation is not one of unmitigated advantages, since the political parties and the relationship to the state unified movements, each of which had its own specificities and usually also defended more limited interests. Today, the integration of different movements is no longer governed by relationships with the state: integration must be direct, and this is much more difficult and involves considerable risk of fragmentation. Yet, how can one fail to see that this is how the autonomy – indeed preponderance – of civil society affirms itself, and that there already exists a commonness of orientation among different movements? One must stress the majority role of women in these new movements, characteristic of professions in which women are highly represented for traditional reasons. These are the sectors involving services to people, assured by women in the traditional society; when these services entered the sphere of market relations, women continued to assure them. But the fact that this situation is rooted in traditional society does not prevent these social formations, found in the sphere of services to persons, from contesting many principles that were and still are at the core of the most radical feminist movements, those that refuse to separate or oppose equality of opportunity and recognition of the biocultural specificity of women.

One should add that between the domain of social movements and that of centralized political action – action directly controlled by the state – there tends very quickly to develop a level intermediary between the social system and the political system, called here the level of public opinion or *öffentlichkeit*. I am not referring merely to television and the major presses, but primarily to organizations of influence-brokering and sometimes even of decision-making, which are distinct from political organizations and, in particular, from parliaments and elected local authorities. It is at this level, that of the pre-political expression and debates of social movements, that the theme of consensus or communication appears. This theme is none other than the direct recognition, by the groups involved, of the similitude of their cultural orientations and therefore of the existence of cultural stakes accepted by all the groups. To cite only one example, but the most important one: committees on biomedical ethics have been constituted in many countries. These committees do not seek to achieve compromises between the suppliers and users of health care, but to identify the common orientations, the fundamental ethical principles that can form the basis of relationships between the parties.

This transformation of the relationships between social movements and political action is so profound that it has prevented many observers from recognizing the existence of the new social movements for, as Charles Tilly puts it, these do not have the same 'repertory' as the older movements. For those, the essential matter was the control of power, and images of violence were considered the most symbolic: the occupation of the Bastille or the Winter Palace, mass demonstrations often violently dispersed by the police, occupations of factories and the theme of the general strike. The new social movements seem as pacific and as interested in consciousness-raising as former ones were violent and interested in the control of power. In brief, the old social movements were associated with the idea of revolution, the new ones are associated with the idea of democracy. Consequently, the idea of democracy can no longer be fully defined by institutional rules. One cannot consider democratic a regime that is not interested in the rights of the personal subject, which we again call, as in the eighteenth century,

the rights of man. However, these are no longer seen as
the rights – always linked to duties – of citizens, but as the
rights of the individual over and against encroaching political power.

Such analyses should, of course, circumvent the most usual
risks of error. The fact that certain demands have taken
shape recently does not mean that they constitute new social
movements. Some currents of opinion and anti-establishment
campaigns are not part of the core of the new social movements as defined above. In particular, following the 1960s
and the major student movements, many Western countries
have seen the formation of leftist-inspired, regionalist, anti-
nuclear, and also feminist movements, which are not clearly
social movements. In some cases, these were highly politicized and ideological forms of old social movements on the
verge of disappearance. Italian and German terrorism is a
case in point. These resorted to physical violence to awaken
a working class that they continued to consider as the revolutionary actor par excellence; but this actor had been fooled,
manipulated and put to sleep, so that it was necessary to
bring it brutally back to consciousness of its true interests.
The terrorists looked towards a working class that, as they
defined it, had long since ceased to exist, probably just as
the anarchists, who became involved in a series of terrorist
incidents at the end of the nineteenth century, looked towards
a world on the borderline of crafts and industry, which had,
by that time, given way in most places to extensive industrialization and mass production. In many countries, the 1970s
were characterized by intermediary movements that voiced
these new demands, in reality more cultural than economic,
though they were expressed in the vocabulary of the old
social movements. The student movements provide the clearest
examples. I have analysed the French movement of May 1968
in these terms, showing the opposition between their content, which was new, and their Trotskyist or Maoist language,
which made them seem reminiscent of the pre-revolutionary period in Russia. This contradiction is very similar to
the one between the content and the language of the revolution of 1848 or of the Paris Commune. As Marx admirably
showed, the new contents, that is, workers' claims, were
subordinated to the exhausted old language of the French

Revolution, almost a century earlier. All these contradictory movements crumbled or divided rapidly, so that by the end of the 1970s, many thought it was time to abandon all reference to social movements, because we live in a type of society that leaves no room for a general but concentrated contestation of the principal forms of social organization. Is it not necessary, today, to revise this judgement? Should we not go beyond the enthusiasm provoked by the collapse of the communist regime and the democratic liberation of peoples subjected to a doubly foreign yoke? Should we not study the appearance of new social movements, and consequently, of new reform strategies in the industrialized and democratic countries themselves?

Some believe that history has reached its end. One could say, on the contrary, that the river of history, which had been diverted through the bogs and meanders of totalitarianism and frozen in the discourse of the state, has resumed its course and is flowing towards one or several futures. For it is only when a society is capable of debating its choices, of recognizing the complementarity of cultural orientations common to most and clearly opposed social interests, that it may have a history. History, which almost stopped in the East, may also halt in the West, if we make the marketplace into a prince as absolute as a political committee, if we believe that the lucid knowledge of the interests of each determines the organization of society by a cascade of rational choices and political compromises. One must, on the contrary, rediscover the existence and efficacity of social actors, East, West and South; one must therefore strive to understand how history, far from having reached its conclusion, resumes its march.

References

Bell, D. (1976) *The Cultural Contradictions of Capitalism* (London: Heinemann).

Fukuyama, Francis (1989) "The End of History?" *The National Interest*, no. 16 (Summer), pp. 3–18.

Toffler, A. (1980) *The Third Wave* (London: Collins).

Part VI

Coda: Social Movements in Sociological Thought

16 Social Theory and Social Movements: Sociology as Sociodicy *

Stanford M. Lyman

In virtually all of their various manifestations in the United States, social movements have proclaimed a salvational message: in effect, each has sought to cure the soul of either the nation, a sodality within society or the individual.[1] In the eighteenth and nineteenth centuries these movements usually arose out of religious revivals, for example the first and second Great Awakenings.[2] Such movements confronted institutionalized systems of social injustice and new or long-established patterns of economic inequity, but always with one eye on remedying a spiritual sickness within the individual soul, while the other surveilled the diseases of the body politic.[3] From 1830 to 1850 transcendentalism, a religiously inspired social movement, not only espoused unitarianism but also took up the causes of utopianists, abolitionists and workers;[4] in the same era but continuing to 1890 a band of New Haven scholars sought scholarly means to evangelical ends.[5] In the latter decades of the nineteenth century a variety of social movements addressed issues inspired by the newly announced social gospel.[6] These movements preached an evangelic message and practiced an inner worldly ethic of responsibility. As missionary endeavors, they widened the scope of their efforts, moving beyond the borders of the United States. Their "errands into the non-Occidental wilderness" took them to such exotic areas as Africa, Oceania and the Orient – that is, places only recently touched by the expansion of commerce, capitalism and Christianity.[7] Domestically and abroad they sought nothing less than the elimination of poverty, cessation of the worst features of

* Published for the first time in this volume.

capitalist exploitation, a purification of the body politic and the imposition and maintenance of moral standards at the levels of both local community life and the national culture.[8] These movements operated from the assumption of an American responsibility to redeem the rest of the world from the ravages, but not the promise, of modernity itself.[9]

America's Protestant-inspired social movements held fast to the idea that the American national state had been established as a beacon to all others. Within the United States religious missions to both immigrants and aborigines sought nothing less than an all-encompassing Christian republic.[10] Not only would American society be continuously improved, but – together with the conversion–assimilation of the foreigner, the Indian, the African and the Asian, the toleration of the Jew, watchful surveillance over Catholics and opposition to the widely alleged Masonic subversion – ultimately it would be made perfect.[11] The means for America's apotheosis as the kingdom of God on earth were within every citizen's reach; their voluntary association for social and moral good might save society as much from the effects of its citizens' individual sins as from its corporations' and politicians' collective corruption. Moreover such movements had an even larger mission: to affirm the truth as well as the righteousness of America's claim, from its inception to the disillusion that set in after the Vietnam War, to be the redeemer nation for the world.[12]

The spiritual element in these social movements derives from America's Puritan heritage. That heritage found its quintessential expression in colonial New England – in the voluntaristic covenant of believers who exercised mutual watchfulness over one another, acceded to legitimate civil authority, but never ceased to recognize the ultimate sovereignty of God over human affairs.[13] All men and women might become brothers and sisters within its broadened vision of the kingdom of God on earth, established in its only seemingly secular polity as the American commonwealth.[14] With the onset of industrialization, immigration and urbanization, however, the inclusive and democratic character of that commonwealth began to falter.[15] It had already been fatally compromised by the colonies' and then the "first new nation's" acquiescence to the enslavement of Africans and the designation of their American-born offspring as chattels,[16] and would be further undercut by the coercive removal and forcible sequestration of the aboriginal peoples of America – their polities and civic identities reduced to that of "domestic, dependent nations."[17] When the Civil War ended the possibility of legalized slavery, the naturalization law was modified to grant citizenship to "free white persons" and "persons of African nativity or African descent." But this change intentionally cast civic status in exclusivist terms, permitting the courts to determine which among the immigrant peoples clamoring at the gates of the seemingly open American society would be declared "aliens ineligible to citizenship in the United States."[18] Race and ethnicity had become troubling elements in the American mosaic – and would continue to be.

Threatened by new forms of worldly success, economic degradation, and social, racial and class divisions, the terms of salvational reference began to shift from theodicy to sociodicy. Convinced that America was still the redeemer nation, the quasi-secular successors of the Puritan divines, the accredited founders[19] of American sociology, took as their project the inner-worldly perfection of American social, economic and political institutions.[20] They became the keepers of the promise of a perfectible society. But although religious believers had accepted theodicies – that is, religious explanations for the apparent arbitrariness of individual suffering, illness, inequality and death, as well as the apparent injustice entailed in the unequal distribution of wealth and social position – sociologists sought to provide an inner-worldly understanding of the same phenomena: Not only would the latter vindicate the ways of society to man, but also, and more significantly, they would reform them. The American sociologists of the *fin de siècle* preached a gospel of individual and social regeneration through an applied social science and an ameliorative social technocracy.[21] In effect it was the new discipline of sociology that provided the ideological justification and inspiriting stimulation for most of the post-religious social movements in America.[22] In the American sociological perspective the responsibility for salvation shifted from prayer to praxis.

Under the intellectual regime of sociodicy new explanations would arise, including, on the one hand, those that rejected religion altogether and sought salvation through various forms of sociocracy,[23] and, on the other, those that rejected the

possibility of salvation altogether and offered either cynical
commentary or doom prophecy.[24] Sociodicy, begun in order
to prove that the Christian future was not an illusion for
America's civil order, found itself having to assume responsibilities that previously had been God's, once He had been
declared either to have removed Himself from the
micromanagement of the earth, to have absented Himself
until humankind would reform itself, or to be but an illusion
that even greater progress in science would expose.

SOCIODICY AND CIVIL SOCIETY

Implicit in the sociological enterprise was a belief that a
covenanted national community could be established within
the boundaries of the United States.[25] In this sense sociology
discovered that many of its fundamental research and policy
problems had arisen out of the race problem[26] and, con-
comitantly, out of the dilemmas and contradictions of an
ever more pluralized civil society.[27] American sociologists did
not then, and for the most part do not now, regard these
dilemmas and contradictions to be insoluble either in their
discipline's theory or in its proposals for a political–economic
praxis. At different moments in the development of the discipline, addressing issues arising out of unresolved elements
of the social question – for example problems of race, ethnicity, nationality, democracy, labor, sex, gender, urbanization, industrialization, leisure, crime, deviance, health,
temperance, poverty, family, the environment, education and
peace – American sociologists have sought to discover how
various socioeconomic and political formations (for example
slavery, capitalism or democratic socialism) might be improved
as institutions or enhanced as processes in order that the
United States of America might move ever more closely toward
its divinely appointed *telos*: a perfected society. Their
"utopianism," however, has always been "pragmatic," expressing itself in an attack on specific problems and on the development of specific methods for problem solving. For this
reason America's sociologists have been much less concerned
with such historical, theoretical or ideological questions as
the origins of capitalism or of the nation's ethnoracial or

economic stratification, class structure or bureaucratization.[28] Rather, defining their problems as arising from the consequences of these "givens," they turned their attention to resolving what they declared to be "the social problems" that arose therefrom.[29] Their perspective rested on the assumption, derived from the Enlightenment and given sociotechnical expression in the works of Comte's teacher, St. Simon, that all problems could be solved by the application of reason and science. In contrast with that of the Europeans,[30] their sociological science was to be put to doing God's work, but in secular, piecemeal, incremental ways.

CONSTITUTING THE SECULAR COVENANT

After 1850 the forging of an American covenant required new understandings of how to transpose earlier voluntaristic submission to the ethical imperatives of a small, homogeneous, Christian community into secular procedures for assigning civic identity within a large, heterogeneous, secular society. Calvin's original interpretation of an ethnically limited covenant – that is, God's election of Israel in which "one people is peculiarly chosen, while others are rejected"[31] – had already foundered on the eighteenth-century missionaries' compromises over slavery and the inner-worldly status of Africans and aborigines in the colonies;[32] it would later find excruciatingly ambivalent expression in the sociologists' formulations of who might be included within America's redemptive social compact. Faced with a society composed of white, red, black, yellow and mixed-blood peoples, and of Catholics, Protestants, Jews, Buddhists and adherents of other non-Western religions, as well as freethinkers, agnostics and atheists, sociologists could not discover a common basis for the secular characteristics they wished to promulgate as scientifically grounded criteria for admission or exclusion.[33] Much of American sociological theory turned on this unresolved question, and puzzled over how the discipline might find an answer that would be commensurate with Christian ideals, and at the same time ensure constitutional guarantees and forward the cause of secular science.

In the movement favoring assimilation, and in their theories that prophesied its inevitability, for example, sociologists thought they had discovered a solvent whereby alien cultures, foreign ethnicities and non-Christian religions might be dissolved in an American melting pot.[34] However a number of socio-historical analysts warned that assimilation was modified not only by deeply engrained prejudices within the white, Anglocentric, Protestant population, but also by a people's assimilating capacity as well as their desire to become fully acculturated congregants in the proposed American communion.[35] The sociologists' designation and measure of that capacity and that desire threatened to exclude altogether or hold back for a considerable time one or several groups; for the sociologists differed among themselves over whether and how ethnoracial and religious prejudices might be eliminated, over who might be capable of voluntary socio-cultural submission to the American ethos, and over how long the testing time for the assimilating group might last.[36] Social-gospel assimilationists, of whom Albion W. Small is a fine example,[37] had no respect for the old-world cultures, customs and folkways of an immigrant people, and did not believe that either the state or civil society owed an obligation to preserve or protect them from what he supposed was the single most important duty of all "foreigners" in America – viz., to immolate their cultural ethos on the altar of Americanism and to dissolve their ethnic identity in the fires of the melting pot. While such sociologists as Small recognized a pluralism of interests, they would not tolerate a plurality of ethnics.[38] Democratic civil society rested on the competition of "objective" or political interests; creedal adherences and collective consciousness of a cultural kind would have to give way to what Robert E. Park called the "coordination of sentiments"[39] necessary for the voluntary association of a civic people. Race, however, continued to confound the assimilationists' hopes, conflating physical, cultural, economic and emotional ties in such bewildering complexities that by the end of the twentieth century the general social process seemed to have proved itself ineffective for constituting the much-vaunted American secular and nonracial commonwealth.[40] In its place is a not-so-civil society marked by varying degrees of ethnogenesis among recently rehyphenated Euro-, Hispanic-, African- and Asian-Americans.[41]

The original movement to Americanize the immigrant was less than successful.[42] By the beginning of the 1980s American social thinkers had begun to call attention to the "decline of the WASP"[43] and the "rise of the unmeltable ethnics,"[44] and were predicting "the end of the American future."[45] As the twentieth century approaches its final years demographers are foretelling a new century in which the social composition of the American population will include many more Hispanic and Asian immigrants and their offspring and much fewer Euroamerican WASPs.[46] Decades earlier, sociologists of the 1950s and thereafter – chastened by the wartime treatment of the highly acculturated Japanese Americans[47] and attuned to the anticommunist exigencies of the Cold War[48] – had begun to redefine the inclusion process such that it would embrace a plurality of culturally and racially distinctive peoples as well as the Negro.[49] All might be admitted if they would bear allegiance to America's destiny in world politics: to thwart the threat of imperialist communism.[50] Differences in race, religion and creed could now be seen as social indicators of a new, tolerant, ethnically differentiated and secular American identity. The ultimate objective of the assimilationist movement would now be reached by sociologists' and opinion leaders' casuistic reconstruction of America's future social organization; what had been seen as the problem of multiple racial, ethnic and religious loyalties was redefined as a national asset: America would realize its destiny by capitalizing on its ethnocultural diversity. The dream of Israel Zangwill's "melting pot" would metamorphose into that of Horace Kallen's "orchestration of mankind."[51] The national ideal was epitomized less as a fiery "melting pot" and more as a cool "salad bowl." However the Vietnam War, the unrest of the 1960s and 1970s and the failure of the civil-rights movement to eradicate the legacy of racism in America challenged this view. By the 1990s America's national solidarity was being viewed with far less sanguinity by sociologists and policy analysts. America, it was acknowledged, had an enduring racial and ethnic dilemma whose resolution transcended the simplicity of the assimilation vs pluralism debate.[52]

MANAGING SOCIAL MOVEMENTS THROUGH THE SECULAR COVENANT

Although America's antiradical tradition had opposed variants of anarchism, socialism and communism for more than a century before the outbreak of the Cold War,[53] after 1947 the vehemence of the latter threatened to undermine the movement for eliminating racial segregation[54] and to marginalize those sociologists who had shown an interest in older resolutions of the race question.[55] The reemergence of the assimilation–pluralism debate seemed to call for new answers to an old but difficult question: how could a secular, civil and plural society legitimately manage its culturally and socially differentiated citizenry?[56] Management – sometimes called social control – has been a theme of American sociology since its beginnings in promoting a moral administration of slavery, and after 1865 it became a *leitmotif* of the discipline's reconstitution of itself as the intellectual agency charged with the task of devising appropriate means for the disposal of the disreputable, dependent, defective and delinquent elements of the American populace.[57] Sociology began to emphasize social control and encourage the administrative guidance of human populations toward eufunctional social changes. One of the antebellum southern Comteans had proposed a casuistic redefinition of slavery as "warranteeism," a reciprocal arrangement between masters and bond-servants guided by Calvinistic precepts and governed by state-supported force.[58] Later, another of these early sociologists extended the thesis to embrace the relations between entrepreneurs and workers as well as the newly freed African Americans.[59] Harvard's early sociology (embodied in the works of Francis Greenwood Peabody and Edward Cummings) focused on the male individual and on his incorporation into right-minded civic associations that would simultaneously enhance societal self-management and ensure moral redemption.[60] To this end Harvard's thinkers would lend their intellectual and ethical guidance to such social movements as might improve and sustain the covenant and the commonwealth.[61] Independently originated movements for change and social reconstruction were not to remain independent – great fears were expressed about the destructive effect the crowd would have on the public interest[62] – but were to be assimilated into the national purpose.

Scientifically guided state administration of civil society and social reconstruction reached its quintessential form as praxiological theory in the works of the sociologists at the University of Wisconsin.[63] There, at a time when the Protestant churches no longer seemed able to provide the moral framework for civil society, and at a time when no less a duo than Karl Marx's daughter and son-in-law were extolling the revolutionary potential of the American working class,[64] Richard T. Ely sought such in another institution, one that would be capable of providing ethical guidance, moral authority and integrative brotherhood.[65] For Ely the only alternative to the church was the state itself, but the newly envisioned ethical state would have to be invested with Protestant benevolence and redemptionist fervor. While the labor movement was to be mobilized by and on behalf of Christian endeavor,[66] the state was to become the successor to, as well as the bearer of, the Protestant mission, not only by absorbing into itself all the problems of the diverse secular interests in civil society, but also by resolving them in accordance with a sacralized secular ethic. A similar kind of effort was imagined by social-gospel whites to be able to guide newly freed blacks into a morally reconstructed but segregated south[67] – a prospect to which the African Methodist Episcopal Church was opposed[68] – and to lead urban African Americans in the north and newly arrived Asians on the Pacific coast into a life enmeshed in racially separated settlement houses and Christian charity.[69] Standing between the state and the people, the university and its professors would become vicars of the new order and policy scientists of the new administration. The state – assuming the disciplinary functions formerly exercised by the Puritan magistrates of the colonial era, and taking the advice offered by such populist–progressive sociologists as Edward Alsworth Ross, who opposed the immigration of Southern and Eastern Europeans, Jews and Asians[70] – would admit to full citizenship only those who exhibited the requisite signs of public spiritedness, and it would encourage the unregenerate to emulate them. What came to be called "The Wisconsin Idea" represented an alternative political direction for American civil society and was motored by the sociologically supported progressive movement. The state would now bear responsibility for the well-being of the soul of society and of all of its citizens. It not only claimed the right to manage the tensions inherent in any of the enunciated secular theodicies,[71] but also the duty either to coopt or to suppress others that attempted to compete with its monopolistic claim.[72] This included especially those movements of a chiliastic character and a revolutionary – rather than reformist – ideology.[73] However any major failure of social or economic policy could leave the ethically progressive state vulnerable to such independently based opposition movements as those that developed during the Great Depression.[74]

In the face of massive threats to civil and social order, the Roosevelt administration combined a secularizing social gospel and Wisconsin progressivism with the recently enunciated Keynesian doctrine,[75] giving the newly centralized welfare state – many of its appointees self-conscious devotees of collective Christian endeavor[76] – an opportunity to become the economic and social manager of the nation.[77] State-administered Keynesianism bid fair to absorb or resist alternative proposals for social reconstruction.[78] Although the Wisconsin Idea, with its nationalization as the New Deal, had virtually eliminated a separate religious check on secular authority – Hubert Humphrey, vice-president under Lyndon Johnson and unsuccessful candidate for the presidency in 1968, was perhaps the last major advocate of a public philosophy rooted in the social gospel[79] – it had not replaced it with a fully developed secular ethic nor had it supplied a grounded moral source for such.

The managerial and technocratic scientist who served this administration assumed that public policies and the political leaders who advocated them arose out of an inherent morality. A new kind of intellectual had in fact emerged, but during the Second World War and immediately after, considerable ambivalence about his or her role continued to prevent its monopolization over policy-making.[80] The positivist policy scientist – George Lundberg provided the ideology for this postwar successor to the secular theodicist sociologist;[81] James Coleman represents a later evolution of the role[82] – surrendered to the state, or to whoever would give him or her a job, the right to decide what the good society would be; the policy scientist would merely demonstrate the most efficacious means to that end.[83] Thereafter social movements as well as civil society would be treated as creatures either in opposition to or in support of the bureaucracy that established state policy.[84] Jimmy Carter, as president and in his post-presidential activities, exhibited the characterological as well as the administrative style of such a religiously inspired technocrat.

THEOLOGIES FOR STATE ADMINISTRATION: SOCIAL-SYSTEMS THEORIES, EAST AND WEST

In the 1940s another foundation for an American secular theodicy began to be enunciated – the theory of social systems.[85] The transformation of Calvinistic religious imperatives into democratic state authority had exposed a sociodicial dilemma: neither ultimate authority nor the catastrophes and injustices of life could be explained by reference to God or to Christian theodicy. Talcott Parsons's theory of the social system found a way around this problem by distributing authority within the harmonics of a dynamically equilibrating universal-achievement system.[86] In his image of American society, each individual occupies one or more specific statuses that define his or her respective rights, privileges, duties and responsibilities. Society itself is comprised of a system of interdependent statuses; hence each has a proper place in the social system according to the function he or she performs. Affective neutrality is the attitudinal and normative propriety for conduct in public places.[87] The maintenance of the system as a whole depends on the proper performance of roles, each individual being called upon to act according to his or her abilities but not necessarily to receive according to his or her needs.[88] Here, then, is a problem requiring a new sociodicy for its resolution. Parsons's sociodicy explains these inequities by reference to "strains" in the system. Hence, in 1945, Parsons could explain both anti-Semitism and racial prejudice as patterned responses to sex-role and job-role "strains" in America's universalistic-achievement system.[89] Two decades later he could announce that the time had come for admission of African Americans to fully fledged citizenship – and that it would occur, but only if nothing interfered.[90] These "strains" give rise to "deviance," but eventually the deviant conduct is absorbed by the system. The system thereby receives a new birth of freedom and proceeds in accordance with its new mode of dynamic equilibrium, having once again achieved stability in the midst of change.

Authority is an attribute of all statuses and roles, but in some of them authority is their major attribute.[91] Authoritative roles are critical for the continued maintenance of the system. Authoritative roles are the agencies of the Protestant ethic's successor – the civil religion. In conception, the civil religion's authority is disembodied: authoritative roles become incumbencies in public offices. Executive functions are no longer attributable to an individual but arise as an artifact of an office that itself is part of a larger system of functioning roles and statuses.[92] The systemic dissolution of authority precludes holding executives responsible for their own acts; moral responsibility is borne by the office or by the system of offices of which it is a part.[93] Hence when a corrupt official is prosecuted as such, the "system" is said to "work." This secular authority has no basis for morality outside its own self-generated processes of integration.[94] Under such a regime official deviance becomes the public version of white-collar crime.[95] And, as such activities as the prosecution of the Iran–Contra principals illustrate, conviction for such crimes is difficult to achieve and even more difficult to sustain.[96] In such a conception of authority there are neither separate moral keepers nor a special subject group of the morally kept; rather, each socialized person is both a moral keeper and a morally kept cog within a system of functionally binding interdependence.[97]

The politics of modern, democratic, social-system ethics depend less upon ownership of than on values-integrative control over the means and media of public social interaction.[98] However such integration as does exist is threatened by the shift from symbolic to strategic interaction in public places.[99] Dissident social movements, as well as other varieties of social protest, moreover, offer challenges to and put in claims for this ownership and control.[100] But the state, making its own all-inclusive sovereign claim, confronts such movements and develops a wide range of strategies and tactics to thwart the objectives of these would-be authorities.[101] In the present era – one wavering between modern and postmodern orientations toward authority and ideology[102] – precisely because of its monopoly over the new ideology of tolerance and pluralism, the state might be able to coopt all but the most intransigent of these movements.[103] When, as in earlier eras, such movements could not be coopted – or when particular individuals or certain peoples were suspected of harboring subversive intentions – intelligence probes, political trials and coercive force might be put into play as defensive elements of the outwardly democratic state's protective arsenal.[104]

Except for those Marxists who had become converts to New-Deal reformism and labor-movement collective bargaining, or who had become converts to a more gradualist and reformist social-systems theory,[105] dissident varieties of Marxism – some of which were tinged with American radical Protestantism and populism – became the single most significant source for oppositional social movements in America (and in the world) during the Cold-War era.[106] For both Parsons and – somewhat more pessimistically – the neo-Utilitarian exchange theorists, the American public philosophy was to be guided by the hidden hand of dynamic equilibrium.[107] However, for some extreme adherents to Cold-War, Marxist sociological thought – guided by their belief that America's role in the world was that of bearer of "late capitalism" – a revitalized Marxism had formulated a praxis that would at the very least be witness to the fulfillment of the promise that was seen to emanate from the irrevocable dialectic of historical materialism.[108] This variant of Marxism also bid fair to become a civil religion; the correct handling of the contradictions disturbing the relations of the people to the state was assigned either to professorial casuists of the Marxist catechism, to cadre leaders of the movement or to the Communist Party. Or, in still another theory-driven variant, it was postponed until an indefinite time in the future, when the party's bureaucratic successor, the dictatorship of the proletariat – that is, the bearer of the state society's eschatology – would complete the task. As a civil religion, such forms of Marxism unite individual, society and state in the pursuit of an historically predetermined *telos*.[109]

Another variant of this civil religion that would affect thought about the outcome of revolutionary social movements is to be found in the convergence of Marxism with positivistic social science. As recast by the late Paul F. Lazarsfeld, "What has become known as Marxist sociology comes closer than any other quest of its kind to [being] the strict model for a theory."[110] As Lazarsfeld conceived the matter, neither state nor civil society in either the then-existent Soviet Union or the United States of America had yet achieved perfect integration. Population segments in both of these political–economic social systems suffered from a persistent sense of alienation. In the USSR, according to Lazarsfeld, research criteria for the resolution of this problem had been set by the Communist Party, which, as "the avant-garde of the working class," took as its task the direction of the "economic and cultural life of the country." Having "accepted empirical social research, or as it is often called, concrete sociology," as a way by which "concrete data on the state of the nation are provided," the party had commissioned sociological investigations that showed – in the words of two Soviet sociologists quoted approvingly by Lazarsfeld – that "in many cases the members of the collectivity, including some of the workers have not yet become aware (*pris conscience*) of how their own fundamental interests and those of socialist society coincide." Apparently Lazarsfeld accepted such a lack of awareness as a true indicator of alienation within the framework of the Soviet system.

Alienation in this perspective, then, is treated as a failure of revolutionary socialization to have overwhelmed all other modes of thought. Through the party the state arrogates to itself the task of remedying this failure. The alienated individual, having not yet submitted him- or herself wholly to the precepts of the Soviet covenant, was perceived as unregenerate. Regeneration was to be accomplished with the technical assistance of Soviet sociologists, who themselves had put forward the claim: "How to suppress the alienation of man in a socialist regime can be scientifically studied through sociological inquiries."[111] In Lazarsfeld's positivist sect of the Marxist civil religion – now virtually moribund because of the dissolution of the Soviet Union and the elimination of its hegemony over the states of Eastern Europe – the state and civil society were to be welded into an undifferentiated unity, a secular social compact, devoted to enforcing a rational-control administration over dysfunctional human alienation and to ensuring there would be no unauthorized deviation from dialectical history's ineluctable path to inner-worldly salvation. As a civil religion for the former USSR, Soviet Marxism was in fact characterized by its demand for "voluntary" submission and by its iron-fisted, concomitant repressiveness, each in effect precluding the necessity for any dissident salvationist social movement to arise.

CLASS, RACE, GENDER: CIVIL vs PLURAL SOCIETY IN AMERICA

From 1945 to the present a revolution of rising ethnoracial consciousness has taken place in America. It has manifested itself as a series of social movements variously espousing desegregation, integration, ethnoracial power, separatism and, at the close of the century, multiculturalism. During the Cold-War era a few American radicals sought to subsume the race question – which in 1944 Gunnar Myrdal had called the "American Dilemma"[112] – into the class issue, thereby hoping to discourage the incipient development of group consciousness among the several ethnoracial solidarities.[113] Although Gumplowicz had predicted such a rise more than a half century earlier, wars of ethnonational liberation and a resistance to assimilation in America were redefined as data for a more complex Marxist theory of development.[114] Some theorists of this persuasion discovered the writings of the Sardinian radical, Antonio Gramsci (1891–1937), who had reformulated Marxism so that its inner-worldly *eskaton* would be a "regulated society," an "ethical state" or a true "civil society."[115] In its penultimate forms it might include a stage wherein "The great majority of human beings who have been at history's margins will come into their own and create a new history, which while still (inevitably) imperfect will contain more positive elements and exhibit fewer errors."[116] Insofar as race consciousness and, in light of later developments, gender consciousness were said to be basic building blocks or stages of development of a future American or global class-based society, the sodalities of race and sex were in effect demarginalized, but at the same time they were invited to participate in their own ultimate disintegration under the hegemony of a benevolent, socialist, civil society. The invitation has not been accepted by leading elements in both groups.[117]

At the end of the Second World War a liberal sociologist, Louis Wirth, had considered a related theoretical modification, one that in effect added a penultimate stage to the already dubiously regarded cyclical theory of race relations formulated earlier by Robert E. Park. Wirth took note of separatist and secessionist tendencies among what he called pluralistic minorities. He proposed that those with power and influence in the dominant society should become sensitive to the fact that "an emerging minority group, as it becomes aware of its ethnic identity . . . seek[s] toleration for its cultural differences." Wirth suggested that the group in question be granted just enough of its wish that when "sufficient toleration and autonomy [had been] attained, the pluralistic minority [would move itself] to the assimilationist stage . . ." The latter stage, he pointedly observed, would be "characterized by the desire for acceptance by an incorporation into the dominant group."[118] Nearly four decades earlier Lester F. Ward, a non-Marxist, radical and antireligious sociologist, had prophesied a resolution of the "woman question" in a similar scenario. He foresaw the coming of a "gynandrocratic" era; it would begin after the forces of romantic love, heterosexual mating and the incentives inspired by the achievement syndrome had worked together to overcome the present but waning period of androcracy.[119]

Neither Ward's nor Wirth's perspectives were recalled by the post-1960s radicals. Rather, conventional sociology was said to have enclosed itself in an orthodox consensus to which they would provide a radical alternative.[120] Some revolutionary theorists pointed to the inherent contradictions in capitalism, contradictions that are alleged to make the capitalist state ever more ineffective in resolving such fundamental problems as those affecting and affected by class, race and gender.[121] For a few years, a few of these projected the dissolution of the capitalist system not only as a basic desideratum, but also as the likely (if not inevitable) outcome of a synthetic, international, ethnoracial–gender–class struggle. The claim that America was now passing through an era of "late" capitalism set temporal limits to the survivability of the American capitalist state and its socio-cultural infrastructure.[122] As secular eschatologists, these social thinkers provided an ultimate sociodicy – a vindication of society (via the dynamic of history) to humanity. Their perspective provided a prophecy of a soon-to-be inaugurated millenium and evoked the praxiological necessity of overcoming those contingencies (countervailing facts and liberal "bourgeois" theories) that stood in the way of its coming to be.[123] However, for the most part, such neo-Marxist sociologists were in the minority – "scientific" prophets with neither a mass nor a class following. Moreover when the Soviet Union disintegrated and the postcommunist states began to adopt a free-market approach, their sociodicy began to lose much of its evocative and vindicative value. Their interest for current sociology resides in their illustration of the distinctiveness that characterizes the chiliastic ideologies of truly revolutionary movements.[124]

Another foundation for social order, as well as a basis for a social movement in pursuit of that order, is the civil religion evangelized in the final days of the waning Cold War by Robert Bellah and his band of disciples. For Bellah, who has gravitated from Marxism through Buddhism to a synthetic Protestant–functionalist position,[125] social science itself becomes the civil religion:

we can . . . say that in contemporary society social science has usurped the traditional position of theology. It is now social science that tells us what kind of creatures we are and what we are about on this planet. It is social science that provides us images of personal behavior and legitimations of the structures that govern us. It is to social science that the task is entrusted, so far as it is entrusted at all, of, in whatever the contemporary terms for it would be, 'justifying the ways of God to man.'[26]

In Bellah's post-1960s sociology, ethics, morality and eschatology become provinces of the religiously oriented scientific intellectual. However in a society wherein there has occurred what Bellah describes as an "erosion of common moral and religious understanding,"[127] there are the dangers of divisiveness, disillusion and decay. The several denominational religions compete with one another; theirs is an antagonism that threatens to turn a struggle over the jurisdiction of America's soul into an uncivil religious war.[128] At the same time alienation from both God and society challenges the grounds for constructing a beneficial civil society,[129] while corruption and official deviance undermine the claim of a public interest.[130] In such a situation each academic discipline might claim the duty to set correct moral standard for society as a whole, as well as the obligation to chart the future for America and every other society.[131] Soon the competitive claims of these civil religions would confront one another in what would likely become a cockpit of creeds. The cockpit is likely to be realized in the universities, where the morals debate becomes a struggle for the souls of colleagues and students.[132] In recent years Bellah and his followers have sought a Comtean resolution of this problem. Just as Comte proposed a "religion of humanity" that would replace Catholicism, they have developed a religio-political public philosophy[133] that seeks to shape the habits of the heart,[134] help students (and everyone else, presumably) to be saved from the 1960s,[135] and formulate a Protestant *manque* ethic for the good society.[136]

TOWARD THE POSTMODERN: SOCIAL MOVEMENTS IN AN AGE OF DIFFUSE ANXIETY

After 1945 the conceptualizations in much of American sociology continued to reflect valuations and transvaluations of the separate and sometimes conflicting themes in Protestantism, populism, ethnicism and Marxism.[137] Since the late 1970s the discipline has become even more fractionalized, as its professional leaders took on the character of an establishment desperately seeking to hold together its increasingly divided members.[138] In the work of Erving Goffman (1922–80) and his followers, however, there is an anticipation of the postmodern.[139] There will be found a description of a social order and a civil religion that exist without dependence on God, the state or historical inevitability.[140]

In Goffman's perspective there has arisen a civil religion of the other-directed; in an age in which charisma is suspect and awe in short supply, it seeks to enhance the faltering confidence and fend off the status-demeaning stigmas that threaten to undermine the socially unconfirmed self.[141] In Goffman's unacknowledged Spinozan outlook, God is not quite dead; rather He has gone away. In His absence His sacred aura has been democratized and diffused. It now resides in the attribution of characterological self-possession that each person is grudgingly willing to grant to the other in the hope that the other will reciprocate.[142] Each self is engaged in its own pursuit, a solitary and minimalist social movement on behalf of itself.

In Goffman's vision of a less than civil but postmodern society, there is neither a religious ethic nor an established set of core values to guide civic or interpersonal conduct; the inscrutability of the ultimately just Calvinist God has been replaced by the inaccessibility of the morally responsible agent.[143] Society becomes a species of communicative conduct[144] wherein each individual presents hopefully efficacious excuses or justifications[145] for acts called into question. Much of life becomes an agonizing quest for self-assurance, self-interest and self-promotion; a voracious but lonely and insecure ego governs the relations of one with the other. Goffman's observations represent a critical endpoint in the analysis of the moral structure of the civil community. The generalized other has disintegrated into a multiplicity of others, and collective action has been reduced to mutual support of or assault upon one another's egos.[146]

Goffman's sociology recalls us to the conflict in and tragedy of modern culture depicted so poignantly by Simmel[147] at the same time that it adumbrates the dilemmas of the post-industrial era delineated by Lyotard.[148] It speaks to a recognition of the anguishing dilemmas that men and women face in a world without God, theodicy or eschatology.[149] This is the postmodern world that Baudrillard has illustrated with his mordant, black-comic essay, *America*.[150] The normlessness of that world drives people to seek eudemonistic distraction in risky ventures, strategic ploys, manipulations of relations in public, game frameworks and adventures, that is, unusual or daring activities carried out in times and places separately carved from their routine world.[151] These seemingly emancipatory acts, attempts to liberate *life* from its constraining iron cages, however, are doomed to be converted into not-yet-imagined, repressive *forms*. An aggressively ambitious but ethically ambiguous and essentially consumer-oriented[152] society places its workers in a labyrinth of alienation,[153] while its business leaders struggle to find their way through the moral mazes of corporate life.[154] Advertising firms coopt the more colorful of the emancipatory forms, transforming them into sales pitches for one or other product or of the several competing life-styles.[155] By this means the once new forms are robbed of both autonomy and integrity and become holograms of the nothingness they personify.

The transvaluation of theodicy into sociodicy has coincided with a general and pervasive secularization and rationalization taking place throughout the Occident. Until the disintegration of the Soviet Union and the end of the Cold War, its central problem was to find a means to cope with the threat of nuclear holocaust.[156] However, with a new world order in the making, the original problems of theodicy remain unresolved: men and women still seek to create a just and peaceful society for themselves and their children. They attempt not only to comprehend the natural and social inequities, injustices and misfortunes that cry out for explanation but also to remedy them. As the successor to Protestant theology, American sociology has been compelled to assume the burden of providing a sociodicy equal to or better than that of its religious predecessor. But although it inherited a world after the twin forces of industrialization and immigration had deprived Puritanism of much of its effectiveness as a theodicy, it has not yet found its own purely secular public philosophy.[157]

Social movements of our time fare no better. If they are revolutionary, they succeed only if they separate the fundamentally radical elements of their ideology from their substantive concerns. They are then absorbed into modern America's secular equivalent of salvation – piecemeal social reform that reconceptualizes the kingdom of God on earth as an already constituted fact or as a gradually-to-be-achieved, inner-worldly utopia of the future.[158] If they are religious,[159] they withdraw either into other-worldly asceticism or hedonic irresponsibility, or they enter into zealous political or criminal action as reactionary or radical movements that substitute ideology for America's failure to have developed a consensually valid and universally just public philosophy.[160] The peoples of the incongruous but beckoning world are still impelled to continue their individual and collective search for both security and identity,[161] but their quest is impeded by the unknown number of cardboard heroes, conniving villains and inveterate fools among their leaders;[162] by the image problems that beset their symbolic leaders;[163] by the inflation of symbols that recent crusades and postmodern praxes have encouraged;[164] and by the less-than-honorable tactics and manipulative strategies of interaction and information that characterize the present and immediately future situation.[165] Sociologists might look for models of social order,[166] but people seek models of the just life.[167]

Notes

1. See, for example, John T. McNeill, *A History of the Cure of Souls*, (New York: Harper Torchbooks, n.d.), pp. 261–86.
2. See the essays by David S. Lovejoy, Patricia U. Bunomi, Rhyo Isaac and James A. Henretta in Margaret C. Jacob and James R. Jacob (eds), *The Origins of Anglo-American Radicalism* (Atlantic Highlands, NJ: Humanities Press International, 1984), pp. 214–57. See also Alan Heimert and Perry Miller (eds), *The Great Awakening: Documents Illustrating the Crisis and Its Consequences* (Indianapolis: Bobbs-Merrill, 1967); and John B. Boles, *The Great Revival: The Origins of the Southern Evangelical Mind* (Lexington: University Press of Kentucky, 1972).
3. See Larzer Ziff, *Puritanism in America: New Culture in a New World* (New York: The Viking Press, 1973), pp. 286–312; two works by Sacvan Bercovitch, *The Puritan Origins of the American Self* (New Haven: Yale University Press, 1975) and *The American Jeremiad* (Madison: University of Wisconsin Press, 1978); as well as Winthrop S. Hudson, *American Protestantism* (University of Chicago Press, 1961), pp. 1–127; Winthrop S. Hudson and John Corrigan, *Religion in America: An Historical Account of the Development of American Religious Life*, 5th edn. (New York: Macmillan, 1992), pp. 1–202; and Timothy L. Smith, *Revivalism and Social Reform: American Protestantism on the Eve of the Civil War* (Baltimore: Johns Hopkins University Press, 1980).
4. Anne C. Rose, *Transcendentalism as a Social Movement, 1830–1850* (New Haven: Yale University Press, 1981).
5. Louise L. Stevenson, *Scholarly Means to Evangelical Ends: The New*

Haven Scholars and the Transformation of Higher Learning in America, 1830–1890 (Baltimore: Johns Hopkins University Press, 1986).

6. See two works by Walter Rauschenbusch, *Christianity and the Social Crisis*, edited by Robert D. Cross (New York: Harper Torchbooks, 1964 [1907]), and *The Social Principles of Jesus* (New York: Association Press, 1919). See also Washington Gladden, *Applied Christianity: Moral Aspects of Social Questions* (Boston: Houghton, Mifflin, 1886; reprint, New York: Arno Press, 1976); and Graham Taylor, *Pioneering on Social Frontiers* (Chicago: University of Chicago Press, 1930; reprint, New York: Arno Press, 1976). In general see Charles Edward Hopkins, *The Rise of the Social Gospel in American Protestantism, 1865–1915* (New Haven: Yale University Press, 1940); Ronald C. White and C. Howard Hopkins with an essay by John C. Bennett, *The Social Gospel: Religion and Reform in Changing America* (Philadelphia: Temple University Press, 1976); and Willem A. Visser 'T Hooft, *The Background of the Social Gospel in America* (St. Louis: The Bethany Press, n.d. [1928]).

7. See William R. Hutchison, *Errand to the World: American Protestant Thought and Foreign Missions* (Chicago: University of Chicago Press, 1987); and Kenton J. Clymer, *Protestant Missionaries in the Philippines, 1898–1916: An Inquiry into the American Colonial Mentality*, (Urbana: University of Illinois Press, 1986).

8. See, for example, Michael B. Katz, *In the Shadow of the Poorhouse: A Social History of Welfare in America* (New York: Basic Books, 1986), pp. 58–109; Arthur C. Holden, *The Settlement Idea: A Vision of Social Justice* (New York: Macmillan, 1922; reprint, New York: Arno Press and the New York Times, 1970); Residents of Hull-House, *Hull-House Maps and Papers: A Presentation of Nationalities and Wages in a Congested District of Chicago, Together with Comments and Essays on Problems Growing Out of the Social Conditions* (Boston: Thomas Y. Crowell, 1895; reprint, New York: Arno Press and the New York Times, 1970); Ken Fones-Wulf, *Trade-Union Gospel: Christianity and Labor in Industrial Philadelphia, 1865–1915* (Philadelphia: Temple University Press, 1989); William G. McLoughlin, *Revivals, Awakenings, and Reform: An Essay on Religion and Social Change in America, 1607–1977* (Chicago: University of Chicago Press, 1978), pp. 141–78; Martin E. Marty, *Pilgrims in Their Own Land: 500 Years of Religion in America* (Boston: Little, Brown, 1984), pp. 307–71.

9. Ernest Lee Tuveson, *Redeemer Nation: The Idea of America's Millenial Role* (Chicago: University of Chicago Press, 1968); Keith W. Stavely, *Puritan Legacies: Paradise Lost and the New England Tradition, 1630–1890*, (Ithaca: Cornell University Press, 1987), pp. 201–43.

10. See T. Scott Miyakawa, *Protestants and Pioneers: Individualism and Conformity on the American Frontier* (Chicago: University of Chicago Press, 1964); Lawrence B. Davis, *Immigrants, Baptists, and the Protestant Mind in America* (Urbana: University of Illinois Press, 1973); and Randall M. Miller and Thomas D. Marzik (eds), *Immigrants and Religion in Urban America* (Philadelphia: Temple University Press, 1977).

11. See Paul Goodman, *Towards a Christian Republic: Antimasonry and*

the *Great Transition in New England, 1826–1836* (New York: Oxford University Press, 1988); Robert T. Handy, *A Christian America: Protestant Hopes and Historical Realities* (New York: Oxford University Press, 1971); Sidney E. Mead, *The Old Religion in the Brave New World: Reflections on the Relations Between Chritendom and the Republic* (Berkeley: University of California Press, 1977); Gustavus Myers, *History of Bigotry in the United States,* edited and revised by Henry M. Christman, (New York: Capricorn Books, 1960), pp. 3–210.

12. Mona Harrington, *The Dream of Deliverance in American Politics* (New York: Alfred A. Knopf, 1986); and Loren Baritz, *Backfire: A History of How American Culture Led Us Into Vietnam and Made Us Fight the Way We Did* (New York: William Morrow, 1985).

13. See three works by Perry Miller, *The New England Mind: The Seventeenth Century* (Cambridge: Harvard University Press, 1939, 1954); *The New England Mind: From Colony to Province* (Cambridge: The Belknap Press of Harvard University Press, 1953); *Errand Into the Wilderness* (Cambridge: The Belknap Press of Harvard University Press, 1956). See also James West Davidson, *The Logic of Millenial Thought: Eighteenth-Century New England* (New Haven: Yale University Press, 1977), esp. pp. 179–297.

14. Perry Miller and Thomas H. Johnson (eds), *The Puritans,* revised edition (New York: Harper Torchbooks, 1963), pp. 181–280.

15. Perry Miller, "Equality in the American Setting," in John Crowell and Stanford J. Searl (eds), *The Responsibility of Mind in a Civilization of Machines: Essays by Perry Miller* (Amherst: University of Massachusetts Press, 1979), pp. 142–60.

16. Lorenzo Johnston Greene, *The Negro in Colonial New England* (New York: Atheneum, 1968), pp. 15–49, 100–289; Forrest G. Wood, *The Arrogance of Faith: Christianity and Race in America from the Colonial Era to the Twentieth Century* (New York: Alfred A. Knopf, 1990), pp. 3–338. See also Marcus Cunliffe, *Chattel Slavery and Wage Slavery: The Anglo-American Context, 1830–1860* (Athens, Ga: University of Georgia Press, 1979).

17. *Cherokee Nation v. Georgia,* 5 Pet. 1 (1831). See Vine Deloria, Jr, "The Application of the Constitution to American Indians," in Oren Lyons *et al.* (eds), *Exiled in the Land of the Free: Democracy, Indian Nations, and the U.S. Constitution* (Santa Fe, NM: Clear Light Publishers, 1992), pp. 281–316; William G. McLoughlin, *Cherokee Renascence in the New Republic* (Princeton University Press, 1986). For a general socio-cultural critique, see Thomas R. Berger, *A Long and Terrible Shadow: White Values, Native Rights in the Americas, 1492–1992* (Seattle: University of Washington Press, 1992). For some representative studies of land control and usage among various Indian tribes, see Terry, L. Anderson (ed.), *Property Rights and Indian Economies* (Lanham, Md: Rowman and Littlefield, 1992); and Emily Benedek, *The Wind Won't Know Me: A History of the Navajo–Hopi Land Dispute* (New York: Alfred A. Knopf, 1992).

18. See Stanford M. Lyman, "The Race Question and Liberalism: Casuistries in American Constitutional Law," *International Journal of*

Politics, Culture, and Society, vol. V, no. 2 (winter 1991), pp. 183–247.

19. I interpose the term "accredited" in belated recognition of the antebellum southern Comteans – Henry Hughes (1829–62), George Fitzhugh (1806–81), George Frederick Holmes (1820–97) and Joseph LeConte (1823–1901) – whose originating contribution to the beginnings of American sociology has been ignored by the discipline's official historians. See two essays by Stanford M. Lyman, "Henry Hughes and the Southern Foundations of American Sociology," in Stanford M. Lyman (ed.), *Selected Writings of Henry Hughes: Antebellum Southerner, Slavocrat, Sociologist* (Jackson: University Press of Mississippi, 1985), pp. 1–72; and "System and Function in Antebellum Southern Sociology," *"International Journal of Politics, Culture, and Society*, vol. II, no. 1 (fall 1988), pp. 95–108.

20. See Arthur J. Vidich and Stanford M. Lyman, *American Sociology: Worldly Rejections of Religion and Their Directions* (New Haven: Yale University Press, 1985).

21. See Cecil Greek, "The Social Gospel Movement and Early American Sociology, 1870–1915," *The Graduate Faculty Journal of Sociology*, vol. III, no. 1 (Fall 1978), pp. 30–42.

22. McLoughlin, op. cit., pp. 141–78.

23. Sociocracy was the conception and end result championed by the thoroughly irreligious Lester Frank Ward. See Ward, *The Psychic Factors of Civilization*, 2nd edn (Boston: Ginn and Co., 1906), pp. 311–31. See also Henry Steele Commager (ed.), *Lester Ward and the Welfare State* (Indianapolis: Bobbs-Merrill, 1967), pp. 416–28.

24. See William Graham Sumner, *Folkways: A Study of the Sociological Importance of Usages, Manners, Customs, Mores, and Morals* (Boston: Ginn and Co., 1940 [1906]), pp. 97–8. See also Stow Persons (ed.), *Social Darwinism: Selected Essays by William Graham Sumner*, (Englewood Cliffs, NJ: Prentice-Hall-Spectrum, 1963), pp. 70–180.

25. See, for example, Albion W. Small, "The Bonds of Nationality," *American Journal of Sociology*, vol. XX, no. 5 (March 1915), pp. 629–83.

26. See Stanford M. Lyman, "Race Relations as Social Process: Sociology's Resistance to a Civil Rights Orientation," in Herbert Hill and James E. Jones (eds), *Race in America: The Struggle for Equality* (Madison: University of Wisconsin Press, 1993), pp. 370–401. See also Vernon J. Williams, Jr, *From a Caste to a Minority: Changing Attitudes of American Sociologists Toward Afro-Americans, 1896–1945* (New York: Greenwood Press, 1989), esp. pp. 5–112.

27. On the dilemmas and contradictions of assimilation and pluralism, see Milton M. Gordon, *Assimilation in American Life: The Role of Race, Religion, and National Origins* (New York: Oxford University Press, 1964); William M. Newman, *American Pluralism: A Study of Minority Groups and Social Theory* (New York: Harper and Row, 1973); two essays by Peter Kivisto, "The Transplanted Then and Now: The Reorientation of Immigration Studies from the Chicago School to the New Social History," *Ethnic and Racial Studies*, vol. XIII, no. 4 (October 1990), pp. 455–81; and "Beyond Assimilation and Pluralism: Toward Situationally Sensitive Theoretic Models of Ethnicity,"

paper presented at the annual meeting of the American Sociological Association, Pittsburgh, Pennsylvania, 20–24 August, 1992; and Rogers M. Smith, "The 'American Creed' and American Identity: The Limits of Liberal Citizenship in the United States," *Western Political Quarterly*, vol. XLI, no. 2 (June 1988), pp. 225–51.

28. For a definitive statement of the original European orientation, see the classic work of Lorenz von Stein, *The History of the Social Movement in France, 1789–1850*, edited and translated by Kaethe Mengelberg (Totowa, NJ: The Bedminster Press, 1964 [1850]).

29. For a recent discursive essay on the subject, see Peter Marris, "Witnesses, Engineers, or Storytellers? Roles of Sociologists in Social Policy," in Herbert J. Gans, (ed.), *Sociology in America* (Newbury Park, CA: Sage Publications, 1990), pp. 75–86.

30. Thus the intellectual beginnings of American sociology stand in sharp contrast to those of Europe, as recently summarized by Alvin Gouldner:

> First, [European] sociology developed a critique of political economy's emphasis on a competitive, market individualism. Second, early sociology opposed institutionalized religions, including both Catholicism and Protestantism, regarded the critique of deism as a necessary foundation of the sciences, and saw the sciences as the necessary basis of modern society. In short, the critique of conventional and established religion was, for early sociologists (particularly St. Simon) as for Marxism, the beginning of all critique. Third, and finally, early sociology rejected the dominance of society by the state, saw the state as undermining society and as essentially archaic insofar as its characteristic form was domination by force (Alvin W. Gouldner, *The Two Marxisms: Contradictions and Anomalies in the Development of Theory* [New York: Seabury Press, 1980], p. 363).

American sociology, with only occasional exceptions, adapted itself to a Manchesterean and, later, Keynesian attitude toward free-market individualism, perceived sociological meliorism as a mission on behalf of an inner-worldly Protestant eschatology, and regarded the state as an agency for the scientific guidance of the people.

31. John Calvin, *Institutes: Institutes of the Christian Religion*, edited by John T. McNeil, translated by Ford Lewis Battles (Philadelphia: Westminster Press, 1961). Quoted from T. Dunbar Moodie, *The Rise of Afrikanerdom: Power, Apartheid, and the Afrikaner Civil Religion* (Berkeley: University of California Press, 1975), p. 25.

32. See the discussion in Stanford M. Lyman, *Militarism, Imperialism, and Racial Accommodation: An Analysis and Interpretation of the Early Writings of Robert E. Park* (Fayetteville: University of Arkansas Press, 1992), pp. 81–104.

33. See Michael W. Hughey and Arthur J. Vidich, "The New American Pluralism: Racial and Ethnic Sodalities and Their Sociological Implications," *International Journal of Politics, Culture, and Society*, vol. VI, no. 2 (winter, 1992), pp. 159–80.

34. See the discussions of this issue presented in two entries in Stephan

Thernstrom (ed.), *The Harvard Encyclopedia of American Ethnic Groups* (Cambridge: The Belknap Press of Harvard University Press, 1980): Philip Gleason, "American Identity and Americanization," pp. 31–58; and Harold J. Abramson, "Assimilation and Pluralism," pp. 150–60.

35. See Lawrence J. Friedman, *Inventors of the Promised Land* (New York: Alfred A. Knopf, 1975); Lawrence H. Fuchs, *The American Kaleidoscope: Race, Ethnicity, and the Civic Culture* (Hanover, NH: Wesleyan University Press, 1990); Ewa Morawska, "The Sociology and Historiography of Immigration," in Virginia Yans-McLaughlin (ed.), *Immigration Reconsidered: History, Sociology, and Politics* (New York: Oxford University Press, 1990), pp. 187–240.

36. See for example, W. Lloyd Warner and Leo Srole, *The Social System of American Ethnic Groups*, Yankee City Series, vol. III (New Haven: Yale University Press, 1945), pp. 283–96; Joel Perlman, *Ethnic Differences: Schooling and Social Structure Among the Irish, Italians, Jews and Blacks in an American City, 1880–1935* (Cambridge University Press, 1988), pp. 203–19; Mary C. Waters, *Ethnic Options: Choosing Identities in America* (Berkeley: University of California Press, 1990), esp. pp. 16–51.

37. See Vernon K. Dibble, *The Legacy of Albion Small* (University of Chicago Press, 1975), p. 248, n. 2.

38. Albion W. Small, *General Sociology: An Exposition of the Main Development in Sociological Theory from Spencer to Ratzenhofer* (University of Chicago Press, 1905; reprint, New York: Arno Press, 1974), pp. 249–322, esp. pp. 256–8.

39. Robert E. Park, "Racial Assimilation in Secondary Groups With Particular Reference to the Negro," in Everett Cherrington Hughes *et al.* (eds), *Race and Culture: The Collected Papers of Robert Ezra Park*, vol. I (Glencoe: The Free Press, 1950), pp. 204–20.

40. Stanford M. Lyman, *Color, Culture, Civilization: Race and Minority Issues in American Society* (Urbana: University of Illinois Press, 1994).

41. See, for example, Eugene E. Roosens, *Creating Ethnicity: The Process of Ethnogenesis*, "Frontiers of Anthropology," vol. 5 (Newbury Park, CA: Sage Publications, 1989), pp. 9–20, 149–62; Richard D. Alba, *Ethnic Identity: The Transformation of White America* (New Haven: Yale University Press, 1990), pp. 290–320; Alejandro Portes and Cynthia G. Truelove, "Making Sense of Diversity: Recent Research on Hispanic Minorities in the United States," in Norman R. Yetman (ed.), *Majority and Minority: The Dynamics of Race and Ethnicity in American Life*, 5th edn (Boston: Allyn and Bacon, 1991), pp. 402–19; Sidney W. Mintz and Richard Price, *The Birth of African-American Culture: An Anthropological Perspective* (Boston: Beacon Press, 1976, 1992); Sucheng Chan, *Asian Americans: An Interpretive History* (Boston: Twayne Publishers, 1991).

42. For various assessments see Edward George Hartmann, *The Movement to Americanize the Immigrant* (New York: AMS Press, 1967 [1948]); Stanley Feldstein and Lawrence Costello (eds), *The Ordeal of Assimilation: A Documentary History of the White Working Class, 1830's to 1970's* (Garden City, NY: Anchor Books, 1974); Colin Greer (ed.),

Divided Society: The Ethnic Experience in America (New York: Basic Books, 1974); Thomas J. Archdeacon, *Becoming American: An Ethnic History* (New York: The Free Press, 1983).

43. Peter Schrag, *The Decline of the WASP* (New York: Simon and Schuster, 1970). For an attempt to recover the WASP hegemony, see Richard Brookhiser, *The Way of the WASP: How It Made America and How It Can Save It* (New York: The Free Press, 1991). For a nostalgic recollection of the era of New England Protestant domination, see Joseph W. Alsop with Adam Platt, *"I've Seen the Best": Memoirs* (New York: Norton, 1992), esp. pp. 17–113.

44. Michael Novak, *The Rise of the Unmeltable Ethnics: Politics and Culture in the Seventies* (New York: Macmillan, 1971).

45. Peter Schrag, *The End of the American Future* (New York: Simon and Schuster, 1973).

46. See Rubén G. Rumbaut, "Passages to America: Perspectives on the New Immigration," in Alan Wolfe (ed.), *America at Century's End* (Berkeley: University of California Press, 1991), pp. 208–44. See also Rita James Simon (ed.), "Immigration and American Public Policy," *Annals of the American Academy of Political and Social Science*, vol. CDLXXXVII (September 1986), pp. 9–217.

47. See Robert Redfield, "The Japanese-Americans," in William Fielding Ogburn (ed.), *American Society in Wartime* (University of Chicago Press, 1943; reprint, New York: Da Capo Press, 1972), pp. 143–64.

48. Cf., for example, two works written forty years apart by Philip Selznick: *The Organizational Weapon: A Study of Bolshevik Strategy and Tactics* (New York: McGraw-Hill, 1952), pp. 115–18, 302–8, and *The Moral Commonwealth: Social Theory and the Promise of Community* (Berkeley: University of California Press, 1992), pp. 95–116, 355–538. On academic sociology and the Cold War, see William Buxton, *Talcott Parsons and the Capitalist Nation-State* (University of Toronto Press, 1985), pp. 117–276; Ellen W. Schrecker, *No Ivory Tower: McCarthyism and the Universities* (New York: Oxford University Press, 1986), pp. 84–342; and Sigmund Diamond, *Compromised Campus: The Collaboration of Universities With the Intelligence Community, 1945–1955* (New York: Oxford University Press, 1992), esp. pp. 24–137.

49. Cf. Talcott Parsons, "Full Citizenship for the Negro American? A Sociological Problem," *Daedalus: Journal of the American Academy of Arts and Sciences*, vol. XCIV, no. 4 (fall 1965), pp. 1009–54.

50. See Mary L. Dudziak, "Desegregation as a Cold War Imperative," *Stanford Law Review*, vol. XLI (1988–9), pp. 61–120.

51. Stanford M. Lyman, "The Assimilation–Pluralism Debate: Toward a Postmodern Resolution of the American Ethnoracial Dilemma," *International Journal of Politics, Culture, and Society*, vol. VI, no. 2 (winter 1992), pp. 181–210.

52. Bart Landry, "The Enduring Dilemma of Race in America," in Wolfe (ed.), op. cit., pp. 185–207; Clint Bolick, *Unfinished Business: A Civil Rights Strategy for America's Third Century* (San Francisco: Pacific Research Institute for Public Policy, 1990).

53. M. J. Heale, *American Anticommunism: Combating the Enemy Within,*

1830–1970 (Baltimore: The Johns Hopkins University Press, 1990); George Sirgiovanni, *An Undercurrent of Suspicion: Anticommunism in America During World War II* (New Brunswick, NJ: Transaction Publishers, 1990); Thomas G. Paterson, *Meeting the Communist Threat: Truman to Reagan* (New York: Oxford University Press, 1988).

54. See Bert Cochran, *Labor and Communism: The Conflict That Shaped American Unions* (Princeton, N.J.: Princeton University Press, 1977), pp. 229–344. For the attitude of the Communist Party toward the race question during its early years, see Theodore Draper, *American Communism and Soviet Russia: The Formative Period* (New York: Viking Press, 1960), pp. 315–56. For the persistence of racism in American labor unions during and after the Second World War, see Herbert Hill, *Black Labor and the American Legal System: Race, Work, and the Law* (Madison: University of Wisconsin Press, 1985). For the effect of the early years of the Cold War on civil rights and other aspects of the race question, see, for example, Douglas T. Miller and Marion Nowak, *The Fifties: The Way We Really Were* (Garden City: Doubleday, 1977), pp. 182–219; and Albert P. Blaustein and Robert L. Zangrando (eds), *Civil Rights and African Americans: A Documentary History* (Evanston: Northwestern University Press, 1991), pp. 355–656. For two analyses of the African-American response in the same era, see Steven F. Lawson, *Running for Freedom: Civil Rights and Black Politics Since 1941* (Philadelphia: Temple University Press, 1991); and Vincent Harding, *The Other American Revolution* (Los Angeles: Center for Afro-American Studies, University of California, 1980), pp. 137–232.

55. Charles U. Smith and Lewis M. Killian, "Sociological Foundations of the Civil Rights Movement," in Gans, op. cit., pp. 105–16. For the Cold-War backlash against a distinguished African-American sociologist, see Anthony M. Platt, *E. Franklin Frazier Reconsidered* (New Brunswick, NJ: Rutgers University Press, 1991), pp. 173–222.

56. For a critique of sociology's failure with respect to civil rights, see Stanford M. Lyman, "Race Relations as Social Process: Sociology's Resistance to a Civil Rights Orientation," op. cit.

57. Henry Hughes, *A Treatise on Sociology: Theoretical and Practical* (Philadelphia: Lippincott, Grambo, 1854; reprint, New York: Negro Universities Press, 1968; and Charles Richmond Henderson, *An Introduction to the Study of the Dependent, Defective, and Delinquent Classes* (Boston: D. C. Heath, 1893).

58. Lyman (ed.), *Selected Writings of Henry Hughes*, op. cit.; Ronald T. Takaki, *A Pro-Slavery Crusade: The Agitation to Reopen the African Slave Trade* (New York: The Free Press, 1971), pp. 86–102.

59. See Harvey Wish (ed.), *Ante-Bellum: Writings of George Fitzhugh and Hinton R. Helper on Slavery* (New York: Capricorn Books, 1960), pp. 3–22, 41–156; Harvey Wish, *George Fitzhugh: Propagandist of the Old South* (Gloucester, Mass: Peter Smith, 1962), pp. 160–340; Cunliffe, op. cit., pp. 1–31; Eugene Genovese, *The World the Slaveholders Made: Two Essays in Interpretation* (New York: Pantheon, 1969), pp. 118–244; Lyman, "System and Function . . ." op. cit.

60. See Paul Buck (ed.), *Social Sciences at Harvard, 1860–1920: From Inculcation to the Open Mind* (Cambridge: Harvard University Press, 1965), pp. 18–128.
61. Arthur J. Vidich and Stanford M. Lyman, *American Sociology: Worldly Rejections of Religion and Their Directions* (New Haven: Yale University Press, 1985), pp. 53–104.
62. Robert E. Park, "The Crowd and the Public," in *The Crowd and the Public and Other Essays*, translated by Charlotte Elsner, edited by Henry Elsner, Jr (University of Chicago Press, 1972), pp. 3–81. Cf. the orientation in Ernest T. Hiller, *The Strike: A Study in Collective Action* (New York: Arno and the New York Times, 1969 [1928]) with that of Alvin W. Gouldner, *Wildcat Strike: A Study in Worker–Management Relationships* (New York: Harper Torchbooks, 1954).
63. The following draws on Arthur J. Vidich and Stanford M. Lyman, "Secular Evangelism at the University of Wisconsin," *Social Research*, vol. XLIX, no. 4 (winter 1982), pp. 1047–72.
64. Edward and Eleanor Marx Aveling, *The Working-Class Movement in America*, 2nd edn (London: Swan Sonnenschein, 1891; reprint, New York: Arno Press and The New York Times, 1969).
65. See two works by Richard T. Ely, *The Labor Movement in America* (New York: Thomas Y. Crowell, 1886; reprint, New York: Arno Press and The New York Times, 1969); and *Studies in the Evolution of Industrial Society* (Port Washington, NY: Kennikat Press, 1971 [1903]), 2 vols, esp. II, pp. 450–490.
66. For a case study, see Fones-Wolf, op. cit.
67. Joe M. Richardson, *Christian Reconstruction: The American Missionary Association and Southern Blacks, 1861–1890* (Athens: University of Georgia Press, 1986); John Patrick McDowell, *The Social Gospel in the South: The Woman's Home Mission Movement in the Methodist Episcopal Church, South, 1886–1939* (Baton Rouge: Louisiana State University Press, 1982), pp. 84–115.
68. See Clarence E. Walker, *A Rock in a Weary Land: The African Methodist Episcopal Church During the Civil War and Reconstruction* (Baton Rouge: Louisiana State University Press, 1982); Calvin S. Morris, *Reverdy C. Ransom: Black Advocate of the Social Gospel* (Lanham, Md: University Press of America, 1990); and Stephen Ward Angell, *Bishop Henry McNeal Turner and Africa-American Religion in the South* (Knoxville: University of Tennessee Press, 1992). See also H. Shelton Smith, *In His Image, But...: Racism in Southern Religion, 1780–1910* (Durham: Duke University Press, 1972), pp. 208–306.
69. Ralph E. Luker, *The Social Gospel in Black and White: American Racial Reform, 1885–1912* (Chapel Hill: University of North Carolina Press, 1991); W. D. Weatherford, *American Churches and the Negro* (Boston: The Christopher Publishing Co., 1957), pp. 246–302; Michael E. Engh, SJ, "A Most Excellent Field for Work: Christian Missionary Efforts in the Los Angeles Chinese Community, 1870–1900," *Gum Saan Journal of the Chinese Historical Society of Southern California*, vol. XV, no. 1 (June 1992), pp. 1–15.
70. See two works by Edward Alsworth Ross, *Changing America: Studies*

426   *Social Theory and Social Movements*

in Contemporary America (New York: The Century Co., 1912), pp. 137–236; *Standing Room Only?* (New York: The Century Co., 1927; reprint, New York: Arno Press, 1977), pp. 285–356.

71. For a sociological analysis, see R. Clyde White and Mary K. White, *Research Memorandum on Social Aspects of Relief Policies in the Depression* (New York: Social Science Research Council, bulletin no. 38, 1937; reprint, New York: Arno Press, 1972).

72. See, for example, Rhonda F. Levine, *Class Struggle and the New Deal: Industrial Labor, Industrial Capital, and the State* (Lawrence: University Press of Kansas, 1988); and Alan Brinkley, *Voices of Protest: Huey Long, Father Coughlin, and the Great Depression* (New York: Vintage Books, 1982).

73. See Franklin Folsom, *Impatient Armies of the Poor: The Story of Collective Action of the Unemployed, 1808–1942* (Niwot, Col.: University Press of Colorado, 1991), pp. 231–430, 464–78.

74. See Roger Biles, *A New Deal for the American People* (DeKalb: Northern Illinois University Press, 1991), pp. 136–234; Frank A. Pinner, Paul Jacobs and Philip Selznick, *Old Age and Political Behavior: A Case Study* (Berkeley: University of California Press, 1959); and Greg Mitchell, *The Campaign of the Century: Upton Sinclair's Race for Governor of California and the Birth of Media Politics* (New York: Random House, 1992); Glen Jeansonne, *Gerald L. K. Smith: Minister of Hate* (New Haven: Yale University Press, 1988).

75. For a thoroughly secular analysis by an economist active in the early New Deal, see Rexford G. Tugwell, *The Battle for Democracy* (New York: Greenwood Press, 1969 [1935]), pp. 46–218.

76. See Barry Dean Karl, *Executive Reorganization and Reform in the New Deal: The Genesis of Administrative Management, 1900–1939* (University of Chicago Press, 1979 [1963]), passim.

77. Walter Trattner, *From Poor Law to Welfare State: A History of Social Welfare in America*, 2nd edn (New York: The Free Press, 1979), pp. 223–74.

78. See Joseph Bensman and Arthur J. Vidich, *American Society: The Welfare State and Beyond*, revised edn (South Hadley, Mass: Bergin and Garvey Publishers, 1987), esp. pp. 161–336.

79. See Charles L. Garrettson, III, *Hubert Humphrey: The Politics of Joy* (New Brunswick, NJ: Transaction Publishers, 1993), pp. 221–302.

80. See Barry D. Karl, *The Uneasy State: The United States From 1915 to 1945* (Chicago: University of Chicago Press, 1983), esp. pp. 205–40; and Richard H. Pells, *The Liberal Mind in a Conservative Age: American Intellectuals in the 1940s and 1950s* (New York: Harper and Row, 1985), pp. 117–261, 346–400.

81. George A. Lundberg, *Can Science Save Us?*, 2nd edn (New York: David McKay, 1947, 1961), esp. pp. 1–65, 119–46.

82. See, for example, James S. Coleman *et al.*, *Equality of Educational Opportunity* (Washington, DC: US Government Printing Office, 1966); and J. Coleman, E. Katz and H. Menzel, *Medical Innovation: A Diffusion Study* (New York: Bobbs-Merrill, 1966).

83. See the discussion in Robert C. Angell, "The Ethical Problems of

Applied Sociology," in Paul F. Lazarsfeld, William H. Sewell and Harold Wilensky, (eds), *The Uses of Sociology* (New York: Basic Books, 1967), pp. 725–40.

84. The economic turndown of the 1980s and the increasing numbers of homeless Americans has led to a revival of the older reformist approach. See Peter H. Rossi, *Down and Out in America: The Origins of Homelessness* (University of Chicago Press, 1989); and Joel Blau, *The Visible Poor: Homelessness in the United States* (New York: Oxford University Press, 1992).

85. Talcott Parsons, *The Social System* (Glencoe: The Free Press, 1951). The concept "social system" was first introduced into American social thought by H[enry] A[ugustine] W[ashington], "The Social System of Virginia," *Southern Literary Messenger*, vol. XIV (February 1848), pp. 65–81.

86. See Talcott Parsons, "The Symbolic Environment of Modern Economies," *Social Research*, vol. XLVI, no. 3 (autumn 1979), pp. 436–53.

87. For an analysis of Parsons' social system theory as a latent sociology of the emotions, see Stanford M. Lyman, *The Seven Deadly Sins: Society and Evil*, revised edn (Dix Hills, NY: General Hall, 1989), pp. 277–98.

88. For the foregoing, see, *inter alia*, Talcott Parsons, "The Marshall Lectures – The Integration of Economic and Sociological Theory," *Sociological Inquiry*, vol. LXI, no. 1 (winter 1991), pp. 10–59. The entire issue of this number of *Sociological Inquiry* is devoted to a symposium on the Marshall lectures – which were delivered at Cambridge University in November 1953.

89. Talcott Parsons, "Certain Primary Sources and Patterns of Aggression in the Social Structure of the Western World," *Essays in Sociological Theory* (New York: The Free Press, 1964), pp. 298–322.

90. Parsons, "Full Citizenship for the Negro American? . . .," op. cit. For a critique, see Stanford M. Lyman, *The Black American in Sociological Thought: A Failure of Perspective* (New York: G. P. Putnam's Sons, 1972), pp. 145–70.

91. See John P. Diggins, "The Socialization of Authority and the Dilemmas of American Liberalism," *Social Research*, vol. XLVI, no. 3 (autumn 1979), pp. 454–86.

92. Talcott Parsons, *Structure and Process in Modern Societies* (Glencoe, Ill.: The Free Press, 1960), pp. 170–98.

93. Cf. Talcott Parsons, "The Hierarchy of Control," in Leon H. Mayhew (ed.), *Talcott Parsons on Institutions and Social Evolution: Selected Writings* (University of Chicago Press, 1982), pp. 157–72.

94. Cf. Talcott Parsons, "Christianity and Modern Industrial Society," *Sociological Theory and Modern Society* (New York: The Free Press, 1967), pp. 385–421 with Parsons, "Jurisdiction," in Mayhew, op. cit., pp. 179–86.

95. See Jack D. Douglas and John M. Johnson (eds), *Official Deviance: Readings in Malfeasance, Misfeasance, and Other Forms of Corruption* (Philadelphia: J. B. Lippincott, 1977); and M. David Ermann and Richard J. Lundman (eds), *Corporate and Governmental Deviance:*

Problems of Organizational Behavior in Contemporary Society, 3rd edn (New York: Oxford University Press, 1987).

96. See Theodore Draper, *A Very Thin Line: The Iran–Contra Affairs* (New York: Hill and Wang, 1991).

97. Cf. Alan Wolfe, *Whose Keeper? Social Science and Moral Obligation* (Berkeley: University of California Press, 1989), esp. pp. 107–211, 256–62.

98. See Talcott Parsons, "Social Interaction," *Social Systems and the Evolution of Action Theory* (New York: The Free Press, 1977), pp. 154–76.

99. See four works by Erving Goffman, *Behavior in Public Places: Notes on the Social Organization of Gatherings* (New York: The Free Press of Glencoe, 1963); *Interaction Ritual: Essays on Face-to-Face Behavior* (Chicago: Aldine Publishing Co., 1967); *Strategic Interaction* (Philadelphia: University of Pennsylvania Press, 1969); *Relations in Public: Microstudies of the Public Order* (New York: Basic Books, 1971). For a contextual analysis, see Stanford M. Lyman, *Civilization: Contents, Discontents, Malcontents, and Other Essays in Social Theory* (Fayetteville: University of Arkansas Press, 1990), pp. 11–21.

100. See T. K. Oommen, "Erving Goffman and the Study of Everyday Protest," in *Beyond Goffman: Studies on Communication, Institution, and Social Interaction* (Berlin and New York: Mouton de Gruyter, 1990), pp. 389–407. See also the anthropological perspective on the relationship of primitive societies and modern states in Pierre Clastres, *Society Against the State: Essays in Political Anthropology*, translated by Robert Hurley in collaboration with Abe Stein (New York: Zone Books, 1987), pp. 189–218.

101. For interesting examples, see Linda J. Medcalf and Kenneth M. Dolbeare, *Neopolitics: American Political Ideas in the 1980s* (New York: Random House, 1985), pp. 74–89, 108–83.

102. See Fred R. Dallmayr, *Twilight of Subjectivity: Contributions to a Post-Individualist Theory of Politics* (Amherst: The University of Massachusetts Press, 1981).

103. See John Patrick Diggins, *The Rise and Fall of the American Left* (New York: W. W. Norton, 1992), esp. pp. 218–384.

104. See, for example, Bob Kumamoto, "The Search for Spies: American Counterintelligence and the Japanese American Community, 1931–1942," *Amerasia Journal*, vol. VI, no. 2 (fall 1979), pp. 45–76; Steven E. Barkan, *Protesters on Trial: Criminal Justice in the Southern Civil Rights and Vietnam Antiwar Movements* (New Brunswick, NJ: Rutgers University Press, 1985), esp. pp. 149–58; Charles De Benedetti with the assistance of Charles Chatfield, *An American Ordeal: The Anti-war Movement of the Vietnam Era* (Syracuse, NY: Syracuse University Press, 1990); Clayborne Carson, *Malcolm X: The FBI File*, edited by David Gallen (New York: Carroll and Graf Publishers, 1991); and Athan Theoharis (ed.), *From the Secret Files of J. Edgar Hoover* (Chicago: Ivan R. Dee, 1991), esp. pp. 86–126.

105. See Maurice Isserman, *If I Had a Hammer . . . The Death of the Old Left and the Birth of the New Left* (New York: Basic Books, 1987), pp. 1–170. The tone for such a synthesis was presented in Robert K.

Merton, "Manifest and Latent Functions," *Social Theory and Social Structure*, revised edn (Glencoe: The Free Press, 1957), pp. 19–84, esp. pp. 38–42. See also Randall Collins, *Sociology Since Midcentury: Essays in Theory Cumulation* (New York: Academic Press, 1981), pp. 297–304.

106. See for example, Richard Flacks, *Making History: The Radical Tradition in American Life* (New York: Columbia University Press, 1988); James Weinstein and David W. Eakins (eds), *For a New America: Essays in History and Politics from "Studies on the Left," 1959–1967* (New York: Vintage Books, 1970); and Franz Schurmann, "System, Contradictions, and Revolution in America," in Roderick Aya and Norman Miller (eds), *The New American Revolution* (New York: The Free Press, 1971), pp. 18–96. The preeminent dissident sociologist – who died long before the denouement of the Cold War was even a fantasy in the sociological imagination – was C. Wright Mills (1916–62). Among his influential works of the period are *The Power Elite* (New York: Oxford University Press, 1956); *The Causes of World War III* (New York: Ballantine Books, 1958, 1960); *The Sociological Imagination* (New York: Oxford University Press, 1959); *Listen, Yankee: The Revolution in Cuba* (New York: Ballantine Books, 1960); and *The Marxists* (New York: Delta-Dell, 1963). Mills' essays have been gathered together: see *Power, Politics and People: The Collected Essays of C. Wright Mills*, edited by Irving Louis Horowitz (New York: Ballantine Books, 1963). For the American Protestant and pragmatic bases of Mills' thought, see Rick Tilman, *C. Wright Mills: A Native Radical and His American Intellectual Roots* (University Park: Pennsylvania State University Press, 1984), esp. pp. 193–202.

107. See Collins, op. cit., pp. 323–32; and Parsons, "On the Concept of Power," *Sociological Theory and Modern Society*, op. cit., pp. 297–354.

108. See Harvey Klehr, *Far Left of Center: The American Radical Left Today* (New Brunswick: Transaction Books, 1988), pp. 87–130. For a brief but insightful discussion of Marx's ambiguous legacy for historical theory, see Louis Schneider, *Classical Theories of Social Change* (Morristown, NJ: General Learning Press, 1976), pp. 81–91.

109. Cf. Paul F. Kress, "Revolution, Liberation, and Utopia: Notes on the Political Thought of Herbert Marcuse," in Aya and Miller, op. cit., pp. 284–317.

110. The following is from Paul F. Lazarsfeld, *Main Trends in Sociology* (New York: Harper Torchbooks, 1973), pp. 40–2.

111. M. Iovtchouk and L. Kogan, "Changement dans le vie spirituelle des ouvries en URSS," in *La Sociologie en URSS* (Rapports des membres de la delegation sovietique au vie Congres international de Sociologie [Moscow: n.p., 1966]), p. 268. Quoted in Lazarsfeld, *Main Trends in Sociology*, op. cit., p. 42.

112. Gunnar Myrdal with the assistance of Richard Sterner and Arnold Rose, *An American Dilemma: The Negro Problem and Modern Democracy* (New York: Harper and Brothers, 1944). For the reception of Myrdal's thesis in America, see David W. Southern, *Gunnar Myrdal and Black–White Relations: The Use and Abuse of An American Dilemma*,

1944–1969 (Baton Rouge: Louisiana State University Press, 1987), pp. 71–306; and Walter A. Jackson, *Gunnar Myrdal and America's Conscience: Social Engineering and Racial Liberalism, 1938–1987* (Chapel Hill: The University of North Carolina Press, 1990), pp. 186–372.

113. See John T. McCartney, *Black Power Ideologies: An Essay in African-American Political Thought* (Philadelphia: Temple University Press, 1992), esp. pp. 91–189. For discontents, discussions and debates over the challenges to both class theory and the assimilation orientation posed by the new "multiculturalist ideology," see Arthur M. Schlesinger, Jr, *The Disuniting of America: Reflections on a Multicultural Society* (Knoxville: Whittle Direct Books, 1991); E. San Juan, Jr, *Racial Formations/Critical Transformations: Articulations of Power in Ethnic and Racial Studies in the United States* (Atlantic Highlands, NJ: Humanities Press, 1992); Charles Taylor *et al.*, *Multiculturalism and "The Politics of Recognition"* (Princeton, N.J.: Princeton University Press, 1992); the essays by Edward Berenson, Henry Louis Gates, Jr, and David Hollinger in the symposium, "Multiculturalism and Beyond: Race and Poverty; Education and Ethnicity," *Contention: Debates in Society, Culture and Science*, vol. II, no. 1 (fall 1992), pp. 51–96; Philip Gleason, *Speaking of Diversity: Language and Ethnicity in Twentieth-Century America* (Baltimore: Johns Hopkins University Press, 1992); Don C. Locke, *Increasing Multicultural Understanding: A Comprehensive Model* (Newbury Park: Sage Publications, 1992); For the rise of Asian American solidarity, see Yen Le Espiritu, *Asian American Panethnicity: Building Institutions and Identities* (Philadelphia: Temple University Press, 1992), esp. pp. 19–111, 134–76.

114. See Norman Miller and Roderick Aya (eds), *National Liberation: Revolution in the Third World* (New York: The Free Press, 1971); Harold Cruse, "Revolutionary Nationalism and the Afro-American" and the exchange between Cruse, Richard Greenleaf and Clark Foreman, in Weinstein and Eakins, op. cit., p. 345–393; Eugene D. Genovese, "The Legacy of Slavery and the Roots of Black Nationalism," *Studies on the Left*, vol. VI, no. 6 (November–December 1966), reprinted in Weinstein and Eakins, op. cit., pp. 394–420; Theodore Draper, *The Rediscovery of Black Nationalism* (New York: Viking, 1970), esp. pp. 57–147, 168–84; Kinfe Abraham, *Politics of Black Nationalism: From Harlem to Soweto* (Trenton, NJ: Africa World Press, 1991), pp. 256–78. For the relations of the Communist Party to the "Negro question in the 1930s," see Harvey Klehr, *The Heyday of American Communism: The Depression Decade* (New York: Basic Books, 1984), pp. 324–48.

115. See Eugene D. Genovese, "On Antonio Gramsci," *Studies On the Left*, vol. VII, no. 2 (March–April 1967). Reprinted in Weinstein and Eakins, op. cit., pp. 284–316.

116. Dante Germino, *Antonio Gramsci: Architect of a New Politics* (Baton Rouge: Louisiana State University Press, 1990), p. 238.

117. See, for example, Gayatri Chakravorty Spivak, *The Post-Colonial Critic: Interviews, Strategies, Dialogues*, edited by Sarah Harasym (New York: Routledge, 1990), pp. 1–74, 152–68; Chantal Mouffe, "Democratic

Citizenship and Political Community," in idem (ed.), *Dimensions of Radical Democracy: Pluralism, Citizenship, Community* (London: Verso, 1992), pp. 225–39; and Paul R. Brass, *Ethnicity and Nationalism: Theory and Comparison* (New Delhi: Sage, 1991), pp. 333–48; Immanuel Wallerstein, "The Ideological Tensions of Capitalism: Universalism Versus Racism and Sexism," in Etienne Balibar and Immanuel Wallerstein (eds), *Race, Nation, Class: Ambiguous Identities* (London: Verso, 1991), pp. 29–36.

118. Louis Wirth, "The Problem of Minority Groups," in Ralph Linton (ed.), *The Science of Man in the World Crisis* (New York: Columbia University Press, 1945), p. 364.

119. Lester F. Ward, *Pure Sociology: A Treatise on the Origin and Spontaneous Development of Society*, 2nd edn (New York: Macmillan, 1907; reprint, New York: Augustus M. Kelley, 1970), pp. 290–456.

120. Dick Atkinson, *Orthodox Consensus and Radical Alternative: A Study in Sociological Theory* (New York: Basic Books, 1972). For the role of Africans and African-Americans in an allegedly coming global revolution, see John Henrik Clarke, *Africans at the Crossroads: Notes for an African World Revolution* (Trenton, NJ: Africa World Press, 1991), esp. pp. 41–78, 171–274.

121. See, for example, the all-too-neglected writings of Oliver Cromwell Cox (1901–74), *Foundations of Capitalism* (New York: Philosophical Library, 1959); *Caste, Class, and Race: A Study in Social Dynamics* (New York: Monthly Review Press, 1959); *Race Relations: Elements and Social Dynamics*, (Detroit: Wayne State University Press, 1976), esp. pp. 288–302; and *Race, Class, and the World System: The Sociology of Oliver C. Cox*, edited by Herbert Hunter and Sameer Y. Abraham (New York: Monthly Review Press, 1987), esp. pp. 71–324. For the dilemmas and contradictions of feminist-Marxism and its confrontation with postmodern thought see, *inter alia*, Nancy Fraser and Linda Nicholson, "Social Criticism Without Philosophy: An Encounter Between Feminism and Postmodernism," *Theory, Culture, and Society*, vol. v, nos 1–2 (June 1988), pp. 373–94; Lieteke van Vucht Tijssen, "Women Between Modernity and Postmodernity," in Bryan S. Turner (ed.), *Theories of Modernity and Postmodernity* (London: Sage Publications, 1990, 1991), pp. 147–63; Sabina Lovibond, "Feminism and Postmodernism," in Roy Boyne and Ali Rattansi (eds), *Postmodernism and Society* (New York: St Martin's Press, 1990), pp. 154–86; Steven Best and Douglas Kellner, *Postmodern Theory: Critical Interrogations* (New York: Guilford Press, 1991), pp. 205–14. In general, see Warren Montag, "What is at Stake in the Debate on Postmodernism?", in E. Ann Kaplan (ed.), *Postmodernism and its Discontents: Theory, Practices* (London: Verso, 1988), pp. 88–104).

122. See, for example, Ernest Mandel, "Late Capitalism and Imperialism," in Tom Bottomore and Patrick Goods (eds), *Readings in Marxist Sociology* (Oxford: Clarendon Press, 1983), pp. 264–8.

123. However, few American Marxist sociologists adapted such Hegelianisms to their versions of neo-Marxism in the 1960s, 1970s or 1980s. See Daniel Bell, *The Social Sciences Since the Second World*

432   *Social Theory and Social Movements*

War (New Brunswick, NJ: Transaction Books, 1985), pp. 83–94; and Immanuel Wallerstein, *Unthinking Social Science: The Limits of Nineteenth-Century Paradigms* (Cambridge: Polity Press, 1991), pp. 23–38, 151–84.

124. Cf. the perspective of Ben Agger, *Socio(onto)logy: A Disciplinary Reading* (Urbana: University of Illinois Press, 1989), pp. 137–228, with that of Samuel Bowles and Herbert Gintis, *Democracy and Capitalism: Property, Community, and the Contradictions of Modern Social Thought* (New York: Basic Books, 1987), pp. ix–xv, 121–51, 176–213. See also Krishan Kumar, *Utopia and Anti-Utopia in Modern Times* (New York: Basil Blackwell, 1987), pp. 50–65, 380–424.

125. Robert N. Bellah, *Beyond Belief: Essays on Religion in a Post-traditional World* (New York: Harper and Row, 1970), pp. xi–xxi, 168–92.

126. Robert Bellah, "The Power of Religion in the Contemporary Society," *Biblical Religion and the Ideology of the Modern World* (New York: Office of University and Young Adult Ministries, General Board of Global Ministries – National Division, December, 1981), part II, p. 10.

127. Robert Bellah, *The Broken Covenant: American Civil Religion in Time of Trial* (New York: Crossroad Books – The Seabury Press, 1975), p. xi.

128. See Robert N. Bellah and Frederick E. Greenspahn (eds), *Uncivil Religion: Inter-religious Hostility in America* (New York: Crossroad, 1987).

129. See, for example, Robert N. Bellah, "New Religious Consciousness and the Crisis in Modernity," in Charles Y. Glock and Robert N. Bellah (eds), *The New Religious Consciousness* (Berkeley: University of California Press, 1976), pp. 333–52.

130. George Armstrong Kelly, "Faith, Freedom, and Disenchantment: Politics and the American Religious Consciousness," in Mary Douglas and Steven M. Tipton (eds), *Religion in America: Spirituality in a Secular Age* (Boston: Beacon Press, 1982, 1983), pp. 207–28.

131. Bellah, *Beyond Belief*, op. cit., pp. 53–167.

132. Barbara Hargrove, "Church Student Ministries and the New Consciousness," in Glock and Bellah (eds), op. cit., pp. 205–26.

133. Cf. the theses presented in Gertrud Lenzer (ed.), *Auguste Comte and Positivism: The Essential Writings* (New York: Harper Torchbooks, 1975), pp. 381–9, with those of William M. Sullivan, *Reconstructing Public Philosophy* (Berkeley: University of California Press, 1982).

134. Robert N. Bellah, Richard Madsen, William M. Sullivan, Ann Swidler and Steven M. Tipton, *Habits of the Heart: Individualism and Commitment in American Life* (Berkeley: University of California Press, 1985), esp. pp. 167–308.

135. Steven M. Tipton, *Getting Saved from the Sixties: Moral Meaning in Conversion and Cultural Change* (Berkeley: University of California Press, 1982).

136. Robert N. Bellah, Richard Madsen, William M. Sullivan, Ann Swidler and Steven M. Tipton, *The Good Society* (New York: Alfred A. Knopf, 1991).

137. Cf. Herbert J. Gans, "Sociology in America: The Discipline and the Public," the 1988 Presidential Address to the American Sociological Association, in Gans (ed.), op. cit., pp. 314–33.

138. See, *inter alia*, Alfred McClung Lee, *Sociology for Whom?*, 2nd edn

(Syracuse, NY: Syracuse University Press, 1986); Christopher G. A. Bryant and Henk A. Becker (eds), *What Has Sociology Achieved?* (New York: St Martin's Press, 1990); Henry Etzkowitz and Ronald M. Glassman (eds), *The Renascence of Sociological Theory: Classical and Contemporary* (Itasca, Ill.: F. E. Peacock, 1991); Terence C. Halliday and Morris Janowitz (eds), *Sociology and its Publics* (University of Chicago Press, 1992). See also Arthur J. Vidich, Stanford M. Lyman and Jeffrey C. Goldfarb, "Sociology and Society: Disciplinary Tensions and Professional Compromises," *Social Research*, vol. XLVIII, no. 2 (summer 1981), pp. 322–61.

139. Since his death Goffman's work has evoked considerable and diverse commentary and criticism. In addition to Riggins, op. cit., see Jason Ditton (ed.), *The View from Goffman* (New York: St Martin's Press, 1980); Paul Drew and Anthony Wootton (eds), *Erving Goffman: Exploring the Interaction Order* (Boston: Northeastern University Press, 1988; and Tom Burns, *Erving Goffman* (London: Routledge, 1992).

140. The following draws on Stanford M. Lyman, *Civilization: Contents, Discontents, Malcontents, and Other Essays in Social Theory* (Fayetteville: University of Arkansas Press, 1990), pp. 11–21.

141. See two works by Erving Goffman, *Stigma: Notes on the Management of Spoiled Identity* (Englewood Cliffs, NJ: Prentice-Hall, Spectrum, 1963, 1964); and *Asylums: Essays on the Social Situation of Mental Patients and Other Inmates* (Garden City, NY: Doubleday-Anchor, 1961).

142. Erving Goffman, *The Presentation of Self in Everyday Life* (Garden City, NY: Doubleday-Anchor, 1959).

143. See Vidich and Lyman, *American Sociology*, op. cit., pp. 272–7, 305–7.

144. Compare Goffman's two postgradunate dissertations: *Some Characteristics of Response to Depicted Experience*, MA dissertation, University of Chicago, December, 1949; and *Communication Conduct in an Island Community*, PhD dissertation, University of Chicago, December, 1953, with his final work, *Forms of Talk* (Philadelphia: University of Pennsylvania Press, 1981) and with Jürgen Habermas, *The Theory of Communicative Action, Vol. 1: Reason and the Rationalization of Society; Vol. II: Lifeworld and System: A Critique of Functionalist Reason*, translated by Thomas McCarthy (Boston: Beacon Press, 1981, 1987).

145. See Stanford M. Lyman and Marvin B. Scott, *A Sociology of the Absurd*, 2nd edn (Dix Hills, NY: General Hall, 1989), pp. 90–155.

146. See Charles Taylor, *Sources of the Self: The Making of the Modern Identity* (Cambridge: Harvard University Press, 1989), esp. pp. 495–522. See also John Shotter, *Social Accountability and Selfhood* (New York: Basil Blackwell, 1984); John Shotter and Kenneth J. Gergen (eds), *Texts of Identity* (London: Sage Publications, 1989); Mike W. Martin (ed.), *Self-Deception and Self-Understanding: New Essays in Philosophy and Psychology* (Lawrence: University Press of Kansas, 1985); Mike W. Martin, *Self-Deception and Morality* (Lawrence: University Press of Kansas, 1986); Efrat Tseëlon, "Self Presentation through Appearance: A Manipulative vs. A Dramaturgical Approach," *Symbolic Interaction*, vol. XV, no. 4 (winter 1992), pp. 501–13.

147. Georg Simmel, *The Conflict in Modern Culture and Other Essays*, translated and edited by K. Peter Etzkorn (New York: Teachers College Press, 1968), pp. 11–46.
148. See Jean-François Lyotard, *The Lyotard Reader*, edited by Andrew Benjamin (Cambridge, Mass: Basil Blackwell, 1989), esp. pp. 314–411.
149. Of course there have long been secular, irreligious sociologies as well as sociologies and cultures of unbelief. For some representative readings, see Colin Campbell, *Toward a Sociology of Irreligion* (New York: Herder and Herder, 1972); James Turner, *Without God or Creed: The Origins of Unbelief in America* (Baltimore: Johns Hopkins University Press, 1985); Rocco Caporale and Antonio Grumelli (eds), *The Culture of Unbelief: Studies and Proceedings from the First International Symposium on Belief Held at Rome, March 22–27, 1969* (Berkeley: University of California Press, 1971); and David Martin, *A General Theory of Secularization* (New York: Harper Colophon, 1979).
150. Jean Baudrillard, *America*, translated by Chris Turner (London: Verso, 1989). See also Jean Baudrillard, *Selected Writings*, edited by Mark Poster (Stanford University Press, 1988), pp. 29–56, 207–19.
151. See Robert E. Park, "Community Organization and the Romantic Temper," in Robert E. Park, Ernest W. Burgess and Roderick D. McKenzie (eds), *The City* (University of Chicago Press, 1925, 1967), pp. 113–22, esp. pp. 117–18; Jessie Bernard, "The Eudaemonists," in Samuel Z. Klausner (ed.), *Why Men Take Chances: Studies in Stress-seeking* (Garden City: Doubleday-Anchor, 1968), pp. 6–47; Lyman and Scott, op. cit., pp. 51–9, 69–89, 98–110, 157–80.
152. For the history and sociology of consumerism in America, see Stuart Ewen, *Captains of Consciousness: Advertising and the Social Roots of the Consumer Culture* (New York: McGraw-Hill, 1976); Stuart and Elizabeth Ewen, *Channels of Desire: Mass Images and the Shaping of American Consciousness* (New York: McGraw-Hill, 1982); Stuart Ewen, *All Consuming Images: The Politics of Style in Contemporary Culture* (New York: Basic Books, 1988); Colin Campbell, *The Romantic Ethic and the Spirit of Modern Consumerism* (New York: Basil Blackwell, 1987).
153. See Robert Jackall, *Workers in a Labyrinth: Jobs and Survival in a Bank Bureaucracy*, (Montclair, NJ: Allanheld, Osmun, 1978).
154. Robert Jackall, *Moral Mazes: The World of Corporate Managers* (New York: Oxford University Press, 1988).
155. See Erving Goffman, *Gender Advertisements* (Cambridge: Harvard University Press, 1979); and Judith Williamson, *Decoding Advertisements: Ideology and Meaning in Advertising* (London: Marion Boyars, 1978). See also George Lipsitz, *Class and Culture in Cold War America: "A Rainbow at Midnight"* (South Hadley, Mass: Bergin and Garvey, 1982), pp. 173–225.
156. See Arthur J. Vidich, "Hiroshima's Legacy: The Theodicy of Man-Made Hazards," *Anthropology Resource Newsletter*, vol. 4, no. 3 (1980), p. 3, and "Prospects for Peace in the Nuclear World," *Journal of Political and Military Sociology*, vol. 8 (1980) pp. 85–97.
157. See Stanford M. Lyman and Arthur J. Vidich, *Social Order and the Public Philosophy: An Analysis and Interpretation of the Work of Herbert*

Blumer (Fayetteville: University of Arkansas Press, 1988), pp. 3–10, 106–20.

158. Cf. Gary J. Dorrien, *Reconstructing the Common Good: Theology and the Social Order*, (Maryknoll, NY: Orbis Books, 1990), pp. 7–76, 160–76. See also George E. McCarthy and Royal W. Rhodes, *Eclipse of Justice: Ethics, Economics, and the Lost Traditions of American Catholicism*, (Maryknoll, NY: Orbis Books, 1992), and "A Symposium on the Catholic Ethic and the Spirit of Socio-Economic Justice," with contributions by Arthur F. McGovern, S. J., James R. Kelly, Joseph A. Varacalli, and José Casanova, *International Journal of Politics, Culture and Society*, vol. VI, no. 2 (Winter, 1992), pp. 299–330.

159. See Peter L. Berger, *A Far Glory: The Quest for Faith in an Age of Credulity* (New York: Free Press, 1992), esp. pp. 191–211.

160. See John B. Judis, *Grand Illusion: Critics and Champions of the American Century*, (New York: Farrar, Straus and Giroux, 1992), esp. pp. 74–317.

161. Orrin E. Klapp, *Collective Search for Identity* (New York: Holt, Rinehart and Winston, 1969).

162. Orrin E. Klapp, *Heroes, Villains, and Fools: The Changing American Character* (Englewood Cliffs, NJ: Prentice-Hall, Spectrum, 1962).

163. Orrin E. Klapp, *Symbolic Leaders: Public Dramas and Public Men* (Chicago: Aldine, 1964), esp. pp. 101–20, 250–64.

164. Orrin E. Klapp, *Inflation of Symbols: Loss of Values in American Culture* (New Brunswick, NJ: Transaction, 1991).

165. Erving Goffman, *Strategic Interaction*, op. cit., pp. 85–145; Orrin E. Klapp, *Opening and Closing: Strategies of Information Adaptation in Society* (Cambridge: Cambridge University Press, 1978), esp. pp. 23–107, 154–90.

166. Orrin E. Klapp, *Models of Social Order: An Introduction to Sociological Theory* (Palo Alto, CA: National Press Books, 1973).

167. See Leonard W. Doob, *Slightly Beyond Skepticism: Social Science and the Search for Morality* (New Haven: Yale University Press, 1987), esp. pp. 195–280.

Acknowledgements

The index was prepared by Paul Cantrell, Ph.D. Joan Schilling typed portions of the M.S. and kept all records, copies, disks, and related items in proper order. The editor thanks both of them.

The editor wishes to acknowledge the original source of publication of the following articles which are reprinted by permission:

Chapter 1, "The General Will," by Robert E. Park, reprinted with the permission of The University of Chicago Press from Robert E. Park, *The Crowd and the Public and Other Essays*, pp. 63–81. Copyright © 1972, The University of Chicago Press.

Chapter 2, "The Religion of Progress," by Albert Salomon, reprinted from *Social Research*, vol. 13, no. 4 (December, 1946), pp. 441–62. Copyright © 1946, New School for Social Research in New York City.

Chapter 3, "Social Movements and Social Order," by Rudolf Heberle, reprinted with the permission of Irvington Publishers from Rudolf Heberle. *Social Movements: An Introduction to Political Sociology*, pp. 447–59 (the retitled "Conclusion", Chapter 20). Copyright © 1951, Irvington Publishers.

Chapter 4, "Social Movements" by Herbert Blumer, reprinted with the permission of Harper Collins Publishers, Inc. from Alfred M. Lee (ed.), *New Outline of the Principles of Sociology* , pp. 199–220. Copyright © 1939, 1946, 1951, 1957, 1969, Barnes & Noble, Inc., renewed in 1967.

Chapter 5, "Dramaturgy and Social Movements: The Social Construction and Communication of Power," by Robert D. Benford and Scott A. Hunt, reprinted with the permission of the authors and University of Texas Press from *Sociological Inquiry*, vol. 62, no. 1 (February 1992), pp. 36–55. Copyright © 1992, University of Texas Press.

Chapter 6, "What's So New About New Social Movements?" by David Plotke, reprinted from *Socialist Review*, vol. 20, no. 1 (January–March 1990), pp. 81–102. Copyright © 1990, Duke University Press.

Chapter 7, "Collective Protest: A Critique of Resource-Mobilization Theory," by Frances Fox Piven and Richard A. Cloward, reprinted with the permission of the authors and Human Sciences Press, Inc. from *International Journal of Politics, Culture, and Society*, vol. 4, no. 4 (Summer 1991), pp. 435–58. Copyright © 1991, Human Sciences Press, Inc.

Chapter 8, "Social Movement Research in the United States: A European Perspective," by Margit Mayer, reprinted with the permission of the author and Human Sciences Press, Inc. from *International Journal of Politics, Culture, and Society*, vol. 4, no. 4 (Summer 1991), pp. 459–80. Copyright © 1991, Human Sciences Press, Inc.

Chapter 9, "It Happened Here: Political Opportunity, the New Institutionalism, and the Townsend Movement," by Edwin Amenta and Yvonne Zylan, reprinted with the permission of the authors and the American Sociological Association from *American Sociological Review*, vol. 56, no. 2 (April 1991), pp. 250–65. Copyright © 1991, American Sociological Association.

Chapter 10, "Ideology as Episodic Discourse: The Case of the Iranian Revolution," by Mansoor Moaddel, reprinted by permission of the author and the American Sociological Association from *American Sociological Review*, vol. 57, no. 3 (June 1992). Copyright © 1992, American Sociological Association.

Chapter 11, "AIDS, the Politically Correct and Social Theory," by Daniel Harris, a combination of two essays reprinted by permission of the author and Lingua Franca, Inc. from "AIDS and Theory," *Lingua Franca: The Review of Academic Life*, n.v. (June 1991), pp. 1, 16–19. Copyright © 1991, Lingua Franca Inc.; and reprinted by permission of the author from "What Is the Politically Correct?" *Salmagundi*, no. 90–91 (Spring–Summer 1991), pp. 45–55. Copyright © 1991, Skidmore College.

Chapter 12, "Environmentalism and Human Emancipation," by Robert J. Brulle, reprinted with the permission of the author and the Society for Human Ecology from a paper presented at the sixth meeting of the Society for Human Ecology (October 1992), Snowbird, Utah. Copyright © 1992, Society for Human Ecology.

Chapter 13, "Rethinking the Sixties Legacy: From New Left to New Social Movements," by Carl Boggs, reprinted with the permission of the author and Transaction Publishers from Michael Peter Smith (ed.), *Breaking Chains: Social Movements and Collective Action*, pp. 50–68. Copyright © 1991, Transaction Publishers.

Chapter 14, "The Left as the Counterculture of Modernity," by Zygmunt Bauman, reprinted with the permission of Telos Press Ltd from *Telos*, no. 70 (Winter 1986–7), pp. 81–93. Copyright © 1986 Telos Press Ltd.

Chapter 15, "Beyond Social Movements?" by Alain Touraine, reprinted with the permission of Sage Publications Ltd from *Theory, Culture and Society*, vol. 9 (1992), pp. 125–45. Copyright © 1992, Sage Publications Ltd.

Notes on the Contributors

SERIES EDITORS

Robert Jackall is Willmott Family Professor of Sociology and Social Thought at Williams College. His most recent book is *Moral Mazes: The World of Corporate Managers*.

Arthur J. Vidich is Senior Lecturer and Professor Emeritus of Sociology and Anthropology at the Graduate Faculty, New School for Social Research. He is the co-author of *Small Town in Mass Society* and *American Society: The Welfare State and Beyond*.

Edwin Amenta, whose research focuses on political sociology, is an Assistant Professor of Sociology at New York University. With Bruce G. Carruthers and Yvonne Zylan, Professor Amenta has co-authored "A Hero for the Aged?" (*American Journal of Sociology*, 1992). He is completing *Bold Relief: The Political Sociology of U.S. Social Spending and Taxation Policies, 1929–1950*.

Zygmunt Bauman, Emeritus Professor of Sociology, University of Leeds, is the author of *Intimations of Postmodernity* (Routledge, 1991); and *Postmodern Ethics* (Blackwell, 1993), as well as many other essays and books in social theory, political sociology, and the sociology of culture.

Robert D. Benford, Associate Professor of Sociology, University of Nebraska-Lincoln, teaches and researches social movements, peace and war, and qualitative methods. His published articles have appeared in *Journal of Contemporary Ethnography, American Sociological Review, Social Forces, The Sociological Quarterly*, and *Sociological Inquiry*.

Herbert Blumer (1900–1987) established "symbolic interactionism" as a distinctive perspective in American sociology. Educated at the University of Missouri and the University of Chicago, Blumer taught for many years at the University of California, Berkeley. Among his works are *Movies and Conduct* (1933); *Critiques of Research in the Social Sciences: An Appraisal of Thomas' and Znaniecki's* The Polish Peasant in Europe and America (1939); *The Rationale of Labor-Management Relations* (1958); and the posthumously published *Industrialization as an Agent of Social Change: A Critical Analysis*. His *Symbolic Interactionism: Perspective and Method* (1969) was reissued in 1986.

Carl Boggs, Professor of Social Sciences at National University in Los Angeles and Visiting Professor of Sociology at UCLA (1993–4), is the author of *Intellectuals and the Crisis of Modernity* as well as *Social Move-*

ments and Political Power; The Two Revolutions; and *The Impasse of European Communism.* Forthcoming in 1994 is his *The Socialist Tradition: From Crisis to Decline.*

Robert J. Brulle is completing a PhD in sociology at George Washington University, Washington, DC. In addition to his dissertation research on the bureaucratic characteristics of environmental organizations, Mr Brulle has investigated discursive analysis and its relation to evolutionary theory and risk assessment in the marine environment. Among his recent publications are "Jürgen Habermas: An Exegesis for Human Ecologists," *Human Ecology Bulletin,* no. 8 (spring/summer, 1992), and "Power, Discourse, and Social Problems: Social Problems from a Rhetorical Perspective," forthcoming in G. Miller (ed.), *Current Perspectives in Social Problems,* vol. 5, 1994.

Richard A. Cloward teaches at the Columbia University School of Social Work. He is the co-author, with Frances Fox Piven, of *Regulating the Poor,* first published in 1971. An updated edition was published in 1993.

Daniel Harris is an essayist and book critic whose work appears in *Harper's, The Los Angeles Times, The Nation, New York Newsday,* and *Salmagundi.* His essay, "Cuteness," will appear in *The Best American Essays of 1993.*

Rudolf Heberle (1896–1991) studied law and economics at the University of Goettingen, but turned to sociology at the University of Kiel, where he studied under his future father-in-law, Ferdinand Toennies. Heberle came to the United States in 1938, a refugee in flight from Nazi tyranny. In America he taught at Louisiana State University until 1963. Among his many works are *From Democracy to Nazism* (1945) and *Social Movements: An Introduction to Political Sociology* (1951). Heberle served as Distinguished Boyd Professor of Sociology at LSU, President of the Southern Sociological Society in 1952, and Vice-President of the American Sociological Association in 1967. In 1991 his name was added to the Roll of Honor of the Southern Sociological Society.

Scott A. Hunt is Assistant Professor of Sociology at the University of Kentucky. Publications include articles in *Sociological Inquiry, Journal of Contemporary Etnography, Rural Sociology, Perspectives on Social Problems, Humanity and Society, Mid-American Review of Sociology,* as well as a chapter (co-authored with Robert D. Benford and David A. Snow) in *From Ideology to Identity in New Social Movements* (edited by Joseph R. Gusfield, Hank Johnston, and Enrique Larana, forthcoming from Temple University Press).

Stanford M. Lyman is the Robert J. Morrow Eminent Scholar and Professor of Social Science at Florida Atlantic University. He is a specialist in the study of minorities, race and ethnic relations, and sociological theory. Lyman is the author of twenty books, among which the most recent are: *Social Order and the Public Philosophy: An Analysis and Interpretation*

440   *Notes on the Contributors*

of the Work of Herbert Blumer, with Arthur J. Vidich; *Civilization: Contents, Discontents, Malcontents, and Other Essays in Social Theory*; and *Militarism, Imperialism, and Racial Accommodation: An Analysis and Interpretation of the Early Writings of Robert E. Park.* In 1994 the University of Illinois Press will publish Lyman's book entitled *Color, Culture, Civilization: Race and Minority Issues in American Society.*

Margit Mayer is a Professor of Politics at the Free University of Berlin. She has written about urban social movements and state responses in the USA and West Germany, the genesis of the American nation state, and the German Green Party. Her in-depth study of social movement research in the United States was published in Dieter Rucht (ed.), *Research on Social Movements: The State of the Art in Western Europe and the USA* (1991).

Mansoor Moaddel, Associate Professor of Sociology at Eastern Michigan University, is the author of *Class, Politics, and Ideology in the Iranian Revolution* (1993); "The Egyptian and Iranian Ulama at the Threshold of Modern Social Change: What Does and What Does Not Account for the Difference," *Arab Studies Quarterly* (summer, 1993); and "Political Conflict in the World-Economy: A Cross-National Analysis of Modernization and World-System Theory," *American Sociological Review* (April 1994). Currently Moaddel is engaged in comparative historical research on Islamic modernism, liberal-nationalism, and religious fundamentalism in the Middle East.

Robert E. Park (1864–1944) was the pre-eminent American figure in sociological studies of race and ethnicity, collective behavior, and urban society at the University of Chicago. After completing undergraduate studies at the University of Michigan, he worked as a journalist for ten years. Under William James at Harvard, he studied philosophy and psychology and then earned a doctorate in Germany under the guidance of Georg Simmel and Wilhelm Windelband. In America Park served as secretary of the Congo Reform Association (1904–7), assistant and ghost writer for Booker T. Washington (1905–13), and then joined the faculty of sociology at the University of Chicago. Since his death, many of his essays have been available in *The Collected Writings of Robert Ezra Park: Race and Culture; Human Communities; Society* (3 vols, 1950, et seq.) His early writings have been reprinted in Stanford M. Lyman, *Militarism, Imperialism, and Racial Accommodation: An Analysis and Interpretation of the Early Writings of Robert E. Park* (1992).

Frances Fox Piven is Distinguished Professor of Political Science and Sociology at the Graduate School and University Center of the City University of New York. She has collaborated with Richard Cloward on *Regulating the Poor, Poor Peoples' Movements, The New Class War*, and numerous other books and articles. She is also the editor of *Labor Parties in Postindustrial Societies*, 1992.

David Plotke is Associate Professor of Political Science at the Graduate

Faculty of Political and Social Science of the New School for Social Research. He is most recently the author of *The Democratic Political Order from the 1930s to the 1970s* (New York: Cambridge University Press, 1994). The article in this volume draws on a manuscript-in-progress entitled, *Political Judgment and Collective Action: Movements and Interest Groups in the Contemporary United States.*

Albert Salomon (1892–1966) was one of the emigre scholars who helped to establish the University-in-Exile at the New School for Social Research. His essays on Max Weber appeared in the New School's journal, *Social Research*, in 1934 and 1935, as did subsequent essays on Ferdinand Toennies (1936), Alfred Weber (1936), and Karl Mannheim (1947). Salomon published *The Tyranny of Progress* in 1955 and *In Praise of Enlightenment* in 1962. A symposium commemorating the one-hundred-and-first year since his birth was held at the New School for Social Research in 1993.

Alain Touraine is a professor in L'Ecole des Lettres et des Sciences Humaines at Paris-Nanterre and the author of *The Self-Production of Society* (1977). Among his contributions to the sociology of social movements are *The Voice and the Eye: An Analysis of Social Movements* (1981); *Solidarity: The Analyses of a Social Movement – Poland, 1980–1981* (1983); *Anti-Nuclear Protest* (1983); and *The Return of the Actor* (1988).

Yvonne Zylan, a graduate student in sociology at New York University, is engaged in research on social movements, political sociology and gender. Her dissertation, "The Divided Female State: Gender and Social Policy, 1945–1990," examines women's changing relationships to the state and markets, and their influence on the emergence of a politics of (in)dependence in the post-Second-World War United States.

Index

Note: indexed materials in endnotes to chapters are signaled by 'n.' after a page number, followed by the endnote number.